P9-DCI-510

MADE BY DAD
67 BLUEPRINTS FOR MAKING COOL STUFF

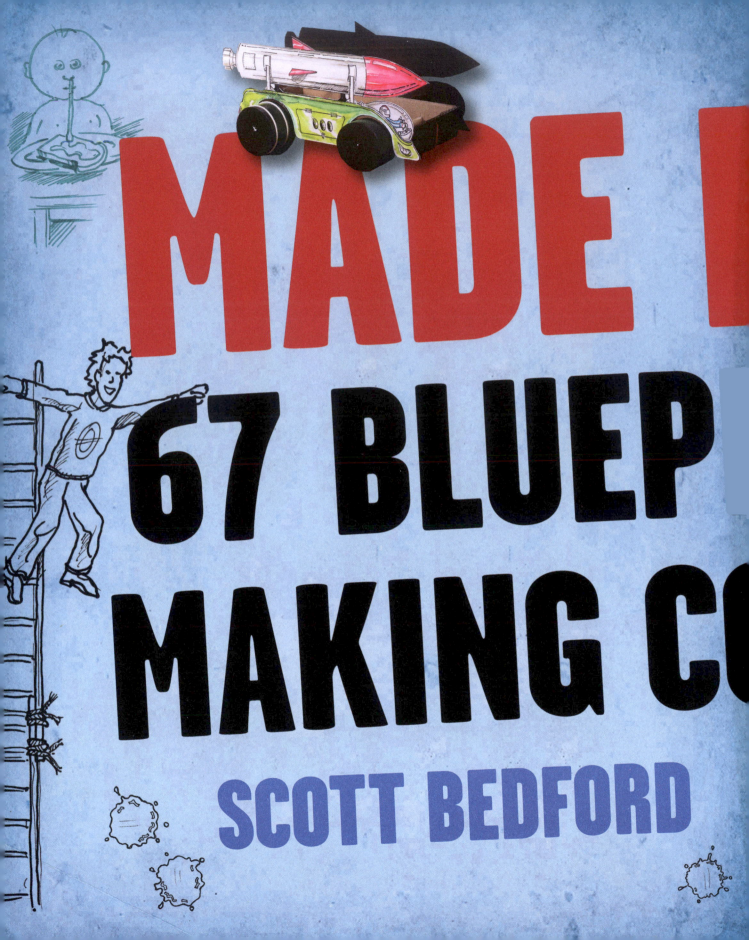

MADE

67 BLUEP
MAKING C

SCOTT BEDFORD

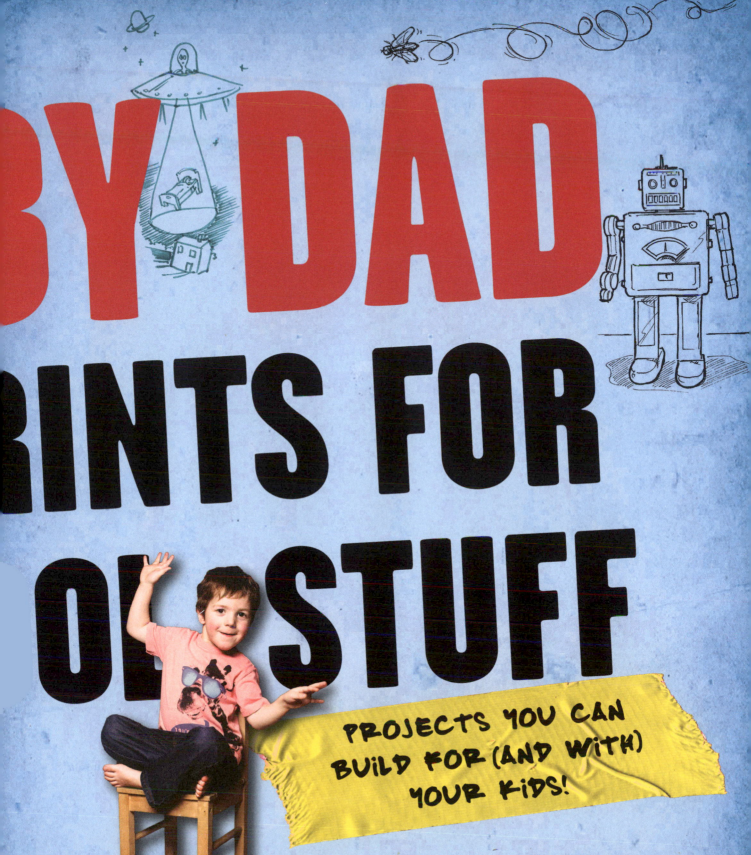

BY DAD

RINTS FOR

OL STUFF

PROJECTS YOU CAN BUILD FOR (AND WITH) YOUR KIDS!

Workman Publishing
New York

Copyright © 2013 by Scott Bedford
Photo and illustration copyright © by Scott Bedford

All rights reserved. No portion of this book may be reproduced—
mechanically, electronically, or by any other means, including photocopying—
without written permission of the publisher. Published simultaneously in
Canada by Thomas Allen & Son Limited.

Library of Congress Cataloging-in-Publication Data is available.

ISBN 978-0-7611-7147-8

Design by Becky Terhune
Cover design by Raquel Jaramillo
Cover photo by Scott Bedford
Author photo by Sharon Bedford

• • •

In creating the projects for this book, the author used products that he had around the house or that
were inspired by familiar movies or cartoons. However, readers can substitute other products or design
home projects inspired by different movies or cartoons. None of the companies whose products are
mentioned in this book have either endorsed or authorized the references to them in *Made by Dad*.

• • •

Workman books are available at special discounts when purchased in bulk
for premiums and sales promotions as well as for fund-raising or educational use.
Special editions or book excerpts also can be created to specification.
For details, contact the Special Sales Director at the address below,
or send an email to specialmarkets@workman.com.

Workman Publishing Company Inc.
225 Varick Street
New York, NY 10014-4381
workman.com

WORKMAN is a registered trademark of Workman Publishing Co., Inc.

Printed in the United States of America
First printing April 2013

10 9 8 7 6 5 4 3 2

CONTENTS

INTRODUCTION

IF YOU HAVE KIDS, some time to kill, and an empty toilet paper roll, this book is definitely for you. (Actually, the kids are optional—although I think they'll be a bit jealous if Dad has all the fun!) But seriously, you don't need a workshop or exotic materials (put your soldering iron away!) to make cool stuff with your kids—just a twinkle in your eye and, of course, this book in your hand. Read it for inspiration, fun, or to get detailed (but playful) blueprints on how to build the sixty-seven projects—the main thing is to get making, and have fun with the kids.

If there is one thing I could put in big, bold, flashing neon letters, it's that the fun is in the *making* and not in creating perfect-looking projects. In other words, wonky, creaky, wobbly, drippy, splashy is cool. Sure, I spent quite a bit of time trying to get all the projects to look as neat as possible so they could be photographed for this book, but the results of some of the early prototypes were far from ideal (see below). They were, however, still very fun to make, and my boys had enormous fun playing with them!

So no excuses. Whether you consider yourself a confident DIYer or someone who up until now has left the crafty stuff to Mom, it's time to show the kids how it's done Dad-style! And if you have any doubt as to whether you're doing it right, look around at the end of a project and ask yourself, "Is the floor covered in paper and cardstock?" . . . "Are the kids covered in paint?" . . . "Have I glued the project to the table?" If you can answer yes to any one of these, then *yes,* I'd say you've got the hang of it. Here's to the fun you'll have, and the messes you'll make.

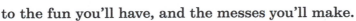

Prototype for the Slingshot Car Launcher, page 76

DAD'S TOOLBOX

MATERIALS

Most of the projects in this book are made from everyday materials, such as soda cans, cardboard tubes, and paper to-go cups (one of my favorites, since you get to enjoy a coffee before you start). Others require materials that might need to be collected over time, such as the old felt-tip markers called for in the Twisted Pen Caddy (page 20) or wooden stirring sticks (in the Jelly Bean Reward Rocket, page 274). Materials that can't be salvaged from around the home can be purchased from stationery and hardware stores, or at the occasional craft shop. Here's an introduction to the key elements in my *Made by Dad* toolbox.

CARD BORED?

One material I turn to again and again is the humble yet versatile corrugated cardboard box—mostly to use as a source for flat panels you can cut from the sides. They can be folded, glued, cut some more—and transformed so fully, that you won't recognize them as the cardboard boxes they once were. The exact size of the box is rarely important, though I will designate small, medium-sized, or large in the project materials lists in order to guide you through your paper recycling bin.

SMALL BOX

8" (203mm)

8" (203mm)

10" (254mm)

MEDIUM-SIZED BOX

16" (406mm)

12" (305mm)

10" (254mm)

LARGE

THIS WAY UP

LARGE BOX (ANY SIZE LARGER THAN MEDIUM)

See the illustration (opposite) for approximate dimensions of each size box. If you don't happen to have any boxes lying around, you can also find them for purchase in a convenient flattened form at most stationery stores. The only other thing to consider when selecting a box to use is the thickness of the cardboard—the sides of some boxes are double layered, which makes them difficult to fold. The sides of the boxes I use are around 3⁄32" (2 mm) thick.

GETTING WIRED

There are a few projects, like Eating Nemo (page 147) and the "Stop the Pigeon" Weather Vane (page 65), that require thick wire. I use #15 gauge (1.5 mm) galvanized steel wire found in the gardening section of a hardware store. A wire coat hanger can work in a pinch, but because it's slightly thicker, it's a lot harder to manipulate.

PAINTING AND DECORATING

I primarily use two materials for painting most of the projects with my boys: spray paint or kids' poster paint. Spray paint is the quickest and the neatest, and the only paint option that doesn't warp cardboard. It's also the most antisocial, so open the windows, or better still, spray outside where the fumes can dissipate. It has the advantage of being able to cover large areas in one go (as in the Priceless Picture Safe, page 197). For other projects, like the Flower Power Tank (page 24), which calls for a camouflage pattern, poster paint is the best option. The challenge is that poster paint causes corrugated cardboard to warp like crazy when painted on one side, so I always recommend painting both sides of a cardboard piece in order to minimize the warping.

COLORING INSIDE THE LINES? NAH!

For decorating projects with fine, colorful details, I'm a huge fan of felt-tip markers. They're not costly, and they come in packs of up to one hundred colors! They work best on uncoated paper or cardstock (which is why, for instance, in the

Balloon Ballast Balancing Act on page 100, I covered the laminated surface of the to-go cup with paper before decorating it). For general, all-purpose outlining, I go with a permanent fine-tip marker, like a Sharpie—it's basic, lasting, and fairly all-terrain when it comes to drawing on different types of surfaces.

TOOLS

My workbench doubles as my dining room table, and my toolbox is the top drawer of a small cupboard—so believe me when I say you really don't need a lot of specialized tools to tackle the projects in this book. But you will need more than a pen knife, so here's an overview of some of the most important equipment, along with a few useful tips, tricks, and hacks.

CUTTING PAPER (AND NOT YOUR HAND)

If you don't own a craft knife, get one. It's a good investment. I recommend going for an X-acto-style knife fitted with a pointed blade that has a flat cutting edge. If you've never used a blade like this before, it may look a little surgical and scary, but I found that even my eight-year-old was able to use it safely (with supervision, of course) and I seized the opportunity to teach him my Golden Rule of Cutting (always cut away from your hand and fingers)— which I recently overheard him reciting to his younger brother!

Along with a good knife, you'll also need a decent supply of replacement blades (what with all the cutting you'll be doing), because there's nothing more frustrating (or unsafe) than cutting with a dull knife edge. I also recommend a steel-edged

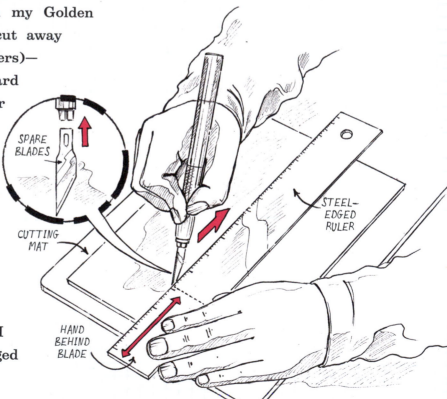

SPARE BLADES

CUTTING MAT

STEEL-EDGED RULER

HAND BEHIND BLADE

ruler, to use as a straightedge when cutting. Craft knives tend to ride up over the edge of plastic or wooden rulers on occasion and can catch fingers! A solid steel ruler is fine, but sometimes troublesome to work with, since it can be awkward to move and position. The best option, in my opinion, is a clear plastic ruler with a stainless steel edge.

Finally, a self-healing cutting mat to go with your craft knife is essential; it will protect the surface of your workspace and prolong the life of the blades. You can, of course, use thin cardboard as a makeshift cutting mat, if necessary—it may dull the blade of the knife faster, but it will protect whatever surface you're working on (floor, kitchen table, priceless antique . . .).

CUTTING HARD STUFF

I know I promised no specialized tools, but this one treads closely into that category: tin snips. I use them to cut soda cans in the "Stop the Pigeon" Weather Vane project (page 65) as well as plastic folders in the Cat-Trap Birdfeeder (page 62). If you decide to invest in a pair of tin snips, I recommend going all out: Forget the ones that look like a pair of heavy-duty scissors; instead, look for the fancy ones with "compound leverage action"—not only are they awesome, they look like they might belong in the Bat Cave!

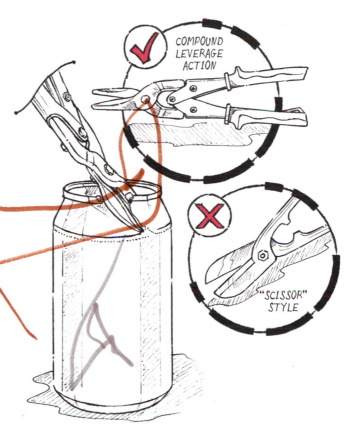

You can also use tin snips to cut wire, which is especially handy if your pliers (see page 7) don't include a cutter, or if you don't own a separate pair of wire cutters (perfect for Eating Nemo on page 147).

The only other tough materials you'll need to slice through are a wooden dowel for making the axles on the Rubber Band Rocket Car on page 110, and

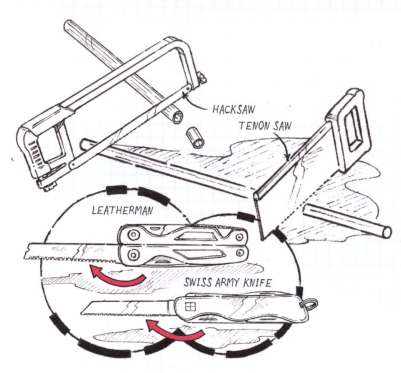

HACKSAW
TENON SAW

LEATHERMAN

SWISS ARMY KNIFE

the dried-up felt-tip pens for the Twisted Pen Caddy on page 20. Both can be trimmed very easily using either a fine-toothed hand saw, a tenon saw, or a hacksaw. But if you really want to be resourceful, you could even use the little saw blade on a Leatherman or Swiss Army knife.

MAKING THINGS STICK

There are several ways of making one material stick to another. In my world, nothing beats hot glue—it's strong, quick-drying, and can join most materials and even fill gaps caused by messy cutting. However, it's less useful for more delicate work, especially for joining small pieces of cardstock and paper, so it's not the only glue you'll want to have on hand. Common alternatives include PVA-based glues that pour as a white liquid and dry transparent, which is a plus, but they take a long time to dry and tend to warp paper or cardstock. I also like to use clear, fast-drying, gel-based glues for adhering hard-to-stick surfaces. In the past, these glues were solvent based and could melt foam, but there are modern varieties that are solvent free.

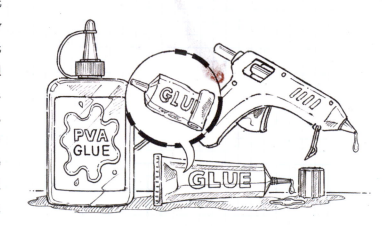

PVA GLUE

GLUE

GLUE

MAKING THINGS BEND OR MELT

Pliers are key for projects where you're bending wire to make levers, hitches, and catches. I particularly like needle-nosed pliers for projects like this because they allow for more dexterity on small parts—*and* they often come with a wire cutter included near the axis of the jaws of the pliers.

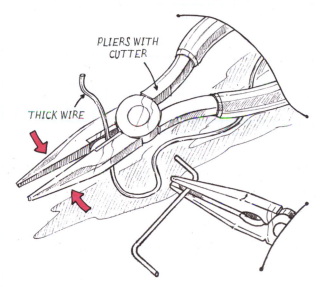

PLIERS WITH CUTTER

THICK WIRE

The only other slightly "out there" tool (besides tin snips) that I use in a couple of projects is a blowtorch—used to warp and twist the plastic casings of felt-tip markers in projects like Beware of Stuffed Animal! (page 40). In my own toolbox, I have a small portable propane torch—the sort of thing you'd use for DIY plumbing—but you can also use a kitchen crème brûlée torch. Obviously, handling a blowtorch of any kind requires some care, but because the felt-tip pens twist and warp so quickly in these projects, I was able to safely complete the melting procedure without taking any major precautions beyond wearing thick leather or canvas gloves. And though it's a fairly obvious point, don't forget to keep the torch away from the kids during and after you've completed the step because the nozzle gets very hot and takes time to cool off.

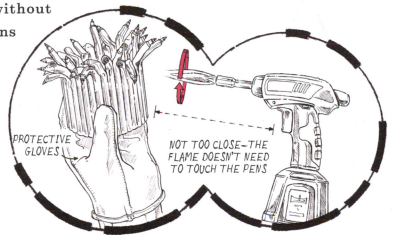

PROTECTIVE GLOVES

NOT TOO CLOSE—THE FLAME DOESN'T NEED TO TOUCH THE PENS

MEASUREMENTS

If you haven't guessed it already from reading, I'm British. All of the projects in this book were originally executed using the metric system of measurement, and adapted to the empirical system. If you have a ruler that includes both measurements, that's great—you can choose whichever system works best for you (some of the smaller measurements may be easier in metric, since you don't have to deal with fractions); just be sure to pick one and stay consistent throughout any given project with either inches or millimeters since not all the measurements are converted directly (some numbers have been rounded for ease of marking).

I recognize that it might be tricky to find some materials (paper to-go cups, for instance) that exactly match the sizes indicated in the projects, since found objects like cups or cardboard tubes or metal cans may vary in size from place to place. In these instances, just try to get as close as possible to the size I've indicated—small differences shouldn't affect the outcome of a project.

TIPS AND TECHNIQUES

Throughout this book, I've included some of my own Pro-Dad Tips—ways to take the project to the next level, or a simple shortcut if you're tight on time. But here are a few that I consistently return to that make the whole messy process of making things a little bit neater.

MAKE A SPRAY BOOTH

Spray paint may be the quickest way to give your projects a nice finish, but having to lay out a protective layer of newspaper each time is a real hassle. And it still tends to get everywhere. So, to minimize the mess (or rather, *contain* it), simply remove the top and front of a large cardboard box, as shown, and use it as a mini-spray booth: Place the elements that need to be sprayed inside it, and the box will collect all the backsplash. When you're finished, make sure it's dry, and store it in a closet or the garage for future use.

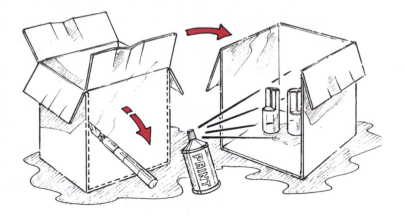

MAKE THE PAINT STICK!

Poster paint may seem all thick and gloppy, but when you paint it onto a shiny surface (like the paper to-go cup in the Snappy Toast Rack project on page 50), you'll struggle to make the paint stick, since it will start to flake off once it's dried. To prevent this from happening, mix some PVA glue in with the paint (approximately one part paint to one part glue).

DRAW STRAIGHT LINES ON A ROUND SURFACE: MAKE A PAPER RULER

The one thing every cardboard tube has in common when it comes to crafting with them, is that they are a real pain to cut! I use a rectangular strip of paper or cardstock to create a "paper ruler" (more accurately, a straightedge) that can be wrapped around the tube. Align the edges of the paper along its overlap and then trace around that edge with a pencil. Remove the paper and then carefully cut along the line using a craft knife.

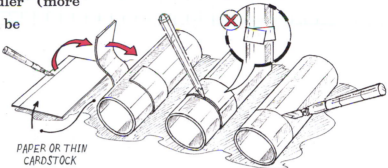

PAPER OR THIN CARDSTOCK

THIS IS NOT COLOR BY NUMBER

I would never prescribe a method for drawing or coloring in—but because I am often asked about my technique, here it is in print: I tend to start with a pencil sketch, which I then outline in black marker (A). I use felt-tip markers to apply patches of color (B), often by moving the marker back and forth to create a series of parallel lines, as in the Cheeky Fortune-Teller (page 202). If I'm drawing on cardstock (because paper is too thin), I dip a paintbrush in water and dab it over the markered parts of the picture (C). The colors will bleed a little to create a very cool watercolor effect (as seen in the Milk Shake Monster project, page 131).

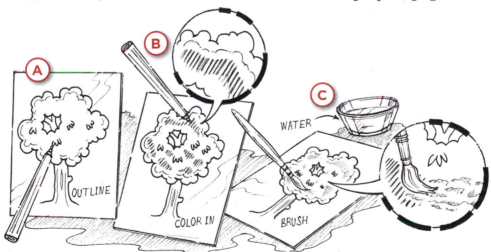

OUTLINE

COLOR IN

WATER

BRUSH

PROPER SCORING

Projects like the Ratapult (page 135) involve making a bespoke box from a piece of corrugated cardboard. If you're new to cardboard, you'll find that accurately folding the corrugated variety can be a bit tricky, especially when folding against the grain; I like to first score along the fold lines using a straightedge and wooden stirring stick, craft (Popsicle) stick, or a blunt knife—the surface of the cardboard may tear slightly but you won't see this once it's folded. (A stirring stick, after all, is not as sharp as a knife, but it also won't go all the way through the layers, which would be bad!)

EARN MOMMY POINTS

This one's a quick one—and more of a tip than a technique—but I've learned over the years that if you're making a supreme mess of the dining room table, your messes will be far more endearing (or at least better tolerated) if Mom's on the receiving end of the thoughtful by-product of the mess (see the "I Love You this Much" Card, page 278, for example). Just look for the "Make It for Mommy" stamp near the project title.

USE THE TEMPLATES

That's what they're there for! I include a lot of drawn elements in my projects because 1) I like to draw and 2) it provides lots of opportunities for the kids to get drawing. But I realize this may backfire. Sometimes kids want their projects to look *exactly* like the ones in the photos, and if that's the case, don't stress, Dad. Just turn to the Appendix in the back of this book (starting on page 281) or log on to workman.com/madebydad and find the relevant template. Look for the illustration of a printer in the instructions for each project, which indicates that there is a template available. You can use the templates in any number of ways— either as a visual reference (A), as a stencil to trace (B), or simply as a template that can be photocopied (or downloaded and printed) onto paper or cardstock (C). Just cut them out and let the kids color them in.

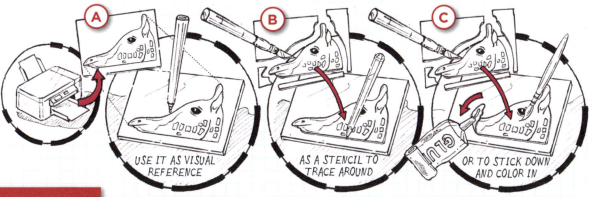

USE IT AS VISUAL REFERENCE — AS A STENCIL TO TRACE AROUND — OR TO STICK DOWN AND COLOR IN

DANGEROUS DECOR

1. GODZILLA SKYLINE

2. MARTIAN DOOR DECAL

3. TWISTED PEN CADDY

4. FLOWER POWER TANK

5. MAGNETIC BOOKENDS

6. EARTHQUAKE COAT HOOK

7. ALIEN ABDUCTION MOBILE

8. BEWARE OF STUFFED ANIMAL!

9. CLAW-THROUGH-THE-WALL PICTURE

10. 1-TON LAMPSHADE

GODZILLA SKYLINE

LEVEL: EASY

MATERIALS
- Ruler
- Scissors
- Black medium-weight cardstock
- Clear or masking tape
- Pencil
- Craft knife and cutting mat
- Mounting putty or double-sided tape

The New York skyline is so iconic, it's just a shame not everyone can wake up to it (including myself). This project attempts to put that right, and in fact, it goes one step further—by throwing Godzilla into the mix. It's a New York skyline straight from the movies!

THAT'S COOL!

EVEN LOOKS GREAT WITH THE CURTAINS CLOSED!

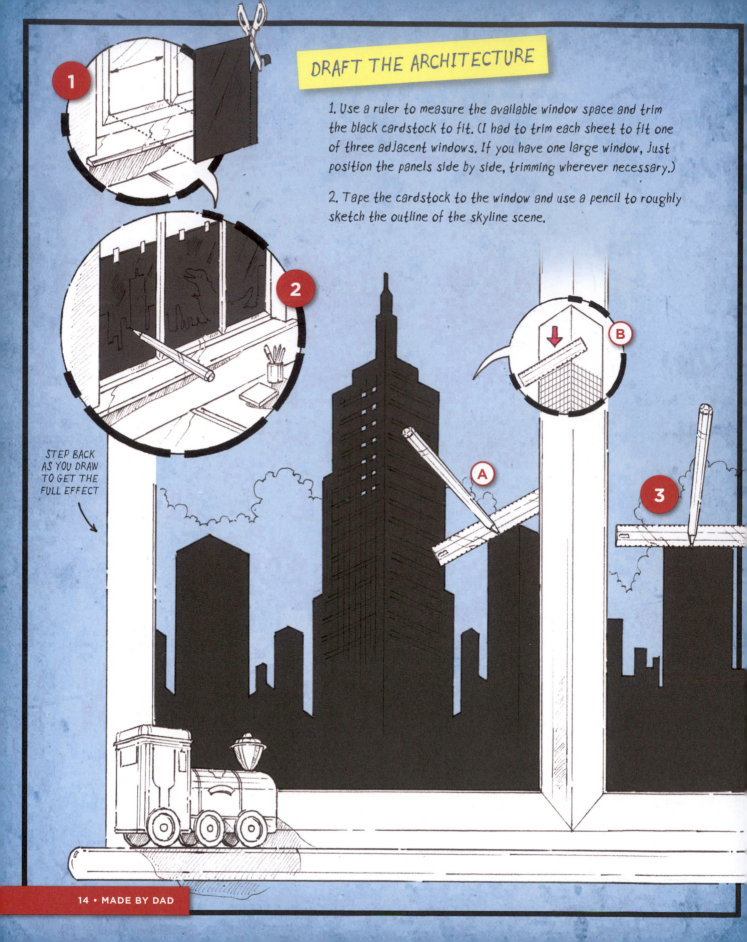

DRAFT THE ARCHITECTURE

1. Use a ruler to measure the available window space and trim the black cardstock to fit. (I had to trim each sheet to fit one of three adjacent windows. If you have one large window, just position the panels side by side, trimming wherever necessary.)

2. Tape the cardstock to the window and use a pencil to roughly sketch the outline of the skyline scene.

STEP BACK AS YOU DRAW TO GET THE FULL EFFECT

FINALIZE THE BLUEPRINTS

3. Remove the skyline panels and neaten the outline using a ruler and pencil. For the ultimate 3-D effect, draw the buildings in perspective with one corner, facing out (A), otherwise, keep things flat.

4. Use the ruler and pencil to draw a grid for the windows. Trace two lines at an angle, as shown (B), for any 3-D skyscrapers.

MAKE MONSTER MAYHEM

5. Don't forget to draw Godzilla! And don't be scared; it's just a simple dinosaur shape. Use the drawings on this page as a guide. For cool extra touches, add a helicopter, draw cracks in neighboring buildings, or stick a water tower in Godzilla's mouth!

WATER TOWER

6

CUTTING MAT

CARVE OUT YOUR CITY

6. Use the craft knife and ruler to cut along the outline of the skyline panels. Mark a selection of squares in the window grid with an X and cut them out. Cut out Godzilla's outline (don't forget his eye!), as well as any extra touches.

EYE

TRY PUTTING DIFFERENT THINGS IN GODZILLA'S MOUTH!

PRO-DAD TIP: If you don't want Mom on your case, have a vacuum with a hose attachment at the ready to suck up any small pieces.

ROOM WITH A WHEW!

MOUNTING PUTTY

7. Reverse the skyline panels so that the pencil marks will face out the window. Use mounting putty to attach the panels to the window. (You can also use double-sided tape, but putty creates a gap that prevents damage from condensation.) Attach Godzilla and any extra touches where desired. Enjoy your new view!

7

AIR GAP

MARTIAN DOOR DECAL

LEVEL: EASY

Why buy generic wall stickers when you can make your own custom creations? This out-of-this-world design features a green Martian pulling down the door, but it could as easily be a castle window with Rapunzel's hair cascading down. Just think big!

MATERIALS

- Black medium-weight cardstock (poster size)
- Ruler
- Pencil
- Craft knife and cutting mat
- White medium-weight cardstock (poster size)
- Poster paint
- Paintbrush
- Black permanent marker
- Paper glue
- Mounting putty or double-sided tape

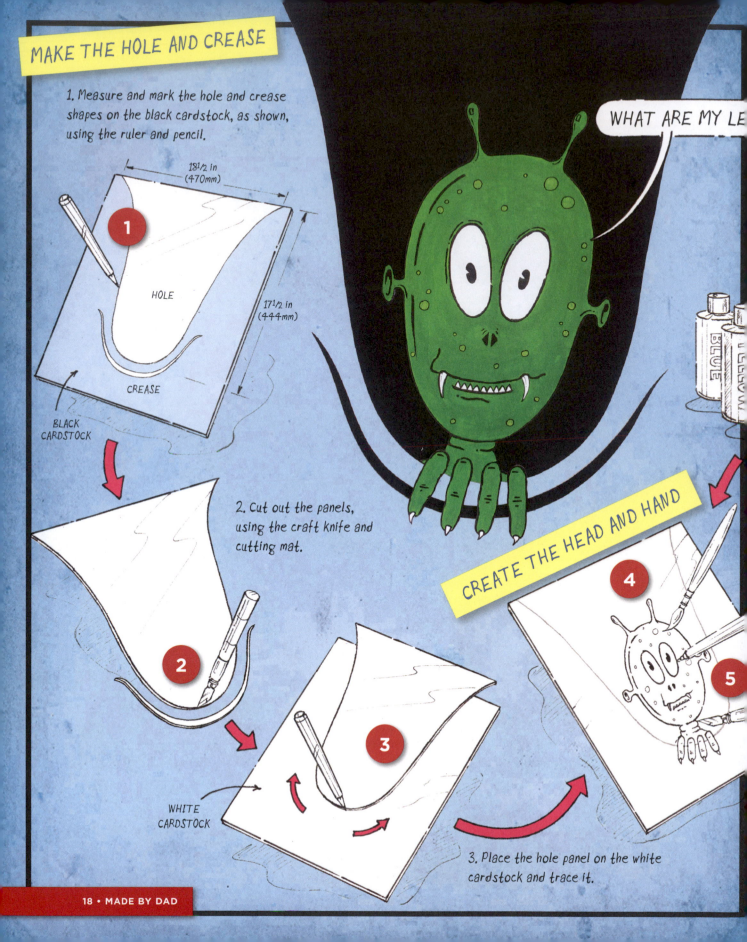

MAKE THE HOLE AND CREASE

1. Measure and mark the hole and crease shapes on the black cardstock, as shown, using the ruler and pencil.

18¹⁄₂ in (470mm)

17¹⁄₂ in (444mm)

HOLE

CREASE

BLACK CARDSTOCK

2. Cut out the panels, using the craft knife and cutting mat.

WHITE CARDSTOCK

3. Place the hole panel on the white cardstock and trace it.

WHAT ARE MY LE

CREATE THE HEAD AND HAND

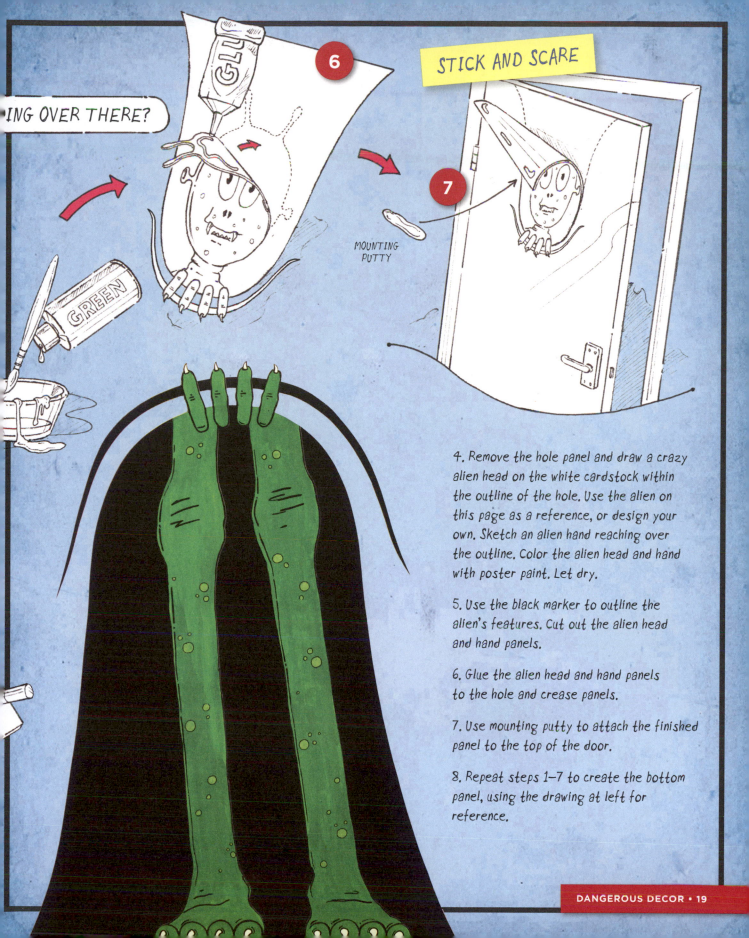

ING OVER THERE?

6

7

GLUE

GREEN

MOUNTING PUTTY

4. Remove the hole panel and draw a crazy alien head on the white cardstock within the outline of the hole. Use the alien on this page as a reference, or design your own. Sketch an alien hand reaching over the outline. Color the alien head and hand with poster paint. Let dry.

5. Use the black marker to outline the alien's features. Cut out the alien head and hand panels.

6. Glue the alien head and hand panels to the hole and crease panels.

7. Use mounting putty to attach the finished panel to the top of the door.

8. Repeat steps 1–7 to create the bottom panel, using the drawing at left for reference.

TWISTED PEN CADDY

LEVEL: MEDIUM

DAD, CAN I HOLD THE BLOWTORCH?

NO!

MATERIALS

- Lightweight cardboard (an old cereal box works well)
- Pencil
- Ruler
- Craft knife and cutting mat
- Tin can
- Clear tape
- 30 dried-up felt-tip markers
- Hot glue gun and glue sticks
- Blowtorch
- Lightweight cardstock
- Scissors
- Paper glue
- Toilet paper tube
- Spray paint (any color)

A guy shouldn't need an excuse to get out the blowtorch and start melting things, but if you do, here's a great one! Made from dried-up felt-tip markers, it's an opportunity to be both destructive and constructive. A lot of fun, but definitely a project for Dad to make and for Junior to watch.

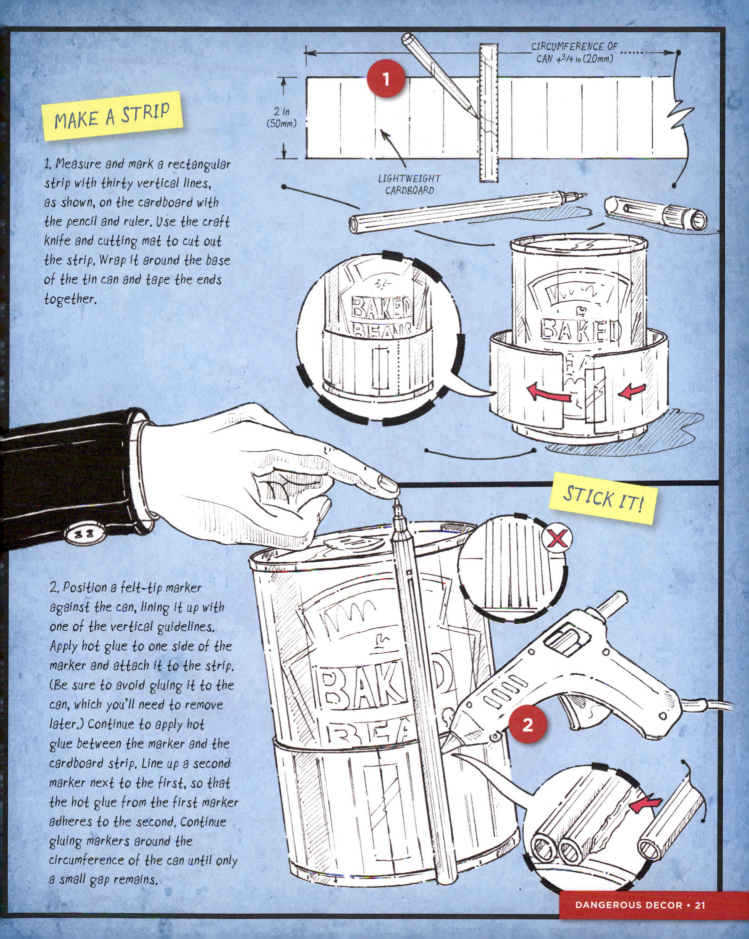

MAKE A STRIP

CIRCUMFERENCE OF
CAN +3/4 in (20mm)

2 in
(50mm)

LIGHTWEIGHT
CARDBOARD

1. Measure and mark a rectangular strip with thirty vertical lines, as shown, on the cardboard with the pencil and ruler. Use the craft knife and cutting mat to cut out the strip. Wrap it around the base of the tin can and tape the ends together.

BAKED

BAKED

STICK IT!

2. Position a felt-tip marker against the can, lining it up with one of the vertical guidelines. Apply hot glue to one side of the marker and attach it to the strip. (Be sure to avoid gluing it to the can, which you'll need to remove later.) Continue to apply hot glue between the marker and the cardboard strip. Line up a second marker next to the first, so that the hot glue from the first marker adheres to the second. Continue gluing markers around the circumference of the can until only a small gap remains.

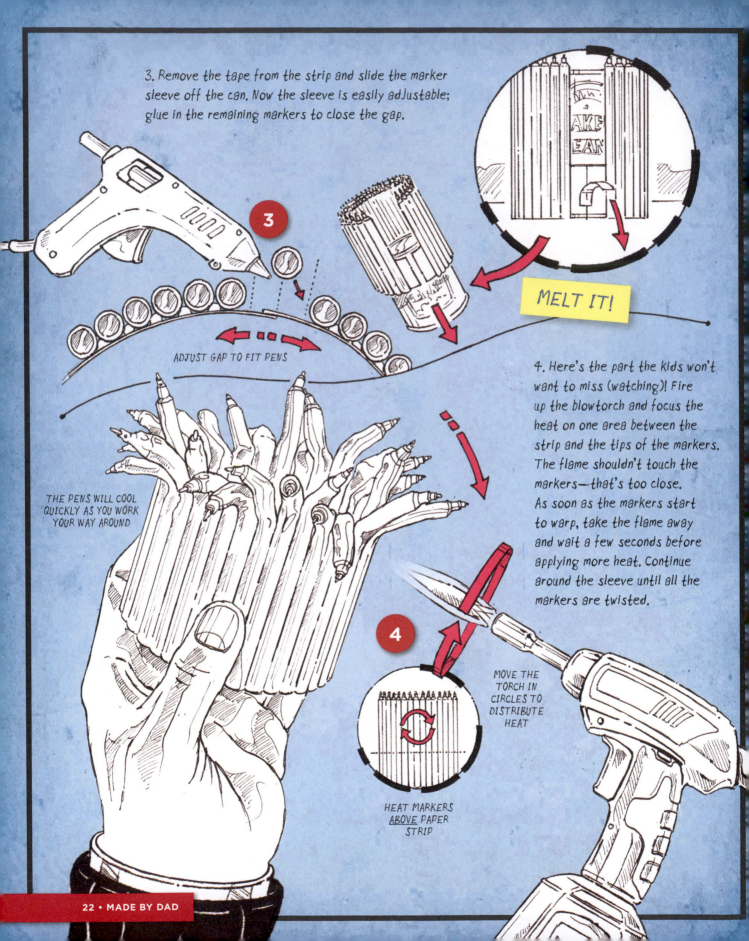

3. Remove the tape from the strip and slide the marker sleeve off the can. Now the sleeve is easily adjustable; glue in the remaining markers to close the gap.

MELT IT!

ADJUST GAP TO FIT PENS

THE PENS WILL COOL QUICKLY AS YOU WORK YOUR WAY AROUND

4. Here's the part the kids won't want to miss (watching)! Fire up the blowtorch and focus the heat on one area between the strip and the tips of the markers. The flame shouldn't touch the markers—that's too close. As soon as the markers start to warp, take the flame away and wait a few seconds before applying more heat. Continue around the sleeve until all the markers are twisted.

MOVE THE TORCH IN CIRCLES TO DISTRIBUTE HEAT

HEAT MARKERS <u>ABOVE</u> PAPER STRIP

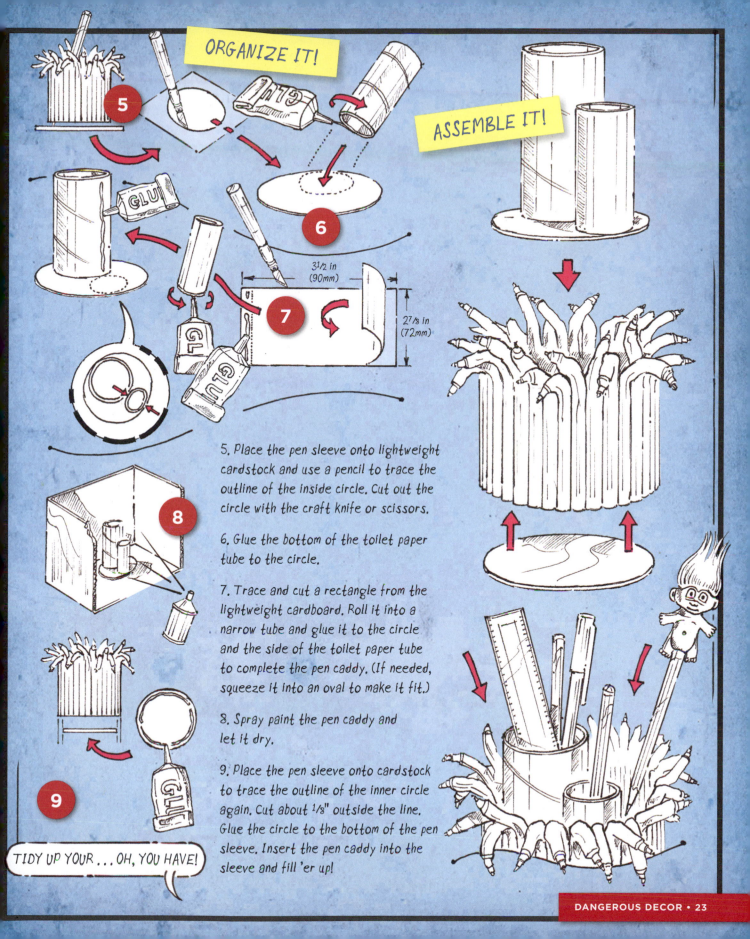

ASSEMBLE IT!

5. Place the pen sleeve onto lightweight cardstock and use a pencil to trace the outline of the inside circle. Cut out the circle with the craft knife or scissors.

6. Glue the bottom of the toilet paper tube to the circle.

7. Trace and cut a rectangle from the lightweight cardboard. Roll it into a narrow tube and glue it to the circle and the side of the toilet paper tube to complete the pen caddy. (If needed, squeeze it into an oval to make it fit.)

8. Spray paint the pen caddy and let it dry.

9. Place the pen sleeve onto cardstock to trace the outline of the inner circle again. Cut about 1/8" outside the line. Glue the circle to the bottom of the pen sleeve. Insert the pen caddy into the sleeve and fill 'er up!

TIDY UP YOUR ... OH, YOU HAVE!

3 1/2 in (90mm)

2 7/8 in (72mm)

FLOWER POWER TANK

LEVEL: MEDIUM

I have a penchant for to-go paper cups.... I'm not sure if it's because it's a great raw material, or because I drink so much coffee. Either way, a paper cup makes a great rotating turret—for "toy mode," add soldiers, and for "decor mode," add flowers.

MATERIALS

- Craft knife and cutting mat
- Medium-sized corrugated cardboard box
- Ruler
- Pencil
- Stirring stick or blunt knife
- Paper glue
- Paper cup (16 oz, 454 g)

- Printer paper
- 2 toilet paper tubes
- Lightweight cardstock
- Coin
- Drafting compass
- 3 empty, clean 15 oz (415 g) tin cans (max. diameter 2¹³/₁₆″, 71 mm)
- Dried-up felt-tip marker
- Hacksaw

- Hot glue gun and glue sticks
- Poster paint (blue and green)
- Paintbrush
- Hammer and nail
- Galvanized wire (#15 gauge, 1.5 mm)
- Wire cutters
- Aluminum foil (optional)

1. Use the craft knife to cut out a large panel from one side of the cardboard box.

2. Use the ruler and pencil to measure and mark the cutting plan onto the panel, as shown. Using a craft knife, carefully cut it out on the cutting mat.

3. Use a stirring stick or blunt knife to score the folds. (Don't worry if the surface tears.)

4. Fold the sides up along the score lines, and apply glue to the side flaps. Apply glue to the end flaps and fold them over to complete the chassis.

5. Measure and mark a series of dots 2³/4" (70 mm) from the top of the paper cup. Wrap a strip of paper around the bottom of the cup and use the ruler to connect the dots with a straight line. Carefully cut along the line. Remove the top of the cup and leave the bottom as the turret.

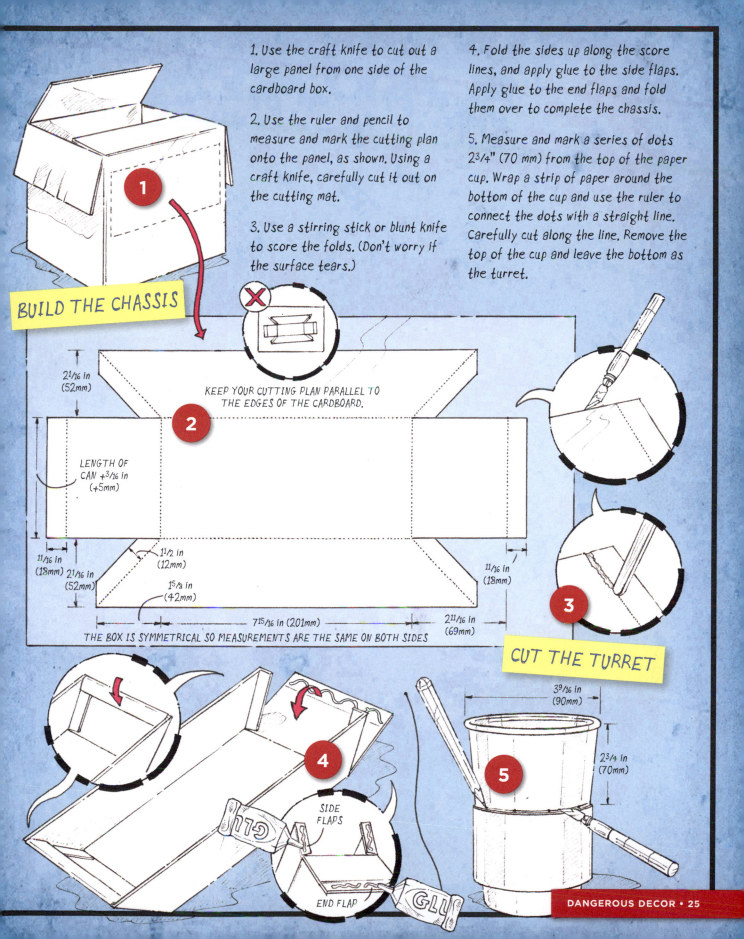

BUILD THE CHASSIS

KEEP YOUR CUTTING PLAN PARALLEL TO THE EDGES OF THE CARDBOARD.

2¹/16 in (52mm)

LENGTH OF CAN +³/16 in (+5mm)

11/16 in (18mm) 2¹/16 in (52mm)

1¹/2 in (12mm)

1⁵/8 in (42mm)

11/16 in (18mm)

7¹⁵/16 in (201mm)

2¹¹/16 in (69mm)

THE BOX IS SYMMETRICAL SO MEASUREMENTS ARE THE SAME ON BOTH SIDES

CUT THE TURRET

3⁹/16 in (90mm)

2³/4 in (70mm)

SIDE FLAPS

END FLAP

GLU

GLU

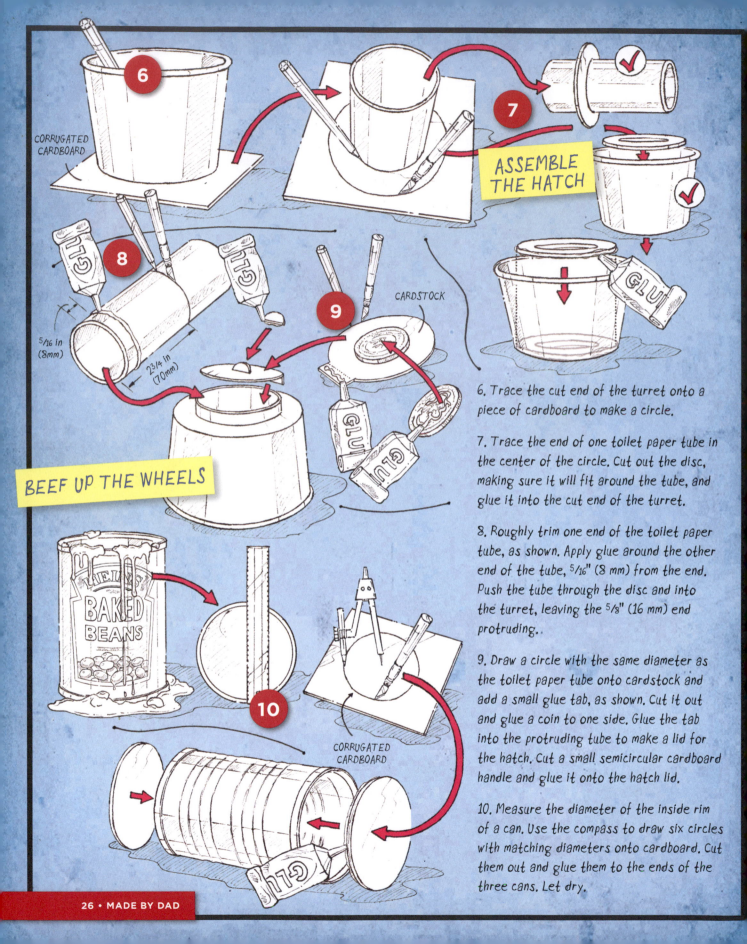

CORRUGATED CARDBOARD

ASSEMBLE THE HATCH

⑥

⑦

⑧

⑨

CARDSTOCK

5/16 in (8mm)

2 3/4 in (70mm)

GLU

GLU

GLU

GLU

BEEF UP THE WHEELS

BAKED BEANS

⑩

CORRUGATED CARDBOARD

GLU

6. Trace the cut end of the turret onto a piece of cardboard to make a circle.

7. Trace the end of one toilet paper tube in the center of the circle. Cut out the disc, making sure it will fit around the tube, and glue it into the cut end of the turret.

8. Roughly trim one end of the toilet paper tube, as shown. Apply glue around the other end of the tube, 5/16" (8 mm) from the end. Push the tube through the disc and into the turret, leaving the 5/8" (16 mm) end protruding.

9. Draw a circle with the same diameter as the toilet paper tube onto cardstock and add a small glue tab, as shown. Cut it out and glue a coin to one side. Glue the tab into the protruding tube to make a lid for the hatch. Cut a small semicircular cardboard handle and glue it onto the hatch lid.

10. Measure the diameter of the inside rim of a can. Use the compass to draw six circles with matching diameters onto cardboard. Cut them out and glue them to the ends of the three cans. Let dry.

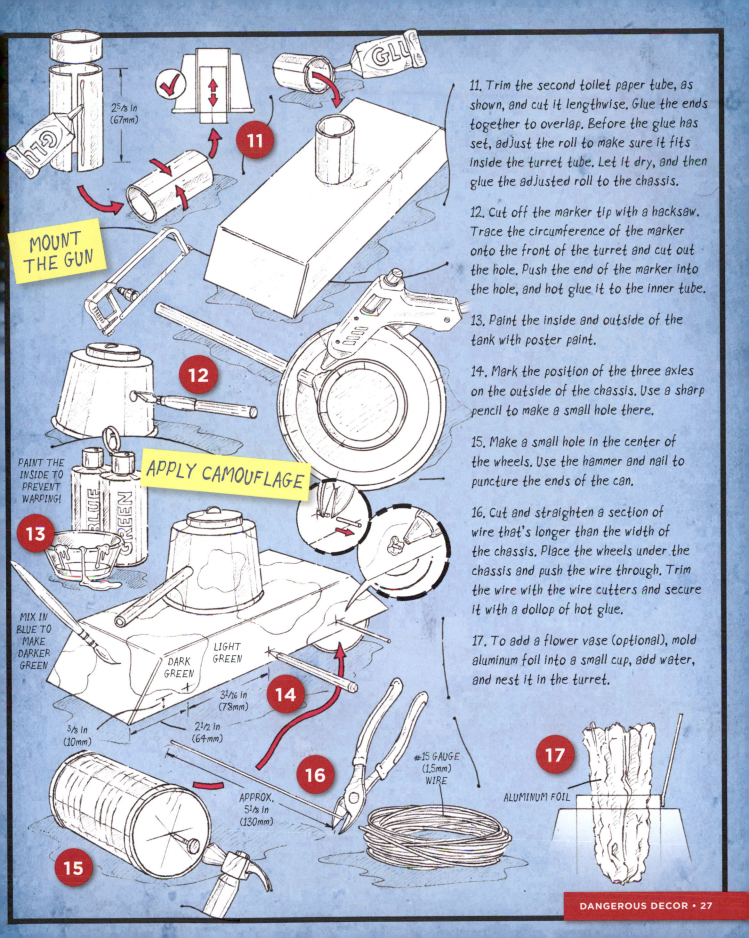

MOUNT THE GUN

APPLY CAMOUFLAGE

2⅝ in (67mm)

PAINT THE INSIDE TO PREVENT WARPING!

BLUE

GREEN

MIX IN BLUE TO MAKE DARKER GREEN

DARK GREEN

LIGHT GREEN

3¹/₁₆ in (78mm)

2½ in (64mm)

⅜ in (10mm)

APPROX. 5⅛ in (130mm)

#15 GAUGE (1.5mm) WIRE

ALUMINUM FOIL

11. Trim the second toilet paper tube, as shown, and cut it lengthwise. Glue the ends together to overlap. Before the glue has set, adjust the roll to make sure it fits inside the turret tube. Let it dry, and then glue the adjusted roll to the chassis.

12. Cut off the marker tip with a hacksaw. Trace the circumference of the marker onto the front of the turret and cut out the hole. Push the end of the marker into the hole, and hot glue it to the inner tube.

13. Paint the inside and outside of the tank with poster paint.

14. Mark the position of the three axles on the outside of the chassis. Use a sharp pencil to make a small hole there.

15. Make a small hole in the center of the wheels. Use the hammer and nail to puncture the ends of the can.

16. Cut and straighten a section of wire that's longer than the width of the chassis. Place the wheels under the chassis and push the wire through. Trim the wire with the wire cutters and secure it with a dollop of hot glue.

17. To add a flower vase (optional), mold aluminum foil into a small cup, add water, and nest it in the turret.

MAGNETIC BOOKENDS

LEVEL: MEDIUM

MATERIALS
- Craft knife and cutting mat
- Medium-sized corrugated cardboard box (sides at least 9″, 229 mm square)
- Pencil
- Drafting compass
- Ruler
- Paper glue
- Books or other heavy object (to use as drying weight)
- Medium-weight cardstock
- Clear tape
- Scissors
- Spray paint (red and silver)
- Newspaper
- Masking tape

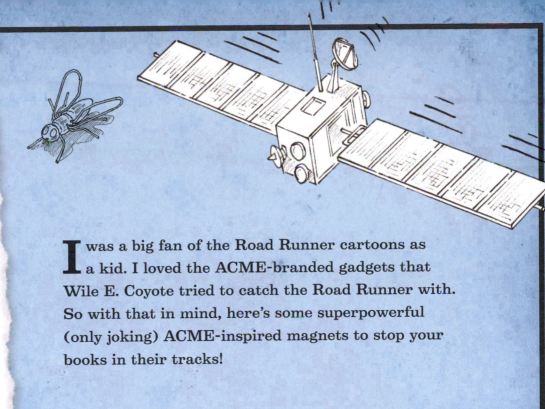

I was a big fan of the Road Runner cartoons as a kid. I loved the ACME-branded gadgets that Wile E. Coyote tried to catch the Road Runner with. So with that in mind, here's some superpowerful (only joking) ACME-inspired magnets to stop your books in their tracks!

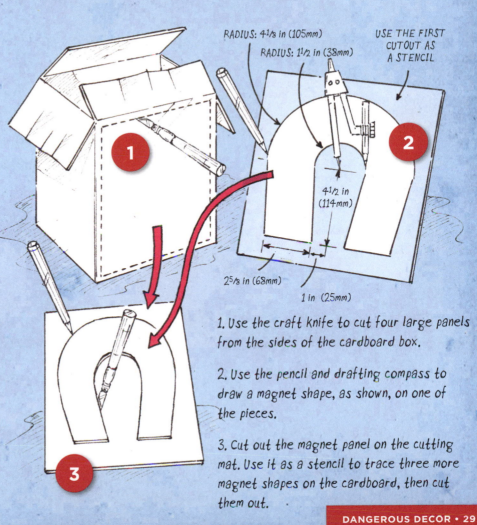

RADIUS: 4⅛ in (105mm)

RADIUS: 1½ in (38mm)

USE THE FIRST CUTOUT AS A STENCIL

4½ in (114mm)

2⅝ in (68mm)

1 in (25mm)

1. Use the craft knife to cut four large panels from the sides of the cardboard box.

2. Use the pencil and drafting compass to draw a magnet shape, as shown, on one of the pieces.

3. Cut out the magnet panel on the cutting mat. Use it as a stencil to trace three more magnet shapes on the cardboard, then cut them out.

WARNING: DON'T POINT AT THE SKY!

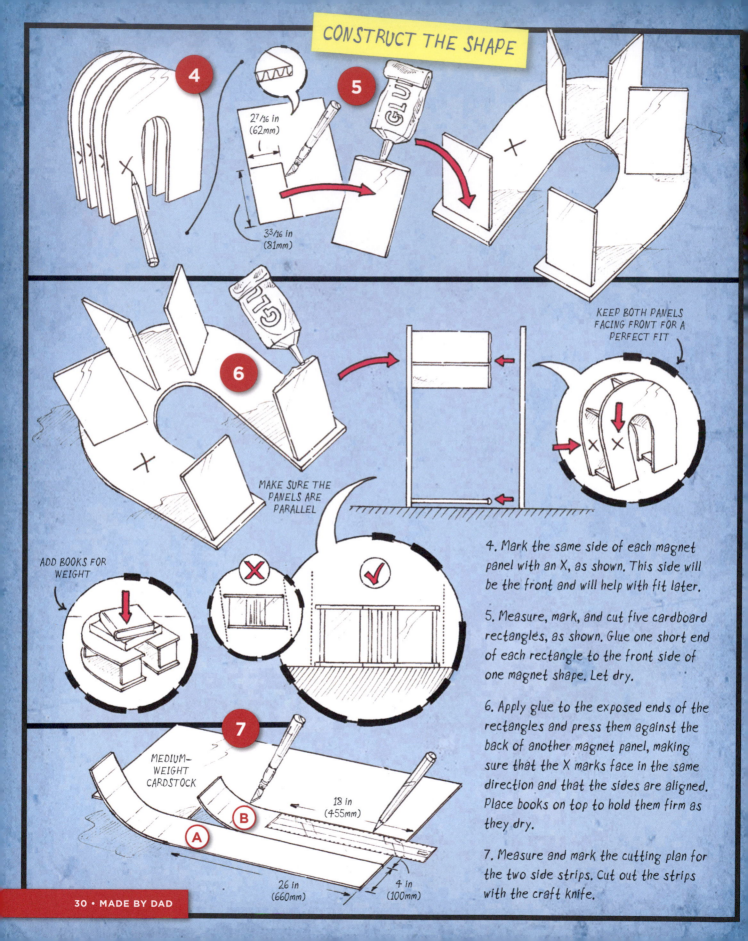

4

2⁷/₁₆ in (62mm)

3³/₁₆ in (81mm)

5

GLUE

6

KEEP BOTH PANELS FACING FRONT FOR A PERFECT FIT

MAKE SURE THE PANELS ARE PARALLEL

ADD BOOKS FOR WEIGHT

7

MEDIUM-WEIGHT CARDSTOCK

Ⓐ Ⓑ

18 in (455mm)

26 in (660mm)

4 in (100mm)

4. Mark the same side of each magnet panel with an X, as shown. This side will be the front and will help with fit later.

5. Measure, mark, and cut five cardboard rectangles, as shown. Glue one short end of each rectangle to the front side of one magnet shape. Let dry.

6. Apply glue to the exposed ends of the rectangles and press them against the back of another magnet panel, making sure that the X marks face in the same direction and that the sides are aligned. Place books on top to hold them firm as they dry.

7. Measure and mark the cutting plan for the two side strips. Cut out the strips with the craft knife.

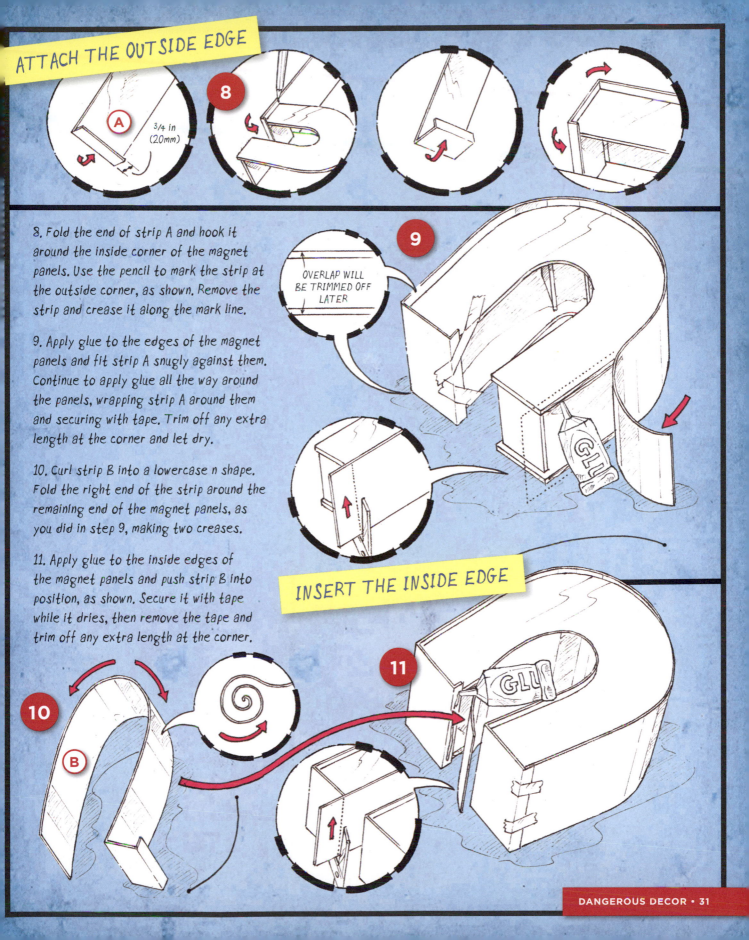

A

3/4 in
(20mm)

8

8. Fold the end of strip A and hook it around the inside corner of the magnet panels. Use the pencil to mark the strip at the outside corner, as shown. Remove the strip and crease it along the mark line.

9. Apply glue to the edges of the magnet panels and fit strip A snugly against them. Continue to apply glue all the way around the panels, wrapping strip A around them and securing with tape. Trim off any extra length at the corner and let dry.

10. Curl strip B into a lowercase n shape. Fold the right end of the strip around the remaining end of the magnet panels, as you did in step 9, making two creases.

11. Apply glue to the inside edges of the magnet panels and push strip B into position, as shown. Secure it with tape while it dries, then remove the tape and trim off any extra length at the corner.

9

OVERLAP WILL
BE TRIMMED OFF
LATER

GLU

INSERT THE INSIDE EDGE

10

B

11

GLU

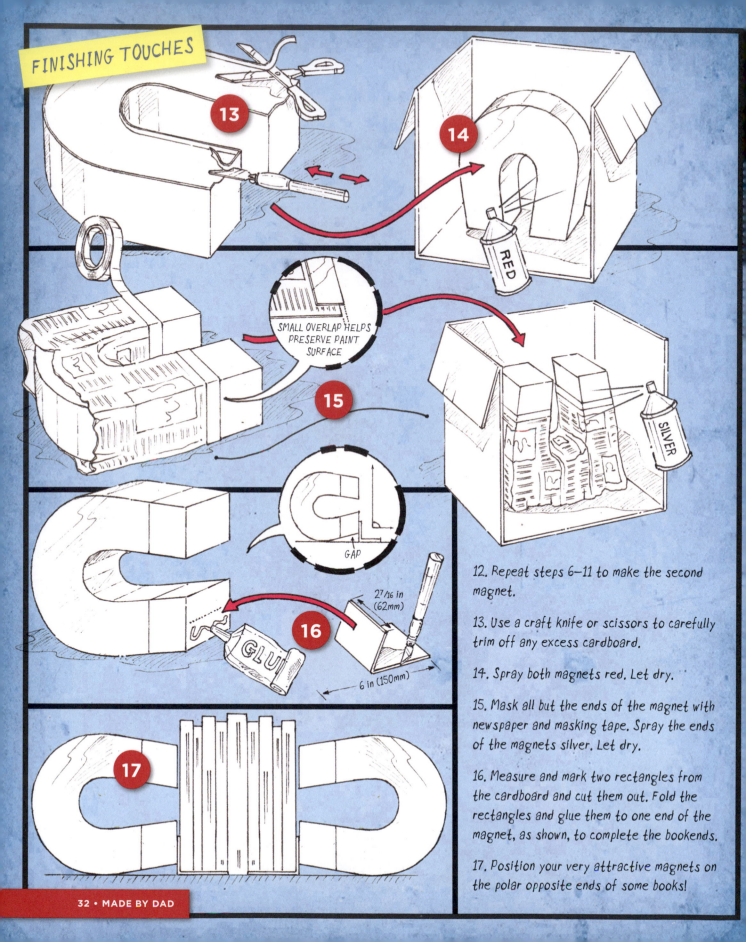

FINISHING TOUCHES

13

14

RED

SMALL OVERLAP HELPS PRESERVE PAINT SURFACE

15

SILVER

GAP

2⁷/₁₆ in (62mm)

16

GLUE

6 in (150mm)

17

12. Repeat steps 6–11 to make the second magnet.

13. Use a craft knife or scissors to carefully trim off any excess cardboard.

14. Spray both magnets red. Let dry.

15. Mask all but the ends of the magnet with newspaper and masking tape. Spray the ends of the magnets silver. Let dry.

16. Measure and mark two rectangles from the cardboard and cut them out. Fold the rectangles and glue them to one end of the magnet, as shown, to complete the bookends.

17. Position your very attractive magnets on the polar opposite ends of some books!

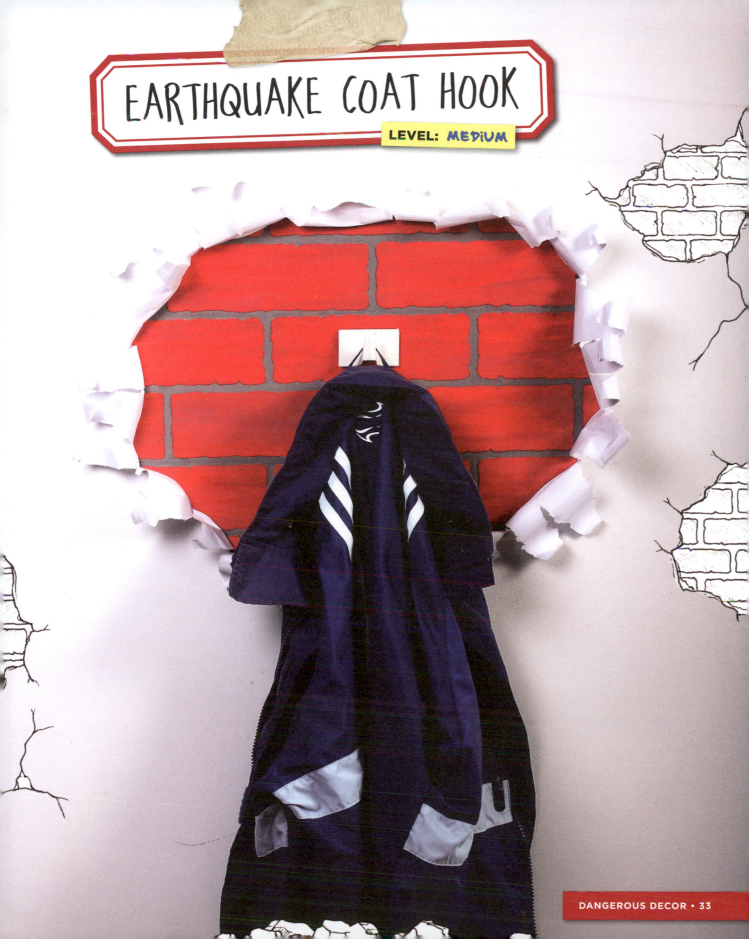

EARTHQUAKE COAT HOOK

LEVEL: MEDIUM

Call it rustic, modern, or the result of a natural disaster—this quirky coat hanger is both useful and fun, which is always a good combination. It's also a cinch to make (no sledgehammers required). As an added bonus, your kids will probably start hanging their coats up!

MATERIALS

- Craft knife and cutting mat
- Medium-sized corrugated cardboard box
- Ruler
- Pencil
- Paper glue
- White medium-weight cardstock
- Scissors
- Poster paint (red, black, and white)
- Paintbrush
- Printer paper
- Craft (Popsicle) stick
- Adhesive plastic hook (3M brand works well)
- Hammer and nail

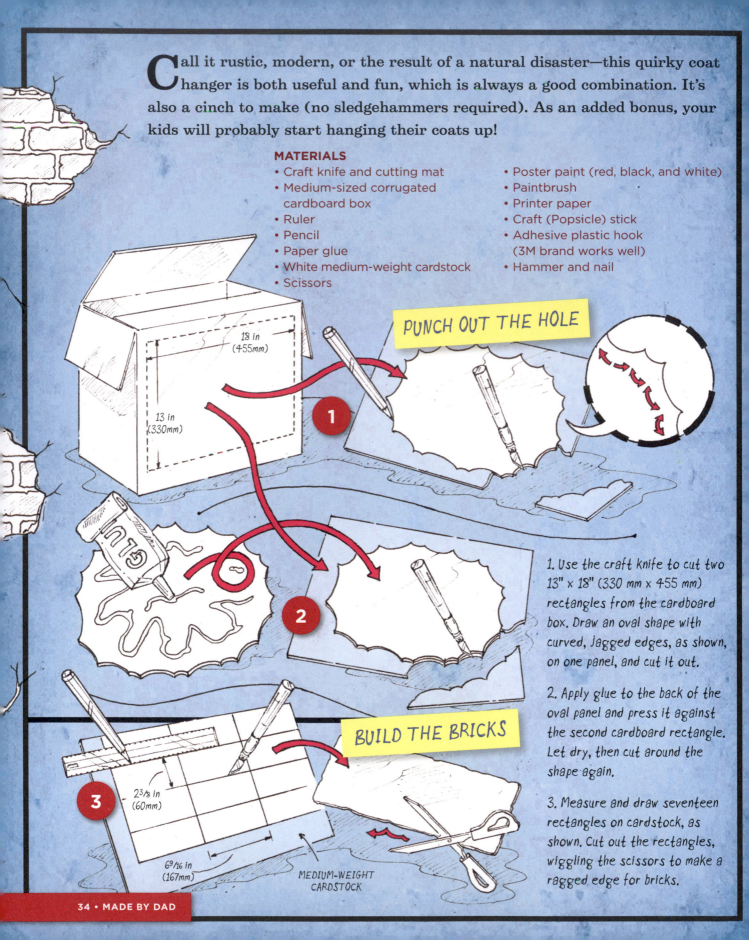

18 in (455mm)

13 in (330mm)

PUNCH OUT THE HOLE

1

GLUE

2

BUILD THE BRICKS

3

2³/₈ in (60mm)

6⁹/₁₆ in (167mm)

MEDIUM-WEIGHT CARDSTOCK

1. Use the craft knife to cut two 13" x 18" (330 mm x 455 mm) rectangles from the cardboard box. Draw an oval shape with curved, jagged edges, as shown, on one panel, and cut it out.

2. Apply glue to the back of the oval panel and press it against the second cardboard rectangle. Let dry, then cut around the shape again.

3. Measure and draw seventeen rectangles on cardstock, as shown. Cut out the rectangles, wiggling the scissors to make a ragged edge for bricks.

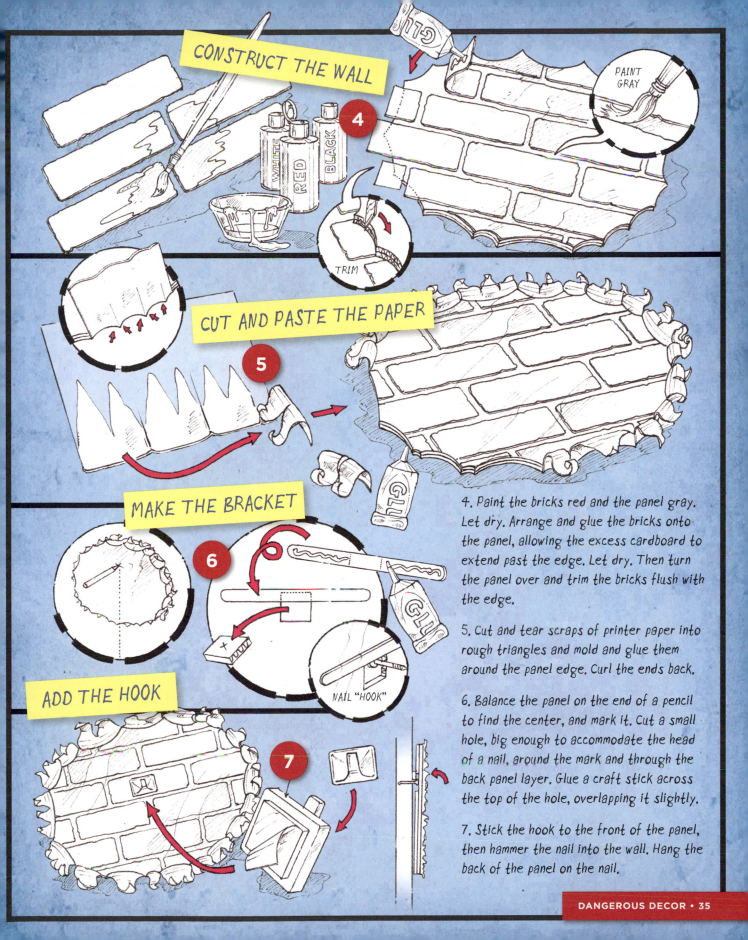

CONSTRUCT THE WALL

PAINT GRAY

WHITE RED BLACK

TRIM

CUT AND PASTE THE PAPER

MAKE THE BRACKET

NAIL "HOOK"

ADD THE HOOK

4. Paint the bricks red and the panel gray. Let dry. Arrange and glue the bricks onto the panel, allowing the excess cardboard to extend past the edge. Let dry. Then turn the panel over and trim the bricks flush with the edge.

5. Cut and tear scraps of printer paper into rough triangles and mold and glue them around the panel edge. Curl the ends back.

6. Balance the panel on the end of a pencil to find the center, and mark it. Cut a small hole, big enough to accommodate the head of a nail, around the mark and through the back panel layer. Glue a craft stick across the top of the hole, overlapping it slightly.

7. Stick the hook to the front of the panel, then hammer the nail into the wall. Hang the back of the panel on the nail.

ALIEN ABDUCTION MOBILE

LEVEL: TRICKY

MATERIALS
- Craft knife and cutting mat
- Medium-sized corrugated cardboard box
- Paper plate
- Paper glue
- Felt-tip markers (in a variety of colors)
- White lightweight cardstock
- Black poster paint
- Paintbrush
- Ruler
- Pencil
- Drafting compass
- Clear plastic cup
- Hot glue gun and glue sticks
- Thread (black or other dark color)
- Mounting putty or coins
- Access to a photocopier or printer
  (optional)

No book for dads would be complete without a flying saucer. And I couldn't resist turning this one into an alien abduction scene with a super powerful tractor beam. It really looks great when it's hung—all the elements slowly rotate as if they are levitating in midair.

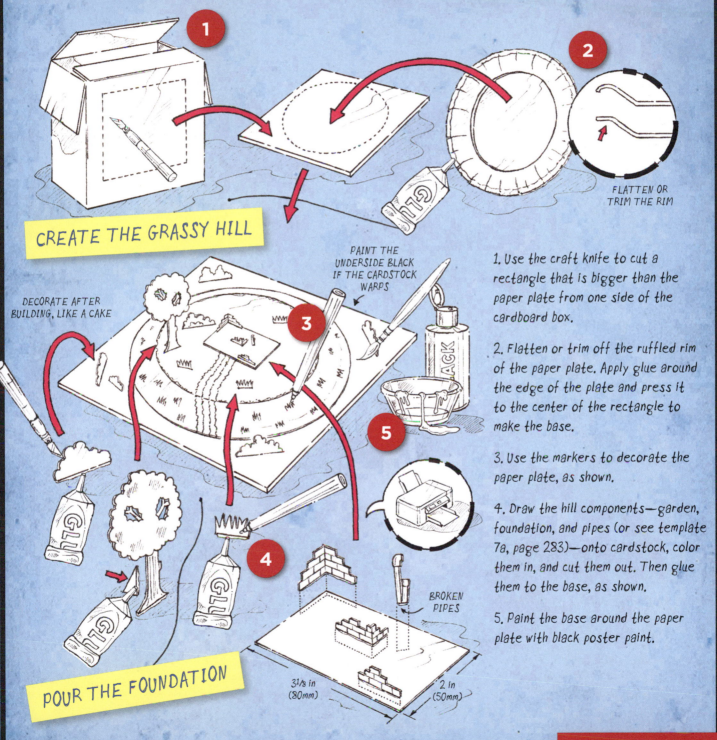

FLATTEN OR TRIM THE RIM

CREATE THE GRASSY HILL

DECORATE AFTER BUILDING, LIKE A CAKE

PAINT THE UNDERSIDE BLACK IF THE CARDSTOCK WARPS

BROKEN PIPES

POUR THE FOUNDATION

3 1/8 in (80mm)

2 in (50mm)

1. Use the craft knife to cut a rectangle that is bigger than the paper plate from one side of the cardboard box.

2. Flatten or trim off the ruffled rim of the paper plate. Apply glue around the edge of the plate and press it to the center of the rectangle to make the base.

3. Use the markers to decorate the paper plate, as shown.

4. Draw the hill components—garden, foundation, and pipes (or see template 7a, page 283)—onto cardstock, color them in, and cut them out. Then glue them to the base, as shown.

5. Paint the base around the paper plate with black poster paint.

6. Measure and mark the cutting plans (or see templates 7a and 7b, pages 283–284) for the house components (walls, ceiling, roof, gables, and chimney) and cut them out. Draw in details. Fold and glue the components, as shown.

7. Measure and mark the cutting plans (or see template 7b, page 284) for the bedroom components (bed, head and footboard, boy, and teddy bear) and cut them out. Draw in details. Fold and glue the components, as shown.

8. Use the compass to measure and mark the cutting plan for the UFO shape. Color it gray and draw in details. Cut it out.

9. Cut the clear plastic cup in half. Form the UFO shape into a cone and position the cup inside the center hole. Overlap the edges of the cone and glue them together. Turn the panel over and secure the cup inside it with hot glue.

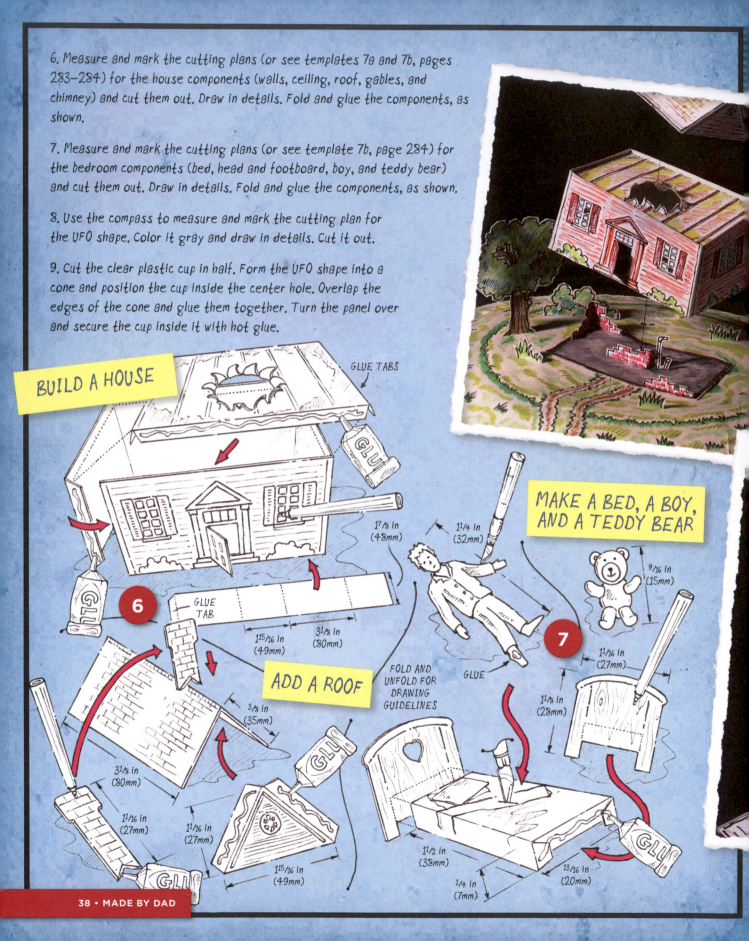

BUILD A HOUSE

GLUE TABS

GLUE

6

GLUE TAB

1⁷⁄₈ in (48mm)

1¹⁵⁄₁₆ in (49mm)

3¹⁄₈ in (80mm)

ADD A ROOF

3⁄₈ in (35mm)

3¹⁄₈ in (80mm)

1¹⁄₁₆ in (27mm)

1¹⁄₁₆ in (27mm)

1¹⁵⁄₁₆ in (49mm)

GLUE

FOLD AND UNFOLD FOR DRAWING GUIDELINES

GLUE

MAKE A BED, A BOY, AND A TEDDY BEAR

1¹⁄₄ in (32mm)

9⁄₁₆ in (15mm)

7

1¹⁄₁₆ in (27mm)

1¹⁄₈ in (28mm)

1¹⁄₂ in (38mm)

¹⁄₄ in (7mm)

¹³⁄₁₆ in (20mm)

GLUE

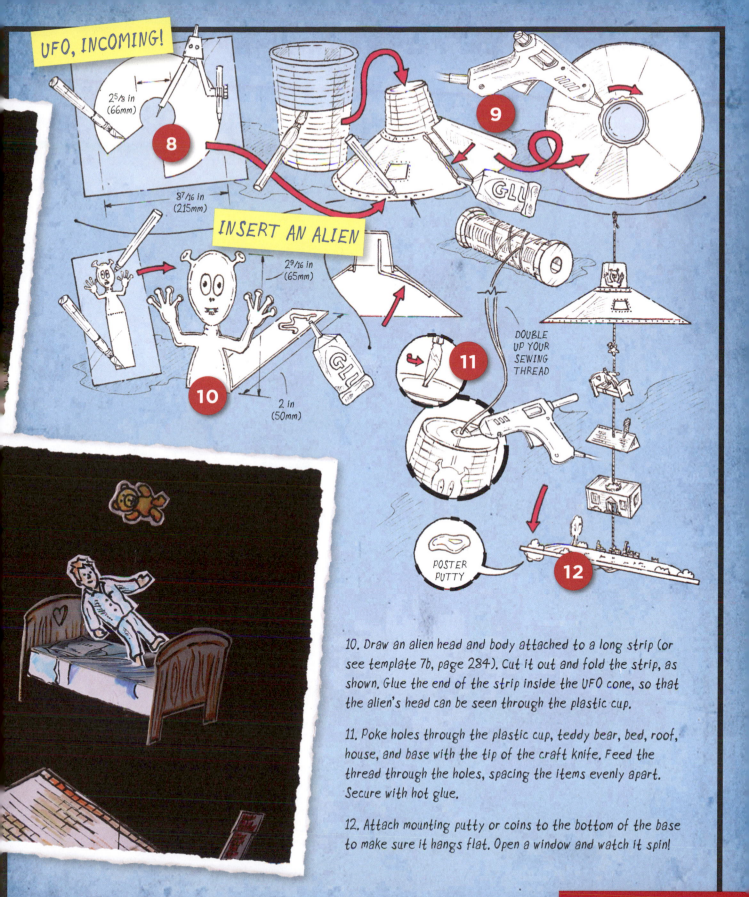

2 5/8 in (66mm)

8 7/16 in (215mm)

INSERT AN ALIEN

2 9/16 in (65mm)

2 in (50mm)

8

9

10

11

12

DOUBLE UP YOUR SEWING THREAD

GLU

GLU

POSTER PUTTY

10. Draw an alien head and body attached to a long strip (or see template 7b, page 284). Cut it out and fold the strip, as shown. Glue the end of the strip inside the UFO cone, so that the alien's head can be seen through the plastic cup.

11. Poke holes through the plastic cup, teddy bear, bed, roof, house, and base with the tip of the craft knife. Feed the thread through the holes, spacing the items evenly apart. Secure with hot glue.

12. Attach mounting putty or coins to the bottom of the base to make sure it hangs flat. Open a window and watch it spin!

BEWARE OF STUFFED ANIMAL!

LEVEL: TRICKY

· DANGEROUS ANIMALS · KEEP OUT ·

Create a cage with a realistic bent bar effect to turn the softest toy animal into the fiercest creature. If cuddly creatures aren't your thing, this mauled crate would also make a great home for a scary dinosaur or mythical monster. Or just leave it empty and stick an "Escaped Alligator" sign on the side!

MATERIALS

- Craft knife and cutting mat
- Ruler
- Small corrugated cardboard box
- Pencil
- Paper glue
- Brown felt-tip marker
- Medium-sized corrugated cardboard box
- Black permanent marker
- Hacksaw
- 10 dried-up felt-tip markers (for the bars)
- Blowtorch
- Silver spray paint
- Hot glue gun and glue sticks
- Plush animal of your choice

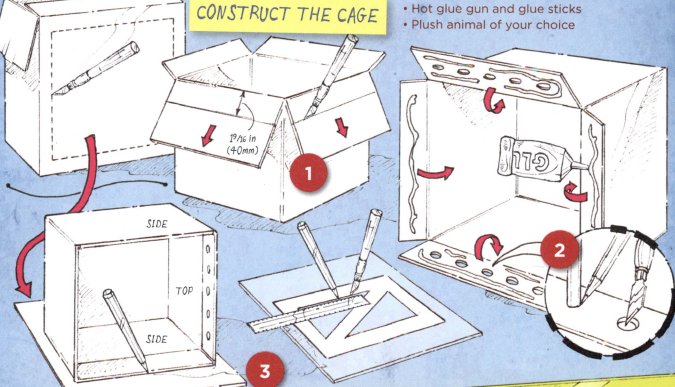

CONSTRUCT THE CAGE

1⁹/₁₆ in (40mm)

SIDE

TOP

SIDE

1

2

3

1. Use the craft knife to trim the flaps on the small cardboard box, as shown.

2. On two opposite flaps, use a pencil to trace the base of a marker to make five evenly spaced circles. Cut out the circles. Apply glue to the flaps and fold them in.

3. Cut three large panels from the medium-sized box. Trace the top and sides of the small box on each panel and cut out the pieces. Use the ruler to mark two right triangles on each piece and cut them out to make three frames.

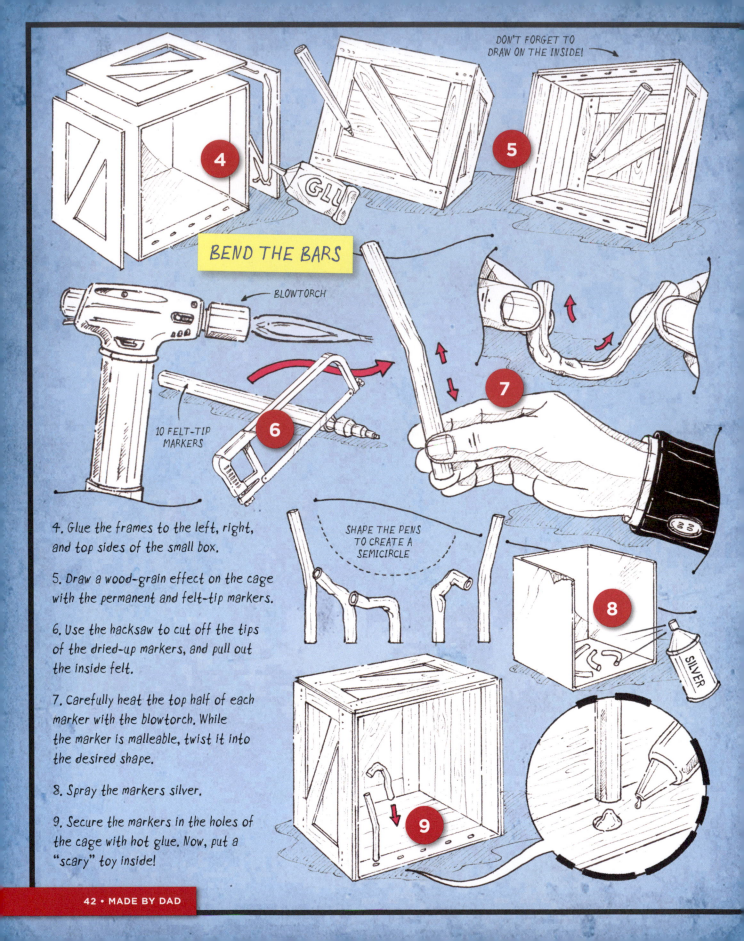

DON'T FORGET TO DRAW ON THE INSIDE!

4

5

BEND THE BARS

BLOWTORCH

6

10 FELT-TIP MARKERS

7

SHAPE THE PENS TO CREATE A SEMICIRCLE

8

SILVER

9

4. Glue the frames to the left, right, and top sides of the small box.

5. Draw a wood-grain effect on the cage with the permanent and felt-tip markers.

6. Use the hacksaw to cut off the tips of the dried-up markers, and pull out the inside felt.

7. Carefully heat the top half of each marker with the blowtorch. While the marker is malleable, twist it into the desired shape.

8. Spray the markers silver.

9. Secure the markers in the holes of the cage with hot glue. Now, put a "scary" toy inside!

CLAW-THROUGH-THE-WALL PICTURE

LEVEL: EASY

MATERIALS

- Craft knife and cutting mat
- Medium-sized corrugated cardboard box
- Ruler
- Pencil
- Felt-tip markers
- Paint
- Paintbrush
- Paper (sized to match frame)
- Paper glue
- Black permanent marker
- Mounting putty

This project will appeal to your kids' destructive side. First, they get to draw a pretty picture and rip it in half, and then they get to put a crack in the wall (yes, a fake one)! A great project for those frustrating rainy days when your rambunctious brood might need to let off steam.

8¹/₂ in (216mm)

11⁵/₈ in (295mm)

1³/₁₆ in (30mm)

1

1. Use the craft knife to cut a large panel from one side of the cardboard box. Measure and mark the cutting plan, as shown. Carefully cut it out on the cutting mat to create the frame.

2. Use markers to draw a wood-grain effect onto the frame.

3. Get your kids to draw or paint a picture on a piece of paper slightly larger than the opening in the frame.

4. Glue the picture onto the back of the frame.

5. Carefully tear the frame and picture in half.

6. Place the two halves, slightly apart, on some paper and use a black marker to draw a crack in between the halves, following the shape of the tear. Color it in and cut it out.

7. Draw four claws, as shown, with the fold tabs at the bottom. Color them and then cut them out. Roll each one so it curves over to conceal the tab.

8. Use mounting putty to attach the claws, crack, and picture halves onto a wall. Now, admire your handiwork and try not to have nightmares!

PUTTY IT UP

VERY THIN SAUSAGES OF MOUNTING PUTTY

MOUNTING PUTTY

MOUNTING PUTTY

8

PAINT A PRETTY PICTURE

INSIDE OF FRAME

OVERLAP

CRAFT THE CLAW

CREATE THE CRACK

RIP!

CURVED

9/16 in (15mm) 1 in (25mm)

1-TON LAMPSHADE

LEVEL: MEDIUM

Bring a bit of old-school Hollywood drama to your home with a 1-ton lampshade. (It certainly brought out the amateur theatrics in my nieces.) It also makes the perfect superhero party prop—get the kids to stand underneath and demonstrate their superhuman strength.

MATERIALS
- Ruler
- Pencil
- Medium-sized corrugated cardboard box
- Craft knife and cutting mat
- Stirring stick or blunt knife
- Hot glue gun and glue sticks
- Black permanent marker
- Poster paint (black and white)
- Paintbrush
- Hanging lightbulb and plastic collar
- Mounting putty
- Plastic chain (optional)

1. Use the ruler and pencil to measure and mark the cutting plan on the cardboard box, as shown. Carefully cut out two S panels and two F panels with the craft knife.

SHAPE YOUR WEIGHT

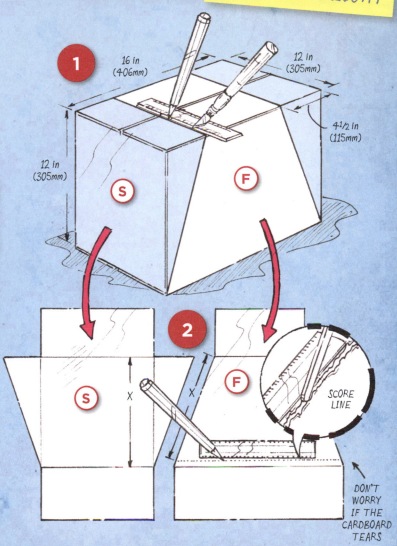

2. Measure the height (x) of one of the S panels. Mark the measurement x along the diagonal edges of F, starting at the narrow end of the panel. Draw a horizontal line connecting the two marks. Use a stirring stick or blunt knife to score the line. Repeat for the second F panel.

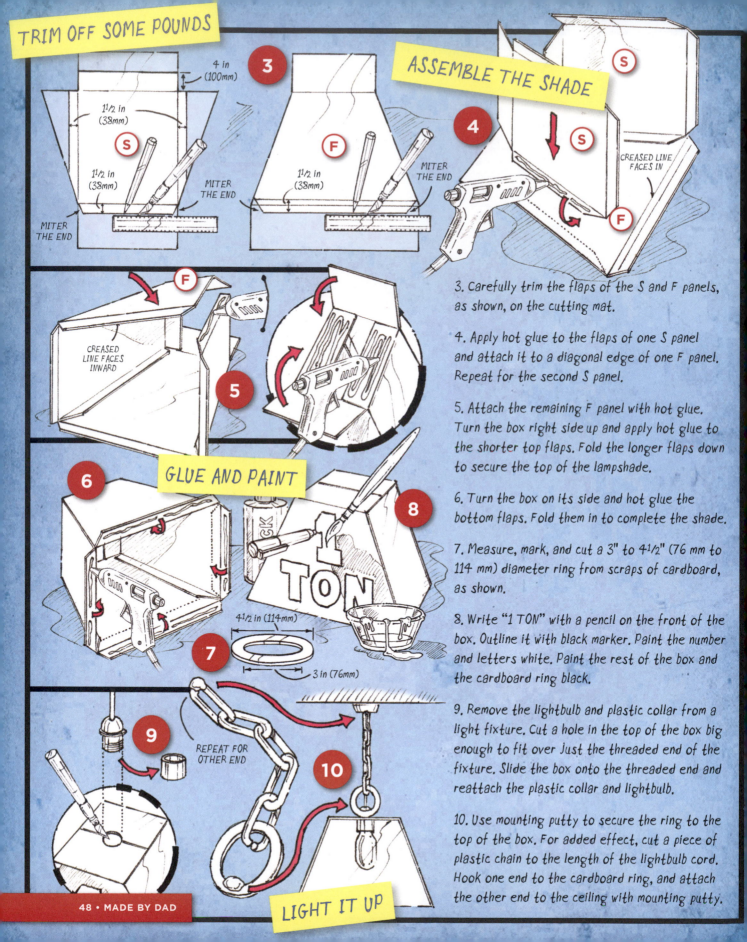

4 in (100mm)

1½ in (38mm)

S

1½ in (38mm)

MITER THE END

MITER THE END

MITER THE END

F

1½ in (38mm)

MITER THE END

ASSEMBLE THE SHADE

S

S

CREASED LINE FACES IN

F

CREASED LINE FACES INWARD

F

GLUE AND PAINT

1 TON

4½ in (114mm)

3 in (76mm)

REPEAT FOR OTHER END

LIGHT IT UP

3. Carefully trim the flaps of the S and F panels, as shown, on the cutting mat.

4. Apply hot glue to the flaps of one S panel and attach it to a diagonal edge of one F panel. Repeat for the second S panel.

5. Attach the remaining F panel with hot glue. Turn the box right side up and apply hot glue to the shorter top flaps. Fold the longer flaps down to secure the top of the lampshade.

6. Turn the box on its side and hot glue the bottom flaps. Fold them in to complete the shade.

7. Measure, mark, and cut a 3" to 4½" (76 mm to 114 mm) diameter ring from scraps of cardboard, as shown.

8. Write "1 TON" with a pencil on the front of the box. Outline it with black marker. Paint the number and letters white. Paint the rest of the box and the cardboard ring black.

9. Remove the lightbulb and plastic collar from a light fixture. Cut a hole in the top of the box big enough to fit over just the threaded end of the fixture. Slide the box onto the threaded end and reattach the plastic collar and lightbulb.

10. Use mounting putty to secure the ring to the top of the box. For added effect, cut a piece of plastic chain to the length of the lightbulb cord. Hook one end to the cardboard ring, and attach the other end to the ceiling with mounting putty.

HOME HACKS

SNAPPY TOAST RACK

LEVEL: EASY

MATERIALS

- Paper cup (16 oz, 454 g)
- Craft knife and cutting mat
- Pencil
- Ruler
- White medium-weight cardstock
- Paper glue
- Drafting compass
- Printer paper
- Poster paint (green, blue, and white)
- PVA glue
- Paintbrush
- Black permanent marker
- Access to a photocopier or printer (optional)

Watch your fingers, this snappy-looking toast rack packs a bite! A combination of two of my favorite things—a grande latte (see if you can score an extra paper cup) and a crocodile—it makes a great breakfast-time accessory!

1. Flip the cup upside down and use a craft knife to remove its base.

2. Use the pencil and ruler to draw a mouth shape extending from the opening at the base on each side of the cup (or see template 11, page 285). Use the craft knife to cut it out.

3. Trace the bottom of the cup onto cardstock. Then remove the cup and add two bumps to the arc of one of the half circles for the nostrils. Close off the arcs by drawing two straight lines. (Or see template 11, page 285.)

4. Cut out both pieces and use paper glue to attach them to the bottom of the cup.

CREATE THE BASE

3 9/16 in (90mm)

5 1/8 in (130mm)

1

ADD CRUSHING JAWS

11/16 in (18mm)

3 in (75mm)

2

DON'T FORGET THE SNOUT

CARDSTOCK

3

4

GLUE

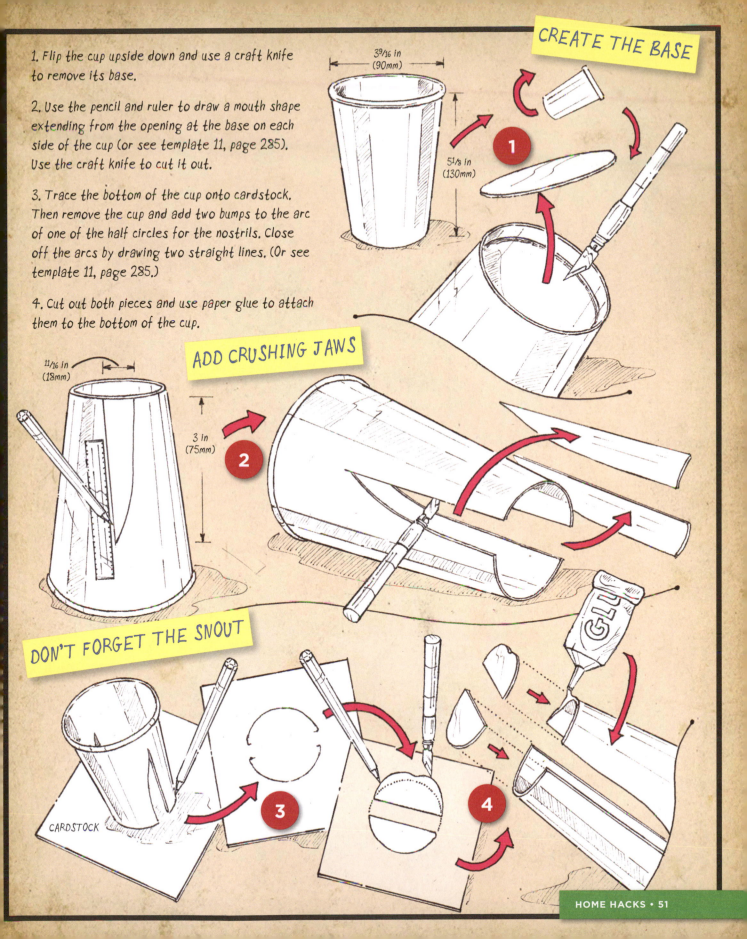

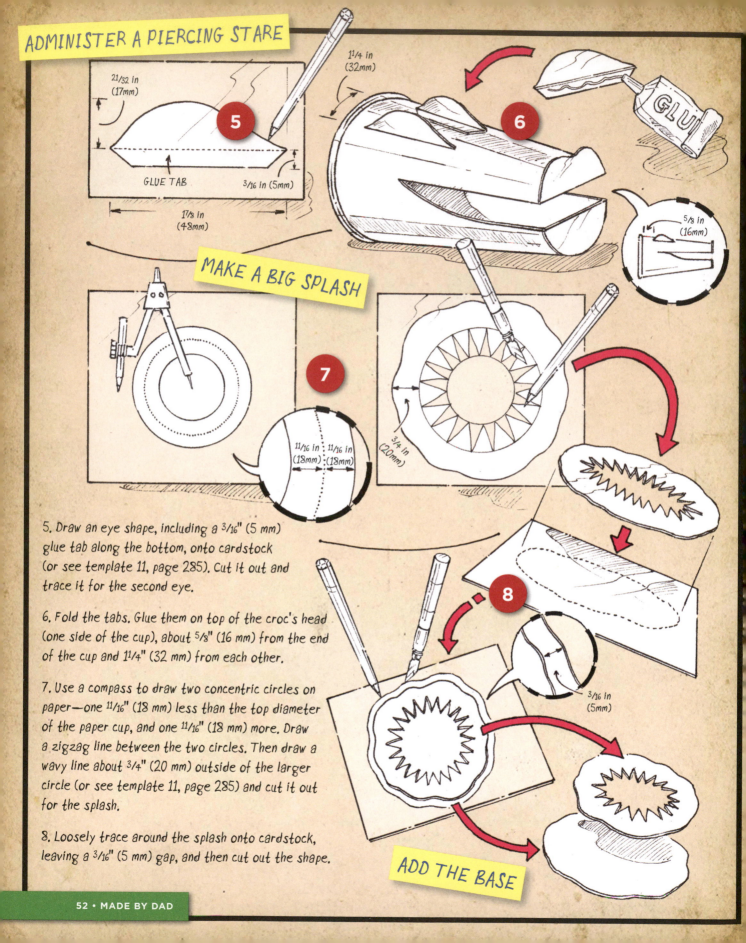

21/32 in (17mm)

1¼ in (32mm)

GLUE TAB

3/16 in (5mm)

1⅞ in (48mm)

5

6

GLUE

5/8 in (16mm)

MAKE A BIG SPLASH

7

11/16 in (18mm) | 11/16 in (18mm)

¾ in (20mm)

8

3/16 in (5mm)

5. Draw an eye shape, including a ³/₁₆" (5 mm) glue tab along the bottom, onto cardstock (or see template 11, page 285). Cut it out and trace it for the second eye.

6. Fold the tabs. Glue them on top of the croc's head (one side of the cup), about ⅝" (16 mm) from the end of the cup and 1¼" (32 mm) from each other.

7. Use a compass to draw two concentric circles on paper—one ¹¹/₁₆" (18 mm) less than the top diameter of the paper cup, and one ¹¹/₁₆" (18 mm) more. Draw a zigzag line between the two circles. Then draw a wavy line about ¾" (20 mm) outside of the larger circle (or see template 11, page 285) and cut it out for the splash.

8. Loosely trace around the splash onto cardstock, leaving a ³/₁₆" (5 mm) gap, and then cut out the shape.

ADD THE BASE

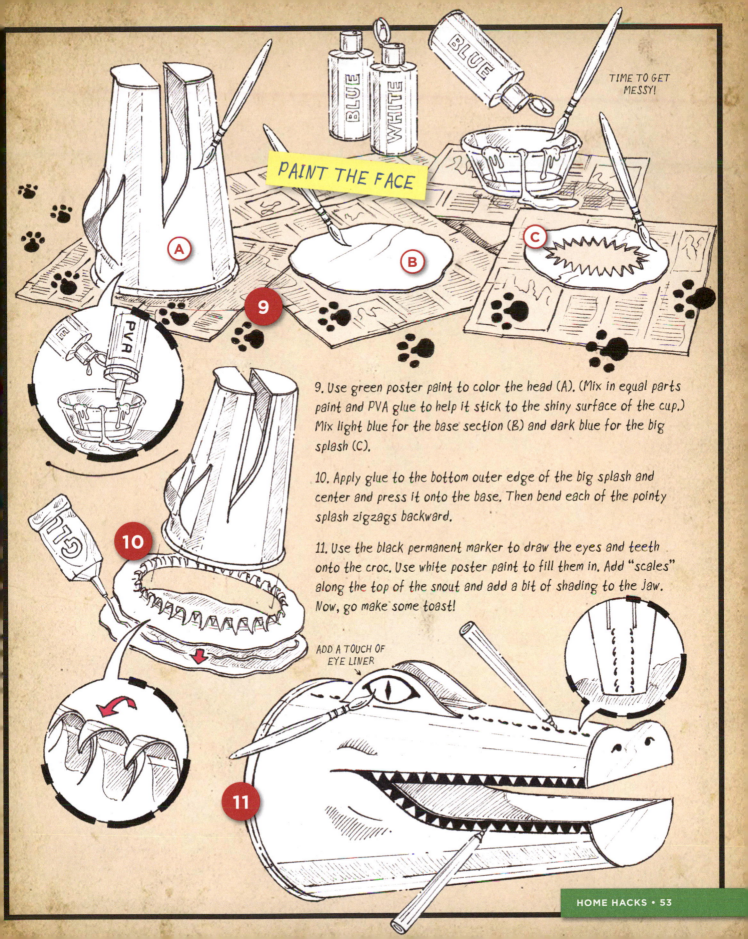

TIME TO GET MESSY!

A

PVA

9

B

C

GLUE

10

11

ADD A TOUCH OF EYE LINER

9. Use green poster paint to color the head (A). (Mix in equal parts paint and PVA glue to help it stick to the shiny surface of the cup.) Mix light blue for the base section (B) and dark blue for the big splash (C).

10. Apply glue to the bottom outer edge of the big splash and center and press it onto the base. Then bend each of the pointy splash zigzags backward.

11. Use the black permanent marker to draw the eyes and teeth onto the croc. Use white poster paint to fill them in. Add "scales" along the top of the snout and add a bit of shading to the jaw. Now, go make some toast!

BLUE
WHITE
BLUE

TRASHY LIGHTS

LEVEL: EASY

Packing away Christmas lights is always a chore, so why not just put them in the trash? Only instead of sending them to a landfill, you'll make this cool wastepaper basket light! It's a piece of cake to make, and when Christmastime comes again, you won't have to rummage in the attic for the lights, you can just rummage through the trash.

MATERIALS
- Scissors
- A string of white LED lights (24 lights or more)
- Colored tissue paper
- Ruler
- Clear tape
- Wire wastepaper basket
- Hot glue gun and glue sticks

COOL, BUT LET'S TURN THE LIGHTS OFF . . .

OFF

ON

AWESOME, THAT'S EVEN COOLER!

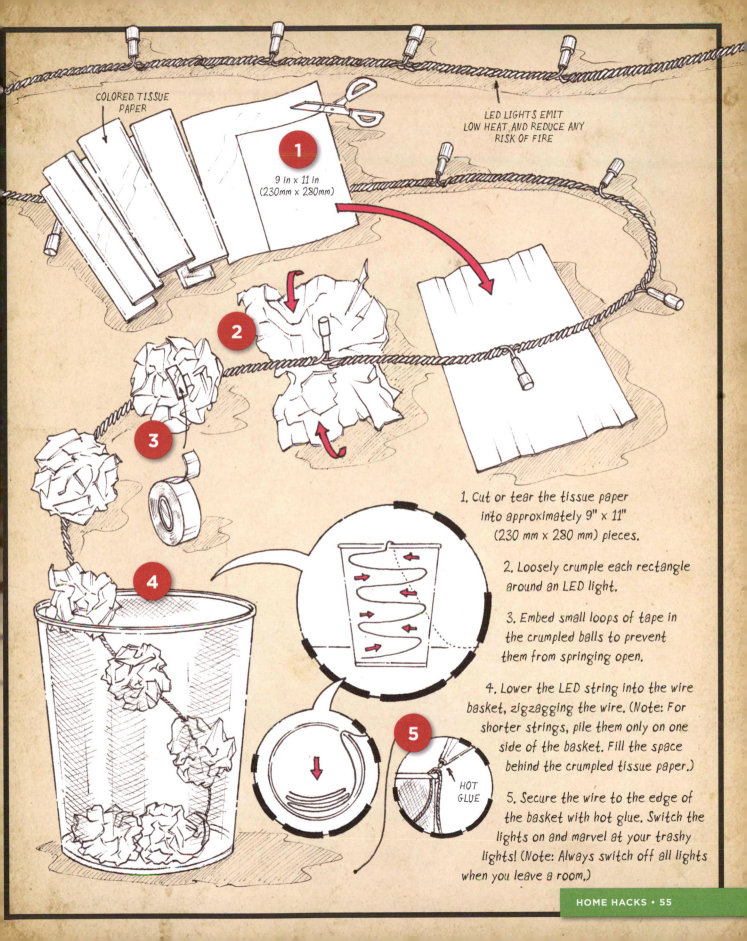

COLORED TISSUE PAPER

LED LIGHTS EMIT LOW HEAT AND REDUCE ANY RISK OF FIRE

1

9 in x 11 in
(230mm x 280mm)

2

3

4

5

HOT GLUE

1. Cut or tear the tissue paper into approximately 9" x 11" (230 mm x 280 mm) pieces.

2. Loosely crumple each rectangle around an LED light.

3. Embed small loops of tape in the crumpled balls to prevent them from springing open.

4. Lower the LED string into the wire basket, zigzagging the wire. (Note: For shorter strings, pile them only on one side of the basket. Fill the space behind the crumpled tissue paper.)

5. Secure the wire to the edge of the basket with hot glue. Switch the lights on and marvel at your trashy lights! (Note: Always switch off all lights when you leave a room.)

TITANIC BOOKSHELF ART

LEVEL: EASY

TITANIC

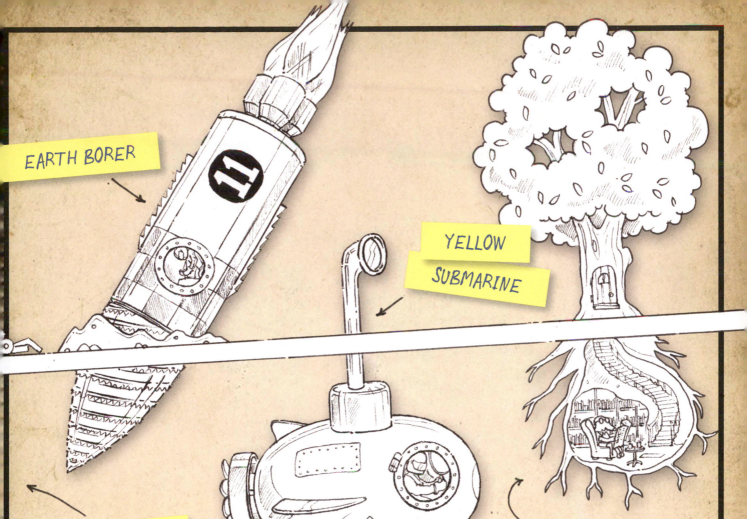

EARTH BORER

YELLOW SUBMARINE

HEAVY ROBOT!

A STUDIOUS MOLE'S LIBRARY

The basic design of this rather humble shelf provides loads of creative opportunities. (No, really, it does!) I'm going to show you how to safely re-create that famous moment in history when the *Titanic* hit the giant iceberg. You can see from the additional ideas above, however, the sky (or sea) is the limit when it comes to shelf decor themes.

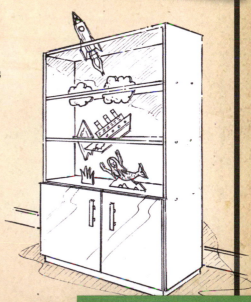

MATERIALS

- Ruler
- Pencil
- Craft knife and cutting mat
- Scissors
- Colored medium-weight cardstock (red and blue)
- Black medium-weight cardstock
- White medium-weight cardstock
- Paper glue
- Cereal box
- Mounting putty or double-sided tape

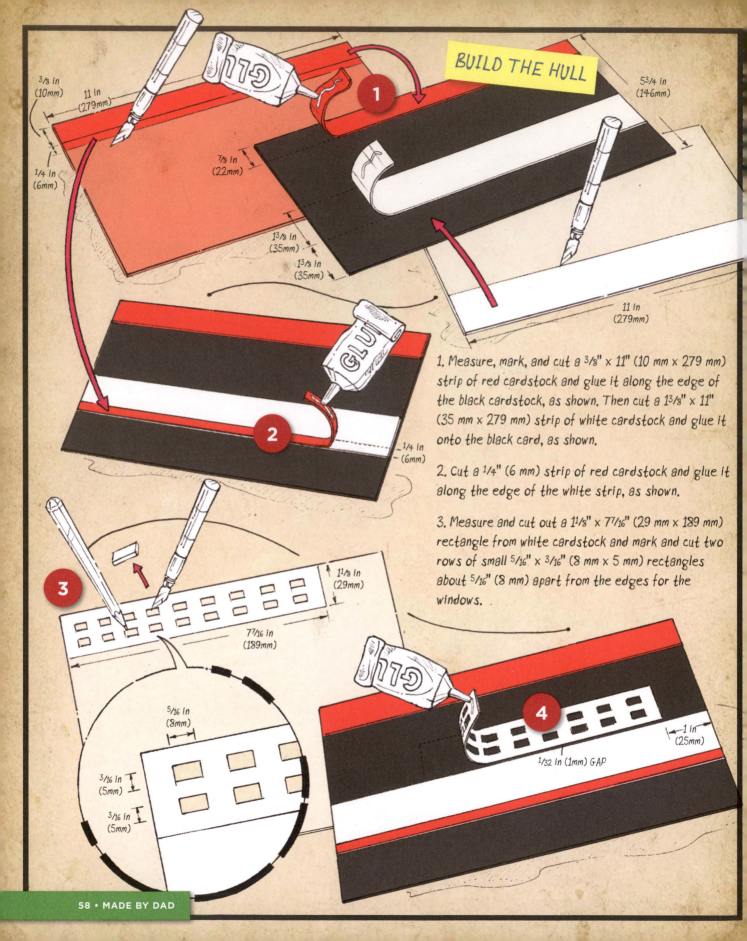

3/8 in (10mm)

11 in (279mm)

1/4 in (6mm)

7/8 in (22mm)

1 3/8 in (35mm)

1 3/8 in (35mm)

5 3/4 in (146mm)

11 in (279mm)

1/4 in (6mm)

1 1/8 in (29mm)

7 7/16 in (189mm)

5/16 in (8mm)

3/16 in (5mm)

3/16 in (5mm)

1 in (25mm)

1/32 in (1mm) GAP

1. Measure, mark, and cut a 3/8" x 11" (10 mm x 279 mm) strip of red cardstock and glue it along the edge of the black cardstock, as shown. Then cut a 1 3/8" x 11" (35 mm x 279 mm) strip of white cardstock and glue it onto the black card, as shown.

2. Cut a 1/4" (6 mm) strip of red cardstock and glue it along the edge of the white strip, as shown.

3. Measure and cut out a 1 1/8" x 7 7/16" (29 mm x 189 mm) rectangle from white cardstock and mark and cut two rows of small 5/16" x 3/16" (8 mm x 5 mm) rectangles about 5/16" (8 mm) apart from the edges for the windows.

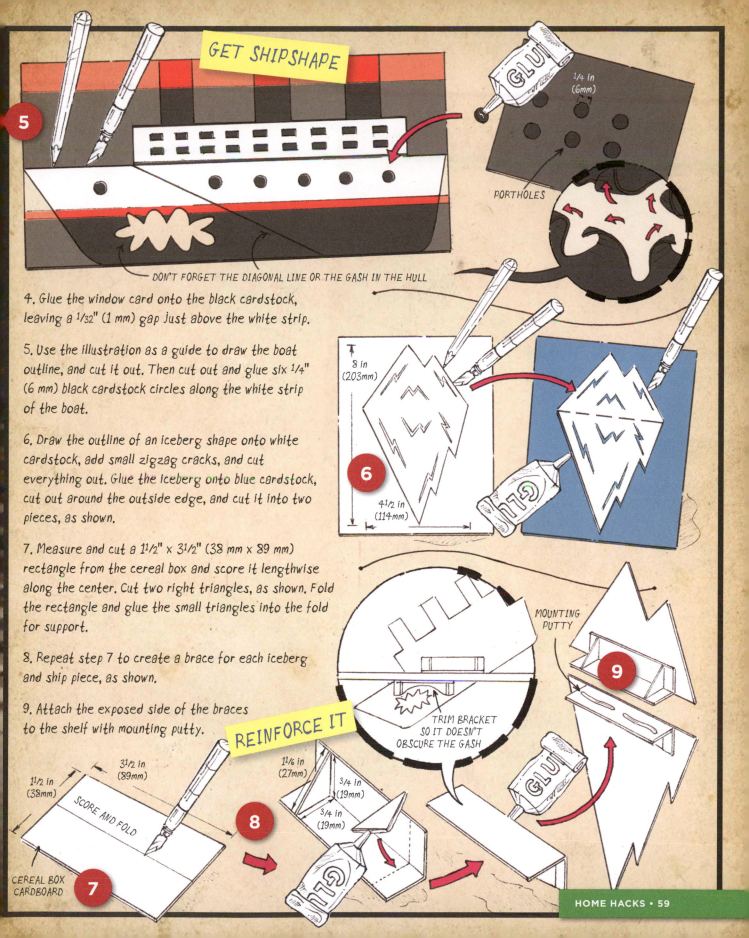

5

1/4 in
(6mm)

PORTHOLES

DON'T FORGET THE DIAGONAL LINE OR THE GASH IN THE HULL

4. Glue the window card onto the black cardstock, leaving a 1/32" (1 mm) gap just above the white strip.

5. Use the illustration as a guide to draw the boat outline, and cut it out. Then cut out and glue six 1/4" (6 mm) black cardstock circles along the white strip of the boat.

6. Draw the outline of an iceberg shape onto white cardstock, add small zigzag cracks, and cut everything out. Glue the iceberg onto blue cardstock, cut out around the outside edge, and cut it into two pieces, as shown.

7. Measure and cut a 1¹/₂" x 3¹/₂" (38 mm x 89 mm) rectangle from the cereal box and score it lengthwise along the center. Cut two right triangles, as shown. Fold the rectangle and glue the small triangles into the fold for support.

8. Repeat step 7 to create a brace for each iceberg and ship piece, as shown.

9. Attach the exposed side of the braces to the shelf with mounting putty.

8 in
(203mm)

4¹/₂ in
(114mm)

6

MOUNTING
PUTTY

9

TRIM BRACKET
SO IT DOESN'T
OBSCURE THE GASH

3¹/₂ in
(89mm)

1¹/₂ in
(38mm)

SCORE AND FOLD

1¹/₆ in
(27mm)

3/4 in
(19mm)

3/4 in
(19mm)

8

CEREAL BOX
CARDBOARD

7

SITTING ON EGGSHELLS

LEVEL: MEDIUM

Give that worn old chair a bit of a lift—literally, by balancing it on four eggs! This quirky IKEA hack is surprisingly easy to do, and even has the added benefit of extending the life of a chair that might be getting a little small for your kids. Of course, that was furthest from my mind when I made it. I just thought it was fun!

MATERIALS

- Kid's chair
- Drill
- 4 Styrofoam craft eggs (2⁵⁄₁₆", 60 mm)
- 4 stainless steel screws (4" x ⁵⁄₃₂", 100 mm x 4 mm)
- Screwdriver
- Poster paint (white, yellow, and red)
- Paintbrush
- PVA glue
- Pencil

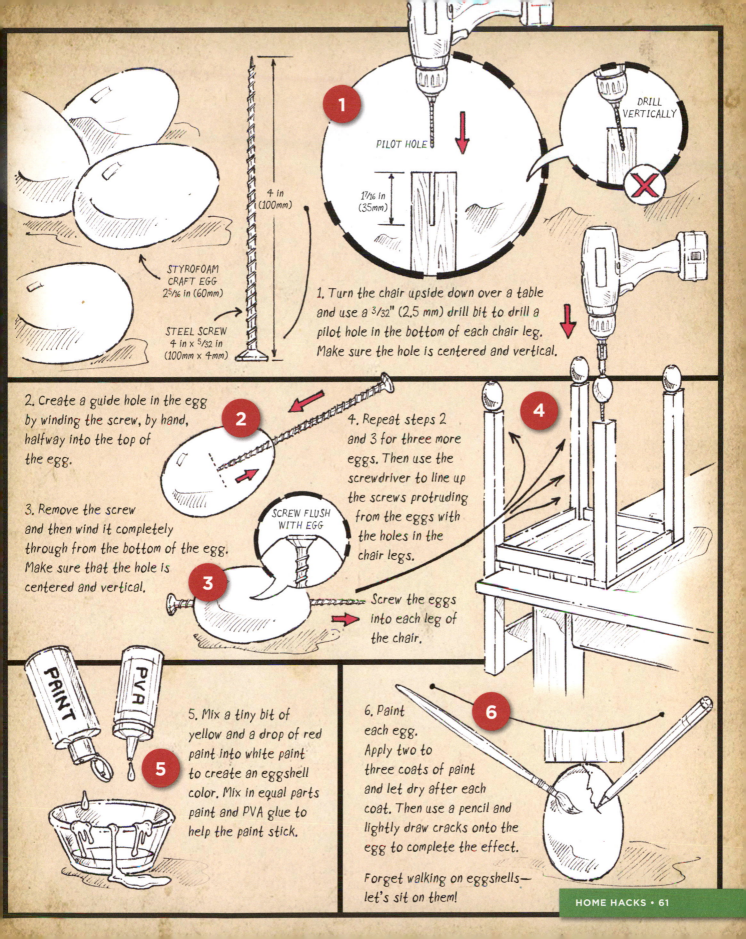

STYROFOAM
CRAFT EGG
2⁵/₁₆ in (60mm)

STEEL SCREW
4 in x ⁵/₃₂ in
(100mm x 4mm)

4 in
(100mm)

1

PILOT HOLE

1⁷/₁₆ in
(35mm)

DRILL
VERTICALLY

1. Turn the chair upside down over a table and use a ³/₃₂" (2.5 mm) drill bit to drill a pilot hole in the bottom of each chair leg. Make sure the hole is centered and vertical.

2

2. Create a guide hole in the egg by winding the screw, by hand, halfway into the top of the egg.

3. Remove the screw and then wind it completely through from the bottom of the egg. Make sure that the hole is centered and vertical.

3

SCREW FLUSH
WITH EGG

4

4. Repeat steps 2 and 3 for three more eggs. Then use the screwdriver to line up the screws protruding from the eggs with the holes in the chair legs.

Screw the eggs into each leg of the chair.

PAINT

PVA

5

5. Mix a tiny bit of yellow and a drop of red paint into white paint to create an eggshell color. Mix in equal parts paint and PVA glue to help the paint stick.

6

6. Paint each egg. Apply two to three coats of paint and let dry after each coat. Then use a pencil and lightly draw cracks onto the egg to complete the effect.

Forget walking on eggshells—let's sit on them!

CAT-TRAP BIRDFEEDER

LEVEL: TRICKY

YOU GO FIRST!

NO, YOU GO FIRST!

MATERIALS
- Tin snips
- 3 plastic folders or binders (1/16", 1.5 mm thick)
- Pencil
- Black permanent marker (thick tip)
- Craft knife
- Hot glue gun and glue sticks or epoxy
- Ruler
- Drill
- Outdoor post
- Screwdriver
- Screws
- Paper cup (16 oz, 454 g) with lid
- Black spray paint
- Thread
- Chopstick or dowel
- Access to a photocopier or printer (optional)

This birdfeeder will set the cat among the pigeons . . . sparrows, starlings, and crows! Made from a few plastic folders and a paper coffee cup, I'm not sure who will be more surprised, your neighbors or the birds!

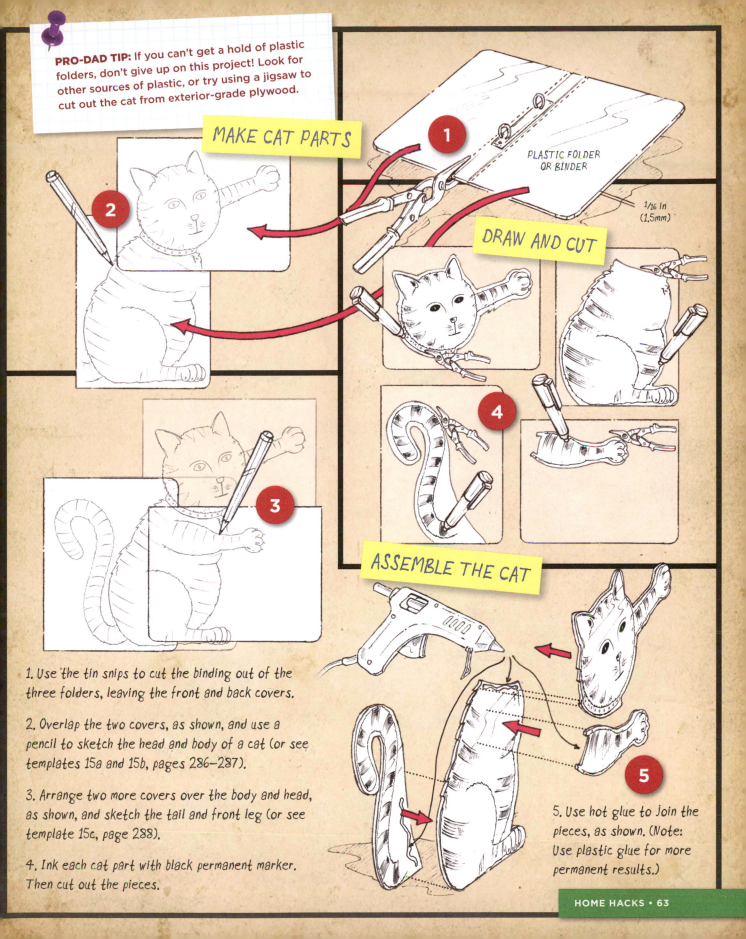

PRO-DAD TIP: If you can't get a hold of plastic folders, don't give up on this project! Look for other sources of plastic, or try using a jigsaw to cut out the cat from exterior-grade plywood.

MAKE CAT PARTS

1

PLASTIC FOLDER OR BINDER

1/16 in (1.5mm)

2

DRAW AND CUT

4

3

ASSEMBLE THE CAT

5

1. Use the tin snips to cut the binding out of the three folders, leaving the front and back covers.

2. Overlap the two covers, as shown, and use a pencil to sketch the head and body of a cat (or see templates 15a and 15b, pages 286–287).

3. Arrange two more covers over the body and head, as shown, and sketch the tail and front leg (or see template 15c, page 288).

4. Ink each cat part with black permanent marker. Then cut out the pieces.

5. Use hot glue to join the pieces, as shown. (Note: Use plastic glue for more permanent results.)

ADD SUPPORT

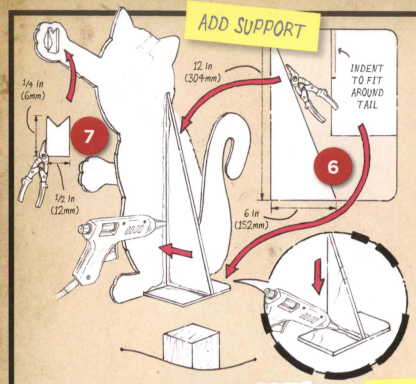

1/4 in (6mm)

1/2 in (12mm)

7

12 in (304mm)

6 in (152mm)

INDENT TO FIT AROUND TAIL

6

6. Measure and cut a 6" x 12" (152 mm x 304 mm) right triangle and a 6" x 4" (152 mm x 100 mm) rectangle from a remaining cover. Assemble the pieces, as shown, and hot glue them along the outside of the joints, then to the back of the cat.

7. Cut a 1/2" x 1 1/2" (12 mm x 40 mm) rectangle with a V-shaped notch on one end. Glue it to the back of the raised paw.

8. Drill two pilot holes through the cat base and into an outdoor post. Then use the screwdriver to secure it with two screws.

9. Mark and use the craft knife to cut two 2" x 2 1/2" (50 mm x 63 mm) arches into the sides of the paper cup. Cut two 3/16" (5 mm) slits in a cross under each. Then spray paint the cup black.

ATTACH THE FEEDER

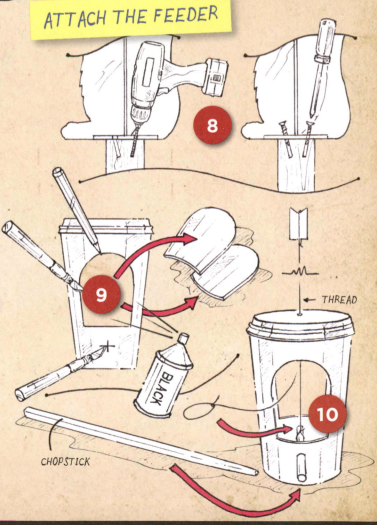

8

9

THREAD

BLACK

10

CHOPSTICK

10. Poke a hole in the lid and feed 12" (304 mm) of thread through it. Tie a loop in the inside end. Push the chopstick through one cross slot in the cup, through the thread loop, and then through the other side of the cup. Tie the other end of the thread around the notch. Then fill the cup with birdseed and wait for the birds!

"STOP THE PIGEON" WEATHER VANE

LEVEL: TRICKY

MUTTLEY! WHERE'S THE GUN!

YOU CAN'T CATCH ME!

As a kid I loved the Hanna-Barbera "Stop the Pigeon" cartoons. In every episode, Dick Dastardly and Muttley attempted to stop Yankee Doodle Pigeon by using a variety of ingenious flying machines. Here's my own ingenious flying machine, made from the not so ingenious soda can.

MATERIALS
- Tin snips
- 6 aluminum soda cans
- Ruler
- Black permanent marker
- Scissors
- Printer paper
- Dowel (1/4", 6 mm)
- Drill
- Hot glue gun and glue sticks
- 6 wooden stirring sticks
- Red spray paint
- White plastic folder
- Galvanized wire (#15 gauge, 1.5 mm)
- Hacksaw
- Dried-up felt-tip markers
- Outdoor post
- Access to a photocopier or printer (optional)

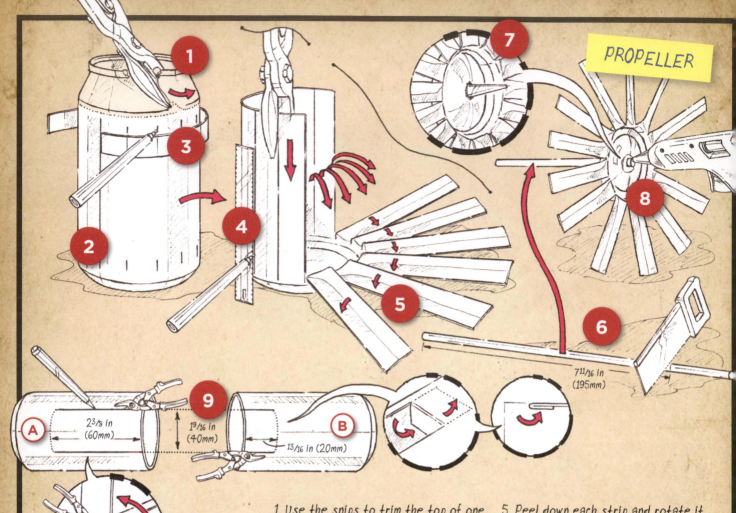

7 11/16 in (195mm)

2 3/8 in (60mm)

1 9/16 in (40mm)

13/16 in (20mm)

A

B

1. Use the snips to trim the top of one of the cans.

2. Use the ruler and marker to draw a vertical line down the side of the can.

3. Cut a 3/4" (20 mm)-wide strip of paper whose length is equal to the circumference of the can. Divide it into thirteen sections. Align the strip with the mark you made in step 2 then wrap it around. Mark each segment onto the can. Repeat at the bottom of the can.

4. Join the lines using a ruler. Then cut along each line with the tin snips.

5. Peel down each strip and rotate it slightly to create the blades of the propeller.

6. Measure and cut the dowel to the length shown.

7. Use a drill (or twist the pointy end of the scissors) to make a 1/4" (6 mm) hole—the size of the dowel—in the center of the propeller.

8. Push the dowel through the hole and secure it with hot glue on both sides.

9. Trim the tops off two more cans (A and B). Mark and cut two slits in each can to make flaps, as shown. Then fold flap A up and trim it into a semicircle. Fold flap B into the can.

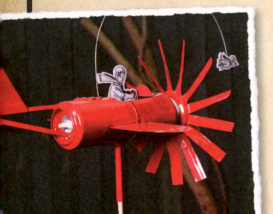

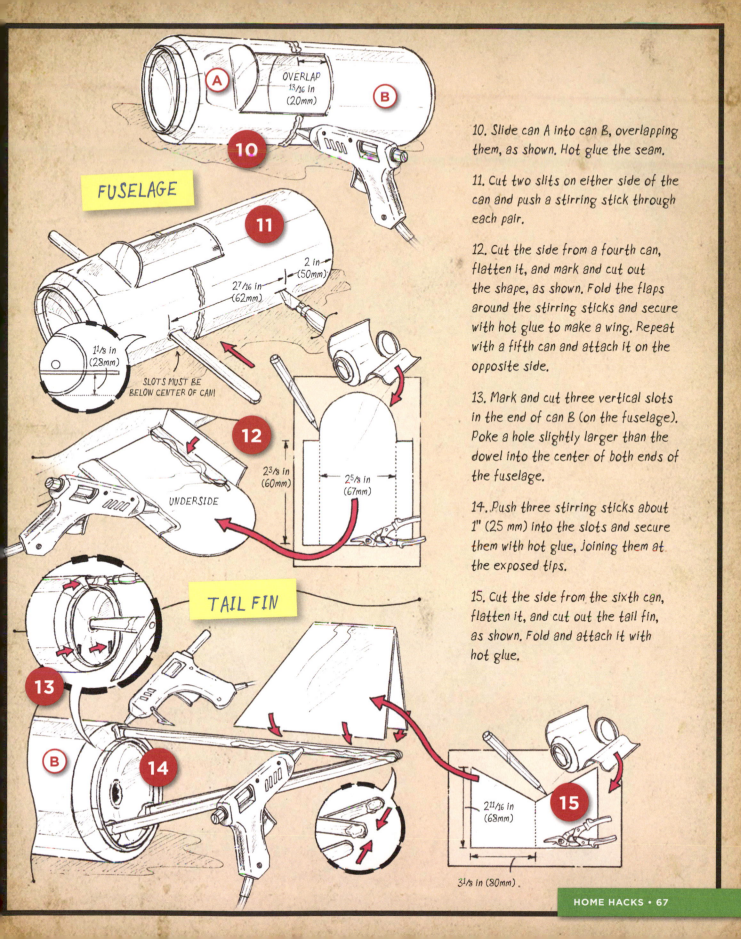

OVERLAP 13/16 in (20mm)

(A) (B)

10

FUSELAGE

11

2 in (50mm)

2 7/16 in (62mm)

1 1/8 in (28mm)

SLOTS MUST BE BELOW CENTER OF CAN!

12

2 3/8 in (60mm)

2 5/8 in (67mm)

UNDERSIDE

TAIL FIN

13

(B)

14

15

2 11/16 in (68mm)

3 1/8 in (80mm)

10. Slide can A into can B, overlapping them, as shown. Hot glue the seam.

11. Cut two slits on either side of the can and push a stirring stick through each pair.

12. Cut the side from a fourth can, flatten it, and mark and cut out the shape, as shown. Fold the flaps around the stirring sticks and secure with hot glue to make a wing. Repeat with a fifth can and attach it on the opposite side.

13. Mark and cut three vertical slots in the end of can B (on the fuselage). Poke a hole slightly larger than the dowel into the center of both ends of the fuselage.

14. Push three stirring sticks about 1" (25 mm) into the slots and secure them with hot glue, joining them at the exposed tips.

15. Cut the side from the sixth can, flatten it, and cut out the tail fin, as shown. Fold and attach it with hot glue.

16. Spray paint the plane and propeller red. Let dry, then push the propeller dowel through the fuselage.

17. Cut a ⅝" (16 mm) washer from aluminum can scraps. Push it onto the back end of the dowel and secure it with hot glue, allowing the propeller at the front to turn freely.

18. Use the marker to draw a pigeon and a pilot onto plastic (or see template 16, page 289). Cut them out with the tin snips. Glue the pilot onto one end of a stirring stick. Glue the stirring stick onto the two wing struts inside the plane.

19. Measure and cut 20" (508 mm) of wire and bend it into a semicircle. Bend one end into a small rectangular loop, and glue it onto the top back of the fuselage. Bend the other end at a 90-degree angle, and glue it to the pigeon.

20. Use the hacksaw to cut the ends off the old felt-tip marker to make a tube. Make sure the dowel fits loosely inside, then glue the tube perpendicular to the underside of the fuselage.

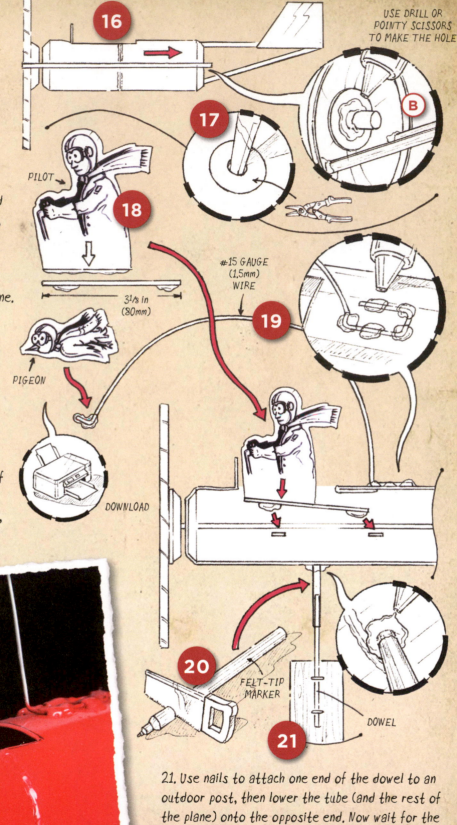

USE DRILL OR POINTY SCISSORS TO MAKE THE HOLE

B

PILOT

3⅛ in (80mm)

PIGEON

#15 GAUGE (1.5mm) WIRE

DOWNLOAD

FELT-TIP MARKER

DOWEL

21. Use nails to attach one end of the dowel to an outdoor post, then lower the tube (and the rest of the plane) onto the opposite end. Now wait for the wind to blow!

TABLE LEG MOON MINE

LEVEL: MEDIUM

MATERIALS

- 3–5 corrugated cardboard boxes of various sizes
- Pencil
- Craft knife and cutting mat
- Hot glue gun and glue sticks
- Colored medium-weight cardstock (various hues)
- Table
- Chair
- Black permanent marker
- Ruler
- Toy cars

Gather up old boxes, a table, and a chair to create an awesome multilevel city. (I just happened to be inspired to create a mine on the moon.) Because everyone's kitchen furniture will be a little bit different, consider the following instructions to be more like guidelines, and enjoy the freedom to do your own thing and build "outside the lines."

PARKING GARAGE TECHNIQUES:
Transform boxes into buildings (A) by using the craft knife to cut open one box to create a flat base and hot gluing another closed box on top. Mark and cut vertical and horizontal doors (B) (think barn doors, garage doors, and house doors) into the sides. To construct a helicopter landing pad (C), or something similar, place the base on the tabletop, then slide it to the edge of the table so a flap extends over. Trim and score the edges of the flap, and fold them down along the score lines to prop the flap, as shown. Decorate accordingly with the permanent marker.

PARKING GARAGE

CUSTOMIZE FURTHER BY ADDING MORE ACCESSORIES WITH GLUE

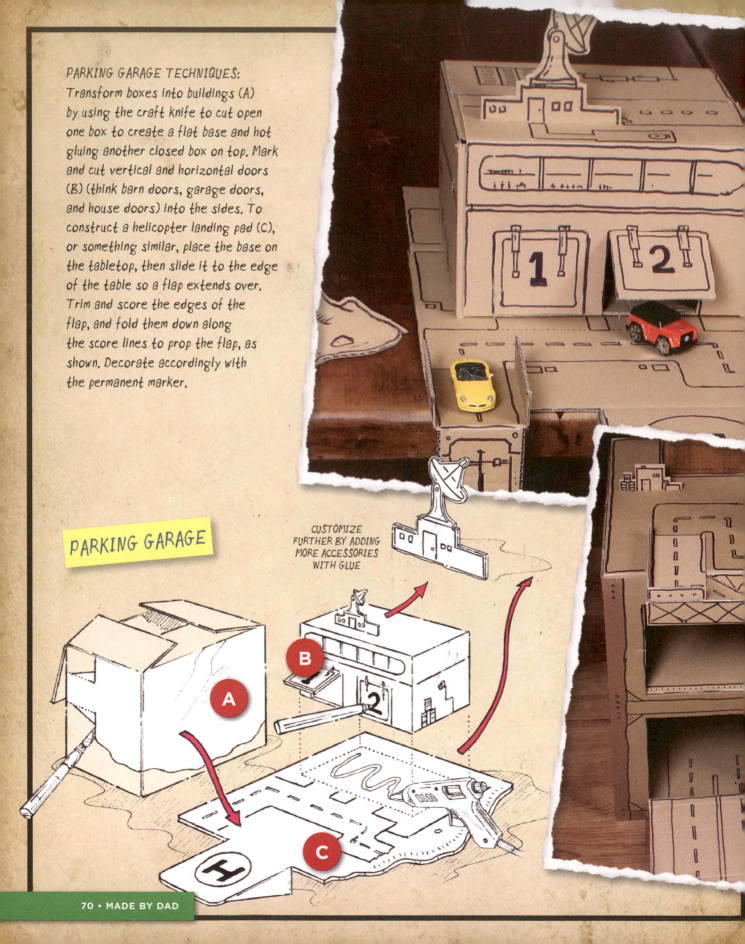

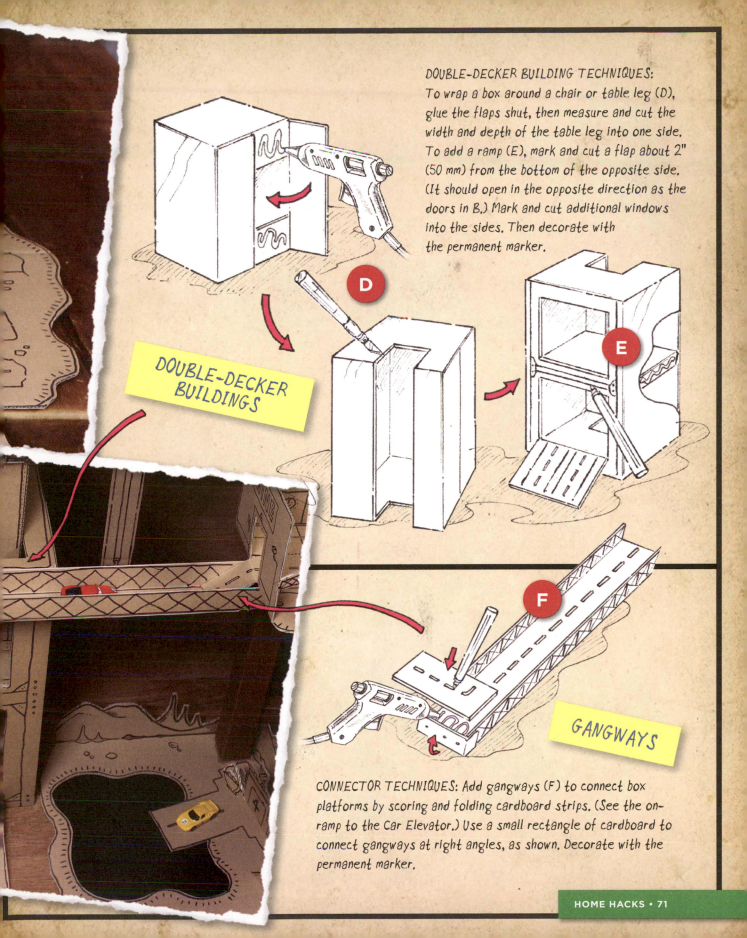

DOUBLE-DECKER BUILDING TECHNIQUES:
To wrap a box around a chair or table leg (D), glue the flaps shut, then measure and cut the width and depth of the table leg into one side. To add a ramp (E), mark and cut a flap about 2" (50 mm) from the bottom of the opposite side. (It should open in the opposite direction as the doors in B.) Mark and cut additional windows into the sides. Then decorate with the permanent marker.

DOUBLE-DECKER BUILDINGS

D

E

F

GANGWAYS

CONNECTOR TECHNIQUES: Add gangways (F) to connect box platforms by scoring and folding cardboard strips. (See the on-ramp to the Car Elevator.) Use a small rectangle of cardboard to connect gangways at right angles, as shown. Decorate with the permanent marker.

CAR ELEVATOR TECHNIQUES: To make the elevator shaft (G), cut a rectangular strip of cardboard about 6" (152 mm) longer than the distance between two levels in your city and about 5" (127 mm) wide, and score and fold along two lines 1¼" (35 mm) in from each edge. Make two snips 6" (152 mm) down from the top along each side of the scored pieces and fold the flap over the top of the top level, then fold the sides up, as shown, to create the on-ramp. Cut a slit down the center of the shaft that starts about 2" (51 mm) in from each end and whose width matches the thickness of the cardboard. To make the elevator platform (H), measure and mark the cutting diagram, as shown. Assemble the front platform pieces at right angles; glue. Then insert the front assembly through the slit in the shaft, and glue the back piece to secure the slide piece.

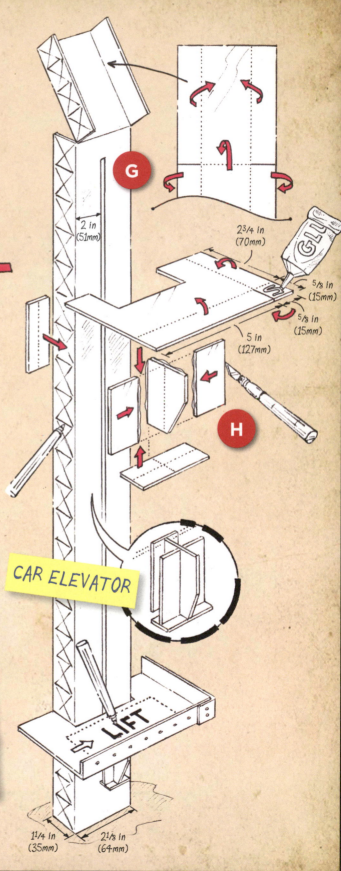

CAR ELEVATOR

LIFT

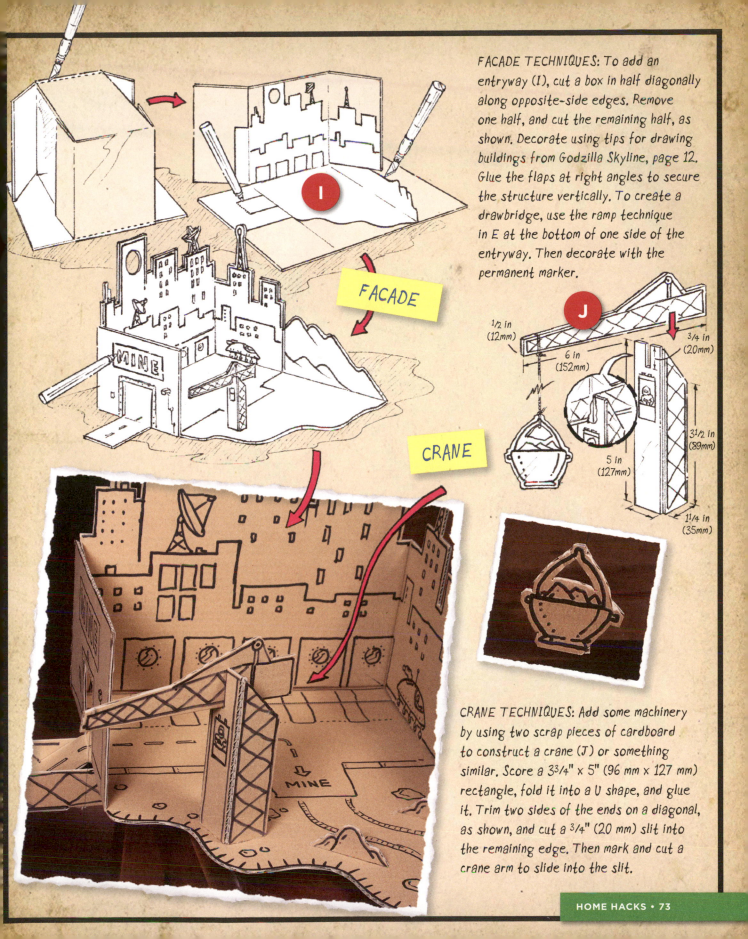

FACADE TECHNIQUES: To add an entryway (I), cut a box in half diagonally along opposite-side edges. Remove one half, and cut the remaining half, as shown. Decorate using tips for drawing buildings from Godzilla Skyline, page 12. Glue the flaps at right angles to secure the structure vertically. To create a drawbridge, use the ramp technique in E at the bottom of one side of the entryway. Then decorate with the permanent marker.

I

FACADE

J

1/2 in (12mm)

6 in (152mm)

3/4 in (20mm)

5 in (127mm)

3 1/2 in (89mm)

1 1/4 in (35mm)

CRANE

MINE

CRANE TECHNIQUES: Add some machinery by using two scrap pieces of cardboard to construct a crane (J) or something similar. Score a 3 3/4" x 5" (96 mm x 127 mm) rectangle, fold it into a U shape, and glue it. Trim two sides of the ends on a diagonal, as shown, and cut a 3/4" (20 mm) slit into the remaining edge. Then mark and cut a crane arm to slide into the slit.

MINE SHAFT TECHNIQUES: To make a mine shaft, pond, puddle, or lake (K), mark and cut a hole in a flat surface of a box (cut it following the steps in I). Glue colored cardstock to the underside.

MINE SHAFT

TERRAIN

TERRAIN TECHNIQUES: Mark, cut, and assemble rocks, hills, or any other stand-alone details (L) by gluing two pieces of cardboard together at a right angle and then reinforcing them in the back with a piece of cardboard cut into a right triangle, as shown. Decorate with the permanent marker.

SUSPECT SCIENCE

SLINGSHOT CAR LAUNCHER

LEVEL: MEDIUM

CRAFTY RELEASE SWITCH

If your kids feel the "need for speed," try turbocharging their toy cars with this rubber band–powered launcher. Simply pull back the launcher, position the car . . . (take a deep breath) and—when you're ready—press the release switch! Of course, your kids will take this opportunity to launch everything from a Lego brick to Barbie's handbag, but that's the joy of it.

MATERIALS

- Craft knife and cutting mat
- Medium-sized corrugated cardboard box
- Ruler
- Pencil
- Stirring stick or blunt knife
- Paper glue
- 4 craft (Popsicle) sticks
- Black spray paint
- 2 cocktail skewers
- 2 rubber bands (6", 150 mm long; ⅛", 3 mm wide)
- Scissors
- Hot glue gun and glue sticks
- White lightweight cardstock
- Colored lightweight cardstock (red and orange)
- Toy car(s)
- Access to a photocopier or printer (optional)

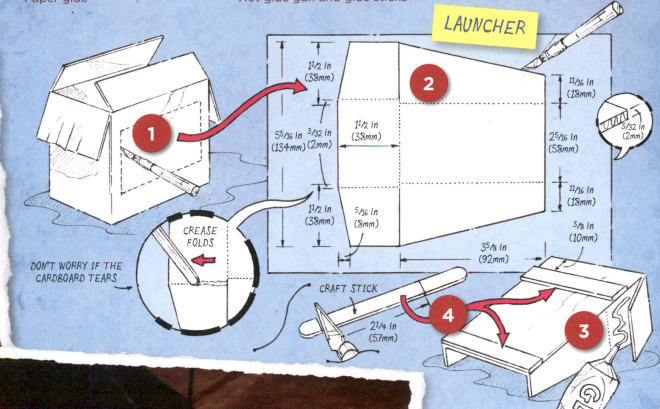

LAUNCHER

1½ in (38mm)

5⁵/₁₆ in (134mm)

³/₃₂ in (2mm)

1½ in (38mm)

1½ in (38mm)

⁵/₁₆ in (8mm)

¹¹/₁₆ in (18mm)

2⁵/₁₆ in (58mm)

¹¹/₁₆ in (18mm)

³/₈ in (10mm)

3⁵/₈ in (92mm)

³/₃₂ in (2mm)

CREASE FOLDS

DON'T WORRY IF THE CARDBOARD TEARS

CRAFT STICK

2¼ in (57mm)

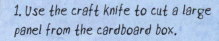

1. Use the craft knife to cut a large panel from the cardboard box.

2. Measure and mark the cutting plan, as shown, then cut it out. Score the folds with the stirring stick.

3. Fold up the sides, and apply paper glue to the end flaps. Fold and press them to the sides to make the launcher.

4. Cut off the ends of two craft sticks, as shown, and glue them onto the bottom of the launcher.

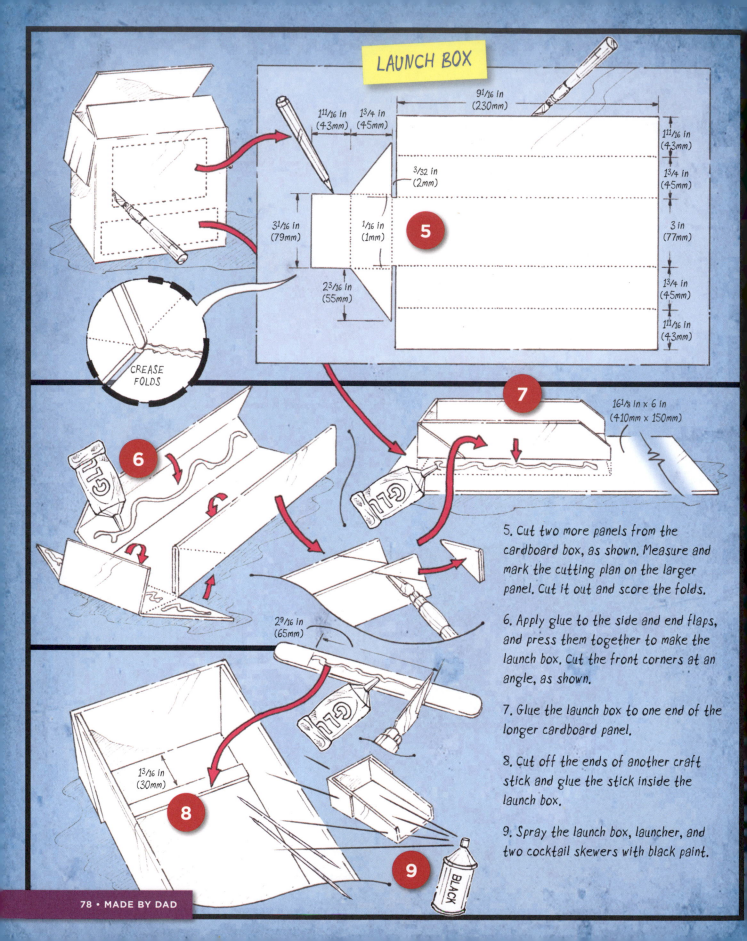

LAUNCH BOX

$9\frac{1}{16}$ in (230mm)

$1\frac{11}{16}$ in (43mm)

$1\frac{3}{4}$ in (45mm)

$\frac{3}{32}$ in (2mm)

$3\frac{1}{16}$ in (79mm)

$\frac{1}{16}$ in (1mm)

$2\frac{3}{16}$ in (55mm)

$1\frac{11}{16}$ in (43mm)

$1\frac{3}{4}$ in (45mm)

3 in (77mm)

$1\frac{3}{4}$ in (45mm)

$1\frac{11}{16}$ in (43mm)

5

CREASE FOLDS

7

$16\frac{1}{8}$ in x 6 in (410mm x 150mm)

6

GLUE

GLUE

$2\frac{9}{16}$ in (65mm)

8

$1\frac{3}{16}$ in (30mm)

GLUE

9

BLACK

5. Cut two more panels from the cardboard box, as shown. Measure and mark the cutting plan on the larger panel. Cut it out and score the folds.

6. Apply glue to the side and end flaps, and press them together to make the launch box. Cut the front corners at an angle, as shown.

7. Glue the launch box to one end of the longer cardboard panel.

8. Cut off the ends of another craft stick and glue the stick inside the launch box.

9. Spray the launch box, launcher, and two cocktail skewers with black paint.

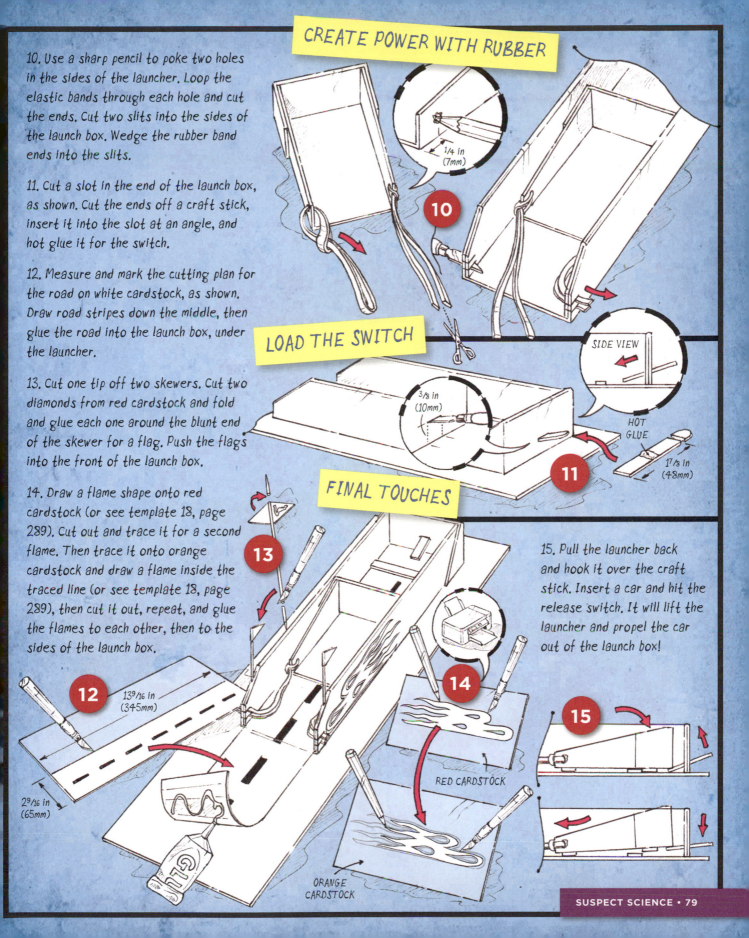

CREATE POWER WITH RUBBER

10. Use a sharp pencil to poke two holes in the sides of the launcher. Loop the elastic bands through each hole and cut the ends. Cut two slits into the sides of the launch box. Wedge the rubber band ends into the slits.

11. Cut a slot in the end of the launch box, as shown. Cut the ends off a craft stick, insert it into the slot at an angle, and hot glue it for the switch.

12. Measure and mark the cutting plan for the road on white cardstock, as shown. Draw road stripes down the middle, then glue the road into the launch box, under the launcher.

13. Cut one tip off two skewers. Cut two diamonds from red cardstock and fold and glue each one around the blunt end of the skewer for a flag. Push the flags into the front of the launch box.

14. Draw a flame shape onto red cardstock (or see template 18, page 289). Cut out and trace it for a second flame. Then trace it onto orange cardstock and draw a flame inside the traced line (or see template 18, page 289), then cut it out, repeat, and glue the flames to each other, then to the sides of the launch box.

15. Pull the launcher back and hook it over the craft stick. Insert a car and hit the release switch. It will lift the launcher and propel the car out of the launch box!

1/4 in (7mm)

LOAD THE SWITCH

SIDE VIEW

HOT GLUE

3/8 in (10mm)

1⁷/₈ in (48mm)

FINAL TOUCHES

13⁹/₁₆ in (345mm)

2⁹/₁₆ in (65mm)

RED CARDSTOCK

ORANGE CARDSTOCK

SPAGHETTI & MARSHMALLOW EIFFEL TOWER

LEVEL: EASY

This project was the first one on my blog to include hand-drawn instructions; it's also turned out to be one of the most downloaded. It seems that the Spaghetti & Marshmallow Eiffel Tower is a very popular science project all around the world! My son won his competition with a variation of this one. . . . I hope it helps.

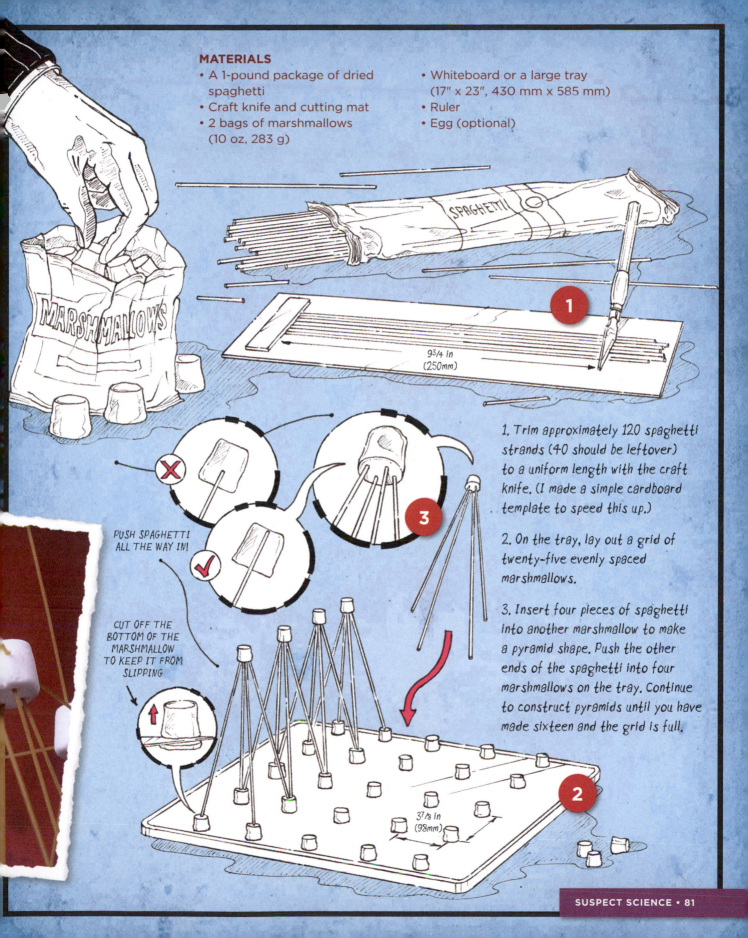

MATERIALS

- A 1-pound package of dried spaghetti
- Craft knife and cutting mat
- 2 bags of marshmallows (10 oz, 283 g)
- Whiteboard or a large tray (17" x 23", 430 mm x 585 mm)
- Ruler
- Egg (optional)

9³/₄ in (250mm)

1

PUSH SPAGHETTI ALL THE WAY IN!

CUT OFF THE BOTTOM OF THE MARSHMALLOW TO KEEP IT FROM SLIPPING

3

1. Trim approximately 120 spaghetti strands (40 should be leftover) to a uniform length with the craft knife. (I made a simple cardboard template to speed this up.)

2. On the tray, lay out a grid of twenty-five evenly spaced marshmallows.

3. Insert four pieces of spaghetti into another marshmallow to make a pyramid shape. Push the other ends of the spaghetti into four marshmallows on the tray. Continue to construct pyramids until you have made sixteen and the grid is full.

3⁷/₈ in (98mm)

2

4. Connect the tops of the pyramids with shorter pieces of spaghetti, as shown. Roughly measure the length by lining up a spaghetti piece with the two marshmallows you want to join, then snap the pieces to fit.

5. Add another layer of pyramids to the top of the first layer, as in step 3. Brace them with shorter pieces of spaghetti.

6. Add a third layer of pyramids to the top of the second layer. Brace the top with shorter pieces of spaghetti.

IF THE STRUCTURE STARTS TO SHIFT, ADD SECOND STRANDS TO THE BOTTOM LAYER WITHOUT DISMANTLING

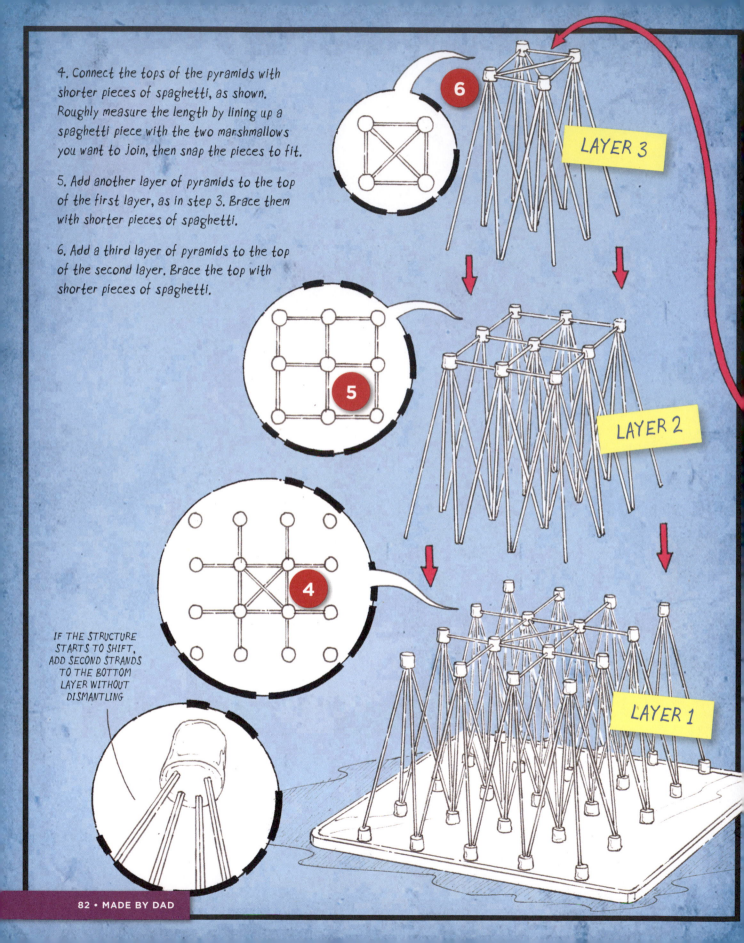

LAYER 3

LAYER 2

LAYER 1

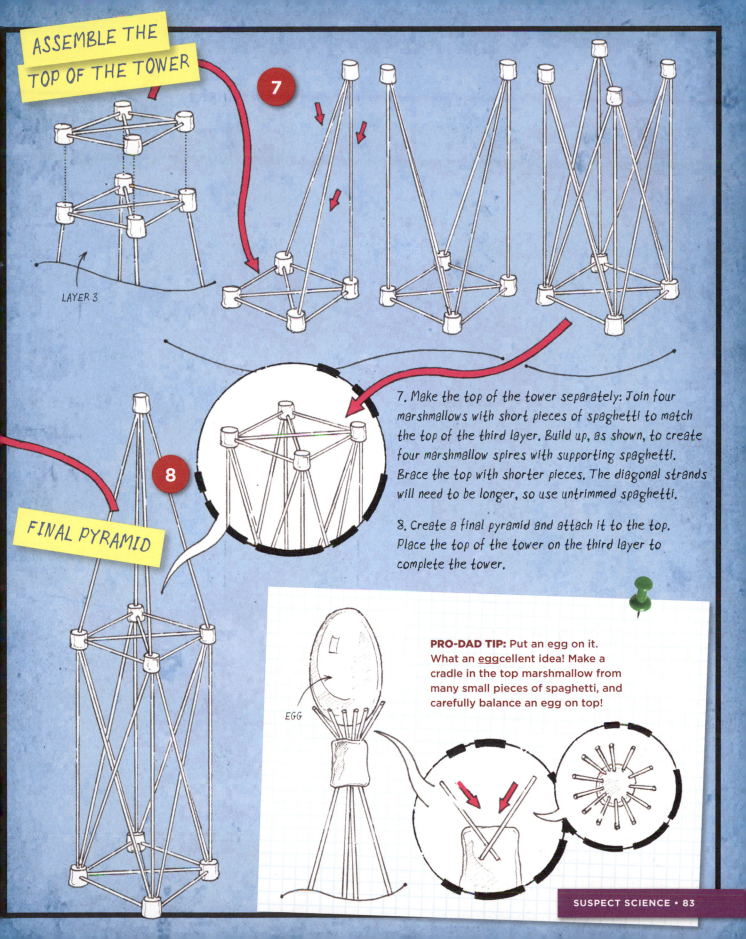

ASSEMBLE THE
TOP OF THE TOWER

7

LAYER 3

FINAL PYRAMID

8

7. Make the top of the tower separately: Join four marshmallows with short pieces of spaghetti to match the top of the third layer. Build up, as shown, to create four marshmallow spires with supporting spaghetti. Brace the top with shorter pieces. The diagonal strands will need to be longer, so use untrimmed spaghetti.

8. Create a final pyramid and attach it to the top. Place the top of the tower on the third layer to complete the tower.

EGG

PRO-DAD TIP: Put an egg on it. What an <u>egg</u>cellent idea! Make a cradle in the top marshmallow from many small pieces of spaghetti, and carefully balance an egg on top!

NO PLACE LIKE HOME TWISTER

LEVEL: MEDIUM

Here's a project that will blow your kids away (as well as the odd toy car and cow!). Perfect for safely adding a touch of disaster to your kids' playtime, it also makes a mean accessory to any train or car set. There's no right or wrong way to make a twister, so I'm not including thousands of measurements . . . but use the view on page 87 as a guide for proportion.

MATERIALS

- Craft knife and cutting mat
- Medium-sized corrugated cardboard box
- Ruler
- Pencil
- White medium-weight cardstock
- Paper glue
- Felt-tip markers
- Toilet paper tube
- Hot glue gun and glue sticks
- Drafting compass

- Long cardboard tube (an empty wrapping paper tube works well)
- Scissors
- Large clear polyethylthene (plastic) bags or sheets (dry cleaning bags work well)
- Clear tape
- Stirring sticks
- Mounting putty
- Access to a photocopier or printer (optional)

IS IT SAFE TO COME OUT YET?

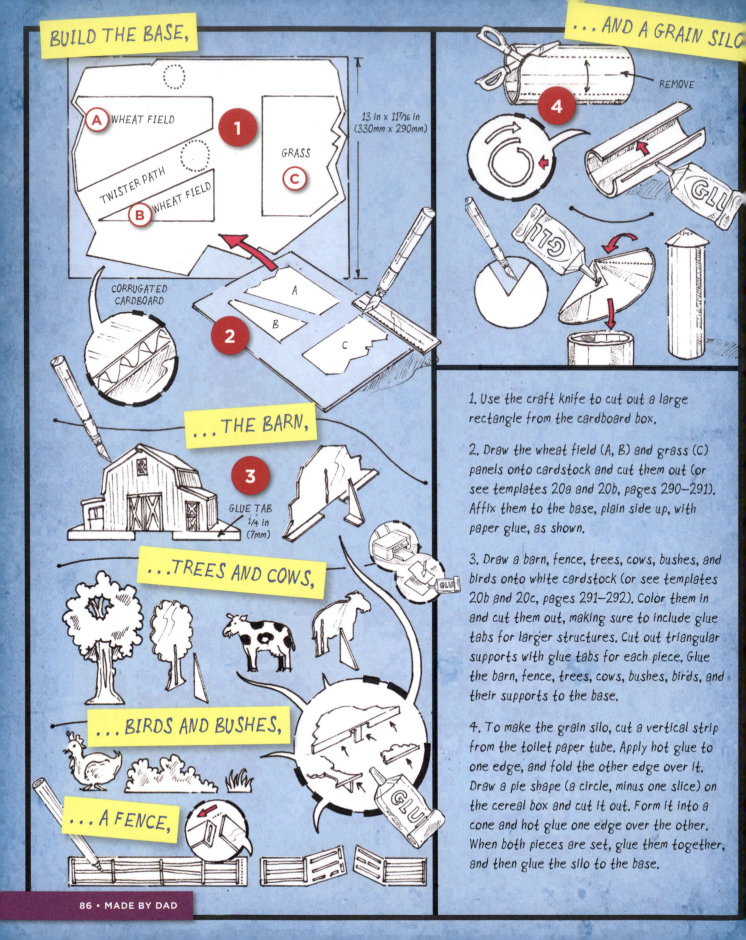

BUILD THE BASE,

A WHEAT FIELD

GRASS

TWISTER PATH

B WHEAT FIELD

C

1

13 in x 11⁷/₁₆ in
(330mm x 290mm)

CORRUGATED
CARDBOARD

2

A

B

C

... THE BARN,

3

GLUE TAB
1/4 in
(7mm)

...TREES AND COWS,

...BIRDS AND BUSHES,

... A FENCE,

... AND A GRAIN SILO

4

REMOVE

GLU

GLU

GLU

GLU

1. Use the craft knife to cut out a large rectangle from the cardboard box.

2. Draw the wheat field (A, B) and grass (C) panels onto cardstock and cut them out (or see templates 20a and 20b, pages 290–291). Affix them to the base, plain side up, with paper glue, as shown.

3. Draw a barn, fence, trees, cows, bushes, and birds onto white cardstock (or see templates 20b and 20c, pages 291–292). Color them in and cut them out, making sure to include glue tabs for larger structures. Cut out triangular supports with glue tabs for each piece. Glue the barn, fence, trees, cows, bushes, birds, and their supports to the base.

4. To make the grain silo, cut a vertical strip from the toilet paper tube. Apply hot glue to one edge, and fold the other edge over it. Draw a pie shape (a circle, minus one slice) on the cereal box and cut it out. Form it into a cone and hot glue one edge over the other. When both pieces are set, glue them together, and then glue the silo to the base.

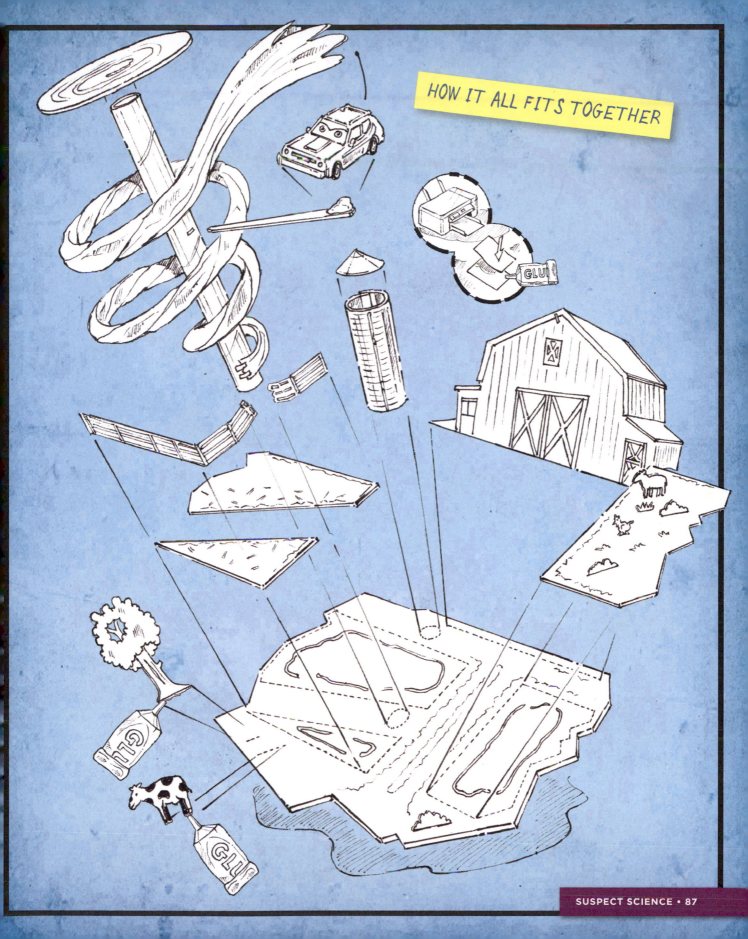

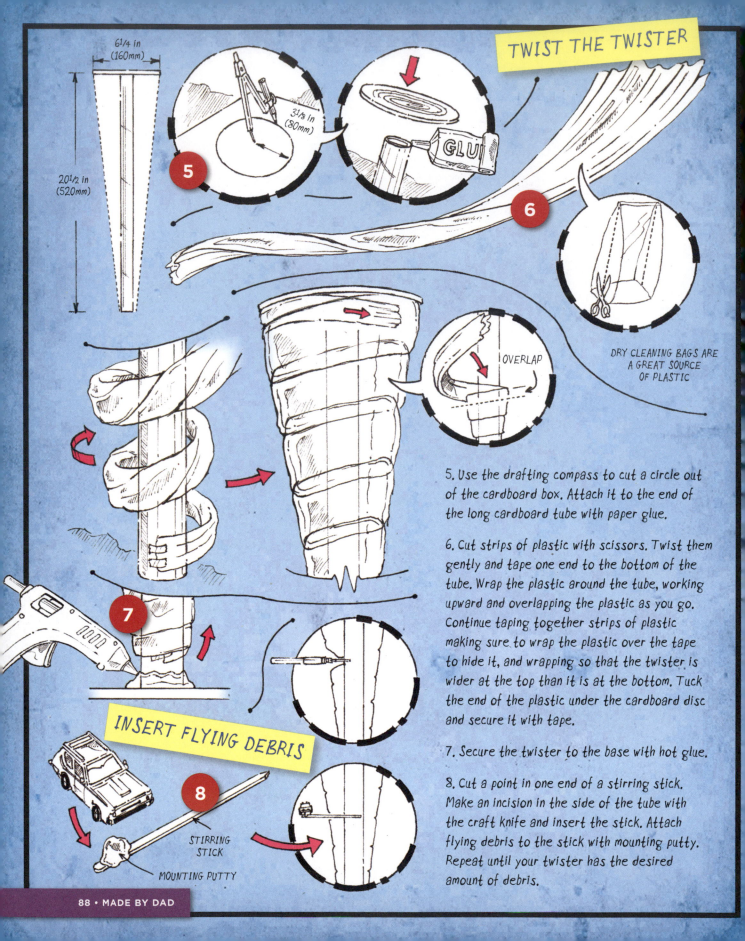

TWIST THE TWISTER

6¼ in
(160mm)

20½ in
(520mm)

3⅛ in
(80mm)

5

GLUE

6

DRY CLEANING BAGS ARE
A GREAT SOURCE
OF PLASTIC

OVERLAP

7

5. Use the drafting compass to cut a circle out
of the cardboard box. Attach it to the end of
the long cardboard tube with paper glue.

6. Cut strips of plastic with scissors. Twist them
gently and tape one end to the bottom of the
tube. Wrap the plastic around the tube, working
upward and overlapping the plastic as you go.
Continue taping together strips of plastic
making sure to wrap the plastic over the tape
to hide it, and wrapping so that the twister is
wider at the top than it is at the bottom. Tuck
the end of the plastic under the cardboard disc
and secure it with tape.

7. Secure the twister to the base with hot glue.

INSERT FLYING DEBRIS

8

STIRRING
STICK

MOUNTING PUTTY

8. Cut a point in one end of a stirring stick.
Make an incision in the side of the tube with
the craft knife and insert the stick. Attach
flying debris to the stick with mounting putty.
Repeat until your twister has the desired
amount of debris.

NONTOPPLING T. REX

LEVEL: MEDIUM

If you think the T. rex dinosaur looks ungainly at the best of times, well, you won't be able to deny that now he positively defies gravity. This nifty optical illusion uses weights to shift the center of gravity—a simple trick that will educate and amaze. And you also get to eat three of those cool little boxes of cereal!

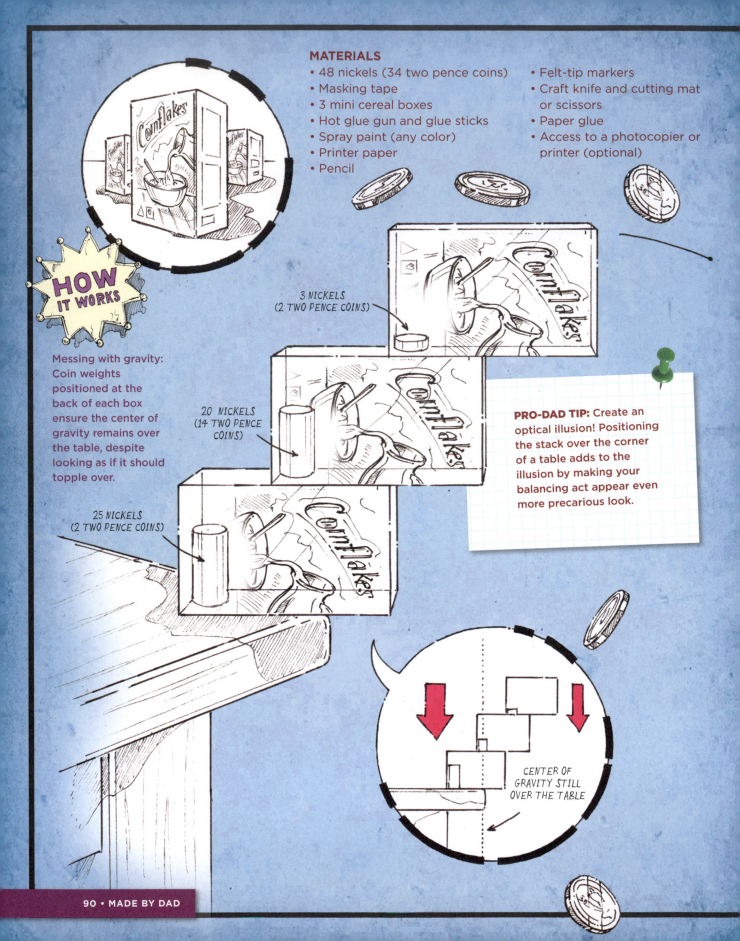

MATERIALS
- 48 nickels (34 two pence coins)
- Masking tape
- 3 mini cereal boxes
- Hot glue gun and glue sticks
- Spray paint (any color)
- Printer paper
- Pencil
- Felt-tip markers
- Craft knife and cutting mat or scissors
- Paper glue
- Access to a photocopier or printer (optional)

HOW IT WORKS

Messing with gravity: Coin weights positioned at the back of each box ensure the center of gravity remains over the table, despite looking as if it should topple over.

3 NICKELS (2 TWO PENCE COINS)

20 NICKELS (14 TWO PENCE COINS)

25 NICKELS (2 TWO PENCE COINS)

PRO-DAD TIP: Create an optical illusion! Positioning the stack over the corner of a table adds to the illusion by making your balancing act appear even more precarious look.

CENTER OF GRAVITY STILL OVER THE TABLE

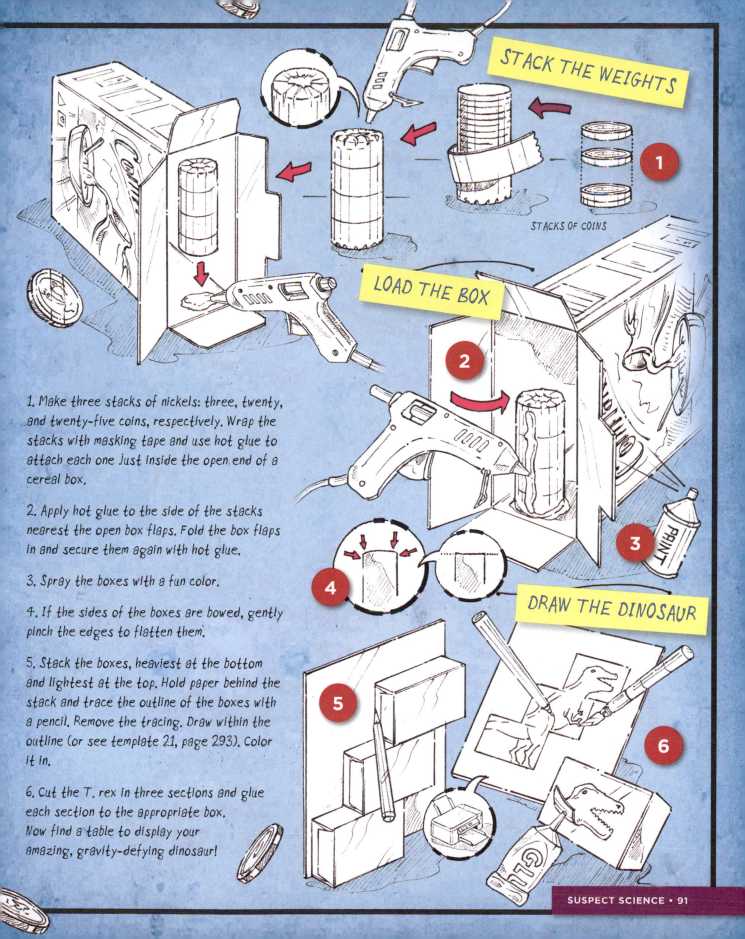

STACKS OF COINS

1

LOAD THE BOX

2

3

4

DRAW THE DINOSAUR

5

6

1. Make three stacks of nickels: three, twenty, and twenty-five coins, respectively. Wrap the stacks with masking tape and use hot glue to attach each one just inside the open end of a cereal box.

2. Apply hot glue to the side of the stacks nearest the open box flaps. Fold the box flaps in and secure them again with hot glue.

3. Spray the boxes with a fun color.

4. If the sides of the boxes are bowed, gently pinch the edges to flatten them.

5. Stack the boxes, heaviest at the bottom and lightest at the top. Hold paper behind the stack and trace the outline of the boxes with a pencil. Remove the tracing. Draw within the outline (or see template 21, page 293). Color it in.

6. Cut the T. rex in three sections and glue each section to the appropriate box. Now find a table to display your amazing, gravity-defying dinosaur!

EXTREME CAR RAMP

LEVEL: MEDIUM

Can you jump five (toy) trains, or perhaps ten gummy bears? Prepare to find out with this "extreme" cereal-box car ramp. When the kids get tired of jumping things, get out a box of Jenga and construct a wall for them to bash down (it will keep them busy at least another half hour).

MATERIALS

- Ruler
- Pencil
- 2 cereal boxes
- Craft knife and cutting mat
- Paper glue
- 1 medium-sized corrugated cardboard box
- Black spray paint
- 4 cocktail skewers
- Black permanent marker
- Lightweight cardboard
- White medium-weight cardstock
- Colored medium-weight cardstock (red and orange)
- Scissors
- Hot glue gun and glue sticks
- Toy car
- Access to a photocopier or printer (optional)

TRANSFORM A BOX INTO

THE TAKEOFF RAMP . . .

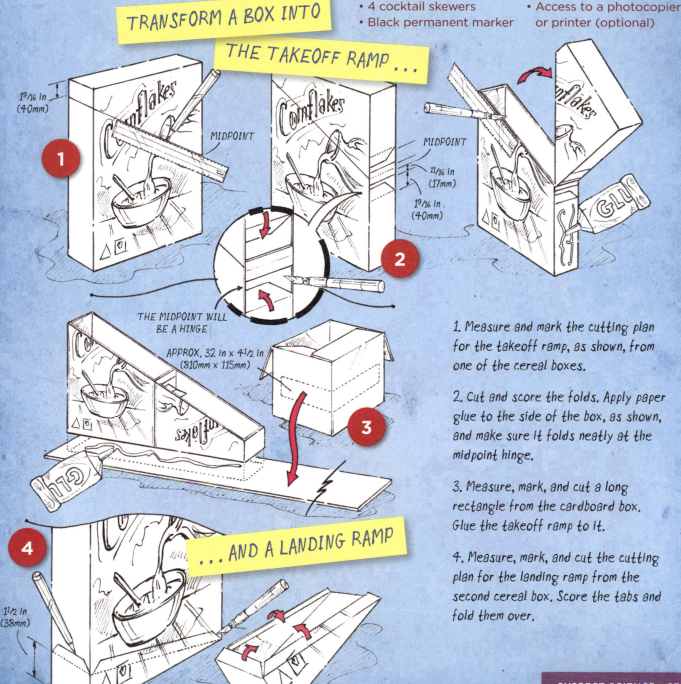

1⁹/₁₆ in (40mm)

MIDPOINT

MIDPOINT

11/16 in (17mm)

1⁹/₁₆ in (40mm)

THE MIDPOINT WILL BE A HINGE

APPROX. 32 in x 4¹/₂ in (810mm x 115mm)

. . . AND A LANDING RAMP

1¹/₂ in (38mm)

1. Measure and mark the cutting plan for the takeoff ramp, as shown, from one of the cereal boxes.

2. Cut and score the folds. Apply paper glue to the side of the box, as shown, and make sure it folds neatly at the midpoint hinge.

3. Measure, mark, and cut a long rectangle from the cardboard box. Glue the takeoff ramp to it.

4. Measure, mark, and cut the cutting plan for the landing ramp from the second cereal box. Score the tabs and fold them over.

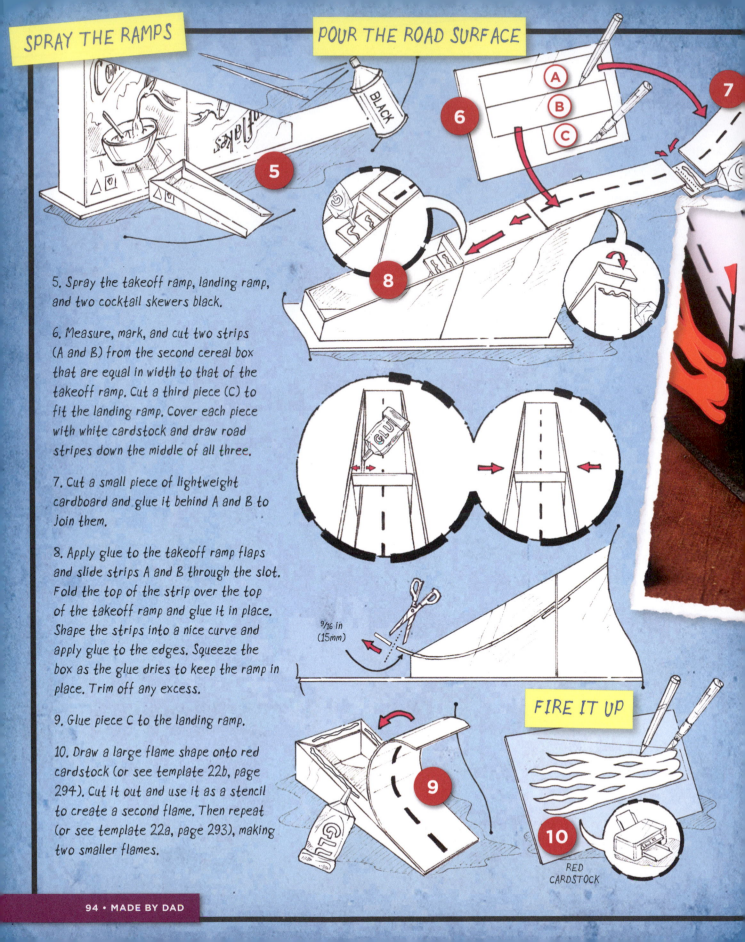

SPRAY THE RAMPS

POUR THE ROAD SURFACE

BLACK

Ⓐ
Ⓑ
Ⓒ

5

6

7

8

GLUE

9/16 in
(15mm)

5. Spray the takeoff ramp, landing ramp, and two cocktail skewers black.

6. Measure, mark, and cut two strips (A and B) from the second cereal box that are equal in width to that of the takeoff ramp. Cut a third piece (C) to fit the landing ramp. Cover each piece with white cardstock and draw road stripes down the middle of all three.

7. Cut a small piece of lightweight cardboard and glue it behind A and B to join them.

8. Apply glue to the takeoff ramp flaps and slide strips A and B through the slot. Fold the top of the strip over the top of the takeoff ramp and glue it in place. Shape the strips into a nice curve and apply glue to the edges. Squeeze the box as the glue dries to keep the ramp in place. Trim off any excess.

9. Glue piece C to the landing ramp.

10. Draw a large flame shape onto red cardstock (or see template 22b, page 294). Cut it out and use it as a stencil to create a second flame. Then repeat (or see template 22a, page 293), making two smaller flames.

FIRE IT UP

GLUE

9

10

RED
CARDSTOCK

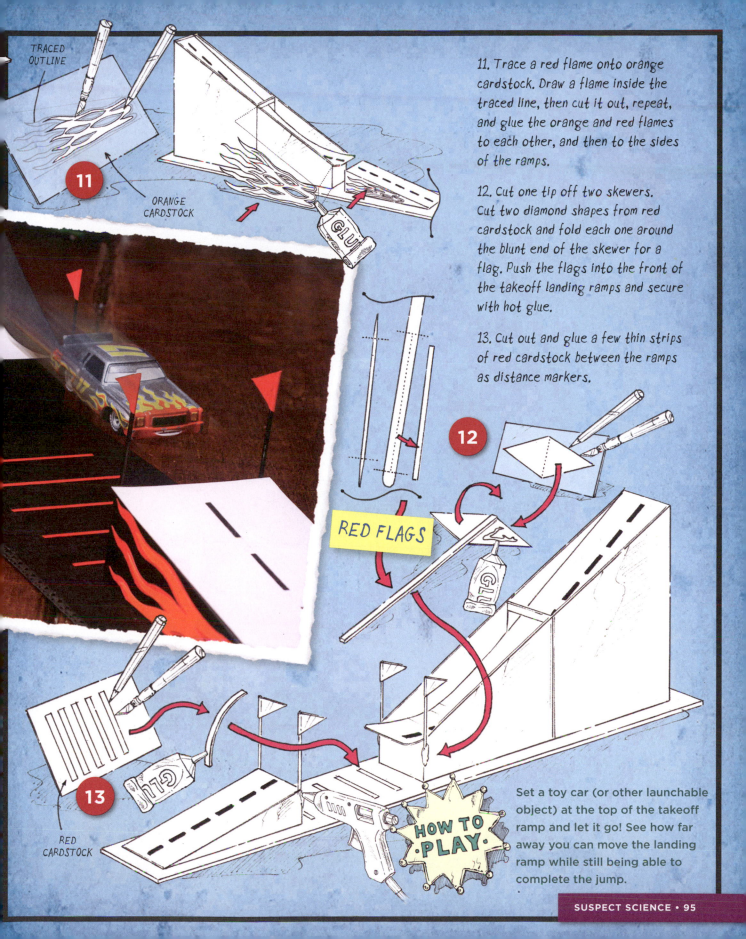

11. Trace a red flame onto orange cardstock. Draw a flame inside the traced line, then cut it out, repeat, and glue the orange and red flames to each other, and then to the sides of the ramps.

12. Cut one tip off two skewers. Cut two diamond shapes from red cardstock and fold each one around the blunt end of the skewer for a flag. Push the flags into the front of the takeoff landing ramps and secure with hot glue.

13. Cut out and glue a few thin strips of red cardstock between the ramps as distance markers.

ORANGE
CARDSTOCK

RED FLAGS

RED
CARDSTOCK

HOW TO
·PLAY·

Set a toy car (or other launchable object) at the top of the takeoff ramp and let it go! See how far away you can move the landing ramp while still being able to complete the jump.

MARVELOUS MARBLE BOUNCER

LEVEL: **MEDIUM**

It's amazing what you can make with practically nothing. Two empty cereal boxes, four empty cereal bowls, some cling wrap, and you've got a crazy triple-jump marble bouncer. This project is inspired by a toy I saw as a kid in Harrods, the famous department store in London—so though you could say it took me thirty years to make, it'll only take you an afternoon.

MATERIALS

- 2 medium-sized cereal boxes
- Paper glue
- Pencil
- Ruler
- Craft knife and cutting mat
- Medium-sized corrugated cardboard box
- Hot glue gun and glue sticks
- 4 cereal bowls
- Cling wrap
- Scissors
- Spray paint (any color)
- Colored lightweight cardstock (in red and orange)
- Gold star stickers

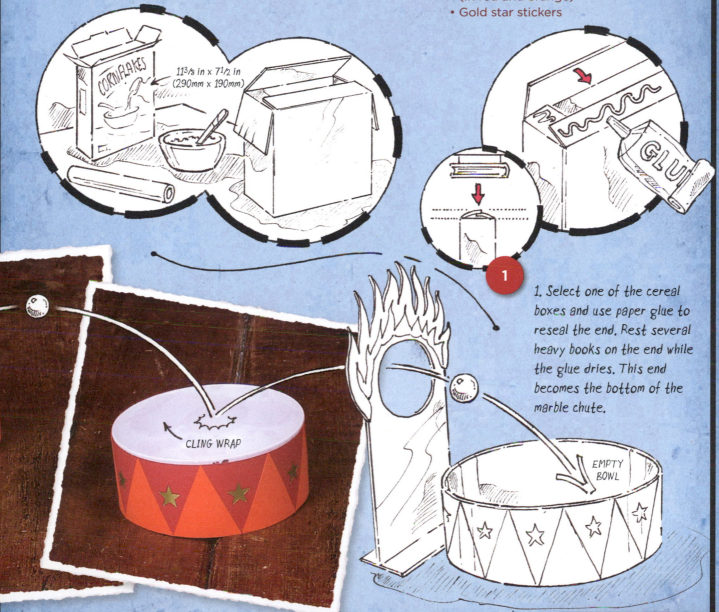

CORNFLAKES

$11^3/_8$ in x $7^1/_2$ in (290mm x 190mm)

GLU

CLING WRAP

EMPTY BOWL

1. Select one of the cereal boxes and use paper glue to reseal the end. Rest several heavy books on the end while the glue dries. This end becomes the bottom of the marble chute.

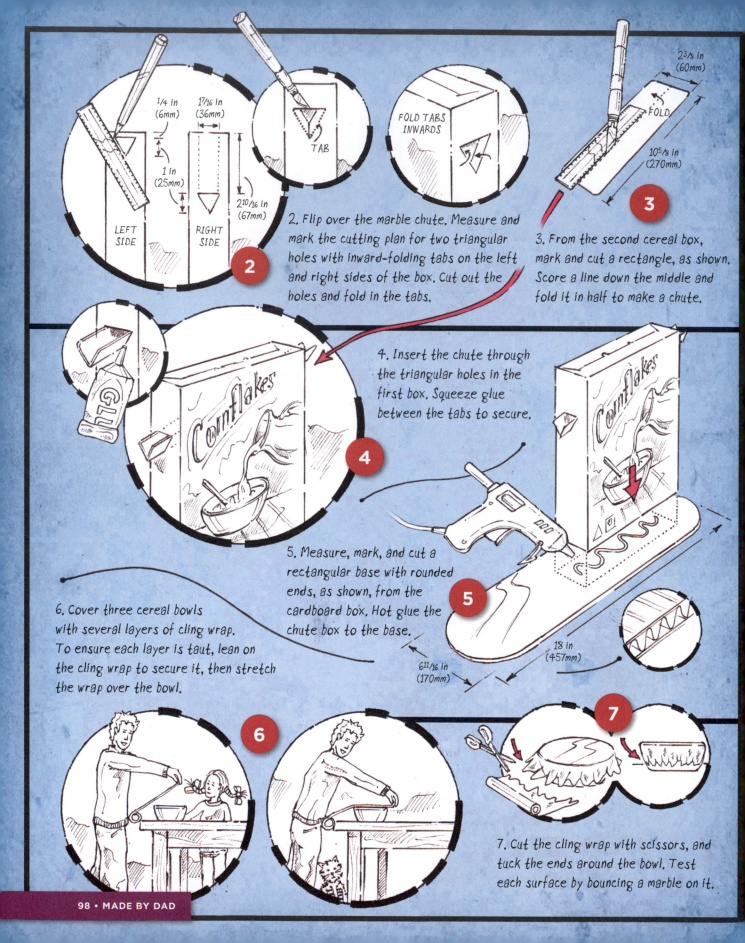

2. Flip over the marble chute. Measure and mark the cutting plan for two triangular holes with inward-folding tabs on the left and right sides of the box. Cut out the holes and fold in the tabs.

1/4 in (6mm)
1 7/16 in (36mm)
1 in (25mm)
2 10/16 in (67mm)

LEFT SIDE

RIGHT SIDE

TAB

FOLD TABS INWARDS

2 3/8 in (60mm)
FOLD
10 5/8 in (270mm)

3. From the second cereal box, mark and cut a rectangle, as shown. Score a line down the middle and fold it in half to make a chute.

GLU

Cornflakes

4. Insert the chute through the triangular holes in the first box. Squeeze glue between the tabs to secure.

Cornflakes

5. Measure, mark, and cut a rectangular base with rounded ends, as shown, from the cardboard box. Hot glue the chute box to the base.

6 11/16 in (170mm)
18 in (457mm)

6. Cover three cereal bowls with several layers of cling wrap. To ensure each layer is taut, lean on the cling wrap to secure it, then stretch the wrap over the bowl.

7. Cut the cling wrap with scissors, and tuck the ends around the bowl. Test each surface by bouncing a marble on it.

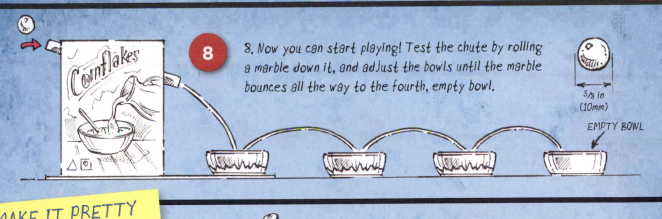

8. Now you can start playing! Test the chute by rolling a marble down it, and adjust the bowls until the marble bounces all the way to the fourth, empty bowl.

3/8 in (10mm)

EMPTY BOWL

MAKE IT PRETTY

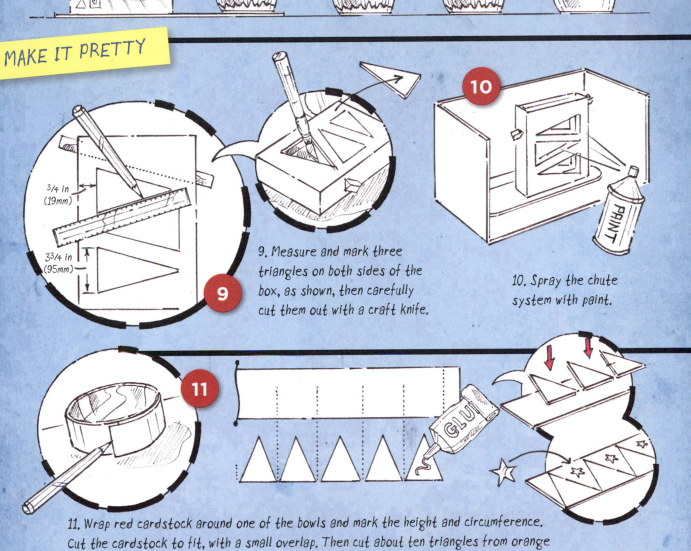

3/4 in (19mm)

3 3/4 in (95mm)

9. Measure and mark three triangles on both sides of the box, as shown, then carefully cut them out with a craft knife.

10. Spray the chute system with paint.

11. Wrap red cardstock around one of the bowls and mark the height and circumference. Cut the cardstock to fit, with a small overlap. Then cut about ten triangles from orange cardstock to fit along the length of the red strip. Glue them to the strip and decorate with gold star stickers.

12. Glue the finished strip around the bowl.

13. Repeat steps 11 and 12 for the three remaining bowls. Cut out red cardstock to fit the protruding ends of the chute and glue it in place. Embellish the chute with gold star stickers.

BALLOON BALLAST BALANCING ACT

LEVEL: CHALLENGING

It's always a kick making something that my boys actually enjoy playing with—especially for extended periods of time! This project was one of those: They spent two days drawing and making their own things to hang on the balloon. It definitely gets a thumbs up!

MATERIALS

- Ruler
- Pencil
- Paper cup (16 oz, 454 g)
- Craft knife and cutting mat
- White lightweight cardstock
- Paper glue
- Felt-tip markers or paint
- Thread
- Scissors
- Balloon
- Dowel (5⁄16", 8 mm)
- Hacksaw
- Drill (1⁄16", 1.5 mm bit)
- 4 small paper clips
- Pliers
- Light fixture
- Hot glue gun and glue sticks
- 2 dried-up AA batteries
- Colored lightweight cardstock (various hues)
- Mounting putty
- Access to a photocopier or printer (optional)

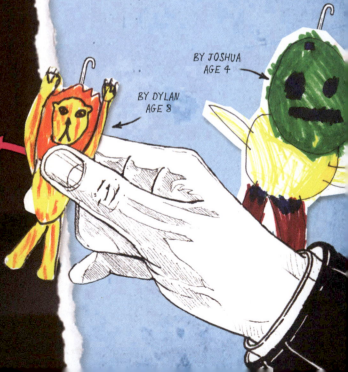

BY JOSHUA AGE 4

BY DYLAN AGE 8

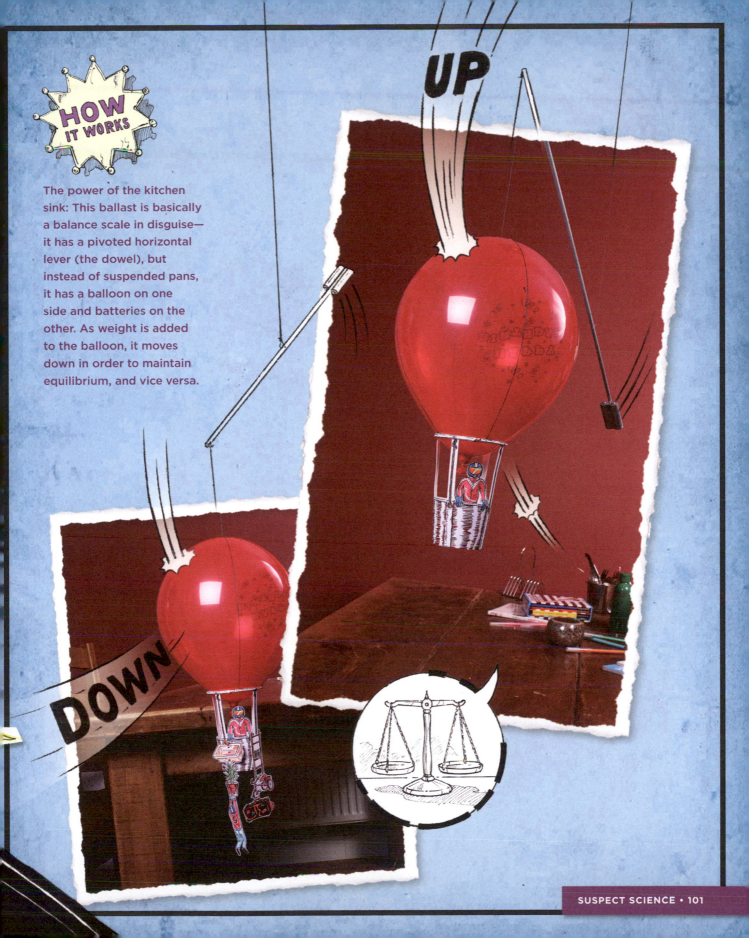

HOW IT WORKS

The power of the kitchen sink: This ballast is basically a balance scale in disguise—it has a pivoted horizontal lever (the dowel), but instead of suspended pans, it has a balloon on one side and batteries on the other. As weight is added to the balloon, it moves down in order to maintain equilibrium, and vice versa.

UP

DOWN

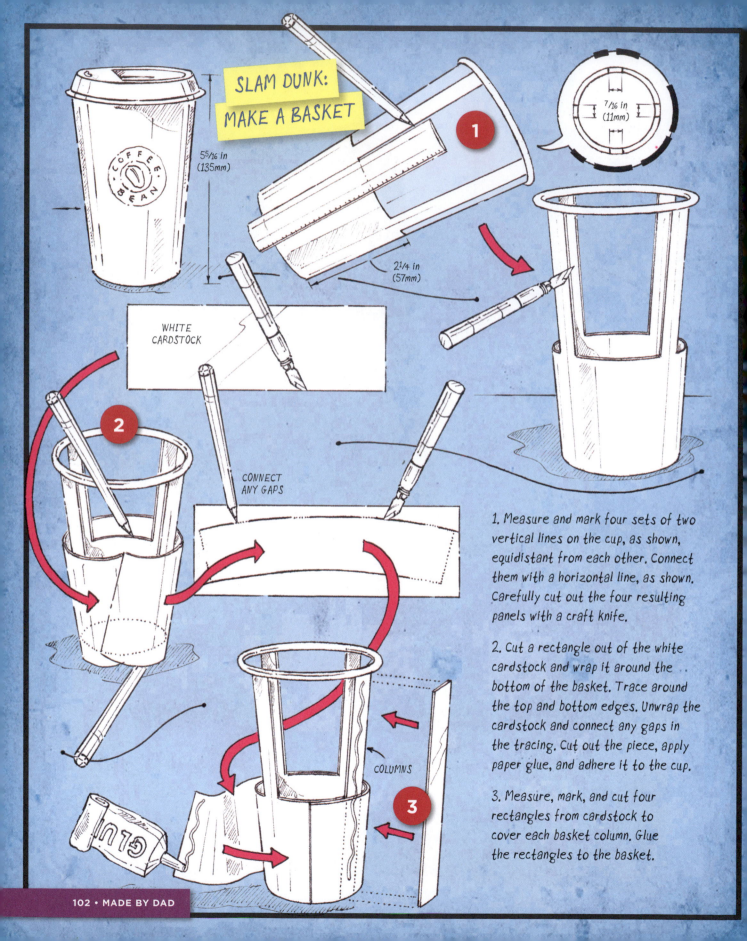

SLAM DUNK: MAKE A BASKET

5⁵/₁₆ in (135mm)

2¹/₄ in (57mm)

7/16 in (11mm)

1

WHITE CARDSTOCK

2

CONNECT ANY GAPS

COLUMNS

GLU

3

1. Measure and mark four sets of two vertical lines on the cup, as shown, equidistant from each other. Connect them with a horizontal line, as shown. Carefully cut out the four resulting panels with a craft knife.

2. Cut a rectangle out of the white cardstock and wrap it around the bottom of the basket. Trace around the top and bottom edges. Unwrap the cardstock and connect any gaps in the tracing. Cut out the piece, apply paper glue, and adhere it to the cup.

3. Measure, mark, and cut four rectangles from cardstock to cover each basket column. Glue the rectangles to the basket.

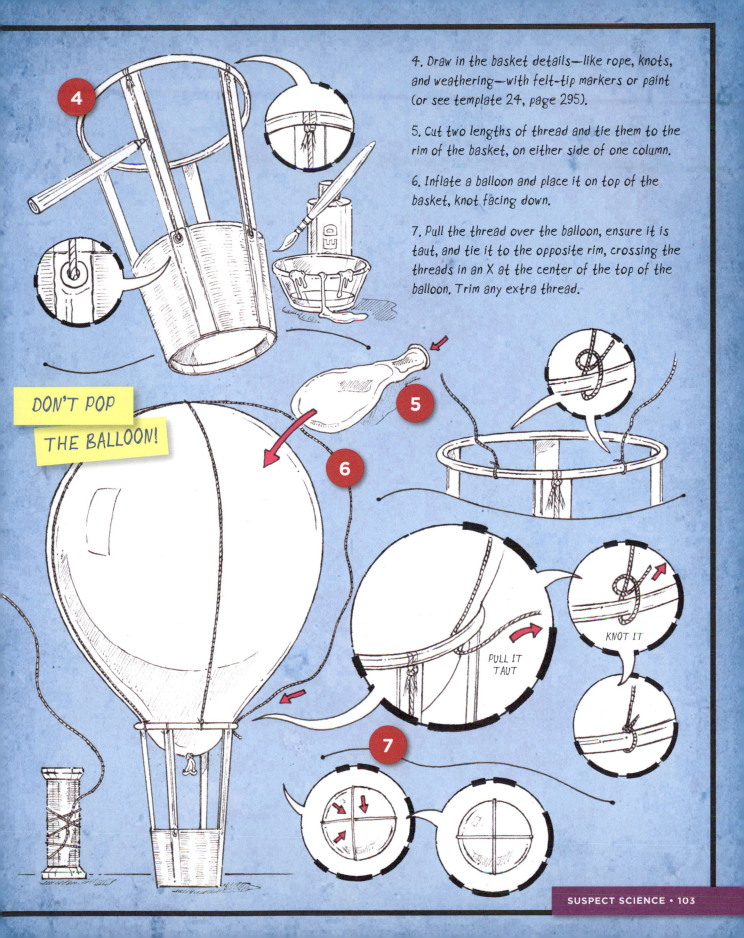

4. Draw in the basket details—like rope, knots, and weathering—with felt-tip markers or paint (or see template 24, page 295).

5. Cut two lengths of thread and tie them to the rim of the basket, on either side of one column.

6. Inflate a balloon and place it on top of the basket, knot facing down.

7. Pull the thread over the balloon, ensure it is taut, and tie it to the opposite rim, crossing the threads in an X at the center of the top of the balloon. Trim any extra thread.

DON'T POP THE BALLOON!

PULL IT TAUT

KNOT IT

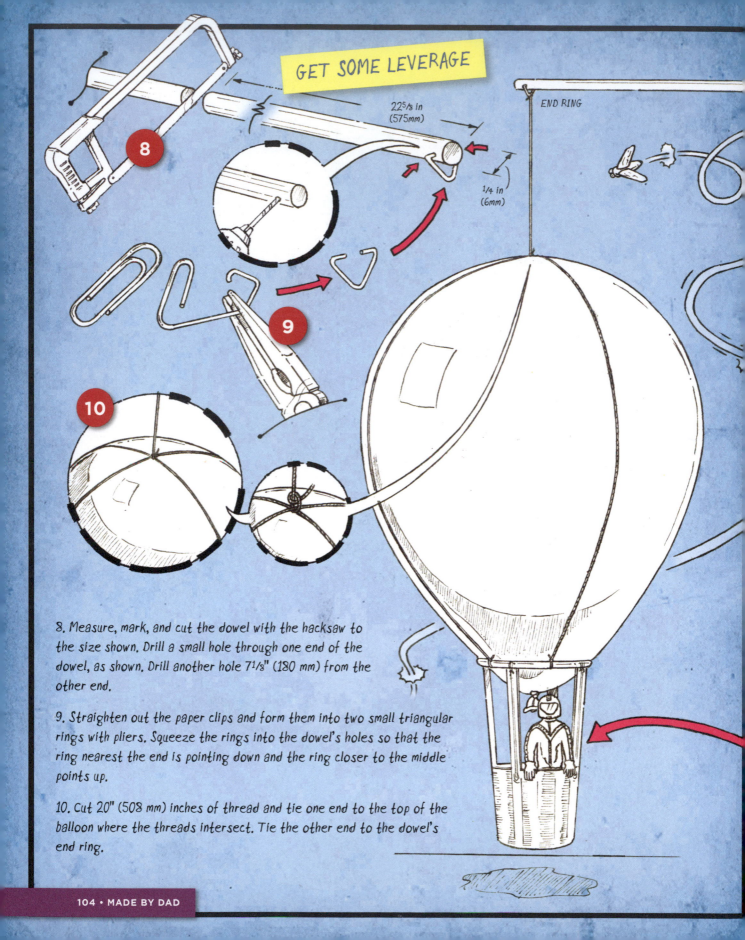

GET SOME LEVERAGE

22⅝ in
(575mm)

END RING

¼ in
(6mm)

8. Measure, mark, and cut the dowel with the hacksaw to the size shown. Drill a small hole through one end of the dowel, as shown. Drill another hole 7⅛" (180 mm) from the other end.

9. Straighten out the paper clips and form them into two small triangular rings with pliers. Squeeze the rings into the dowel's holes so that the ring nearest the end is pointing down and the ring closer to the middle points up.

10. Cut 20" (508 mm) inches of thread and tie one end to the top of the balloon where the threads intersect. Tie the other end to the dowel's end ring.

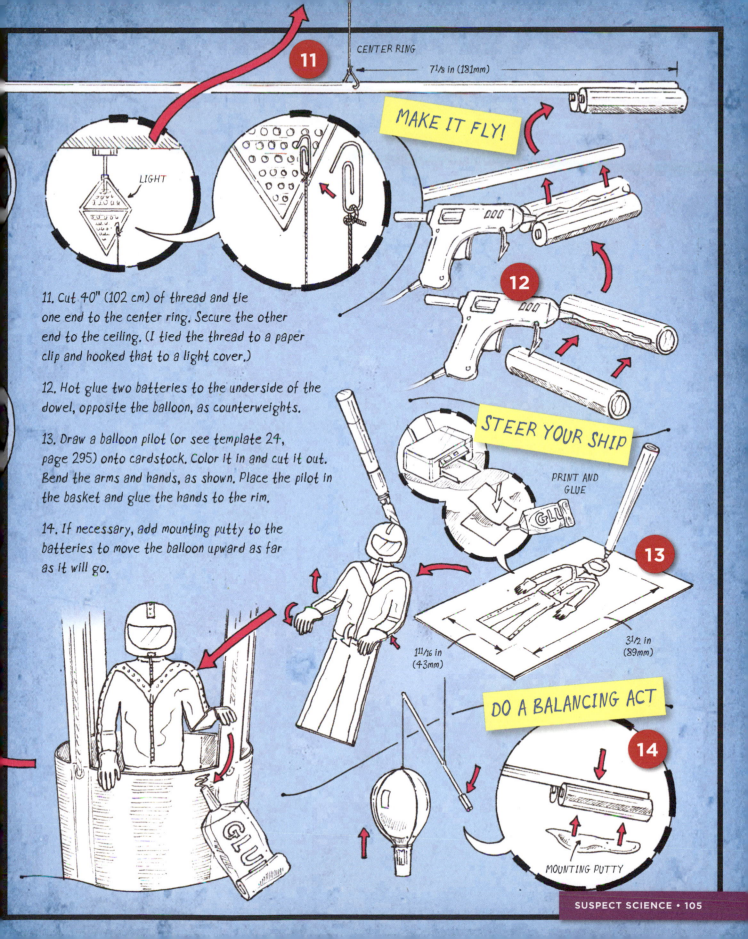

CENTER RING

7⅛ in (181mm)

MAKE IT FLY!

LIGHT

11. Cut 40" (102 cm) of thread and tie one end to the center ring. Secure the other end to the ceiling. (I tied the thread to a paper clip and hooked that to a light cover.)

12. Hot glue two batteries to the underside of the dowel, opposite the balloon, as counterweights.

13. Draw a balloon pilot (or see template 24, page 295) onto cardstock. Color it in and cut it out. Bend the arms and hands, as shown. Place the pilot in the basket and glue the hands to the rim.

14. If necessary, add mounting putty to the batteries to move the balloon upward as far as it will go.

STEER YOUR SHIP

PRINT AND GLUE

GLUE

3½ in (89mm)

1¹¹⁄₁₆ in (43mm)

GLUE

DO A BALANCING ACT

MOUNTING PUTTY

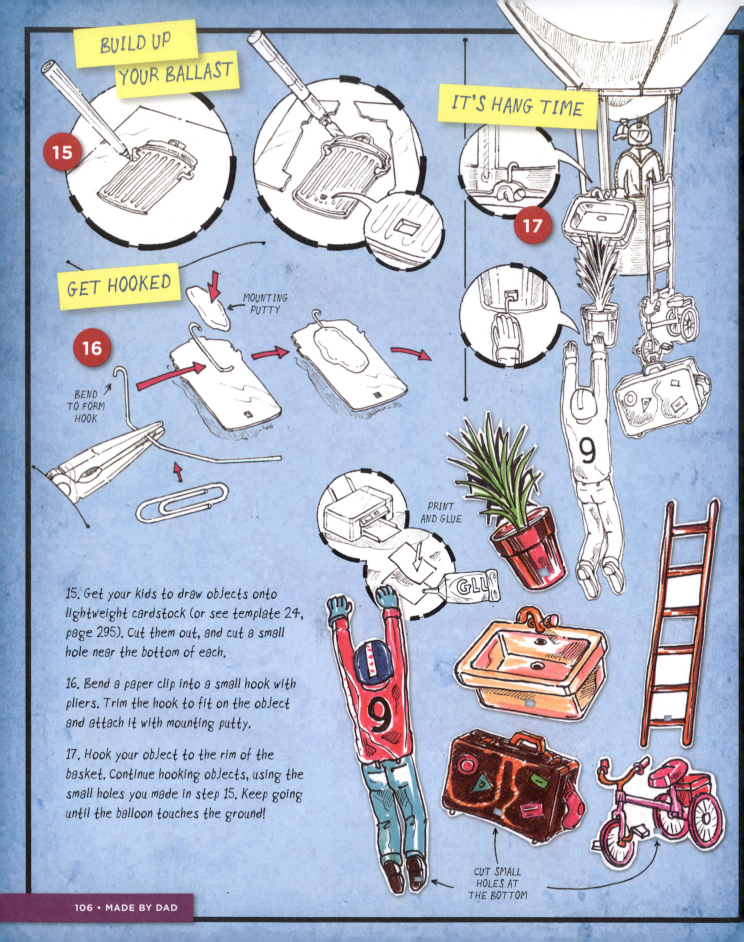

BUILD UP YOUR BALLAST

15

IT'S HANG TIME

17

GET HOOKED

16

MOUNTING PUTTY

BEND TO FORM HOOK

PRINT AND GLUE

GLU

9

9

CUT SMALL HOLES AT THE BOTTOM

15. Get your kids to draw objects onto lightweight cardstock (or see template 24, page 295). Cut them out, and cut a small hole near the bottom of each.

16. Bend a paper clip into a small hook with pliers. Trim the hook to fit on the object and attach it with mounting putty.

17. Hook your object to the rim of the basket. Continue hooking objects, using the small holes you made in step 15. Keep going until the balloon touches the ground!

Be amazed as Teddy travels through the center of the Earth and pops out in China having mysteriously swapped his Stars and Stripes along the way. Turn the tube around, give him a little push, and watch him surface back in the USA waving the red, white, and blue again. Magic.

MATERIALS
- Pencil
- Ruler
- Toilet paper tube
- Craft knife and cutting mat
- Paper glue
- Long cardboard tube (an empty wrapping-paper tube works well)
- White lightweight cardstock (poster size)
- Lightweight cardstock
- Felt-tip markers
- Small corrugated cardboard box
- Sponge
- Masking tape
- Drafting compass
- Access to a photocopier or printer (optional)

TEDDY THROUGH THE CENTER OF THE EARTH

LEVEL: MEDIUM

MAKE THE INNER TUBES

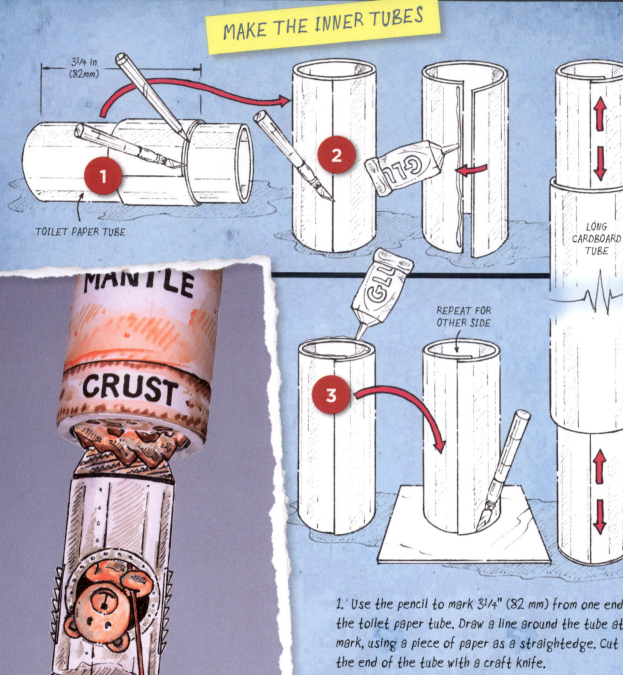

3¼ in (82mm)

1

TOILET PAPER TUBE

2

GLU

LONG
CARDBOARD
TUBE

3

GLU

REPEAT FOR
OTHER SIDE

1. Use the pencil to mark 3¼" (82 mm) from one end of
the toilet paper tube. Draw a line around the tube at the
mark, using a piece of paper as a straightedge. Cut off
the end of the tube with a craft knife.

2. Cut the shortened tube vertically and apply paper glue
to one edge. Rejoin the edges so that it will be able to
slide inside the long cardboard tube and let it dry.

3. Apply glue to one end of the inner tube and press it
onto a piece of cardstock. Let dry, then trim around
the tube, making sure it will still slide through the long
cardboard tube. Repeat for the other end.

MANTLE

CRUST

4. Draw two bears, one with a US flag, and one with a Chinese flag onto cardstock (or see template 25, page 296). Color them in and cut them out.

5. Measure, mark, and cut two supports from the cardboard box, as shown (or see template 25, page 296). Glue the supports to the back of the teddies and then to each end of the covered inner tube.

6. Cut a rectangle out of each end of the long tube. Then cut two strips of sponge slightly longer and wider than the rectangles. Poke the middle of one sponge through one of the holes so that it protrudes on the inside. Tape around the outside of the tube, securing the sponge. Repeat with the second sponge. The sponges will gently grip the inner tube.

ADD SUPPORT

DIAMETER OF INNER TUBE: MINUS 1/8 in (4mm)

1/16 in (2mm) GAP

MAKE THE SPONGE GRIP

1/2 in (12mm)

5/16 in (8mm)

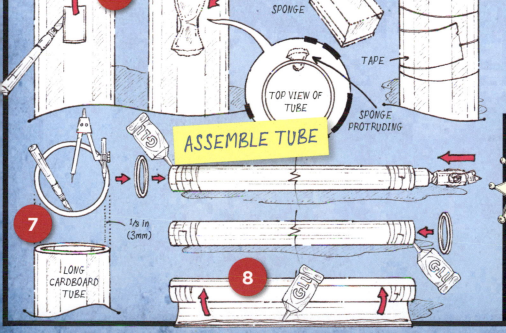

SPONGE

TOP VIEW OF TUBE

TAPE

SPONGE PROTRUDING

ASSEMBLE TUBE

1/8 in (3mm)

LONG CARDBOARD TUBE

7. Use the compass to draw two narrow rings onto cardstock. Cut them out. Insert the inner tube into the long tube, and glue one ring to each end of the long tube, so the inner tube can't fall out.

8. Decorate the large sheet of cardstock with the layers of the Earth, and wrap it around the tube. Secure it with glue.

HOW TO PLAY

Hold the tube so Teddy pokes out the bottom. Rotate it until Teddy is at the top. Give him a gentle push through the center of the earth! Repeat endlessly.

RUBBER BAND ROCKET CAR

LEVEL: **Tricky**

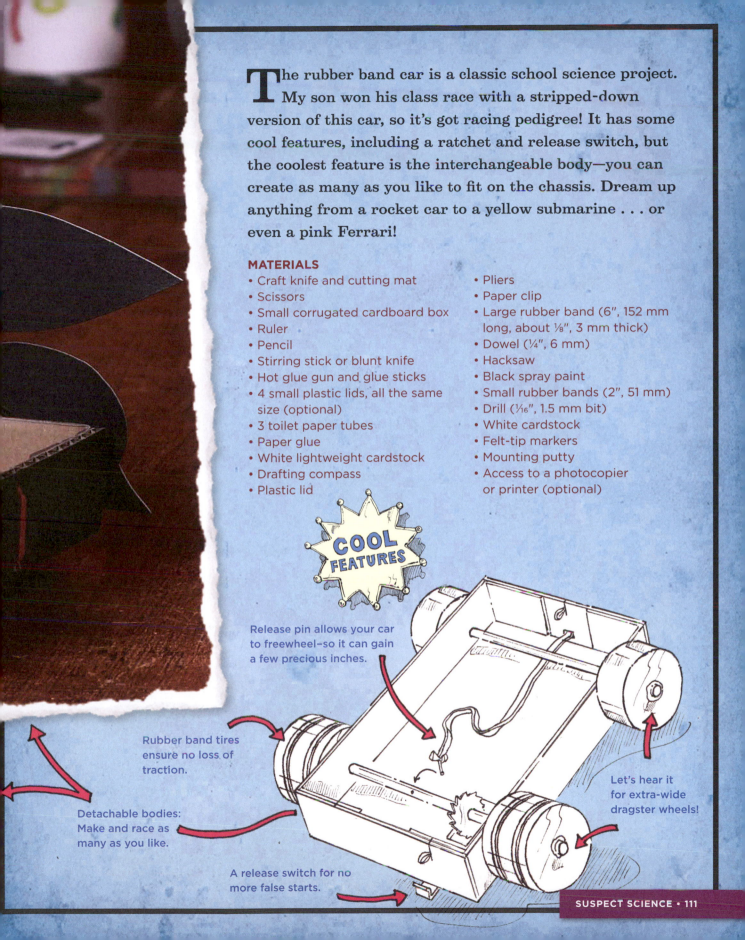

The rubber band car is a classic school science project. My son won his class race with a stripped-down version of this car, so it's got racing pedigree! It has some cool features, including a ratchet and release switch, but the coolest feature is the interchangeable body—you can create as many as you like to fit on the chassis. Dream up anything from a rocket car to a yellow submarine . . . or even a pink Ferrari!

MATERIALS

- Craft knife and cutting mat
- Scissors
- Small corrugated cardboard box
- Ruler
- Pencil
- Stirring stick or blunt knife
- Hot glue gun and glue sticks
- 4 small plastic lids, all the same size (optional)
- 3 toilet paper tubes
- Paper glue
- White lightweight cardstock
- Drafting compass
- Plastic lid
- Pliers
- Paper clip
- Large rubber band (6", 152 mm long, about ⅛", 3 mm thick)
- Dowel (¼", 6 mm)
- Hacksaw
- Black spray paint
- Small rubber bands (2", 51 mm)
- Drill (1/16", 1.5 mm bit)
- White cardstock
- Felt-tip markers
- Mounting putty
- Access to a photocopier or printer (optional)

COOL FEATURES

Release pin allows your car to freewheel—so it can gain a few precious inches.

Rubber band tires ensure no loss of traction.

Detachable bodies: Make and race as many as you like.

A release switch for no more false starts.

Let's hear it for extra-wide dragster wheels!

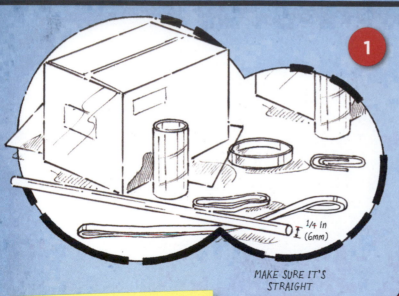

MAKE SURE IT'S STRAIGHT

1/4 in (6mm)

1. Use scissors or a craft knife to cut off one side of the cardboard box.

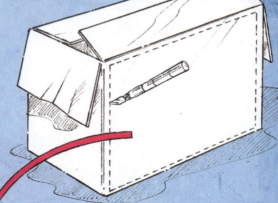

BUILD THE CHASSIS

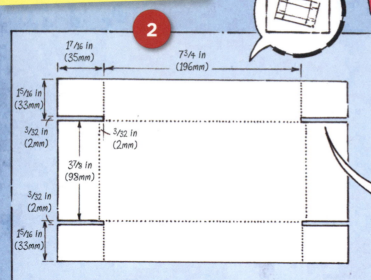

17/16 in (35mm)

73/4 in (196mm)

15/16 in (33mm)

3/32 in (2mm)

3/32 in (2mm)

37/8 in (98mm)

3/32 in (2mm)

15/16 in (33mm)

THE BOX IS SYMMETRICAL SO MEASUREMENTS ARE THE SAME ON BOTH SIDES

2. Measure and mark the cutting plan for the chassis on the panel. Carefully cut it out with the craft knife on the cutting mat.

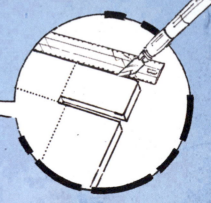

3. Score the fold lines with a stirring stick, as shown.

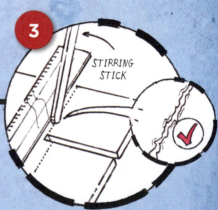

STIRRING STICK

DON'T WORRY IF THE CARDBOARD SURFACE TEARS

4. Fold up the ends and side panels and secure them with hot glue to complete the chassis.

SHORTCUT ALERT!

For fast and easy wheel assembly (and if you don't care about having extra-wide dragster wheels), use four plastic lids and skip to step 9 to cut a hole for the axle.

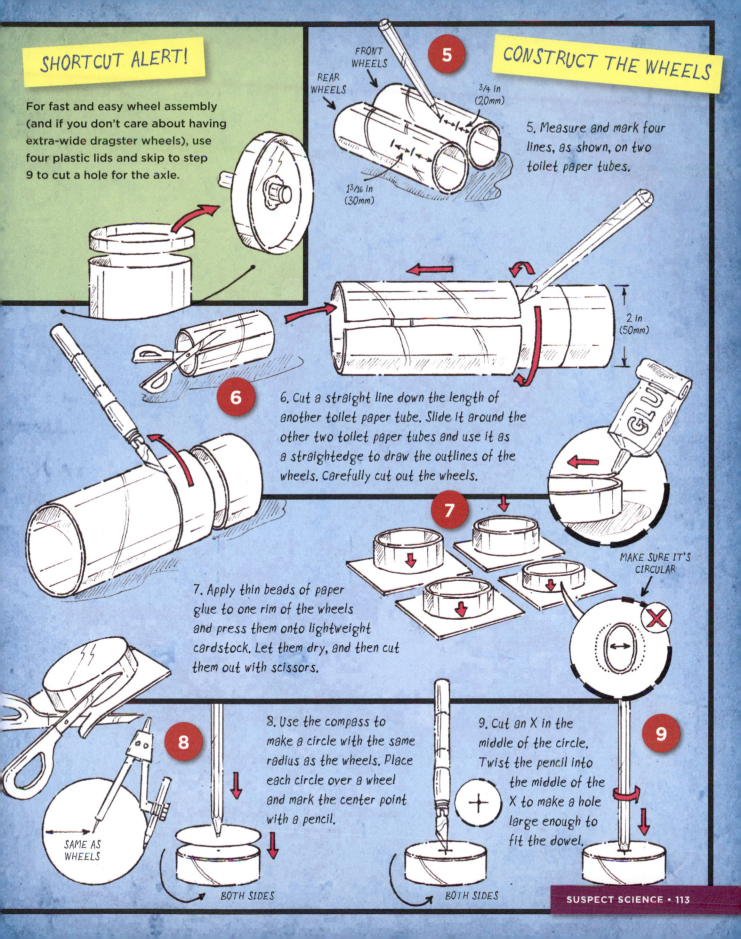

CONSTRUCT THE WHEELS

5. Measure and mark four lines, as shown, on two toilet paper tubes.

FRONT WHEELS
REAR WHEELS
3/4 in (20mm)
1 3/16 in (30mm)
2 in (50mm)

6. Cut a straight line down the length of another toilet paper tube. Slide it around the other two toilet paper tubes and use it as a straightedge to draw the outlines of the wheels. Carefully cut out the wheels.

GLUE

MAKE SURE IT'S CIRCULAR

7. Apply thin beads of paper glue to one rim of the wheels and press them onto lightweight cardstock. Let them dry, and then cut them out with scissors.

8. Use the compass to make a circle with the same radius as the wheels. Place each circle over a wheel and mark the center point with a pencil.

SAME AS WHEELS

BOTH SIDES

9. Cut an X in the middle of the circle. Twist the pencil into the middle of the X to make a hole large enough to fit the dowel.

BOTH SIDES

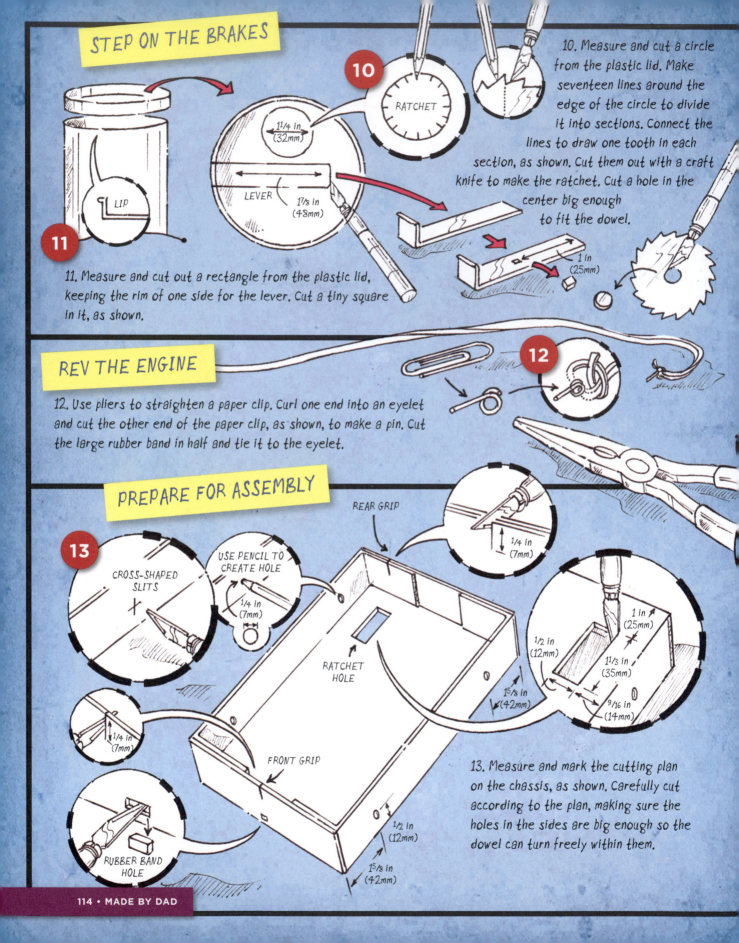

STEP ON THE BRAKES

10

RATCHET

1¼ in (32mm)

LEVER

1⅞ in (48mm)

1 in (25mm)

10. Measure and cut a circle from the plastic lid. Make seventeen lines around the edge of the circle to divide it into sections. Connect the lines to draw one tooth in each section, as shown. Cut them out with a craft knife to make the ratchet. Cut a hole in the center big enough to fit the dowel.

11

LIP

11. Measure and cut out a rectangle from the plastic lid, keeping the rim of one side for the lever. Cut a tiny square in it, as shown.

REV THE ENGINE

12

12. Use pliers to straighten a paper clip. Curl one end into an eyelet and cut the other end of the paper clip, as shown, to make a pin. Cut the large rubber band in half and tie it to the eyelet.

PREPARE FOR ASSEMBLY

REAR GRIP

13

CROSS-SHAPED SLITS

USE PENCIL TO CREATE HOLE

¼ in (7mm)

¼ in (7mm)

1 in (25mm)

½ in (12mm)

1⅓ in (35mm)

1⅝ in (42mm)

9/16 in (14mm)

RATCHET HOLE

¼ in (7mm)

FRONT GRIP

RUBBER BAND HOLE

½ in (12mm)

1⅝ in (42mm)

13. Measure and mark the cutting plan on the chassis, as shown. Carefully cut according to the plan, making sure the holes in the sides are big enough so the dowel can turn freely within them.

CUT THE AXLES

14. Slide the dowel through the chassis at one axle, attaching the wheels to either end. Allow $3/32$" (2 mm) between the wheel and the chassis, and another $1/8$" (3 mm) protruding from the wheel. Mark the dowel with a pencil, remove it, and then cut it with the hacksaw. Repeat for the second axle.

Note: If your wheels are larger than $2^9/16$" (65 mm), allow $7/32$" (5 mm) between the wheel and chassis.

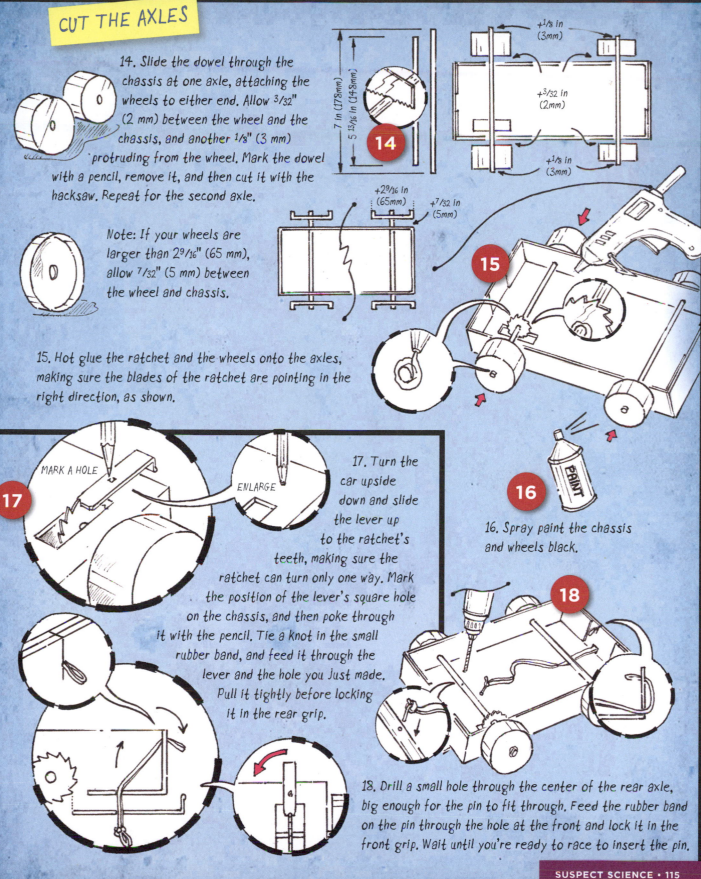

+$1/8$ in (3mm)

+$3/32$ in (2mm)

+$1/8$ in (3mm)

7 in (178mm)

5 13/16 in (148mm)

+$2^9/16$ in (65mm)

+$7/32$ in (5mm)

15. Hot glue the ratchet and the wheels onto the axles, making sure the blades of the ratchet are pointing in the right direction, as shown.

MARK A HOLE

ENLARGE

17. Turn the car upside down and slide the lever up to the ratchet's teeth, making sure the ratchet can turn only one way. Mark the position of the lever's square hole on the chassis, and then poke through it with the pencil. Tie a knot in the small rubber band, and feed it through the lever and the hole you just made. Pull it tightly before locking it in the rear grip.

16. Spray paint the chassis and wheels black.

18. Drill a small hole through the center of the rear axle, big enough for the pin to fit through. Feed the rubber band on the pin through the hole at the front and lock it in the front grip. Wait until you're ready to race to insert the pin.

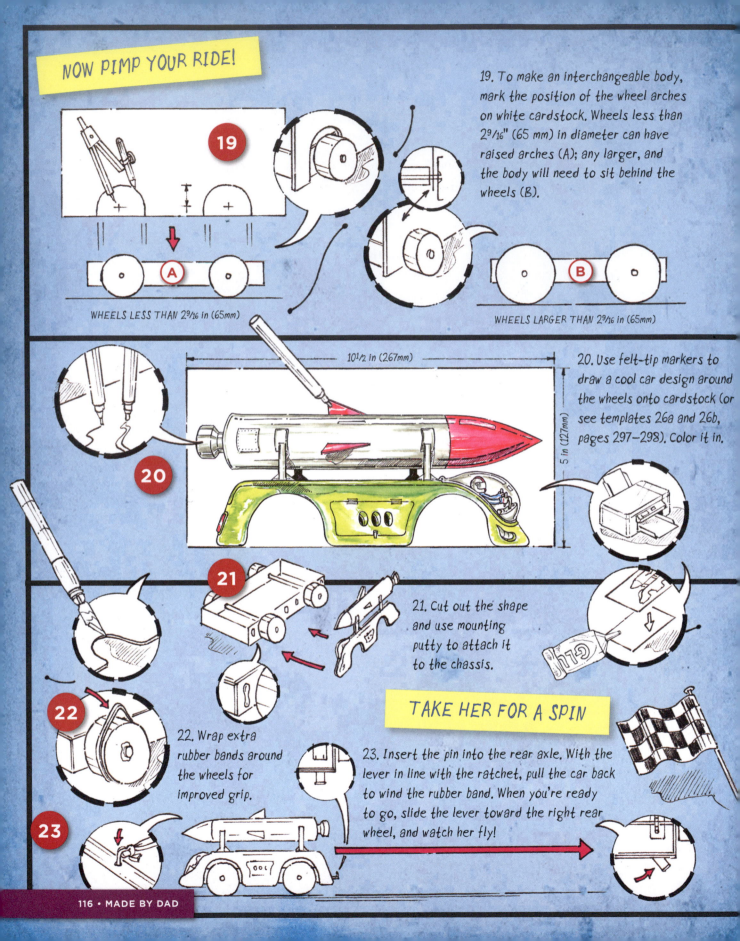

NOW PIMP YOUR RIDE!

19. To make an interchangeable body, mark the position of the wheel arches on white cardstock. Wheels less than 2⁹/₁₆" (65 mm) in diameter can have raised arches (A); any larger, and the body will need to sit behind the wheels (B).

WHEELS LESS THAN 2⁹/₁₆ in (65mm)

(A)

WHEELS LARGER THAN 2⁹/₁₆ in (65mm)

(B)

10½ in (267mm)

5 in (127mm)

20. Use felt-tip markers to draw a cool car design around the wheels onto cardstock (or see templates 26a and 26b, pages 297–298). Color it in.

21. Cut out the shape and use mounting putty to attach it to the chassis.

TAKE HER FOR A SPIN

22. Wrap extra rubber bands around the wheels for improved grip.

23. Insert the pin into the rear axle. With the lever in line with the ratchet, pull the car back to wind the rubber band. When you're ready to go, slide the lever toward the right rear wheel, and watch her fly!

BLAZING VOLCANO

LEVEL: EASY

The "volcano" is such a science fair staple that I was desperate to give it my own twist. I opted to play with fire. Now you, too, can take pleasure in setting random household items ablaze . . . without getting a visit from the fire department!

MATERIALS
- Pencil
- Ruler
- Colored medium-weight cardstock (red, yellow, dark brown, and green)
- Craft knife and cutting mat
- Paper glue
- Drafting compass
- Medium-sized corrugated cardboard box
- Mounting putty
- Coffee mug

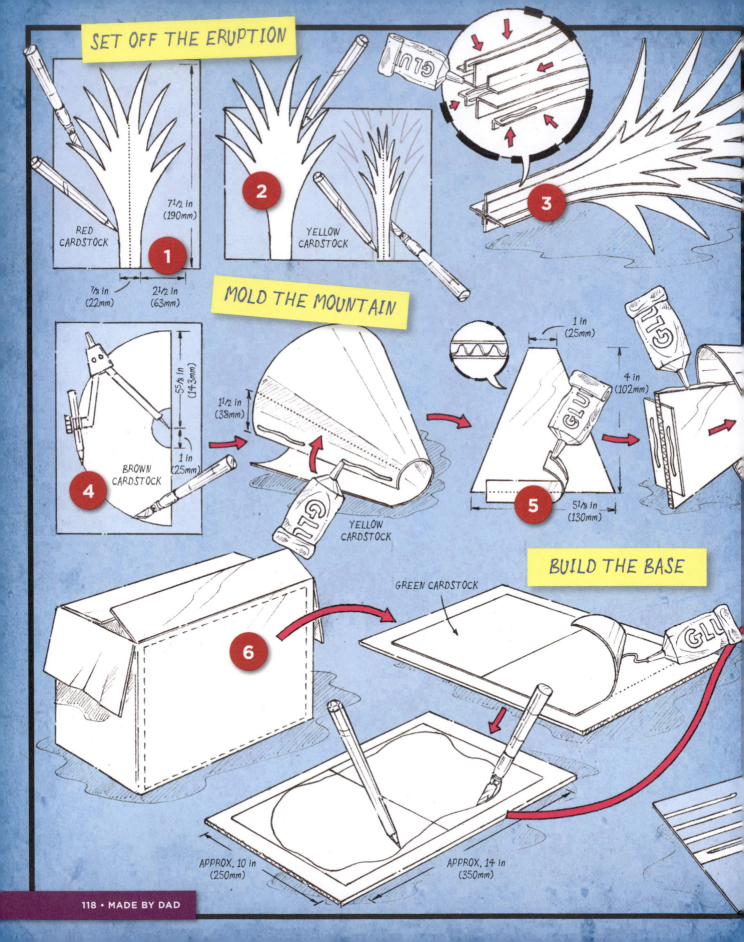

SET OFF THE ERUPTION

1 RED CARDSTOCK
7½ in (190mm)
⅞ in (22mm)
2½ in (63mm)

2 YELLOW CARDSTOCK

3 GLU

MOLD THE MOUNTAIN

4 BROWN CARDSTOCK
5⅝ in (143mm)
1 in (25mm)

1½ in (38mm)
YELLOW CARDSTOCK
GLU

5 1 in (25mm)
4 in (102mm)
5⅛ in (130mm)
GLU

BUILD THE BASE

6 GREEN CARDSTOCK
GLU

APPROX. 10 in (250mm)
APPROX. 14 in (350mm)

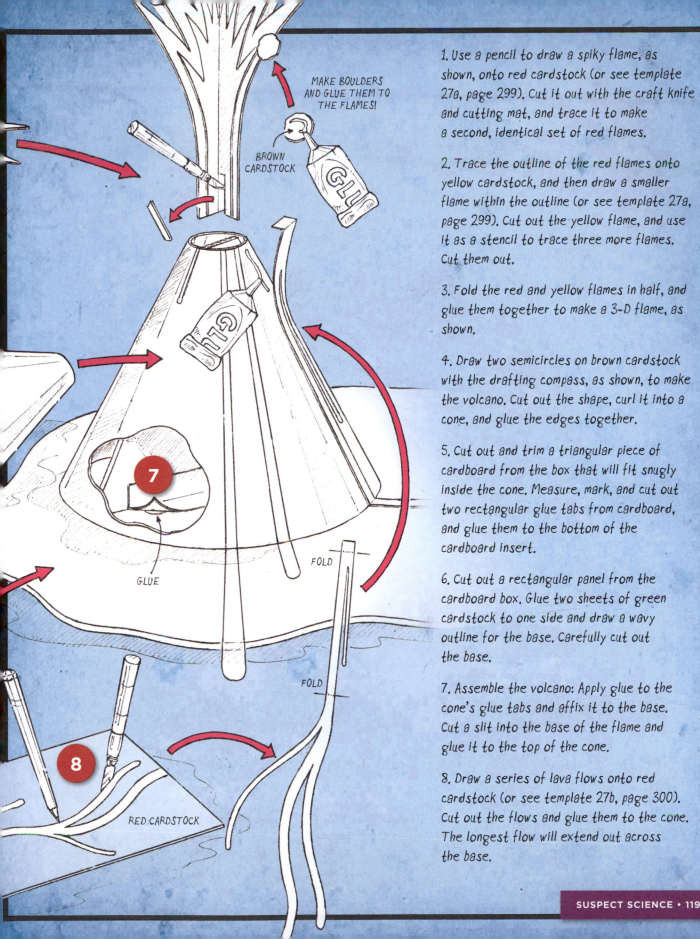

MAKE BOULDERS AND GLUE THEM TO THE FLAMES!

BROWN CARDSTOCK

GLU

GLU

7

GLUE

FOLD

FOLD

8

RED CARDSTOCK

1. Use a pencil to draw a spiky flame, as shown, onto red cardstock (or see template 27a, page 299). Cut it out with the craft knife and cutting mat, and trace it to make a second, identical set of red flames.

2. Trace the outline of the red flames onto yellow cardstock, and then draw a smaller flame within the outline (or see template 27a, page 299). Cut out the yellow flame, and use it as a stencil to trace three more flames. Cut them out.

3. Fold the red and yellow flames in half, and glue them together to make a 3-D flame, as shown.

4. Draw two semicircles on brown cardstock with the drafting compass, as shown, to make the volcano. Cut out the shape, curl it into a cone, and glue the edges together.

5. Cut out and trim a triangular piece of cardboard from the box that will fit snugly inside the cone. Measure, mark, and cut out two rectangular glue tabs from cardboard, and glue them to the bottom of the cardboard insert.

6. Cut out a rectangular panel from the cardboard box. Glue two sheets of green cardstock to one side and draw a wavy outline for the base. Carefully cut out the base.

7. Assemble the volcano: Apply glue to the cone's glue tabs and affix it to the base. Cut a slit into the base of the flame and glue it to the top of the cone.

8. Draw a series of lava flows onto red cardstock (or see template 27b, page 300). Cut out the flows and glue them to the cone. The longest flow will extend out across the base.

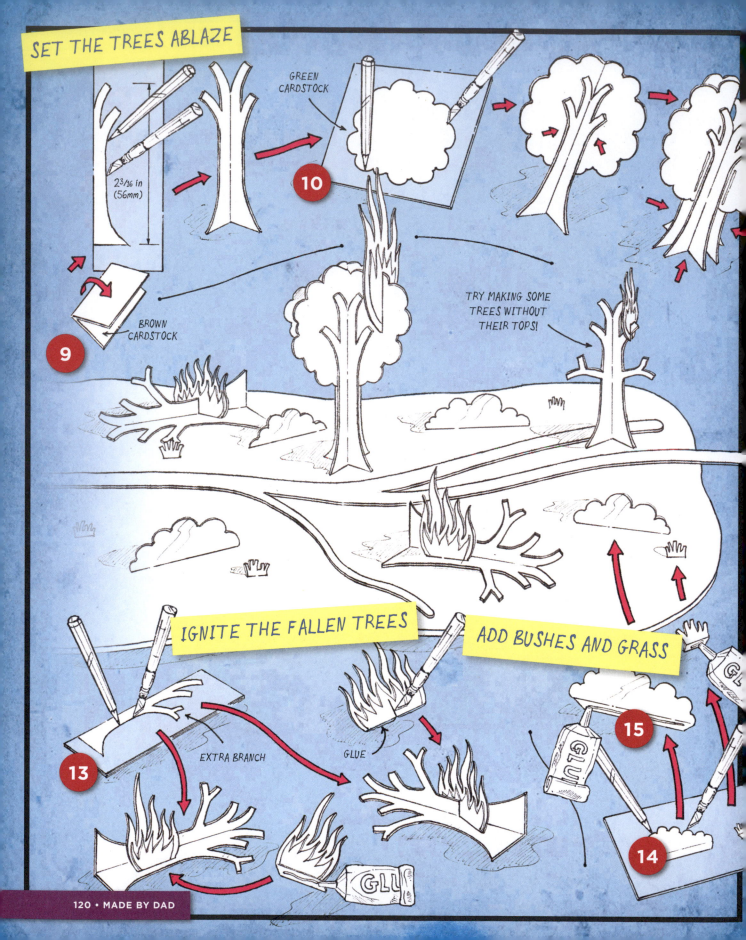

SET THE TREES ABLAZE

2³/₁₆ in (56mm)

BROWN CARDSTOCK

9

10

GREEN CARDSTOCK

TRY MAKING SOME TREES WITHOUT THEIR TOPS!

IGNITE THE FALLEN TREES

ADD BUSHES AND GRASS

EXTRA BRANCH

GLUE

13

14

15

GLUE

GLU

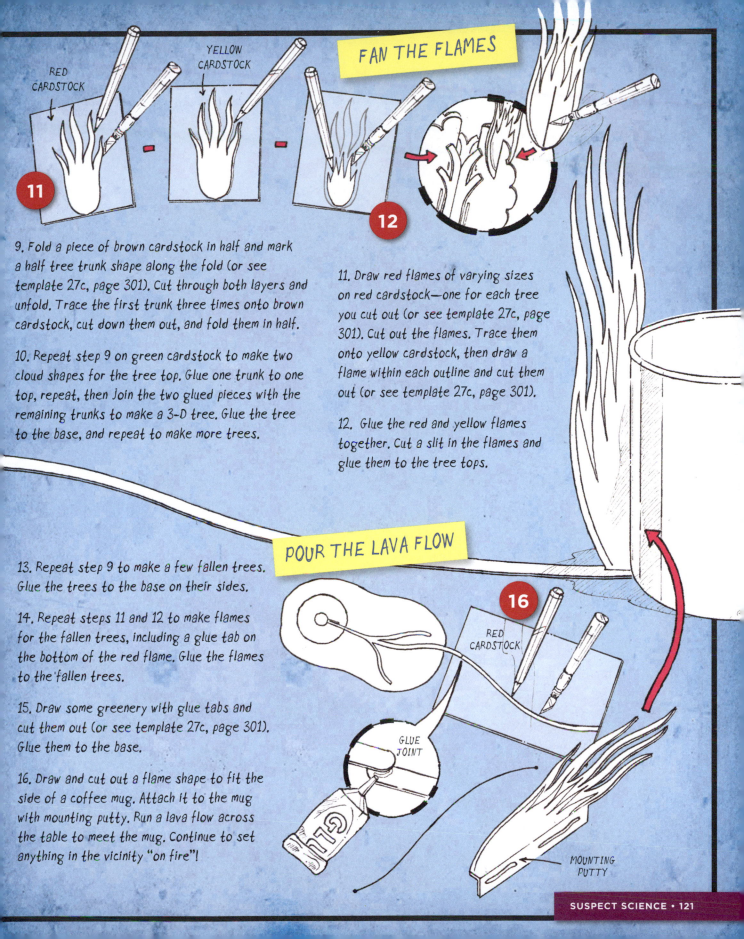

RED CARDSTOCK

YELLOW CARDSTOCK

11

12

9. Fold a piece of brown cardstock in half and mark a half tree trunk shape along the fold (or see template 27c, page 301). Cut through both layers and unfold. Trace the first trunk three times onto brown cardstock, cut down them out, and fold them in half.

10. Repeat step 9 on green cardstock to make two cloud shapes for the tree top. Glue one trunk to one top, repeat, then join the two glued pieces with the remaining trunks to make a 3-D tree. Glue the tree to the base, and repeat to make more trees.

11. Draw red flames of varying sizes on red cardstock—one for each tree you cut out (or see template 27c, page 301). Cut out the flames. Trace them onto yellow cardstock, then draw a flame within each outline and cut them out (or see template 27c, page 301).

12. Glue the red and yellow flames together. Cut a slit in the flames and glue them to the tree tops.

POUR THE LAVA FLOW

13. Repeat step 9 to make a few fallen trees. Glue the trees to the base on their sides.

14. Repeat steps 11 and 12 to make flames for the fallen trees, including a glue tab on the bottom of the red flame. Glue the flames to the fallen trees.

15. Draw some greenery with glue tabs and cut them out (or see template 27c, page 301). Glue them to the base.

16. Draw and cut out a flame shape to fit the side of a coffee mug. Attach it to the mug with mounting putty. Run a lava flow across the table to meet the mug. Continue to set anything in the vicinity "on fire"!

16

RED CARDSTOCK

GLUE JOINT

MOUNTING PUTTY

Subvert Newton's laws using nothing more than black cardstock and some mounting putty. This fun project is really easy to construct and very eye-catching. . . . In fact, it's quite good at catching anything: Cars, people, and even the Statue of Liberty are helpless against its powerful pull.

MATERIALS
- Lightweight cardboard
- Pencil
- Ruler
- Craft knife and cutting mat or scissors
- Black heavyweight cardstock (poster size)
- Mounting putty
- Lots of small toys and objects that you don't mind losing to the black hole
- Access to a photocopier or printer (optional)

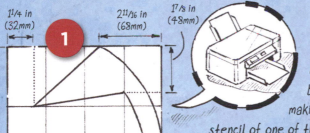

1. The art of creating a twirly black hole lies in making a cardboard stencil of one of the arms. Measure and mark the cutting plan, as shown, onto lightweight cardboard (or see template 28, page 302). Cut out the stencil with a craft knife and cutting mat.

1¼ in (32mm) 2¹¹/₁₆ in (68mm) 1⅞ in (48mm)

10⅝ in (270mm)

6⅝ in (168mm)

ARM SECTION

PIVOT POINT

16½ in (420mm)

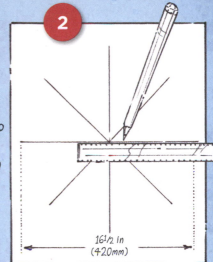

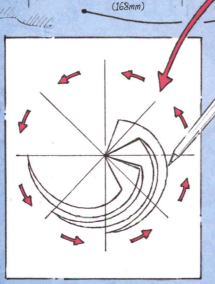

2. Mark a grid, as shown, on the cardstock. Position the stencil so the pivot point is at the center of the intersecting lines and the tip touches the end of one of the lines. Trace around the stencil, then rotate it so the end point touches the next grid line. Trace around the stencil again. Repeat all the way around the grid, and carefully cut out the spiral.

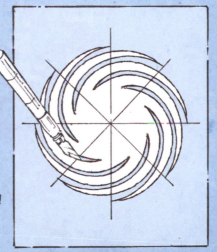

3. Following the "Sticky Tutorial" at right (A through E), add mounting putty to each arm of the black hole and then stick it to the wall.

3

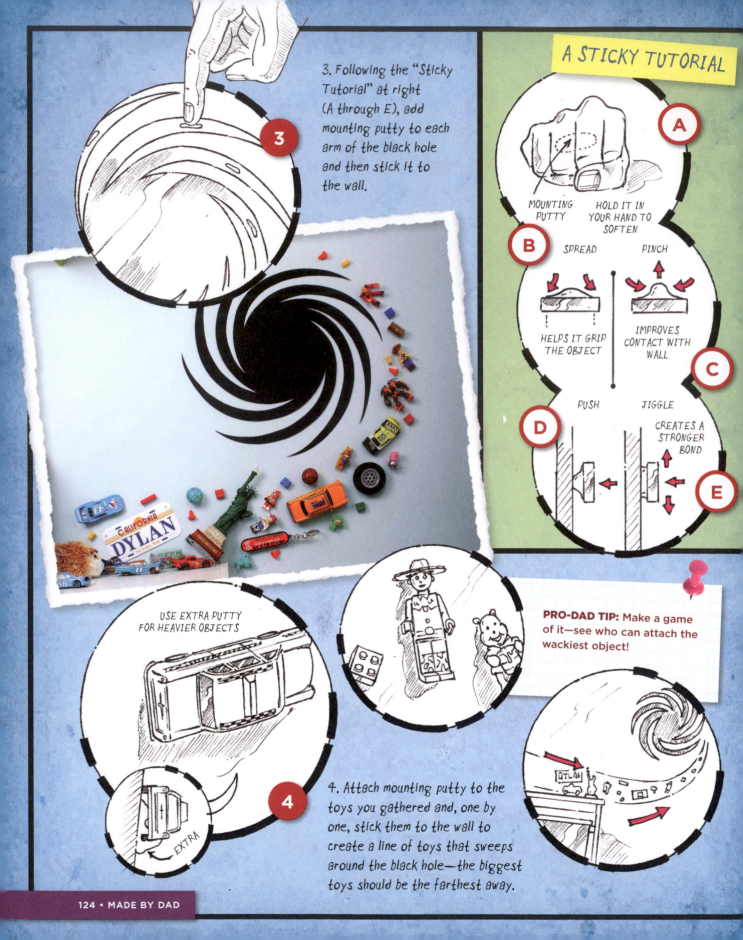

A

MOUNTING PUTTY — HOLD IT IN YOUR HAND TO SOFTEN

B

SPREAD — PINCH

HELPS IT GRIP THE OBJECT — IMPROVES CONTACT WITH WALL

C

PUSH — JIGGLE

CREATES A STRONGER BOND

D

E

USE EXTRA PUTTY FOR HEAVIER OBJECTS

EXTRA

4

PRO-DAD TIP: Make a game of it—see who can attach the wackiest object!

4. Attach mounting putty to the toys you gathered and, one by one, stick them to the wall to create a line of toys that sweeps around the black hole—the biggest toys should be the farthest away.

GEEKY GADGETS

SUBMARINE VS. SQUID

LEVEL: MEDIUM

GIANT SQUID! TO THE ESCAPE SUB!

MATERIALS

- Ruler
- Long cardboard tube
  (an empty wrapping paper tube,
  about 1½", 38 mm diameter works well)
- Paper
- Pencil
- Craft knife and cutting mat
- Paper glue
- White lightweight cardstock
- White medium-weight cardstock
- Drafting compass
- Silver spray paint
- Black permanent marker
- Felt-tip markers
- Access to a photocopier or printer
  (optional)

As a kid, I loved the old *20,000 Leagues Under the Sea* movie, which inspired this homage to the famous squid battle. I have also added one extra twist to the classic: My submarine boasts a very neat little escape pod—more James Bond than Captain Nemo.

YOU CAN'T CATCH US!

EAT OUR BUBBLES!

1. Measure 2½" (63 mm) from the end of the cardboard tube. Wrap a strip of paper around the tube at the mark and draw along the edge.

2. Cut along the line with a craft knife until tube A separates. Using the same technique, cut another piece 7½" (190 mm) long; this will be the hull (tube B).

3. Cut a third piece of tube 1¾" (44 mm) long. Squash it into an oval shape to make the conning tower (tube C). Glue one end and attach it to the lightweight cardstock.

4. Trim the excess cardstock around the edge.

5. Use the illustration as a guide to mark and cut the opposite end into a curve.

6. Apply glue along the curved edge and attach it 4⅜" (111 mm) from one end of the hull (B).

7. Draw a "stern blade," as shown, on medium-weight cardstock, and cut it out.

8. Glue along the edges to attach it to the hull and conning tower.

9. Draw a circle on medium-weight cardstock and divide it into eight rounded sections for propeller blades. Cut it out, and once the tail is complete, attach it with glue.

10. Mark and cut a V shape from the end of tube A, as shown.

11. Curl a piece of lightweight cardstock around the cut end of tube A and trace the edge with a pencil. Extend the lines to complete the tracing as shown.

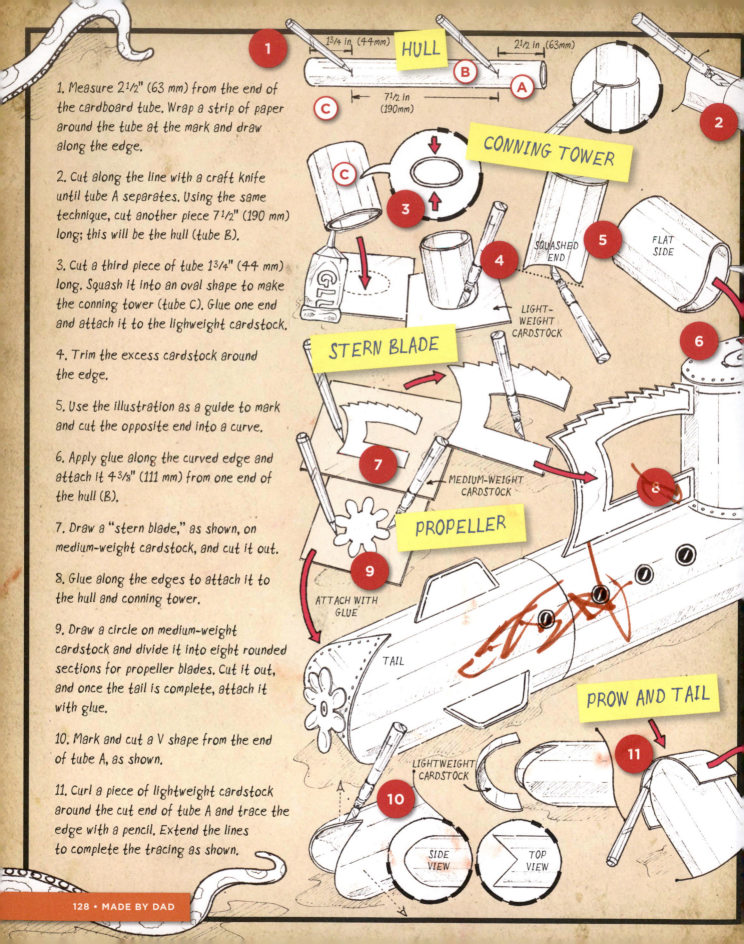

HULL

1¾ in (44mm)

2½ in (63mm)

7½ in (190mm)

CONNING TOWER

STERN BLADE

PROPELLER

SQUASHED END

FLAT SIDE

LIGHT-WEIGHT CARDSTOCK

MEDIUM-WEIGHT CARDSTOCK

ATTACH WITH GLUE

TAIL

PROW AND TAIL

LIGHTWEIGHT CARDSTOCK

SIDE VIEW

TOP VIEW

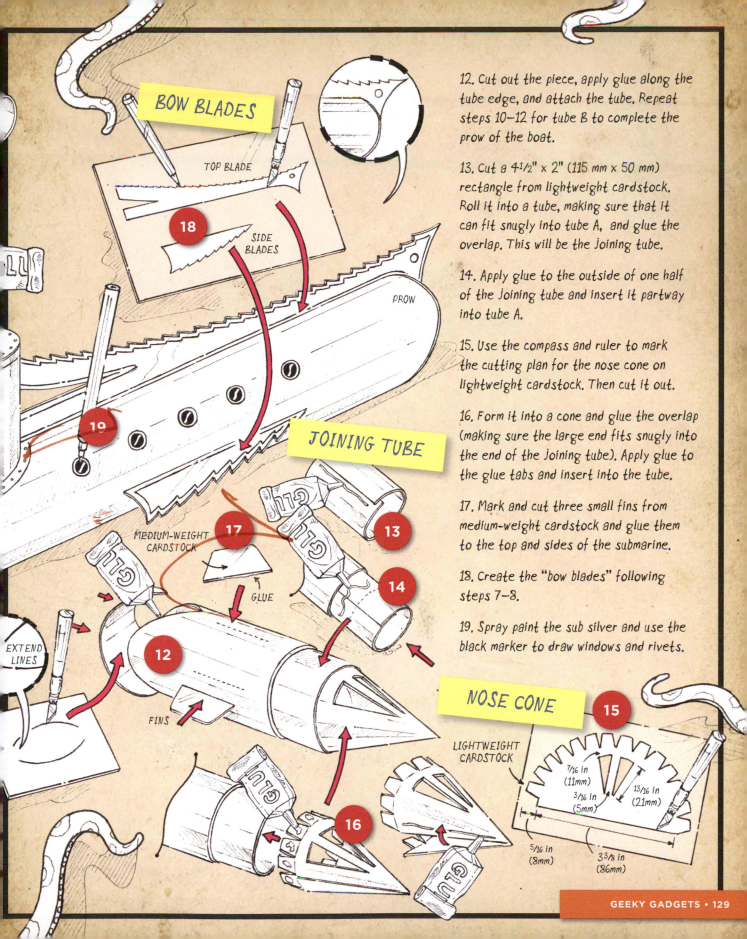

TOP BLADE

18

SIDE BLADES

PROW

19

MEDIUM-WEIGHT CARDSTOCK

17

13

14

GLUE

EXTEND LINES

12

FINS

16

12. Cut out the piece, apply glue along the tube edge, and attach the tube. Repeat steps 10–12 for tube B to complete the prow of the boat.

13. Cut a 4½" x 2" (115 mm x 50 mm) rectangle from lightweight cardstock. Roll it into a tube, making sure that it can fit snugly into tube A, and glue the overlap. This will be the Joining tube.

14. Apply glue to the outside of one half of the Joining tube and insert it partway into tube A.

15. Use the compass and ruler to mark the cutting plan for the nose cone on lightweight cardstock. Then cut it out.

16. Form it into a cone and glue the overlap (making sure the large end fits snugly into the end of the Joining tube). Apply glue to the glue tabs and insert into the tube.

17. Mark and cut three small fins from medium-weight cardstock and glue them to the top and sides of the submarine.

18. Create the "bow blades" following steps 7–8.

19. Spray paint the sub silver and use the black marker to draw windows and rivets.

15

LIGHTWEIGHT CARDSTOCK

7/16 in (11mm)

3/16 in (5mm)

13/16 in (21mm)

5/16 in (8mm)

3 3/8 in (86mm)

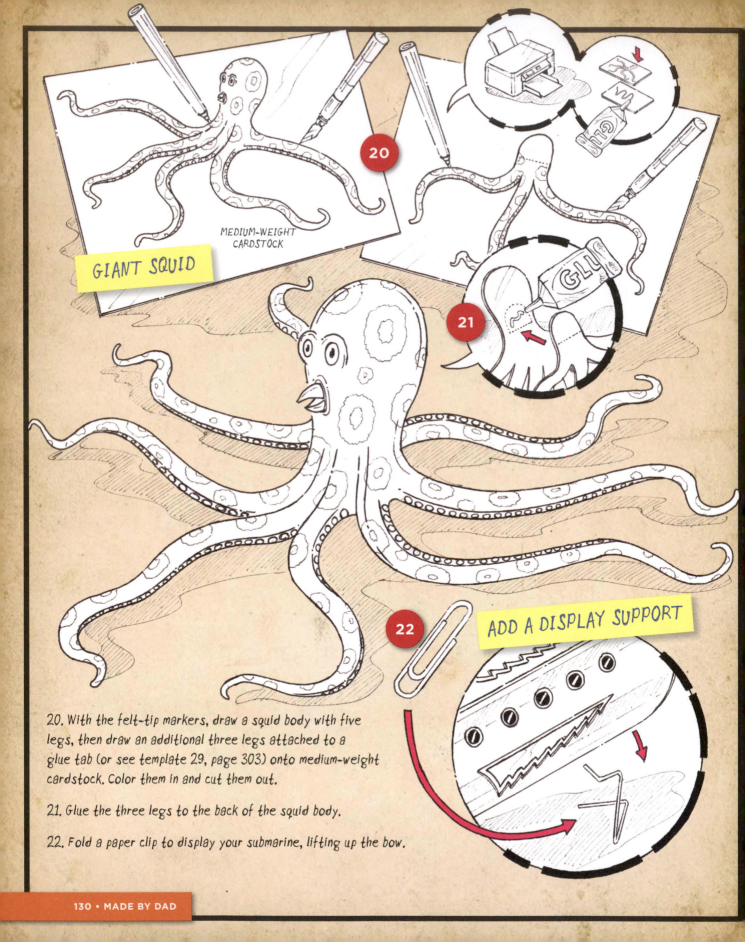

GIANT SQUID

MEDIUM-WEIGHT CARDSTOCK

20

21

22

ADD A DISPLAY SUPPORT

20. With the felt-tip markers, draw a squid body with five legs, then draw an additional three legs attached to a glue tab (or see template 29, page 303) onto medium-weight cardstock. Color them in and cut them out.

21. Glue the three legs to the back of the squid body.

22. Fold a paper clip to display your submarine, lifting up the bow.

MILK SHAKE MONSTER

LEVEL: MEDIUM

This milk shake will surprise you, and not because it's an unusual flavor well, sort of—just press the straw (turn the page) to find out. This project uses a neat little trick to create a reverse telescopic effect, but mainly it's just a lot of fun.

WHAT MONSTER?

BOO!

APPROX. 4 in (100mm)

1

7

MATERIALS

- 2 toilet paper tubes
- Paper to-go cup (with plastic lid and thick straw)
- Pencil
- White lightweight cardstock

- Craft knife and cutting mat
- Drafting compass
- Scissors
- Pliers
- 2 paper clips
- Clippers

- Hot glue gun and glue sticks
- Thread
- Felt-tip markers
- Paper glue
- Acess to a photocopier or printer (optional)

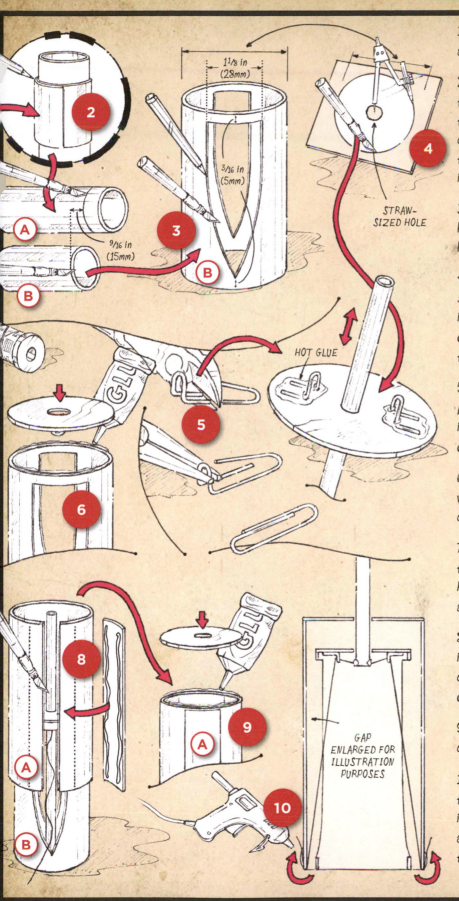

STRAW-SIZED HOLE

HOT GLUE

GAP
ENLARGED FOR
ILLUSTRATION
PURPOSES

1. Place a toilet paper tube in the paper cup and mark the height of the cup on it.

2. Wrap a strip of cardstock around the tube, in line with the mark, and draw along the edge. Then cut around the line with the craft knife, separating tube A. Repeat the technique with the second tube (B), but make it 9/16" (15 mm) shorter.

3. Follow the cutting plan to cut two large holes into the sides of tube B (you don't have to be precise).

4. Use the compass to mark a circle the same diameter as tube B on cardstock; cut it out using the craft knife and cutting mat or scissors. Cut a hole large enough to fit the straw in the center.

5. Use pliers to bend up the end of two paper clips. Then use clippers to cut them in half. Hot glue the pieces opposite each other on the cardstock circle, as shown.

6. Glue the circle onto the end of tube B, with the paper clips lined up with the two cutouts on the inside.

7. Feed thread through one cutout, the two paper clips, and the second cutout. Push the straw through the center hole and hot glue the end to the thread.

8. Cut open the length of tube A. Slide it over tube B. Cut and glue a strip of cardstock over the gap. Make sure the outer tube can move freely.

9. Repeat step 4 to cut another cardstock circle and glue it onto the end of tube A.

10. With tube A over tube B, feed the thread ends out through the two side holes in tube B, pull them taut (so the straw is at its highest point), and hot glue the ends to the bottom edge of tube A.

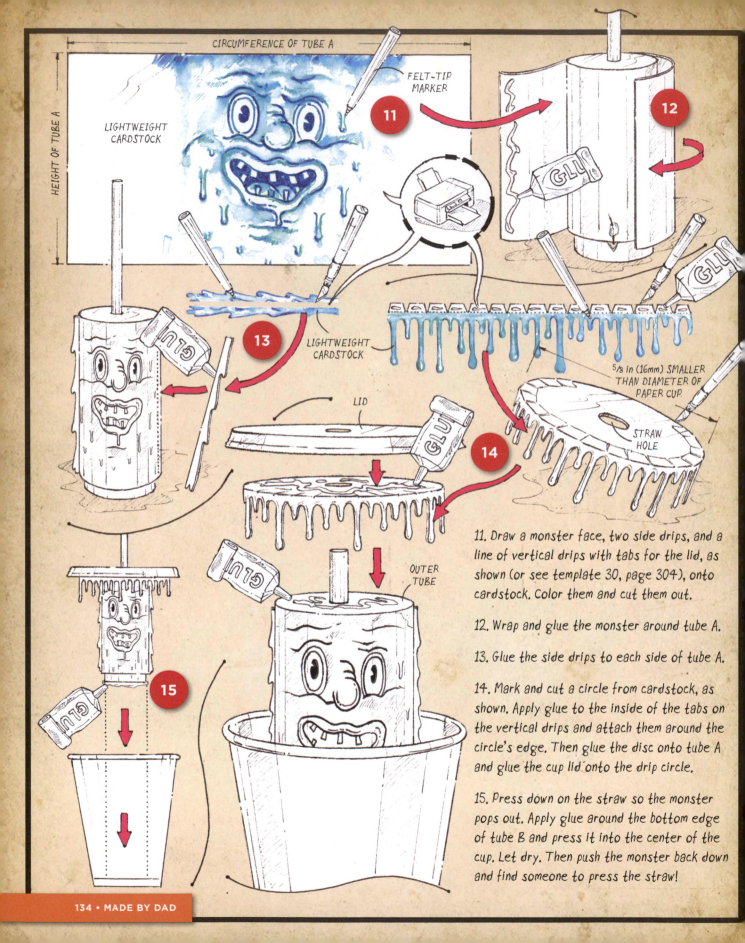

CIRCUMFERENCE OF TUBE A

HEIGHT OF TUBE A

LIGHTWEIGHT CARDSTOCK

FELT-TIP MARKER

LIGHTWEIGHT CARDSTOCK

GLU

GLU

5/8 in (16mm) SMALLER THAN DIAMETER OF PAPER CUP

STRAW HOLE

LID

GLU

GLU

OUTER TUBE

GLU

GLU

11. Draw a monster face, two side drips, and a line of vertical drips with tabs for the lid, as shown (or see template 30, page 304), onto cardstock. Color them and cut them out.

12. Wrap and glue the monster around tube A.

13. Glue the side drips to each side of tube A.

14. Mark and cut a circle from cardstock, as shown. Apply glue to the inside of the tabs on the vertical drips and attach them around the circle's edge. Then glue the disc onto tube A and glue the cup lid onto the drip circle.

15. Press down on the straw so the monster pops out. Apply glue around the bottom edge of tube B and press it into the center of the cup. Let dry. Then push the monster back down and find someone to press the straw!

RATAPULT

LEVEL: MEDIUM

Catapults have always come across as a little anti-feline to me, so to even things up, I've concocted the world's first Ratapult. (NOTE: No rats were injured in the making of this project—each was provided with a crash helmet.) If you are inclined to propel other paper mammals, you are free to experiment! There's no reason you can't make a dogapult; it just doesn't rhyme.

MATERIALS

- Medium-sized corrugated cardboard box
- Craft knife and cutting mat
- Stirring stick or blunt knife
- Hot glue gun and glue sticks
- 12" (30 cm) shatter-resistant ruler
- Clear tape
- Craft (Popsicle) sticks
- Felt-tip markers
- Black poster paint
- Paintbrush
- Paper glue
- Scissors
- 2 thin rubber bands (3", 75 mm)
- Access to photocopier or printer (optional)

DON'T YOU DARE PRESS THAT STICK!

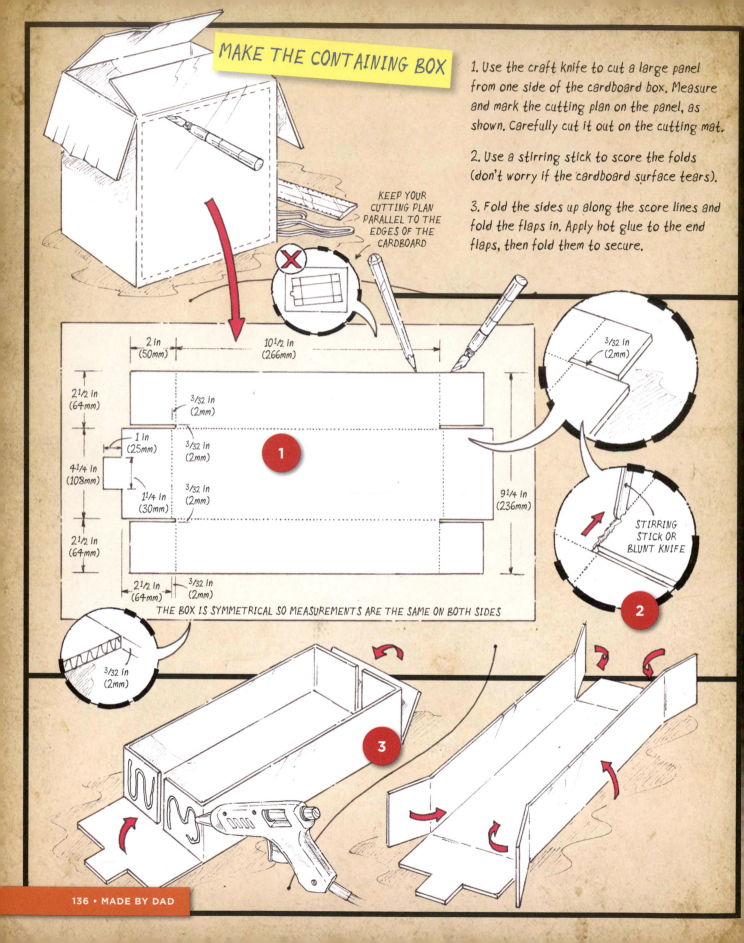

MAKE THE CONTAINING BOX

1. Use the craft knife to cut a large panel from one side of the cardboard box. Measure and mark the cutting plan on the panel, as shown. Carefully cut it out on the cutting mat.

2. Use a stirring stick to score the folds (don't worry if the cardboard surface tears).

3. Fold the sides up along the score lines and fold the flaps in. Apply hot glue to the end flaps, then fold them to secure.

KEEP YOUR CUTTING PLAN PARALLEL TO THE EDGES OF THE CARDBOARD

2 in (50mm)

10½ in (266mm)

2½ in (64mm)

3/32 in (2mm)

1 in (25mm)

3/32 in (2mm)

4¼ in (108mm)

1¼ in (30mm)

3/32 in (2mm)

9¼ in (236mm)

2½ in (64mm)

2½ in (64mm)

3/32 in (2mm)

THE BOX IS SYMMETRICAL SO MEASUREMENTS ARE THE SAME ON BOTH SIDES

3/32 in (2mm)

3/32 in (2mm)

STIRRING STICK OR BLUNT KNIFE

3/32 in (2mm)

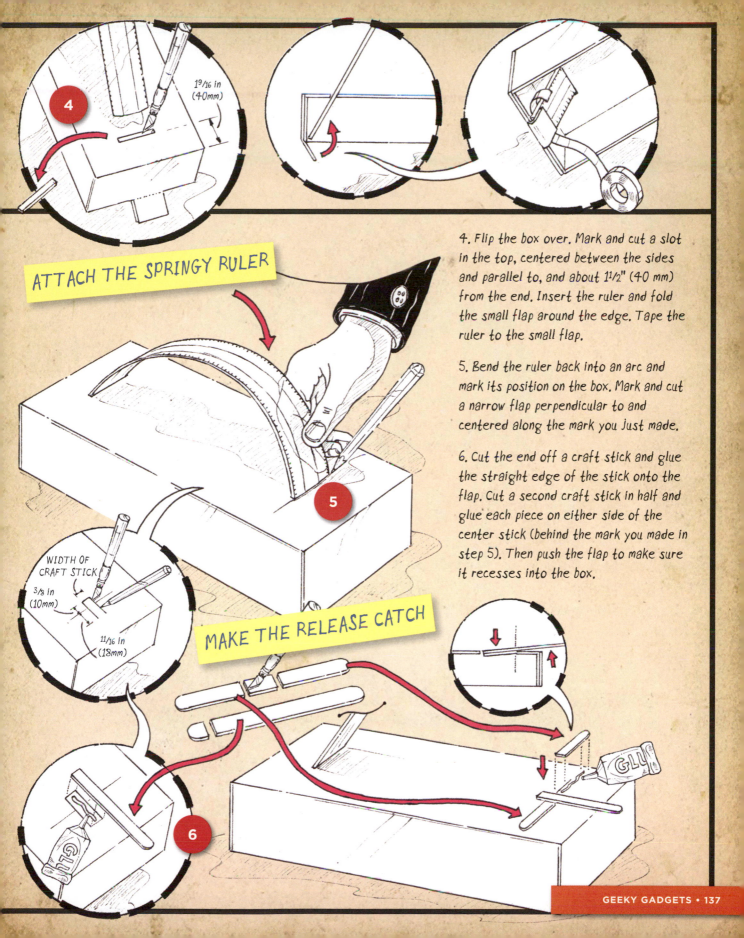

4 1⁹/₁₆ in (40mm)

ATTACH THE SPRINGY RULER

5

WIDTH OF CRAFT STICK

³/₈ in (10mm)

¹¹/₁₆ in (18mm)

MAKE THE RELEASE CATCH

6

4. Flip the box over. Mark and cut a slot in the top, centered between the sides and parallel to, and about 1½" (40 mm) from the end. Insert the ruler and fold the small flap around the edge. Tape the ruler to the small flap.

5. Bend the ruler back into an arc and mark its position on the box. Mark and cut a narrow flap perpendicular to and centered along the mark you just made.

6. Cut the end off a craft stick and glue the straight edge of the stick onto the flap. Cut a second craft stick in half and glue each piece on either side of the center stick (behind the mark you made in step 5). Then push the flap to make sure it recesses into the box.

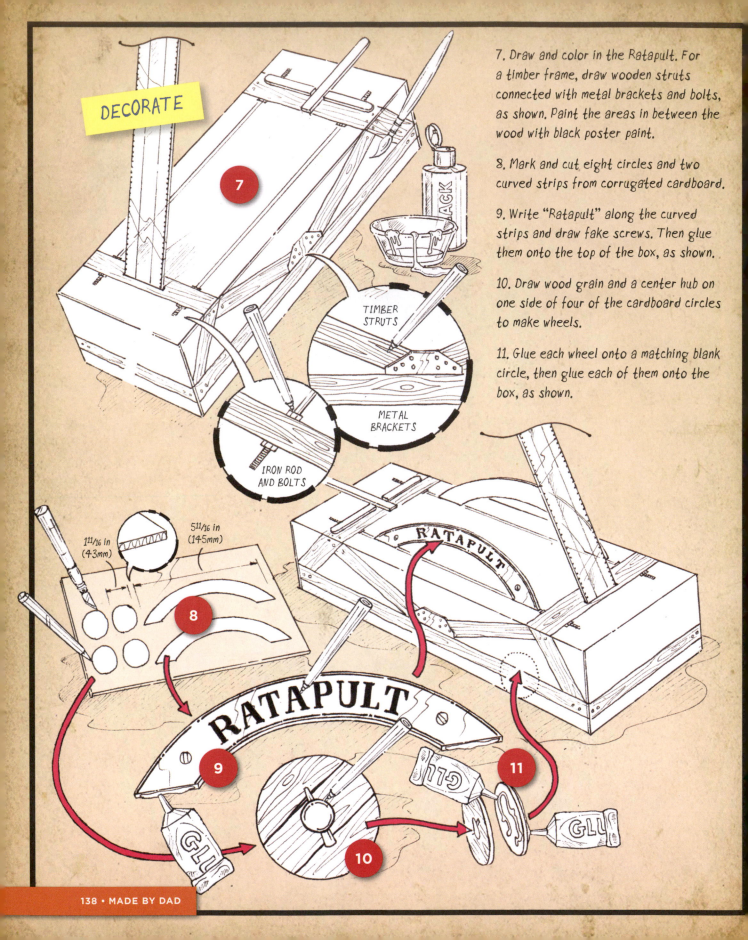

DECORATE

7. Draw and color in the Ratapult. For a timber frame, draw wooden struts connected with metal brackets and bolts, as shown. Paint the areas in between the wood with black poster paint.

8. Mark and cut eight circles and two curved strips from corrugated cardboard.

9. Write "Ratapult" along the curved strips and draw fake screws. Then glue them onto the top of the box, as shown.

10. Draw wood grain and a center hub on one side of four of the cardboard circles to make wheels.

11. Glue each wheel onto a matching blank circle, then glue each of them onto the box, as shown.

TIMBER STRUTS

METAL BRACKETS

IRON ROD AND BOLTS

1 11/16 in (43mm)

5 11/16 in (145mm)

RATAPULT

RATAPULT

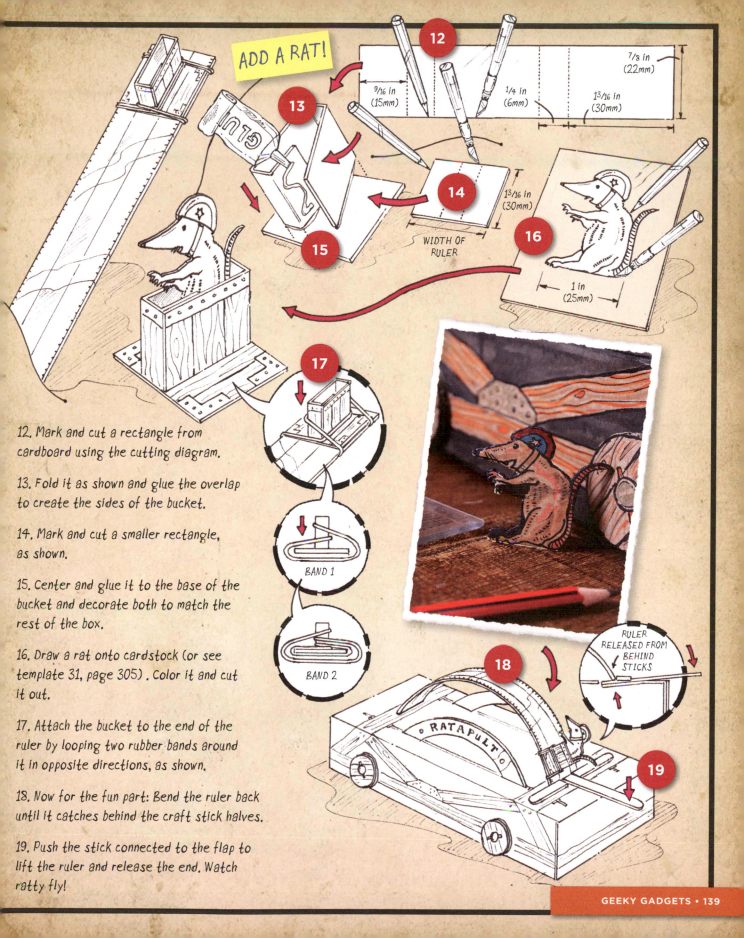

ADD A RAT!

7/8 in (22mm)

9/16 in (15mm) 1/4 in (6mm) 1 3/16 in (30mm)

1 3/16 in (30mm)

WIDTH OF RULER

1 in (25mm)

BAND 1

BAND 2

RATAPULT

RULER RELEASED FROM BEHIND STICKS

12. Mark and cut a rectangle from cardboard using the cutting diagram.

13. Fold it as shown and glue the overlap to create the sides of the bucket.

14. Mark and cut a smaller rectangle, as shown.

15. Center and glue it to the base of the bucket and decorate both to match the rest of the box.

16. Draw a rat onto cardstock (or see template 31, page 305). Color it and cut it out.

17. Attach the bucket to the end of the ruler by looping two rubber bands around it in opposite directions, as shown.

18. Now for the fun part: Bend the ruler back until it catches behind the craft stick halves.

19. Push the stick connected to the flap to lift the ruler and release the end. Watch ratty fly!

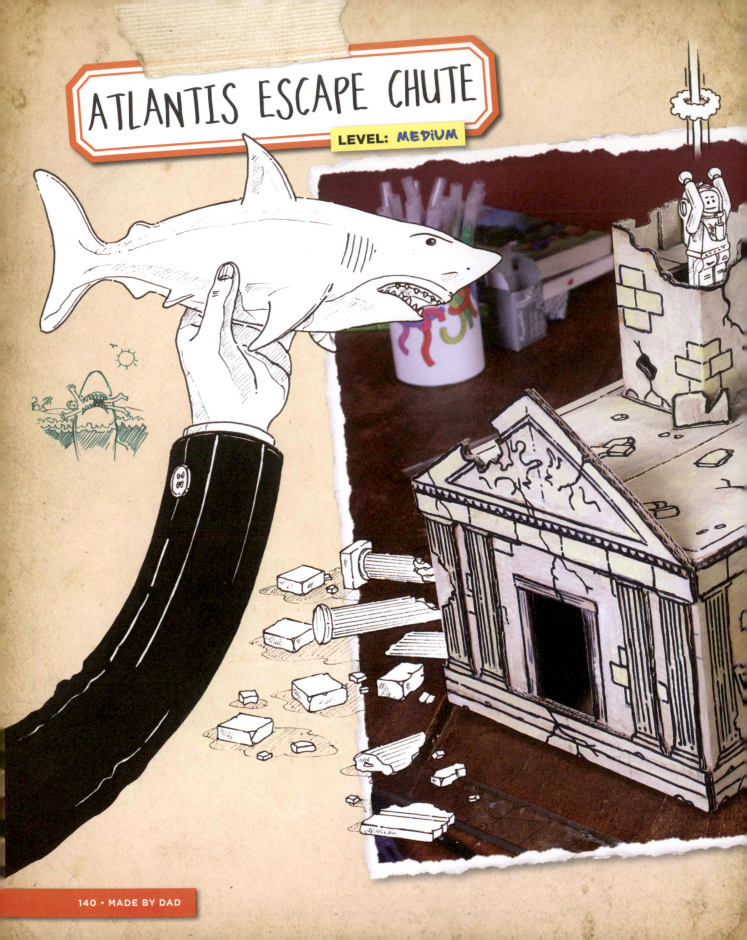

ATLANTIS ESCAPE CHUTE

LEVEL: MEDIUM

At first glance, this may look like an ordinary, run-of-the-mill ancient underwater ruin. But when a menacing shark approaches, a secret escape chute beneath the tower whisks the diver to safety! Here, I've given this project the complete Atlantis treatment, but it could as easily be a princess's castle or a knight's fortress, with a naughty dragon threatening instead of a nasty shark.

MATERIALS
- Small corrugated cardboard box
- Pencil
- Ruler
- Craft knife and cutting mat
- Medium-sized corrugated cardboard box
- Black permanent marker
- Hot glue gun and glue sticks or paper glue
- Paper towel tube
- Toy figurines
- Poster paint (optional)
- Paintbrush (optional)

I'M OFF! YOU'LL FIND ME IN THE ESCAPE SUB ON PAGE 126!

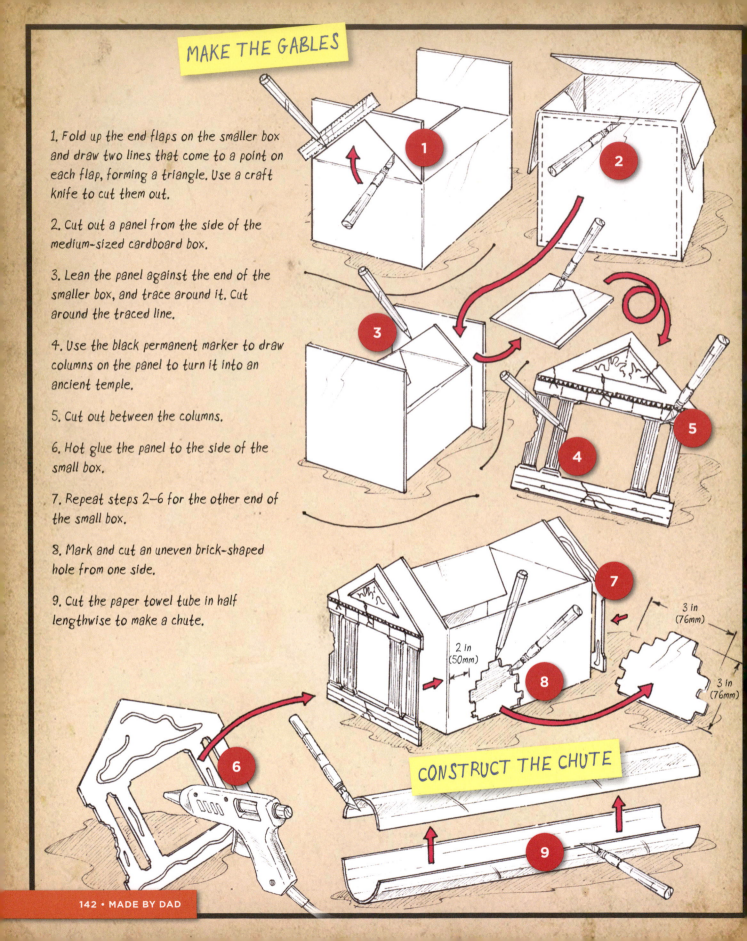

MAKE THE GABLES

1. Fold up the end flaps on the smaller box and draw two lines that come to a point on each flap, forming a triangle. Use a craft knife to cut them out.

2. Cut out a panel from the side of the medium-sized cardboard box.

3. Lean the panel against the end of the smaller box, and trace around it. Cut around the traced line.

4. Use the black permanent marker to draw columns on the panel to turn it into an ancient temple.

5. Cut out between the columns.

6. Hot glue the panel to the side of the small box.

7. Repeat steps 2–6 for the other end of the small box.

8. Mark and cut an uneven brick-shaped hole from one side.

9. Cut the paper towel tube in half lengthwise to make a chute.

3 in
(76mm)

2 in
(50mm)

3 in
(76mm)

CONSTRUCT THE CHUTE

10. Cut the end of the chute at an angle and cut slits along the edge to form glue tabs. Then position the chute at an angle in the box, as shown. Mark the point at which it protrudes from the hole and trim it.

11. Apply glue to the glue tabs and under the end of the chute near the hole. Secure the chute into the box, with the tabbed end raised at a steep angle, and pressed into the inside of the box. Close the box flaps.

12. Mark and cut a 11" x 5½" (280 mm x 140 mm) rectangle from cardboard and fold and glue the overlap to form a tower. Use the craft knife to roughly hack off the top quarter of the tower.

13. Cut a small hole into the box flap above the chute. Push a pencil through it to check that it is in line with the chute. Then place the tower over the hole and trace around the inside.

14. Cut along the traced line, hot glue the box flaps in place, and glue the large tower piece over the hole and the small, broken piece onto the roof.

15. Cut a small rectangle of cardboard and glue it into the tower to form a platform. Add toy figurines to explore the platform (then help them jump down the chute should danger approach).

16. Draw and cut out a hole for the doorway. Use the black marker to draw additional columns, cracks, and stones. Optional: Use poster paint to paint the building a sandy color.

BUILD THE TOWER

2½ in (64mm)

5½ in (140mm)

GLUE

REMOTE RELEASE ZIP LINE

LEVEL: EASY

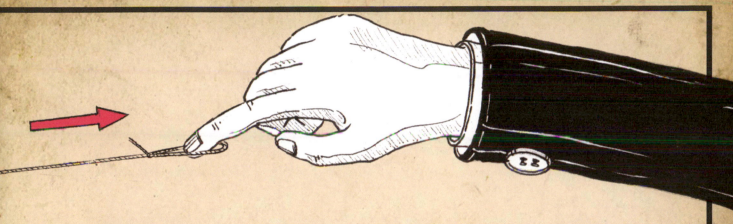

Even toys sometimes need to make a quick escape, and a remote release zip line is the perfect solution! This one was rigged up between two chairs, but you could easily go bigger and better with a bit of improvising. My son also lined up a number of "baddies" for the hero to knock over as he swooshed down the wire.

WHOOSH!

AWESOME! BUT WHAT'S BEHIND THAT HOLE . . . ?

MATERIALS
- Two paper clips
- One rubber band
- Two chairs
- Thread
- Toy figurine (zip line rider)
- Mounting putty

HOW IT WORKS

It's all in the paper clip release switch: Pull the cord and the hook tips off the bump and away it goes!

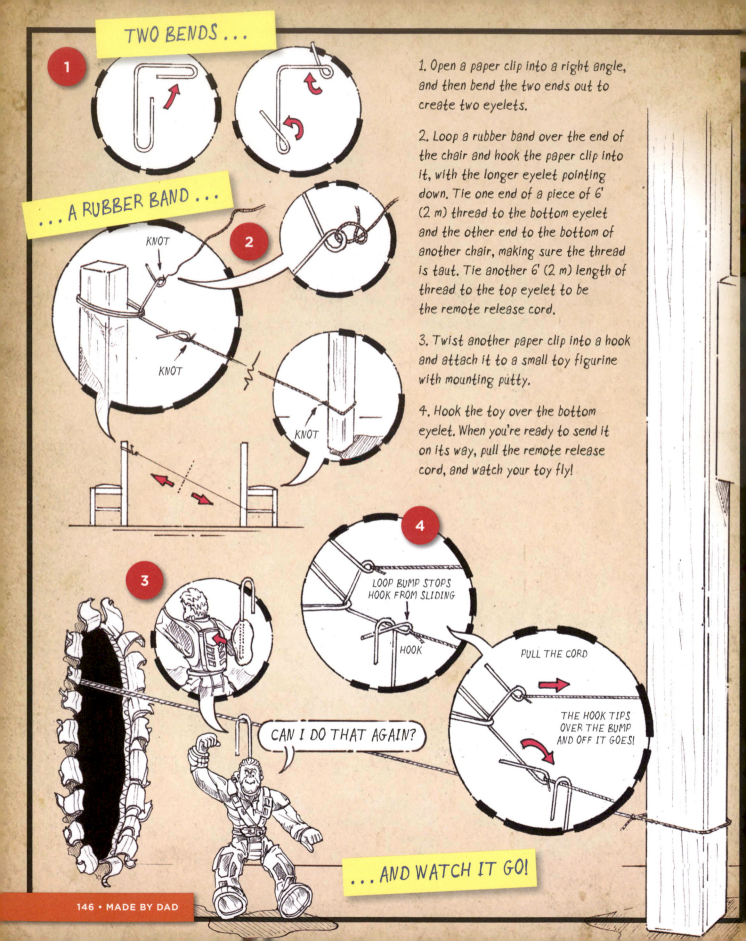

TWO BENDS...

1

...A RUBBER BAND...

KNOT

2

KNOT

KNOT

1. Open a paper clip into a right angle, and then bend the two ends out to create two eyelets.

2. Loop a rubber band over the end of the chair and hook the paper clip into it, with the longer eyelet pointing down. Tie one end of a piece of 6' (2 m) thread to the bottom eyelet and the other end to the bottom of another chair, making sure the thread is taut. Tie another 6' (2 m) length of thread to the top eyelet to be the remote release cord.

3. Twist another paper clip into a hook and attach it to a small toy figurine with mounting putty.

4. Hook the toy over the bottom eyelet. When you're ready to send it on its way, pull the remote release cord, and watch your toy fly!

3

4

LOOP BUMP STOPS HOOK FROM SLIDING

HOOK

PULL THE CORD

THE HOOK TIPS OVER THE BUMP AND OFF IT GOES!

CAN I DO THAT AGAIN?

...AND WATCH IT GO!

EATING NEMO

LEVEL: TRICKY

Has Nemo's luck finally run out? Well . . . no, I couldn't be that cruel! You can, however, take pleasure in watching him being eaten over and over again—safe in the knowledge that he'll always be burped out. My nieces loved this creation—it's definitely not just for boys!

MATERIALS

- Medium-sized corrugated cardboard box or lightweight cardboard (see step 1)
- Ruler
- Pencil
- Craft knife and cutting mat, or scissors
- Dried-up felt-tip marker
- Hot glue gun and glue sticks
- White lightweight cardstock
- Drafting compass
- Wire (about #15 gauge, 1.5 mm)
- Pliers with wire cutters
- Two coins
- Printer paper
- Paper glue
- Felt-tip markers
- Access to photocopier or printer (optional)

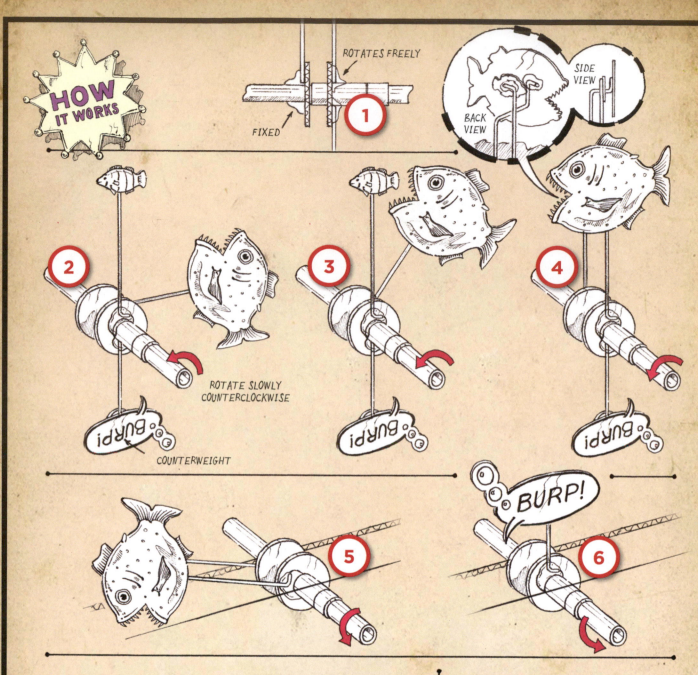

HOW IT WORKS

1 ROTATES FREELY / FIXED

BACK VIEW / SIDE VIEW

2 ROTATE SLOWLY COUNTERCLOCKWISE / COUNTERWEIGHT

3

4

5

6 BURP!

Eating Nemo explained: Before you get started, it's important to know exactly how cool this contraption is. Here's the trick: Nemo, the clownfish, is not fixed to the axle, but rotates freely. A counterweight keeps him upright. The big fish, however, is fixed to the axle. As the axle rotates, the big fish moves in front of Nemo to "eat" him, and then pushes Nemo down and out of view. Eventually as Nemo moves out of view, the "Burp!" bubble rotates up to the top before spinning around, returning Nemo to his original position.

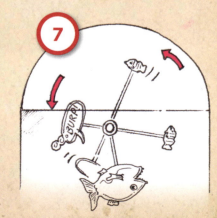

7

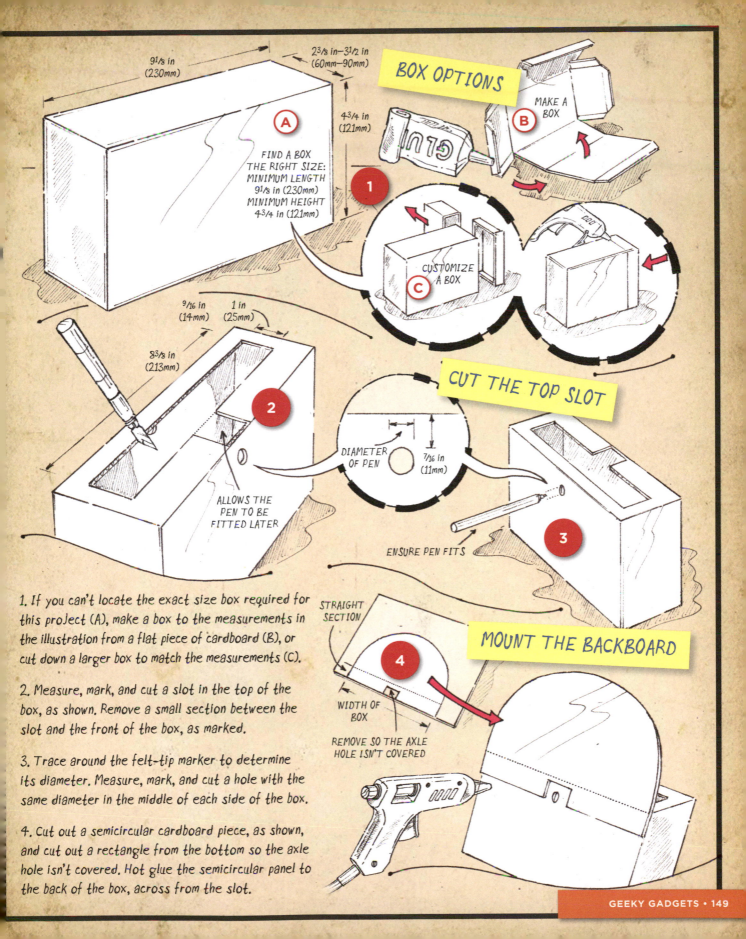

BOX OPTIONS

A FIND A BOX THE RIGHT SIZE: MINIMUM LENGTH 9 1/8 in (230mm) MINIMUM HEIGHT 4 3/4 in (121mm)

9 1/8 in (230mm)

2 3/8 in–3 1/2 in (60mm–90mm)

4 3/4 in (121mm)

B MAKE A BOX

1

C CUSTOMIZE A BOX

9/16 in (14mm)

1 in (25mm)

8 3/8 in (213mm)

2 ALLOWS THE PEN TO BE FITTED LATER

CUT THE TOP SLOT

DIAMETER OF PEN

7/16 in (11mm)

ENSURE PEN FITS

3

MOUNT THE BACKBOARD

STRAIGHT SECTION

4

WIDTH OF BOX

REMOVE SO THE AXLE HOLE ISN'T COVERED

1. If you can't locate the exact size box required for this project (A), make a box to the measurements in the illustration from a flat piece of cardboard (B), or cut down a larger box to match the measurements (C).

2. Measure, mark, and cut a slot in the top of the box, as shown. Remove a small section between the slot and the front of the box, as marked.

3. Trace around the felt-tip marker to determine its diameter. Measure, mark, and cut a hole with the same diameter in the middle of each side of the box.

4. Cut out a semicircular cardboard piece, as shown, and cut out a rectangle from the bottom so the axle hole isn't covered. Hot glue the semicircular panel to the back of the box, across from the slot.

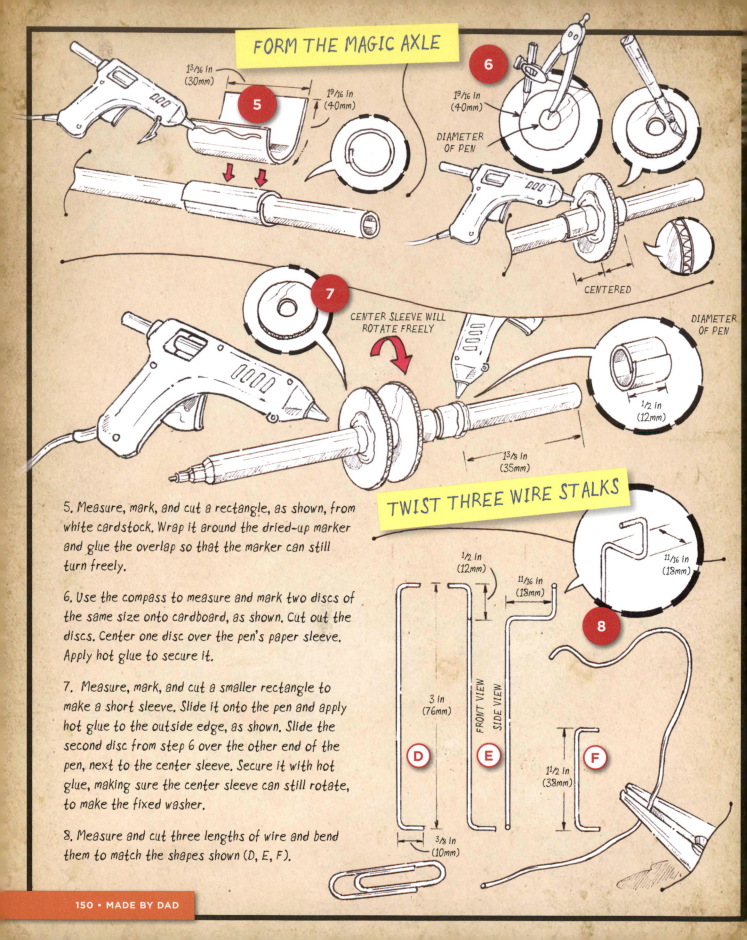

FORM THE MAGIC AXLE

5

1 3/16 in (30mm)

1 9/16 in (40mm)

6

1 9/16 in (40mm)

DIAMETER OF PEN

CENTERED

7

CENTER SLEEVE WILL ROTATE FREELY

DIAMETER OF PEN

1/2 in (12mm)

1 3/8 in (35mm)

TWIST THREE WIRE STALKS

8

11/16 in (18mm)

1/2 in (12mm)

11/16 in (18mm)

3 in (76mm)

FRONT VIEW

SIDE VIEW

1 1/2 in (38mm)

D

E

F

3/8 in (10mm)

5. Measure, mark, and cut a rectangle, as shown, from white cardstock. Wrap it around the dried-up marker and glue the overlap so that the marker can still turn freely.

6. Use the compass to measure and mark two discs of the same size onto cardboard, as shown. Cut out the discs. Center one disc over the pen's paper sleeve. Apply hot glue to secure it.

7. Measure, mark, and cut a smaller rectangle to make a short sleeve. Slide it onto the pen and apply hot glue to the outside edge, as shown. Slide the second disc from step 6 over the other end of the pen, next to the center sleeve. Secure it with hot glue, making sure the center sleeve can still rotate, to make the fixed washer.

8. Measure and cut three lengths of wire and bend them to match the shapes shown (D, E, F).

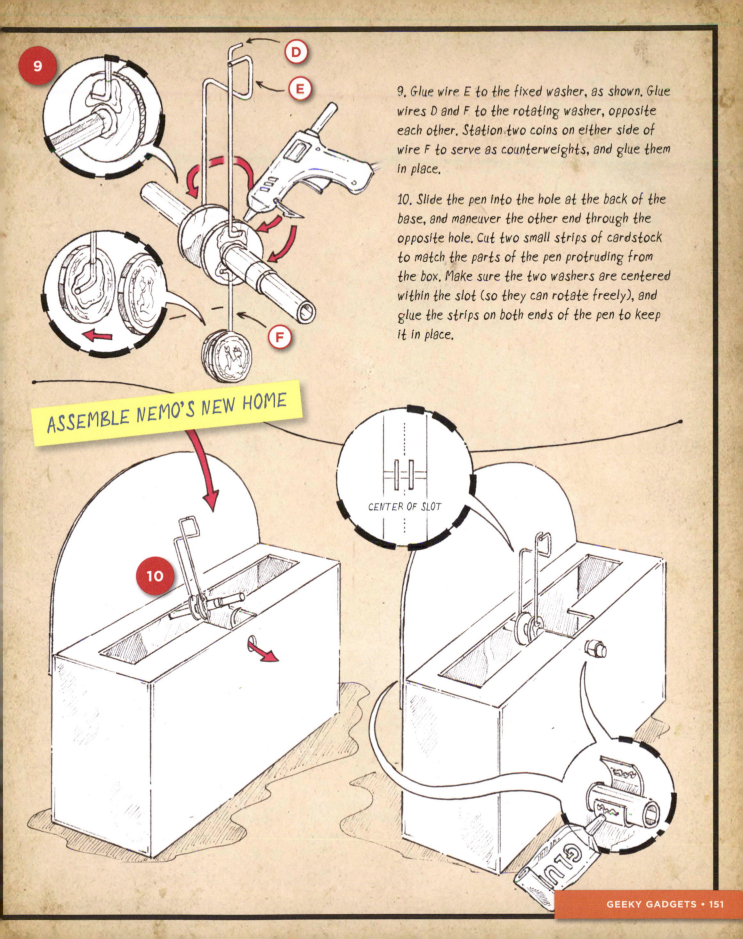

9. Glue wire E to the fixed washer, as shown. Glue wires D and F to the rotating washer, opposite each other. Station two coins on either side of wire F to serve as counterweights, and glue them in place.

10. Slide the pen into the hole at the back of the base, and maneuver the other end through the opposite hole. Cut two small strips of cardstock to match the parts of the pen protruding from the box. Make sure the two washers are centered within the slot (so they can rotate freely), and glue the strips on both ends of the pen to keep it in place.

ASSEMBLE NEMO'S NEW HOME

CENTER OF SLOT

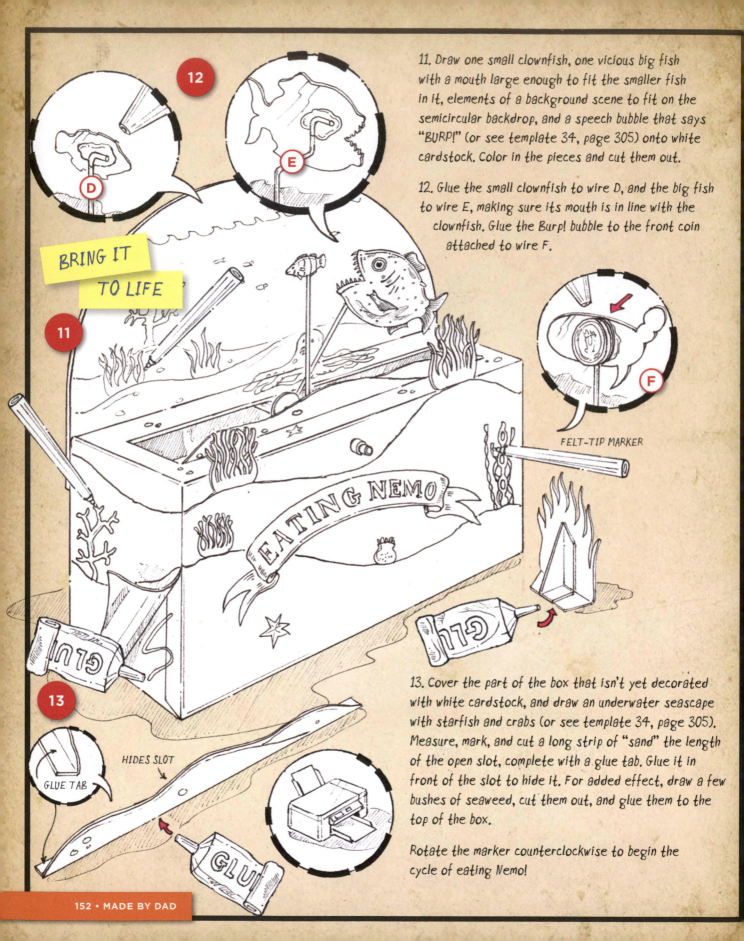

11. Draw one small clownfish, one vicious big fish with a mouth large enough to fit the smaller fish in it, elements of a background scene to fit on the semicircular backdrop, and a speech bubble that says "BURP!" (or see template 34, page 305) onto white cardstock. Color in the pieces and cut them out.

12. Glue the small clownfish to wire D, and the big fish to wire E, making sure its mouth is in line with the clownfish. Glue the Burp! bubble to the front coin attached to wire F.

FELT-TIP MARKER

BRING IT TO LIFE

EATING NEMO

HIDES SLOT

GLUE TAB

13. Cover the part of the box that isn't yet decorated with white cardstock, and draw an underwater seascape with starfish and crabs (or see template 34, page 305). Measure, mark, and cut a long strip of "sand" the length of the open slot, complete with a glue tab. Glue it in front of the slot to hide it. For added effect, draw a few bushes of seaweed, cut them out, and glue them to the top of the box.

Rotate the marker counterclockwise to begin the cycle of eating Nemo!

STEAMPUNK BALANCING ROBOT

LEVEL: TRICKY

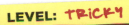

MATERIALS

- Toilet paper tube
- Paper glue
- White light- or medium-weight cardstock
- Craft knife and cutting mat
- Spray paint (red, silver, and gold)
- Black permanent marker
- Thin rubber band
- Paper clip
- Galvanized wire (#15 gauge, 1.5 mm)
- Colored light- or medium-weight cardstock (red and yellow)
- Hot glue gun and glue sticks
- Pliers with wire cutters
- Dried-up AA battery

This retro-looking bot has features a Swiss Army knife couldn't muster—not bad for what was once a toilet paper tube and some cardstock! Although I'll show you how to make the robot above exactly, this project is ripe for improvisation, depending on the time and materials you have available.

Rotating head with four different robot expressions.

COOL FEATURES

Cogtastic telescopic steampunk-style brain.

Amazing "hover effect" created using a wire counterbalance.

Independently rotating arms.

1. Glue the end of a toilet paper tube to lightweight cardstock. Cut around the tube with a craft knife.

2. Measure and mark a line 1/4" (7 mm) from the closed end of the tube. Using a strip of paper as a straightedge, continue the line all the way around the tube. Carefully cut out the top of the robot with a craft knife.

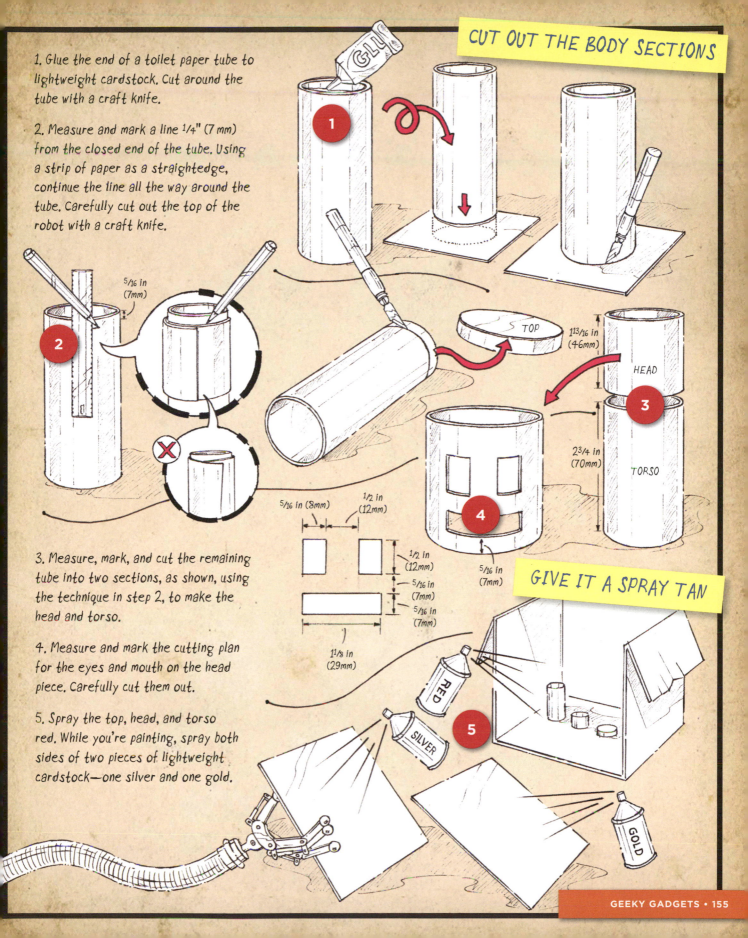

5/16 in (7mm)

TOP

1 13/16 in (46mm)

HEAD

3

2 3/4 in (70mm)

TORSO

5/16 in (7mm)

5/16 in (8mm)   1/2 in (12mm)

1/2 in (12mm)

5/16 in (7mm)

5/16 in (7mm)

1 1/8 in (29mm)

3. Measure, mark, and cut the remaining tube into two sections, as shown, using the technique in step 2, to make the head and torso.

4. Measure and mark the cutting plan for the eyes and mouth on the head piece. Carefully cut them out.

5. Spray the top, head, and torso red. While you're painting, spray both sides of two pieces of lightweight cardstock—one silver and one gold.

RED

SILVER

GOLD

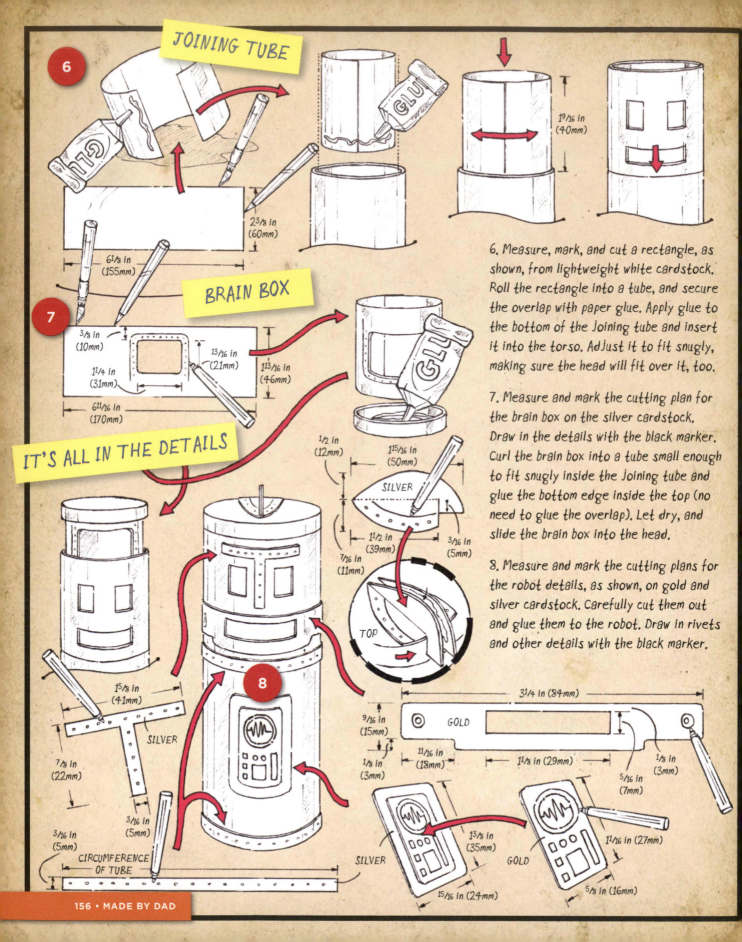

JOINING TUBE

2³⁄₈ in (60mm)

6¹⁄₈ in (155mm)

1⁹⁄₁₆ in (40mm)

BRAIN BOX

³⁄₈ in (10mm)

1¹⁄₄ in (31mm)

13⁄₁₆ in (21mm)

1¹³⁄₁₆ in (46mm)

6¹¹⁄₁₆ in (170mm)

IT'S ALL IN THE DETAILS

GLU

½ in (12mm)

1¹⁵⁄₁₆ in (50mm)

SILVER

1¹⁄₂ in (39mm)

³⁄₁₆ in (5mm)

7⁄₁₆ in (11mm)

TOP

1⁵⁄₈ in (41mm)

SILVER

7⁄₈ in (22mm)

³⁄₁₆ in (5mm)

³⁄₁₆ in (5mm)

CIRCUMFERENCE OF TUBE

9⁄₁₆ in (15mm)

1⁄₈ in (3mm)

3¹⁄₄ in (84mm)

GOLD

11⁄₁₆ in (18mm)

1¹⁄₈ in (29mm)

1⁄₈ in (3mm)

5⁄₁₆ in (7mm)

SILVER

1³⁄₈ in (35mm)

GOLD

1¹⁄₁₆ in (27mm)

15⁄₁₆ in (24mm)

5⁄₈ in (16mm)

6. Measure, mark, and cut a rectangle, as shown, from lightweight white cardstock. Roll the rectangle into a tube, and secure the overlap with paper glue. Apply glue to the bottom of the Joining tube and insert it into the torso. Adjust it to fit snugly, making sure the head will fit over it, too.

7. Measure and mark the cutting plan for the brain box on the silver cardstock. Draw in the details with the black marker. Curl the brain box into a tube small enough to fit snugly inside the Joining tube and glue the bottom edge inside the top (no need to glue the overlap). Let dry, and slide the brain box into the head.

8. Measure and mark the cutting plans for the robot details, as shown, on gold and silver cardstock. Carefully cut them out and glue them to the robot. Draw in rivets and other details with the black marker.

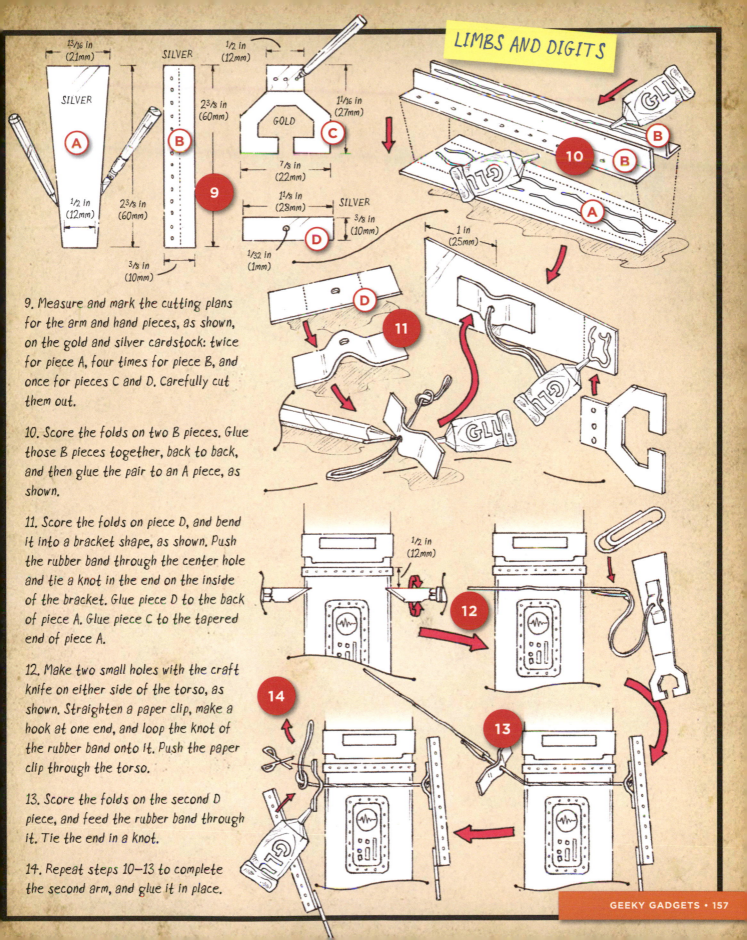

9. Measure and mark the cutting plans for the arm and hand pieces, as shown, on the gold and silver cardstock: twice for piece A, four times for piece B, and once for pieces C and D. Carefully cut them out.

10. Score the folds on two B pieces. Glue those B pieces together, back to back, and then glue the pair to an A piece, as shown.

11. Score the folds on piece D, and bend it into a bracket shape, as shown. Push the rubber band through the center hole and tie a knot in the end on the inside of the bracket. Glue piece D to the back of piece A. Glue piece C to the tapered end of piece A.

12. Make two small holes with the craft knife on either side of the torso, as shown. Straighten a paper clip, make a hook at one end, and loop the knot of the rubber band onto it. Push the paper clip through the torso.

13. Score the folds on the second D piece, and feed the rubber band through it. Tie the end in a knot.

14. Repeat steps 10–13 to complete the second arm, and glue it in place.

MAKE IT SMART

MAKE IT EXPRESSIVE (X4)

15

16

12⅛ in
(35mm)

DIAMETER
OF BRAIN
BOX

PREPARE THE ENGINE

17

¾ in
(19mm)

7/16 in
(11mm)

9 in (230mm)

15. Pivot the head to face forward, and draw a mouth and eyes inside the holes with the black marker. Rotate the head a quarter turn and draw a different set of features. Repeat until you've made four faces.

16. Measure, mark, and cut out a piece of gold cardstock, as shown. Draw in a set of cogs with the black marker, and cut around the shapes. Glue the panel in place, inside the brain box.

17. Place the robot on a piece of cardstock and trace around the base. Cut out the circle, and measure and mark a hole in its center, as shown. Measure, mark, and cut out a strip of cardstock. Glue along the strip's length and curl it into an overlapping circle. Glue it onto the cardstock disc, around the hole in the center, to make the engine nozzle.

THREAD THE BALANCING WIRE

18

1¾ in
(45mm)

18. Measure and cut a hole in the back of the torso, as shown. Feed the wire through the hole, and out the bottom of the robot. Bend the end of the wire, and push it back into the robot body.

GALVANIZED
WIRE

1¼ in
(32mm)

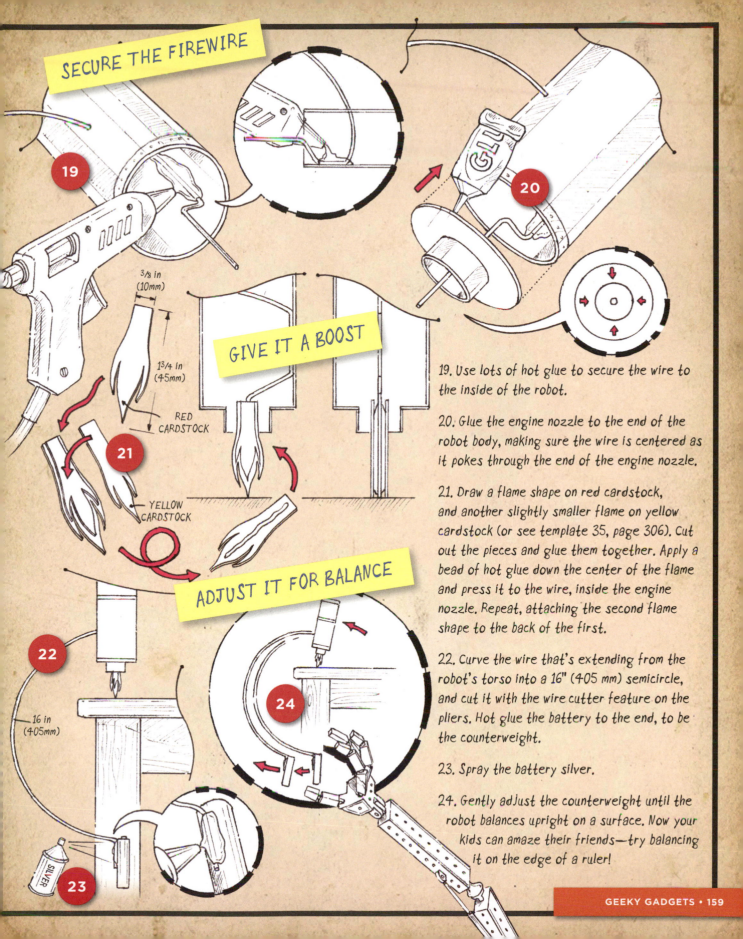

SECURE THE FIREWIRE

19

3/8 in (10mm)

1 3/4 in (45mm)

RED CARDSTOCK

GIVE IT A BOOST

20

21

YELLOW CARDSTOCK

ADJUST IT FOR BALANCE

22

24

16 in (405mm)

SILVER

23

19. Use lots of hot glue to secure the wire to the inside of the robot.

20. Glue the engine nozzle to the end of the robot body, making sure the wire is centered as it pokes through the end of the engine nozzle.

21. Draw a flame shape on red cardstock, and another slightly smaller flame on yellow cardstock (or see template 35, page 306). Cut out the pieces and glue them together. Apply a bead of hot glue down the center of the flame and press it to the wire, inside the engine nozzle. Repeat, attaching the second flame shape to the back of the first.

22. Curve the wire that's extending from the robot's torso into a 16" (405 mm) semicircle, and cut it with the wire cutter feature on the pliers. Hot glue the battery to the end, to be the counterweight.

23. Spray the battery silver.

24. Gently adjust the counterweight until the robot balances upright on a surface. Now your kids can amaze their friends—try balancing it on the edge of a ruler!

TOWERING TOY CRANE

LEVEL: TRICKY

A door is one of the few things attached to your home that has moving parts. With a little imagination, you can turn it into a very cool crane, complete with handmade winder, ratchet, and release switch.

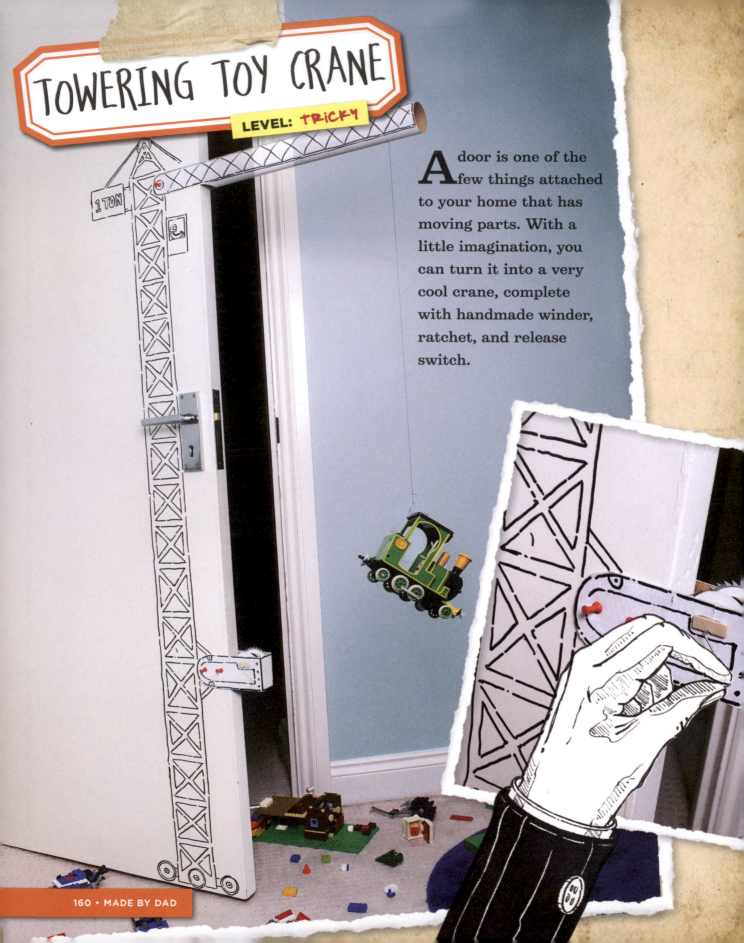

1 TON

MATERIALS

- Craft knife and cutting mat
- Cardboard parcel tube (about 21", 530 mm long; 2", 51 mm in diameter)
- Ruler
- Pencil
- 8 pushpins
- 2 paper clips

- Thread
- Small corrugated cardboard box
- Stirring stick or blunt knife
- Hot glue gun and glue sticks
- Toilet paper tube
- Drafting compass
- White lightweight cardstock
- Paper glue

- Small piece of flat plastic (the side of a milk container works well)
- Pliers with wire cutters
- Wire (#15 gauge, 1.5 mm)
- Craft (Popsicle) stick
- Toy
- Black permanent marker
- Whiteboard marker (optional)
- Printer paper (optional)

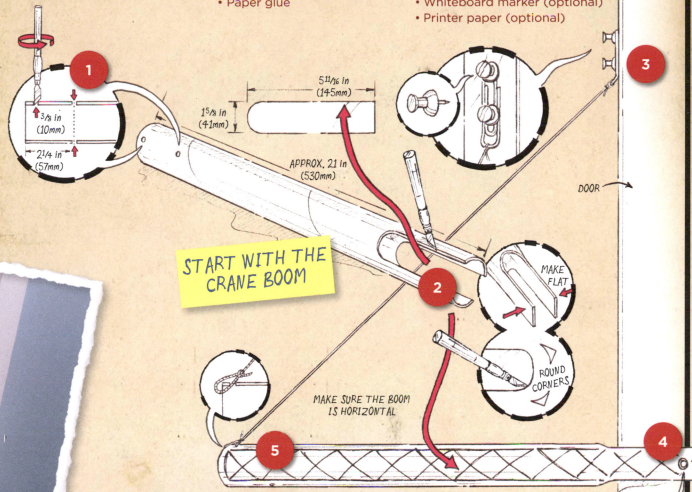

START WITH THE CRANE BOOM

3/8 in (10mm)

2 1/4 in (57mm)

1 5/8 in (41mm)

5 11/16 in (145mm)

APPROX. 21 in (530mm)

MAKE FLAT

ROUND CORNERS

DOOR

MAKE SURE THE BOOM IS HORIZONTAL

1. Use the craft knife to make three small holes in one end of the long tube.

2. Measure, mark, and cut two arched sections from the other end of the tube to make the crane boom. Flatten the ends and round off the corners.

3. Use two pushpins to attach a paper clip to the edge of the door, near the top, as shown. Tie one end of a 3' (1 m) piece of thread to the bottom of the paper clip.

4. Attach the tube to the edge of the door, securing each side with a pushpin.

5. Tie the other end of the thread through the outermost hole in the crane boom and around the end of the boom.

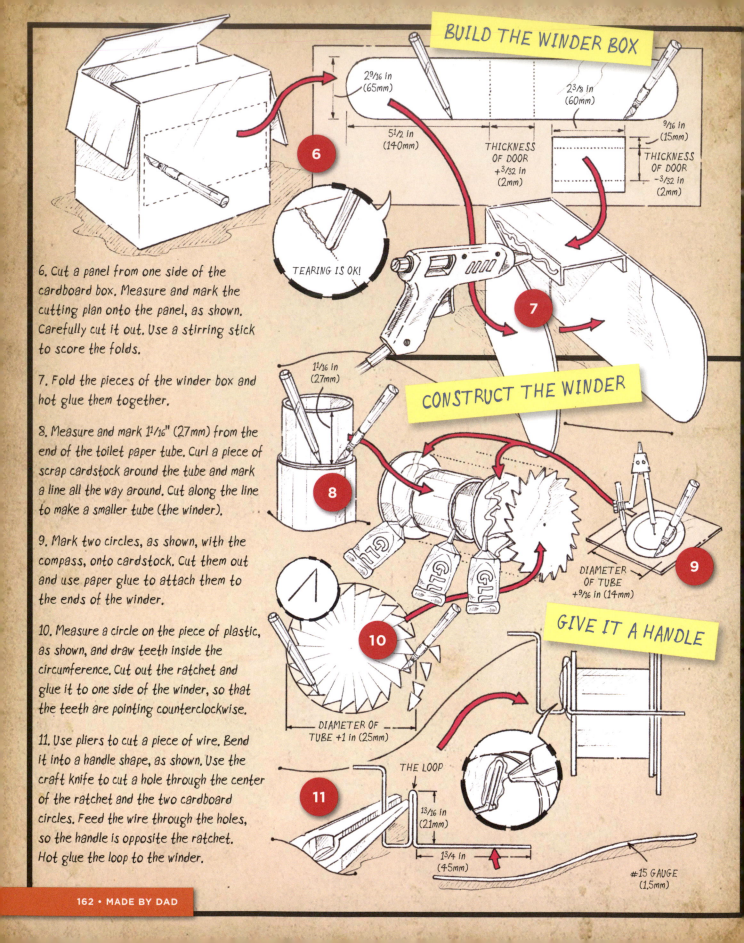

2⁹/₁₆ in (65mm)

2³/₈ in (60mm)

5¹/₂ in (140mm)

THICKNESS OF DOOR +³/₃₂ in (2mm)

⁹/₁₆ in (15mm)

THICKNESS OF DOOR −³/₃₂ in (2mm)

6

TEARING IS OK!

7

CONSTRUCT THE WINDER

1¹/₁₆ in (27mm)

8

DIAMETER OF TUBE +⁹/₁₆ in (14mm)

9

GLU GLU GLU

DIAMETER OF TUBE +1 in (25mm)

10

GIVE IT A HANDLE

THE LOOP

13/16 in (21mm)

1³/₄ in (45mm)

#15 GAUGE (1.5mm)

11

6. Cut a panel from one side of the cardboard box. Measure and mark the cutting plan onto the panel, as shown. Carefully cut it out. Use a stirring stick to score the folds.

7. Fold the pieces of the winder box and hot glue them together.

8. Measure and mark 1¹/₁₆" (27mm) from the end of the toilet paper tube. Curl a piece of scrap cardstock around the tube and mark a line all the way around. Cut along the line to make a smaller tube (the winder).

9. Mark two circles, as shown, with the compass, onto cardstock. Cut them out and use paper glue to attach them to the ends of the winder.

10. Measure a circle on the piece of plastic, as shown, and draw teeth inside the circumference. Cut out the ratchet and glue it to one side of the winder, so that the teeth are pointing counterclockwise.

11. Use pliers to cut a piece of wire. Bend it into a handle shape, as shown. Use the craft knife to cut a hole through the center of the ratchet and the two cardboard circles. Feed the wire through the holes, so the handle is opposite the ratchet. Hot glue the loop to the winder.

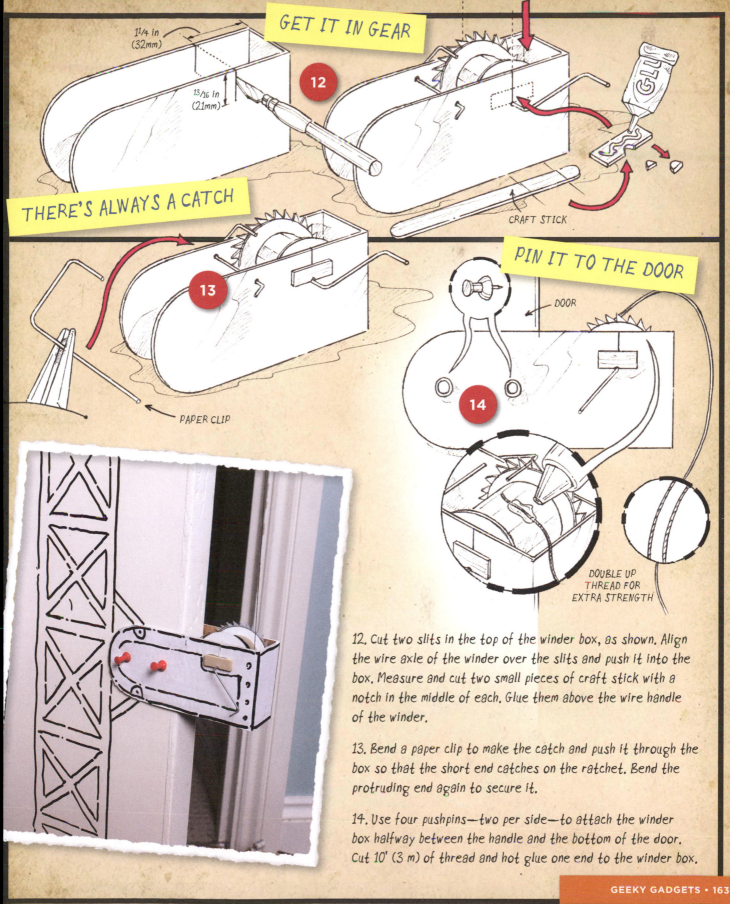

GET IT IN GEAR

1¼ in (32mm)

13/16 in (21mm)

12

CRAFT STICK

THERE'S ALWAYS A CATCH

13

PAPER CLIP

PIN IT TO THE DOOR

DOOR

14

DOUBLE UP THREAD FOR EXTRA STRENGTH

12. Cut two slits in the top of the winder box, as shown. Align the wire axle of the winder over the slits and push it into the box. Measure and cut two small pieces of craft stick with a notch in the middle of each. Glue them above the wire handle of the winder.

13. Bend a paper clip to make the catch and push it through the box so that the short end catches on the ratchet. Bend the protruding end again to secure it.

14. Use four pushpins—two per side—to attach the winder box halfway between the handle and the bottom of the door. Cut 10' (3 m) of thread and hot glue one end to the winder box.

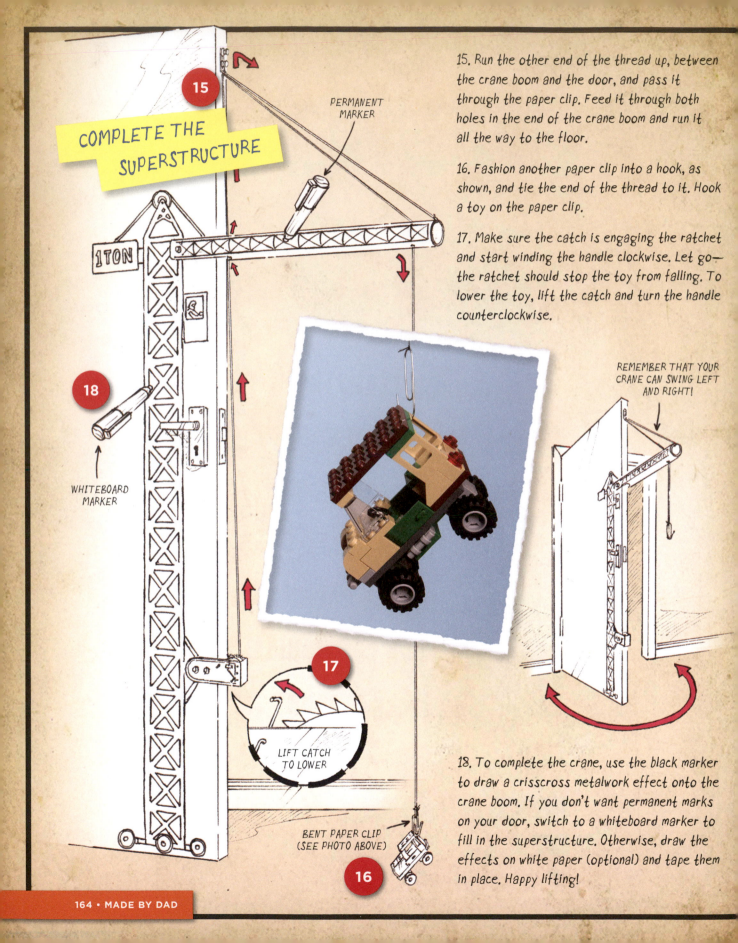

COMPLETE THE SUPERSTRUCTURE

PERMANENT MARKER

1 TON

18

WHITEBOARD MARKER

15. Run the other end of the thread up, between the crane boom and the door, and pass it through the paper clip. Feed it through both holes in the end of the crane boom and run it all the way to the floor.

16. Fashion another paper clip into a hook, as shown, and tie the end of the thread to it. Hook a toy on the paper clip.

17. Make sure the catch is engaging the ratchet and start winding the handle clockwise. Let go—the ratchet should stop the toy from falling. To lower the toy, lift the catch and turn the handle counterclockwise.

REMEMBER THAT YOUR CRANE CAN SWING LEFT AND RIGHT!

17

LIFT CATCH TO LOWER

BENT PAPER CLIP
(SEE PHOTO ABOVE)

16

18. To complete the crane, use the black marker to draw a crisscross metalwork effect onto the crane boom. If you don't want permanent marks on your door, switch to a whiteboard marker to fill in the superstructure. Otherwise, draw the effects on white paper (optional) and tape them in place. Happy lifting!

COVERT CREATIONS

SWOOSH!

A wobbly ruler one second, a fearsome sword the next. Granted, this isn't exactly Optimus Prime turning from an 18-wheeler into the leader of the Autobots, but it's still quite cool! It also boasts a gleaming metallic blade (silver-painted cardstock) and jewel-encrusted hand guard (felt-tip marker drawings), and dispatches a mean paper cut (just kidding)!

MATERIALS

- White medium-weight cardstock (poster size)
- 18" (46 cm) plastic shatterproof ruler
- Pencil
- Craft knife and cutting mat
- Paper glue
- Silver spray paint
- Felt-tip markers
- Access to a photocopier or printer (optional)

BEWARE OF PAPER CUTS!

SWORD BLADE

RULER

HOW IT WORKS

Once it's constructed, you can easily transform the ruler into a sword and back again—depending on whether it's needed for doing homework or defending a castle. Simply remove the handle butt and slide the ruler in or out.

HANDLE BUTT

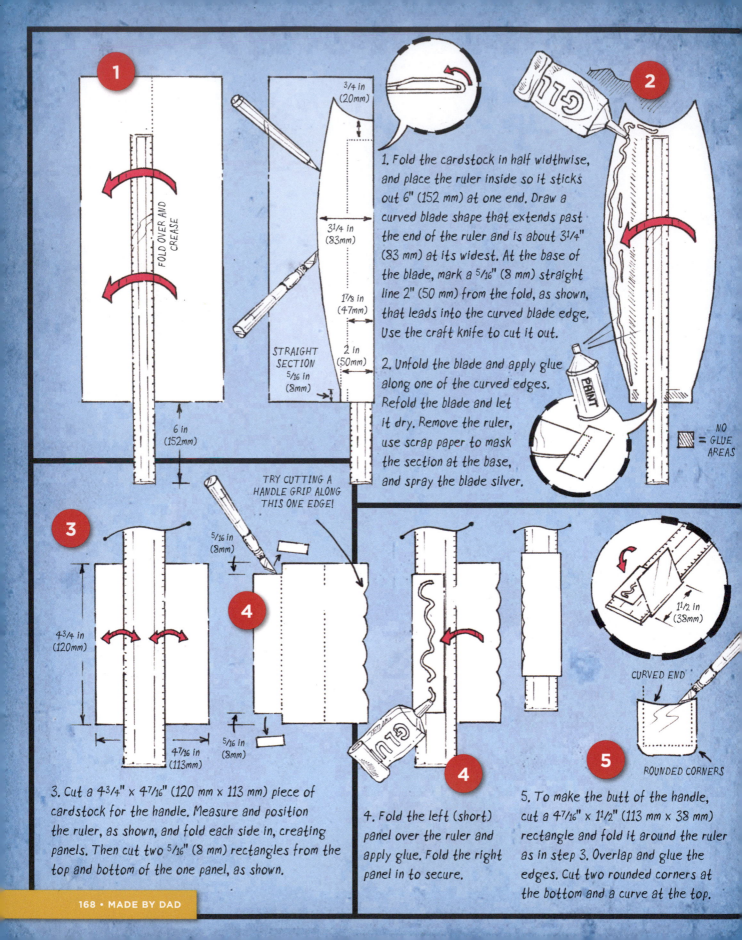

1

FOLD OVER AND CREASE

3/4 in (20mm)

3 1/4 in (83mm)

1 7/8 in (47mm)

STRAIGHT SECTION 5/16 in (8mm)

2 in (50mm)

6 in (152mm)

2

= GLUE AREAS

NO

1. Fold the cardstock in half widthwise, and place the ruler inside so it sticks out 6" (152 mm) at one end. Draw a curved blade shape that extends past the end of the ruler and is about 3 1/4" (83 mm) at its widest. At the base of the blade, mark a 5/16" (8 mm) straight line 2" (50 mm) from the fold, as shown, that leads into the curved blade edge. Use the craft knife to cut it out.

2. Unfold the blade and apply glue along one of the curved edges. Refold the blade and let it dry. Remove the ruler, use scrap paper to mask the section at the base, and spray the blade silver.

3

4 3/4 in (120mm)

4 7/16 in (113mm)

5/16 in (8mm)

TRY CUTTING A HANDLE GRIP ALONG THIS ONE EDGE!

5/16 in (8mm)

4

4

1 1/2 in (38mm)

CURVED END

5

ROUNDED CORNERS

3. Cut a 4 3/4" x 4 7/16" (120 mm x 113 mm) piece of cardstock for the handle. Measure and position the ruler, as shown, and fold each side in, creating panels. Then cut two 5/16" (8 mm) rectangles from the top and bottom of the one panel, as shown.

4. Fold the left (short) panel over the ruler and apply glue. Fold the right panel in to secure.

5. To make the butt of the handle, cut a 4 7/16" x 1 1/2" (113 mm x 38 mm) rectangle and fold it around the ruler as in step 3. Overlap and glue the edges. Cut two rounded corners at the bottom and a curve at the top.

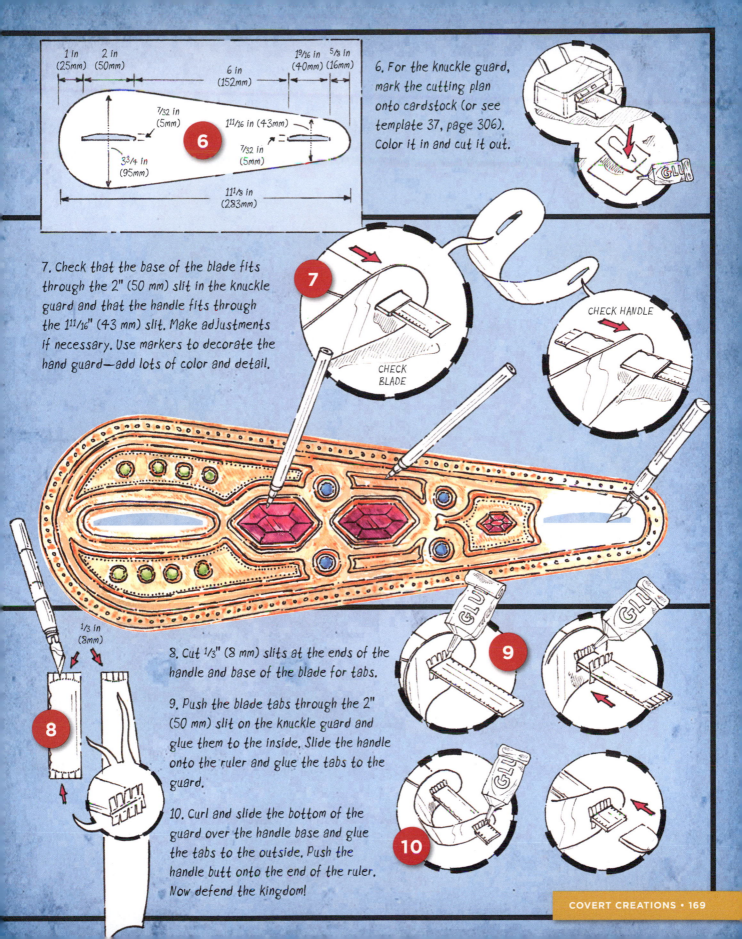

1 in
(25mm)
2 in
(50mm)
6 in
(152mm)
1⁹/₁₆ in
(40mm)
⁵/₈ in
(16mm)

⁷/₃₂ in
(5mm)
1¹¹/₁₆ in (43mm)
⁷/₃₂ in
(5mm)

3³/₄ in
(95mm)

11¹/₈ in
(283mm)

6. For the knuckle guard, mark the cutting plan onto cardstock (or see template 37, page 306). Color it in and cut it out.

7. Check that the base of the blade fits through the 2" (50 mm) slit in the knuckle guard and that the handle fits through the 1¹¹/₁₆" (43 mm) slit. Make adjustments if necessary. Use markers to decorate the hand guard—add lots of color and detail.

CHECK HANDLE

CHECK BLADE

¹/₃ in
(8mm)

8. Cut ¹/₃" (8 mm) slits at the ends of the handle and base of the blade for tabs.

9. Push the blade tabs through the 2" (50 mm) slit on the knuckle guard and glue them to the inside. Slide the handle onto the ruler and glue the tabs to the guard.

10. Curl and slide the bottom of the guard over the handle base and glue the tabs to the outside. Push the handle butt onto the end of the ruler. Now defend the kingdom!

REVERSIBLE CASTLE

LEVEL: EASY

THIS IS MY CASTLE!

MATERIALS

- 2 sheets of white heavyweight cardstock (poster size)
- Ruler
- Pencil
- Craft knife and cutting mat
- Scissors
- Felt-tip markers

Ideal for stories that feature a "goodie" and "baddie" castle, or for a brother and sister who can't agree on whether it's a fort or a palace, this clever castle can change its color quicker than a chameleon. It's also good for keeping your kids occupied; most of the hard work is coloring it in.

1. For the wall, measure and cut a 24⁷/₁₆" x 11¹³/₁₆" (620 mm x 300 mm) rectangle from one sheet of cardstock. For the tower, measure and cut a 23¹/₄" x 9¹³/₁₆" (590 mm x 246 mm) rectangle from the second sheet.

2. Fold the tower piece in half widthwise and crease. Fold the wall piece in half lengthwise and crease.

NO, IT'S MY CASTLE!

24⁷/₁₆ in x 11¹³/₁₆ in (620mm x 300mm)

23¹/₄ in x 9¹³/₁₆ in (590mm x 246mm)

TOWER CARD

WALL CARD

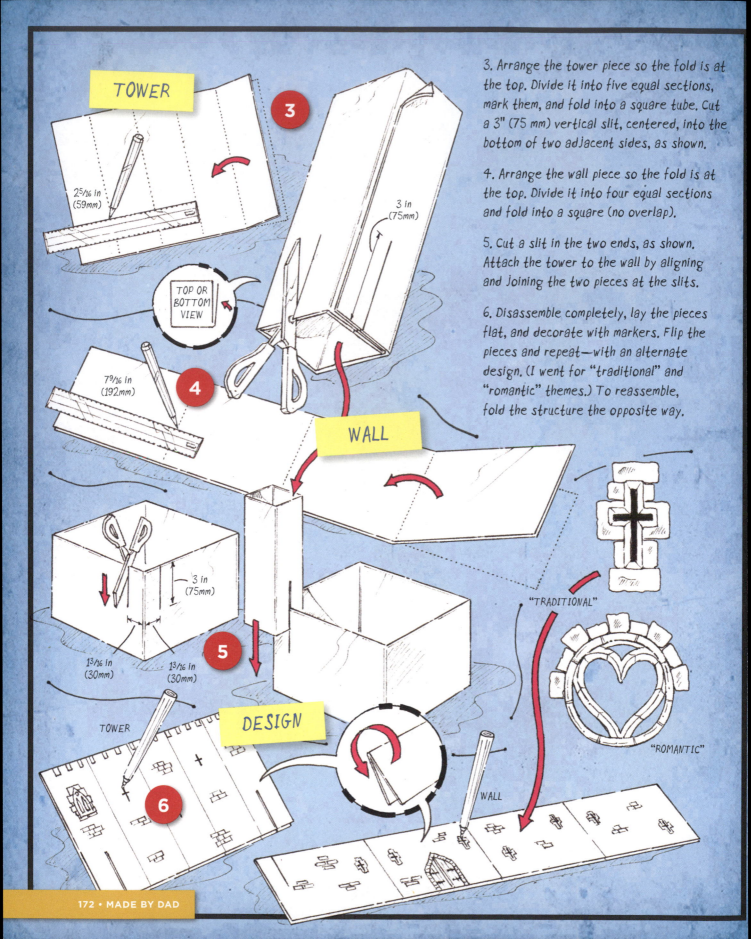

TOWER

2 5/16 in (59mm)

3

3 in (75mm)

TOP OR BOTTOM VIEW

7 9/16 in (192mm)

4

WALL

3 in (75mm)

1 3/16 in (30mm)   1 3/16 in (30mm)

5

TOWER

DESIGN

6

WALL

"TRADITIONAL"

"ROMANTIC"

3. Arrange the tower piece so the fold is at the top. Divide it into five equal sections, mark them, and fold into a square tube. Cut a 3" (75 mm) vertical slit, centered, into the bottom of two adjacent sides, as shown.

4. Arrange the wall piece so the fold is at the top. Divide it into four equal sections and fold into a square (no overlap).

5. Cut a slit in the two ends, as shown. Attach the tower to the wall by aligning and joining the two pieces at the slits.

6. Disassemble completely, lay the pieces flat, and decorate with markers. Flip the pieces and repeat—with an alternate design. (I went for "traditional" and "romantic" themes.) To reassemble, fold the structure the opposite way.

SNAIL SOUP DECOY

LEVEL: MEDIUM

MATERIALS

- Empty tin can (15.5 oz, 439 g)
- Pencil
- Small corrugated cardboard box
- Craft knife and cutting mat
- Old spoon
- Hacksaw
- Plastic bowl
- PVA glue
- Poster paint (yellow, green, and orange)
- Paintbrush
- Drafting compass
- White lightweight cardstock
- Paper glue
- Clear tape
- Silver spray paint
- Black permanent marker
- Ruler
- Scissors
- Felt-tip markers
- Access to a photocopier or printer (optional)

GROSS! NOTHING TO STEAL HERE!

Every kid needs a secret place to hide treasures, especially if there's a nosy sibling on the prowl! Inspired by the *Home Alone* movies, this decoy looks like a disgusting can of Snail Soup, unpalatable to both burglars and annoying little brothers and sisters.

From snail goo to secret treasure: Unless your burglar has a taste for cold snail soup, this decoy is foolproof! But if he attempts to sneak a mouthful of the delicious goo, he will be pleasantly surprised—a gentle tug on the spoon's handle reveals a super-reinforced cardboard safe concealed inside. And inside that? Sweets, coins, and Nintendo DS games—all of life's most valuable treasures!

FAVORITE NINTENDO GAME

TREASURE MAP

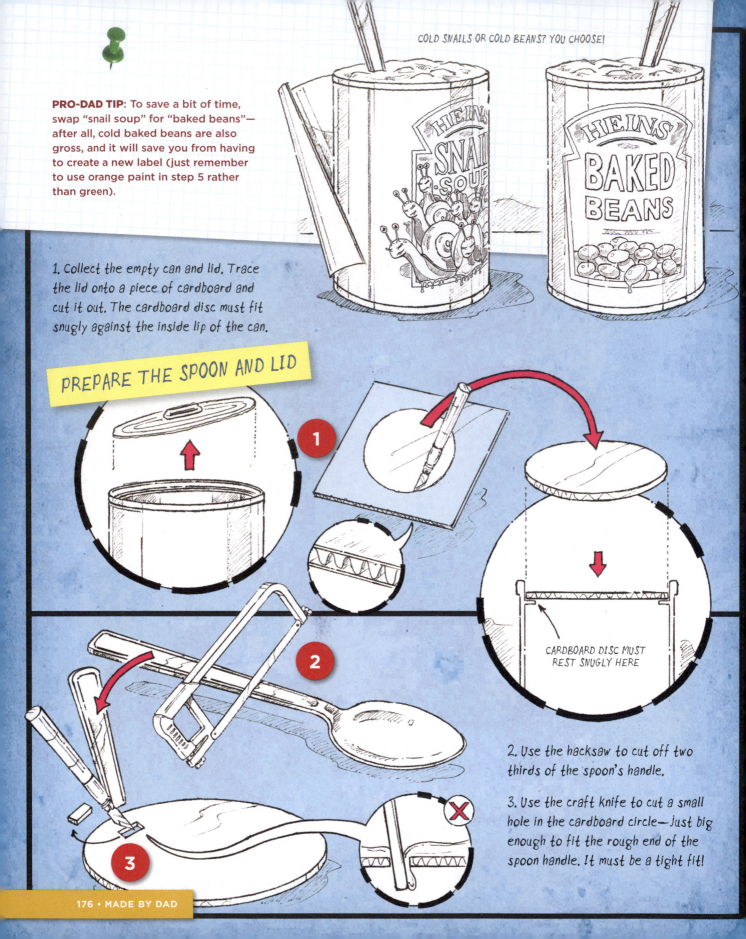

COLD SNAILS OR COLD BEANS? YOU CHOOSE!

PRO-DAD TIP: To save a bit of time, swap "snail soup" for "baked beans"—after all, cold baked beans are also gross, and it will save you from having to create a new label (just remember to use orange paint in step 5 rather than green).

1. Collect the empty can and lid. Trace the lid onto a piece of cardboard and cut it out. The cardboard disc must fit snugly against the inside lip of the can.

PREPARE THE SPOON AND LID

CARDBOARD DISC MUST REST SNUGLY HERE

2. Use the hacksaw to cut off two thirds of the spoon's handle.

3. Use the craft knife to cut a small hole in the cardboard circle—just big enough to fit the rough end of the spoon handle. It must be a tight fit!

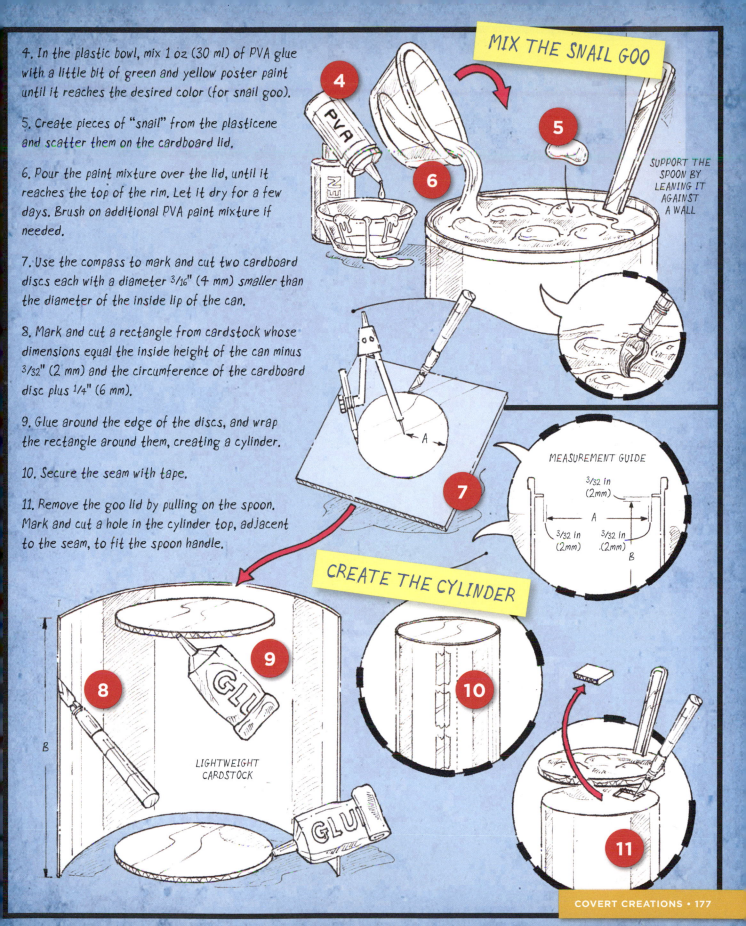

4. In the plastic bowl, mix 1 oz (30 ml) of PVA glue with a little bit of green and yellow poster paint until it reaches the desired color (for snail goo).

5. Create pieces of "snail" from the plasticene and scatter them on the cardboard lid.

6. Pour the paint mixture over the lid, until it reaches the top of the rim. Let it dry for a few days. Brush on additional PVA paint mixture if needed.

7. Use the compass to mark and cut two cardboard discs each with a diameter 3/16" (4 mm) smaller than the diameter of the inside lip of the can.

8. Mark and cut a rectangle from cardstock whose dimensions equal the inside height of the can minus 3/32" (2 mm) and the circumference of the cardboard disc plus 1/4" (6 mm).

9. Glue around the edge of the discs, and wrap the rectangle around them, creating a cylinder.

10. Secure the seam with tape.

11. Remove the goo lid by pulling on the spoon. Mark and cut a hole in the cylinder top, adjacent to the seam, to fit the spoon handle.

MIX THE SNAIL GOO

SUPPORT THE SPOON BY LEANING IT AGAINST A WALL

MEASUREMENT GUIDE

3/32 in (2mm)

A

3/32 in (2mm)   3/32 in .(2mm)

B

CREATE THE CYLINDER

LIGHTWEIGHT CARDSTOCK

GLU

GLU

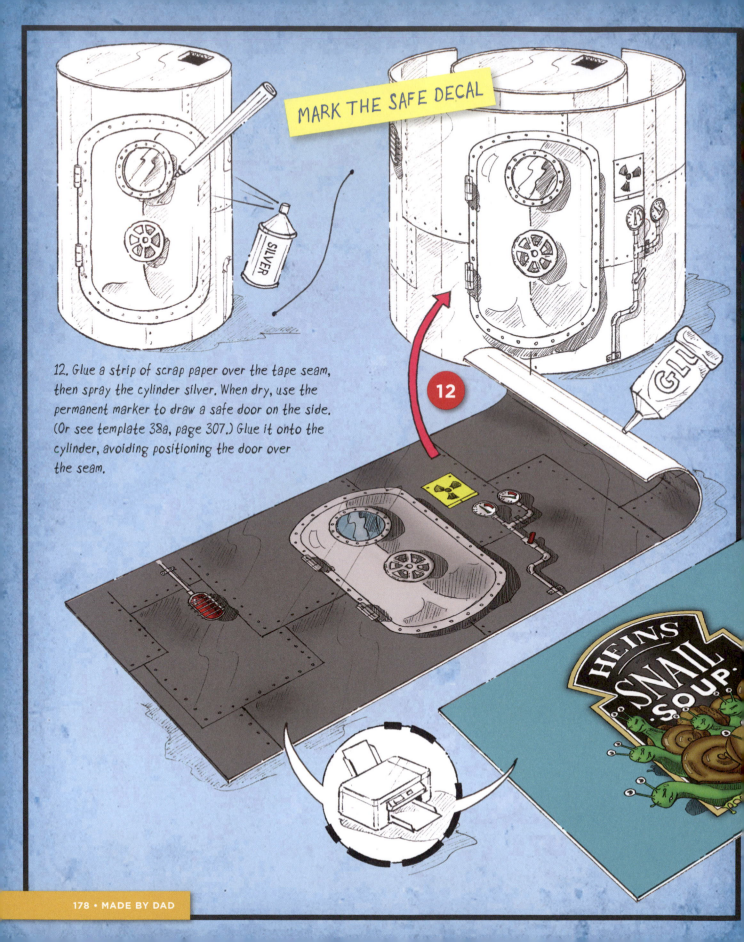

MARK THE SAFE DECAL

12. Glue a strip of scrap paper over the tape seam, then spray the cylinder silver. When dry, use the permanent marker to draw a safe door on the side. (Or see template 38a, page 307.) Glue it onto the cylinder, avoiding positioning the door over the seam.

12

SILVER

GL

HEINS SNAIL SOUP

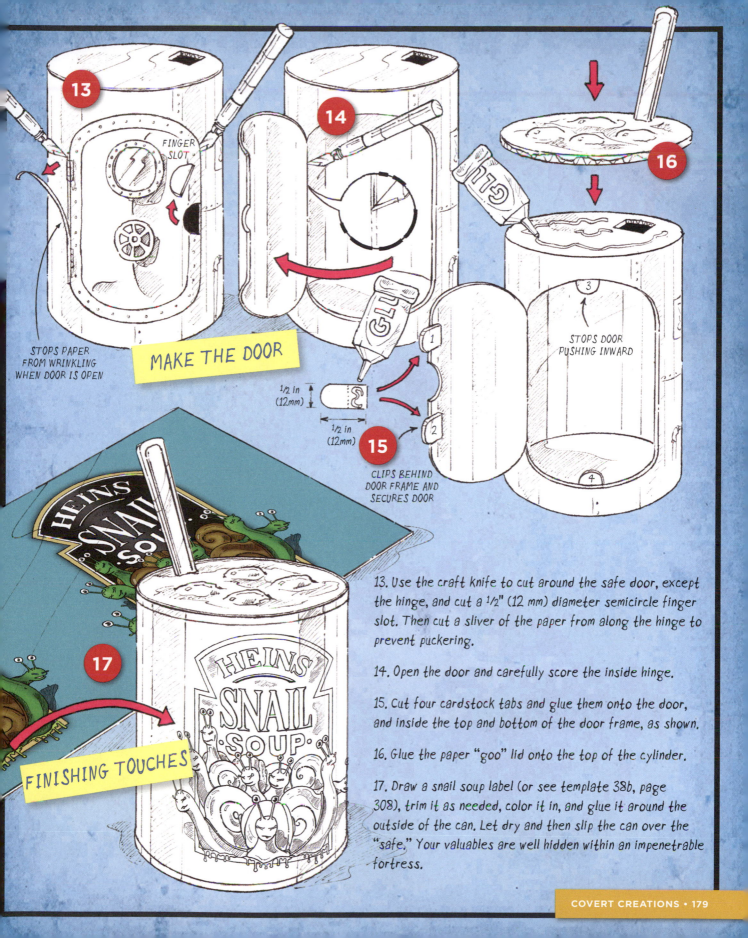

FINGER SLOT

STOPS PAPER FROM WRINKLING WHEN DOOR IS OPEN

MAKE THE DOOR

1/2 in (12mm)

1/2 in (12mm)

CLIPS BEHIND DOOR FRAME AND SECURES DOOR

STOPS DOOR PUSHING INWARD

GLU

FINISHING TOUCHES

HEINS SNAIL SOUP

13. Use the craft knife to cut around the safe door, except the hinge, and cut a 1/2" (12 mm) diameter semicircle finger slot. Then cut a sliver of the paper from along the hinge to prevent puckering.

14. Open the door and carefully score the inside hinge.

15. Cut four cardstock tabs and glue them onto the door, and inside the top and bottom of the door frame, as shown.

16. Glue the paper "goo" lid onto the top of the cylinder.

17. Draw a snail soup label (or see template 38b, page 308), trim it as needed, color it in, and glue it around the outside of the can. Let dry and then slip the can over the "safe." Your valuables are well hidden within an impenetrable fortress.

A "keep out" sign for every occasion—well, three occasions, to be precise, because that's the number that fits on a 12" x 18" (A3) piece of paper. Of course, it could just as easily be a "Welcome, cake being served" sign—it's up to you how cranky or cordial you want to be—and making your own personalized messages is half the fun.

MATERIALS

- Craft knife and cutting mat
- Small corrugated cardboard box
- Ruler
- Pencil
- Stirring stick or blunt knife
- Paper glue
- 2 dried-up felt-tip markers or a $\frac{5}{16}$" (8 mm) dowel
- White lightweight cardstock
- Hacksaw
- Hot glue gun and glue sticks
- Printer paper (12" x 18", A3)
- Pliers
- Galvanized wire (#15 gauge, 1.5 mm)
- Silver spray paint

TOXIC GAS

ENTER AT YOUR **PERIL**

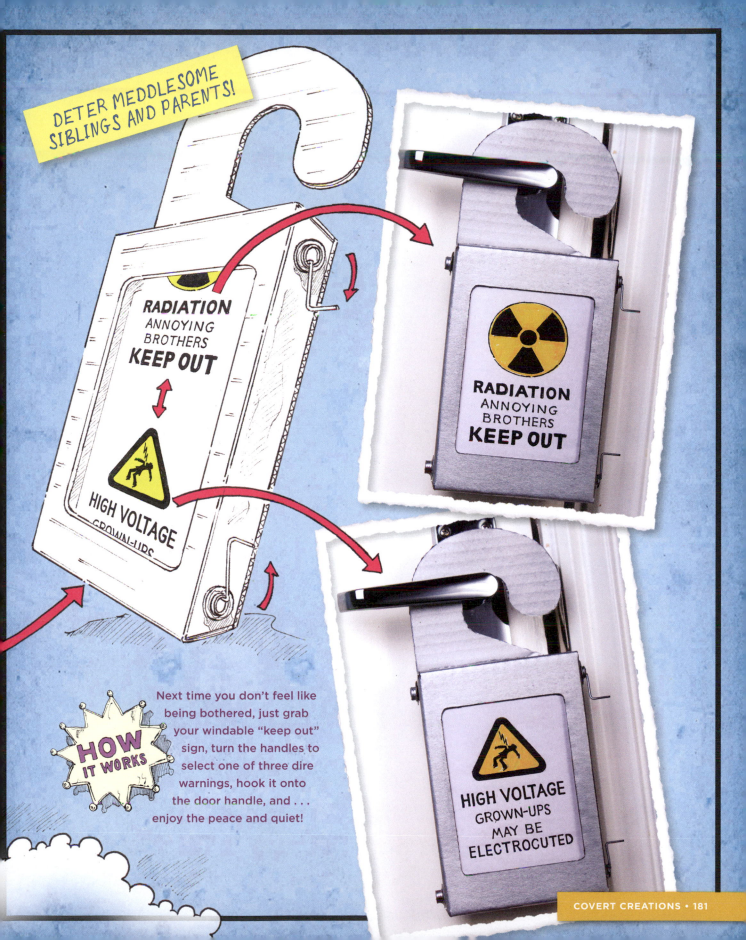

DETER MEDDLESOME SIBLINGS AND PARENTS!

RADIATION
ANNOYING
BROTHERS
KEEP OUT

HIGH VOLTAGE
GROWN-UPS

RADIATION
ANNOYING
BROTHERS
KEEP OUT

HIGH VOLTAGE
GROWN-UPS
MAY BE
ELECTROCUTED

HOW IT WORKS

Next time you don't feel like being bothered, just grab your windable "keep out" sign, turn the handles to select one of three dire warnings, hook it onto the door handle, and . . . enjoy the peace and quiet!

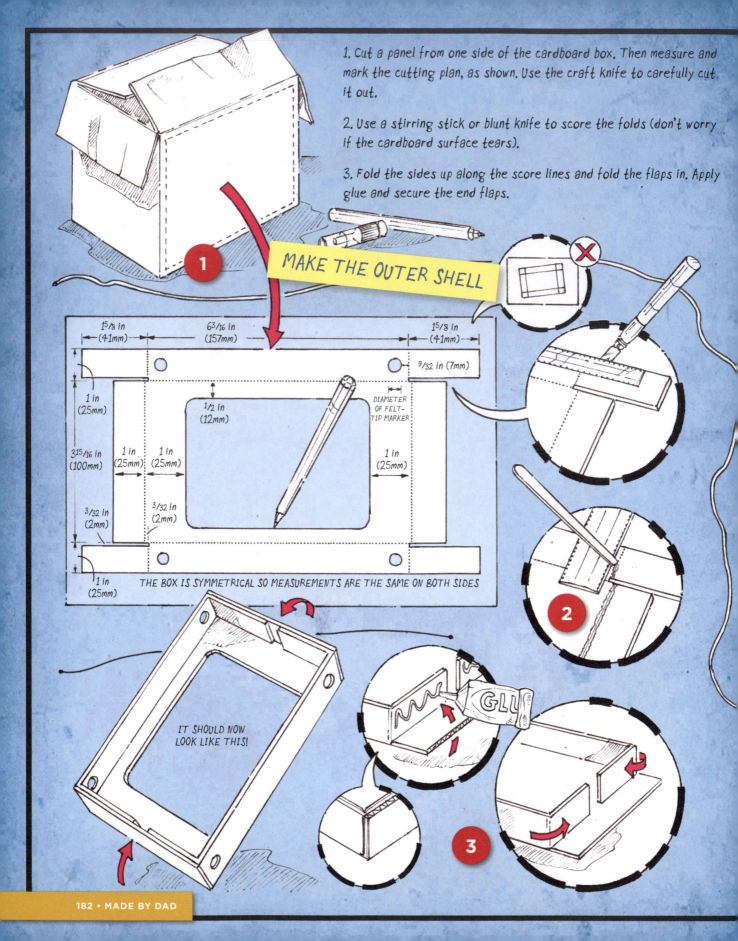

1. Cut a panel from one side of the cardboard box. Then measure and mark the cutting plan, as shown. Use the craft knife to carefully cut it out.

2. Use a stirring stick or blunt knife to score the folds (don't worry if the cardboard surface tears).

3. Fold the sides up along the score lines and fold the flaps in. Apply glue and secure the end flaps.

MAKE THE OUTER SHELL

1⁵/₈ in (41mm) 6³/₁₆ in (157mm) 1⁵/₈ in (41mm)

⁹/₃₂ in (7mm)

1 in (25mm)

¹/₂ in (12mm)

DIAMETER OF FELT-TIP MARKER

3¹⁵/₁₆ in (100mm)   1 in (25mm)   1 in (25mm)   1 in (25mm)

³/₃₂ in (2mm)   ³/₃₂ in (2mm)

1 in (25mm)

THE BOX IS SYMMETRICAL SO MEASUREMENTS ARE THE SAME ON BOTH SIDES

GLU

IT SHOULD NOW LOOK LIKE THIS!

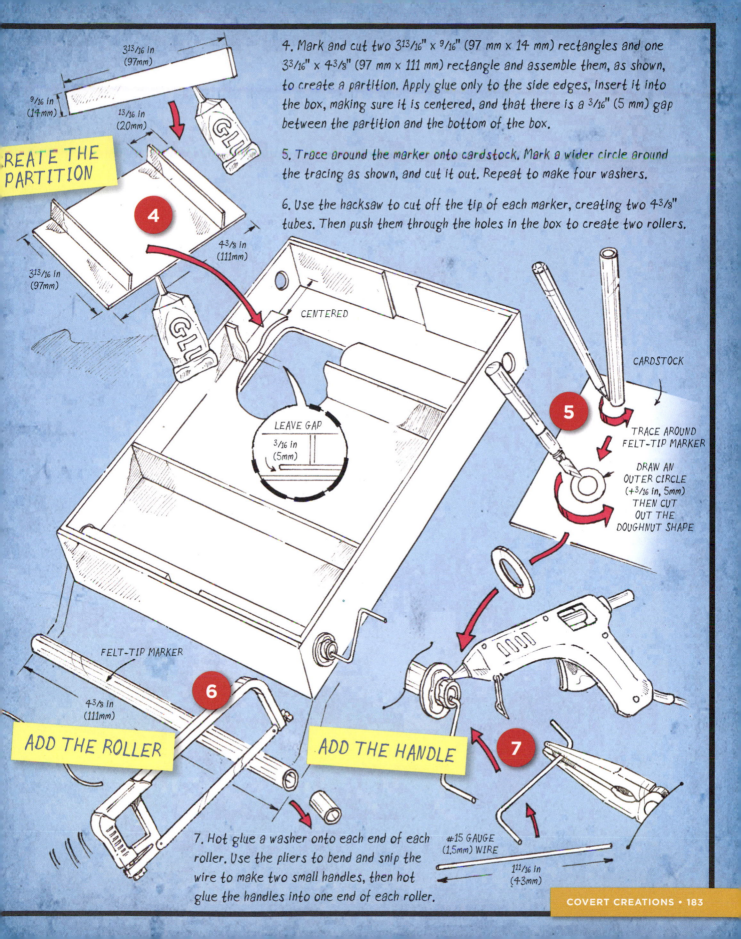

3¹³/₁₆ in (97mm)

9/16 in (14mm)

13/16 in (20mm)

4

3¹³/₁₆ in (97mm)

4³/₈ in (111mm)

4. Mark and cut two 3¹³/₁₆" x ⁹/₁₆" (97 mm x 14 mm) rectangles and one 3³/₁₆" x 4³/₈" (97 mm x 111 mm) rectangle and assemble them, as shown, to create a partition. Apply glue only to the side edges, insert it into the box, making sure it is centered, and that there is a ³/₁₆" (5 mm) gap between the partition and the bottom of the box.

5. Trace around the marker onto cardstock. Mark a wider circle around the tracing as shown, and cut it out. Repeat to make four washers.

6. Use the hacksaw to cut off the tip of each marker, creating two 4³/₈" tubes. Then push them through the holes in the box to create two rollers.

CENTERED

LEAVE GAP
³/₁₆ in
(5mm)

CARDSTOCK

5

TRACE AROUND FELT-TIP MARKER

DRAW AN OUTER CIRCLE (+³/₁₆ in, 5mm) THEN CUT OUT THE DOUGHNUT SHAPE

FELT-TIP MARKER

6

4³/₈ in (111mm)

7

7. Hot glue a washer onto each end of each roller. Use the pliers to bend and snip the wire to make two small handles, then hot glue the handles into one end of each roller.

#15 GAUGE (1.5mm) WIRE

1¹¹/₁₆ in (43mm)

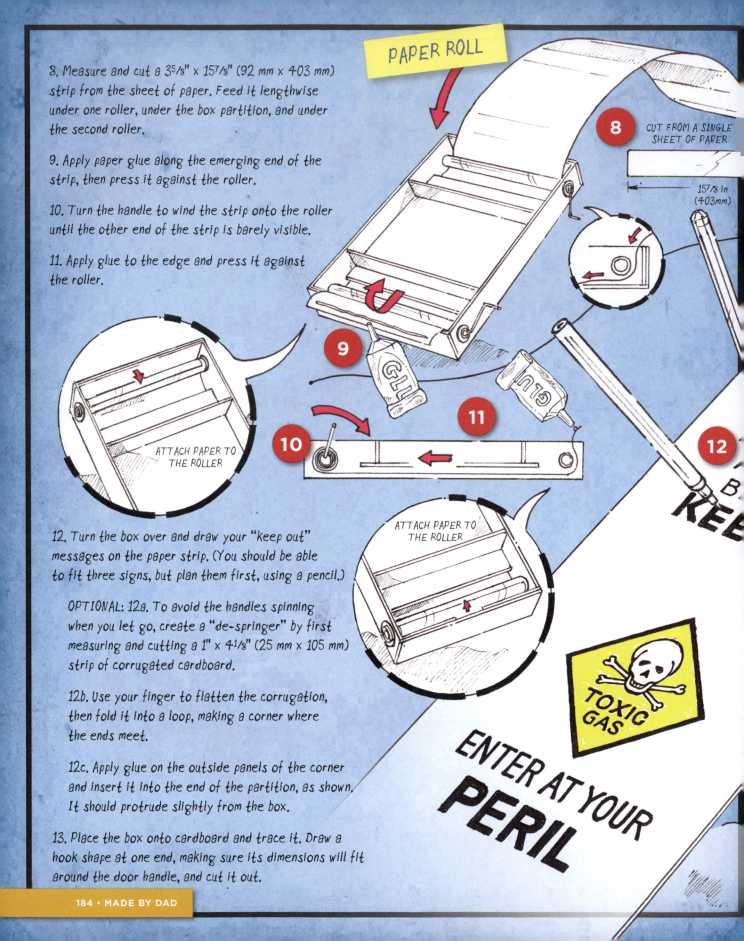

8. Measure and cut a 3⁵/₈" x 15⁷/₈" (92 mm x 403 mm) strip from the sheet of paper. Feed it lengthwise under one roller, under the box partition, and under the second roller.

9. Apply paper glue along the emerging end of the strip, then press it against the roller.

10. Turn the handle to wind the strip onto the roller until the other end of the strip is barely visible.

11. Apply glue to the edge and press it against the roller.

8 CUT FROM A SINGLE SHEET OF PAPER

15⁷/₈ in (403mm)

ATTACH PAPER TO THE ROLLER

9

10

11

12

ATTACH PAPER TO THE ROLLER

12. Turn the box over and draw your "keep out" messages on the paper strip. (You should be able to fit three signs, but plan them first, using a pencil.)

OPTIONAL: 12a. To avoid the handles spinning when you let go, create a "de-springer" by first measuring and cutting a 1" x 4¹/₈" (25 mm x 105 mm) strip of corrugated cardboard.

12b. Use your finger to flatten the corrugation, then fold it into a loop, making a corner where the ends meet.

12c. Apply glue on the outside panels of the corner and insert it into the end of the partition, as shown. It should protrude slightly from the box.

13. Place the box onto cardboard and trace it. Draw a hook shape at one end, making sure its dimensions will fit around the door handle, and cut it out.

TOXIC GAS

B. KEE...

ENTER AT YOUR PERIL

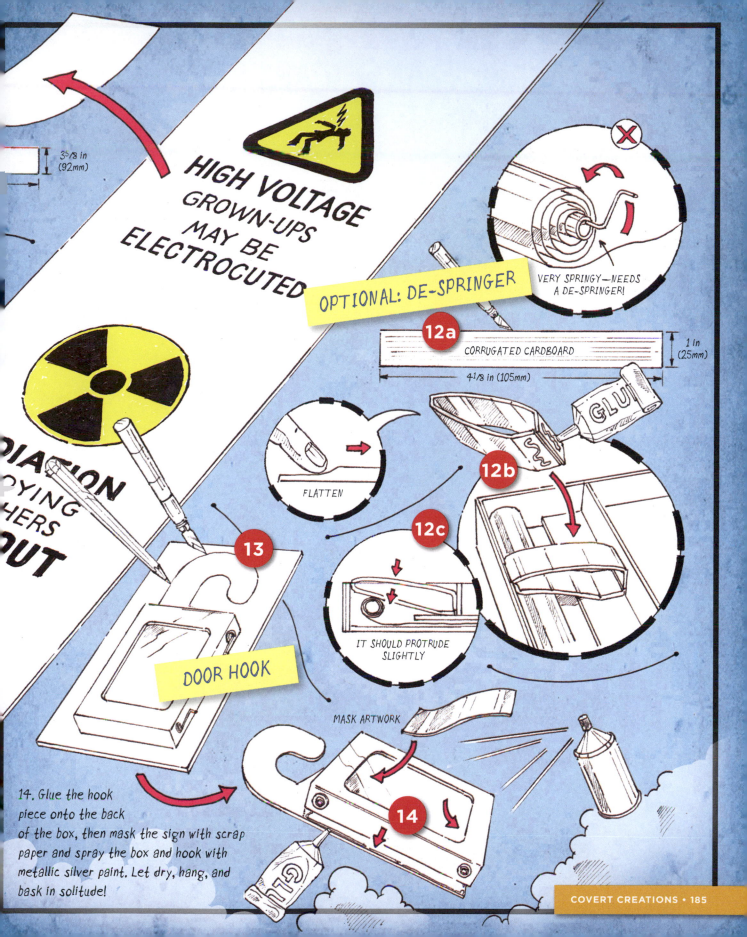

HIGH VOLTAGE
GROWN-UPS
MAY BE
ELECTROCUTED

3⅝ in
(92mm)

VERY SPRINGY—NEEDS
A DE-SPRINGER!

OPTIONAL: DE-SPRINGER

12a
CORRUGATED CARDBOARD

1 in
(25mm)

4⅛ in (105mm)

FLATTEN

12b

GLUE

12c
IT SHOULD PROTRUDE
SLIGHTLY

DIATION
PYING
HERS
OUT

13

DOOR HOOK

MASK ARTWORK

14

GLUE

14. Glue the hook
piece onto the back
of the box, then mask the sign with scrap
paper and spray the box and hook with
metallic silver paint. Let dry, hang, and
bask in solitude!

LEVEL: TRICKY

Protect your treasures by installing a realistic-looking surveillance camera, and then double-protect your treasures by hiding them inside the camera itself. A double-decoy that is clever enough to thwart even the smartest thief among sneaky siblings and curious cousins.

MATERIALS

- Craft knife and cutting mat
- Large corrugated cardboard box
- Ruler
- Pencil
- Stirring stick or blunt knife
- Hot glue gun and glue sticks
- Cereal box
- Paper glue
- Dried-up felt-tip marker
- Spray paint (white, black, and silver)
- Plastic bottle cap (approximately 1½", 38 mm in diameter; ½", 13 mm tall)
- Black permanent marker
- Clear plastic or transparency film
- Velcro tabs

A SURVEILLANCE CAMERA . . . I GIVE UP!

1. Cut out a panel from the side of the corrugated cardboard box.

2. Measure and mark the cutting plan, as shown. Use the craft knife to carefully cut it out.

3. Use a stirring stick or blunt knife to score the folds. (Don't worry if the cardboard surface tears.)

4. Fold the sides up along the score lines and fold the flaps.

5. Apply hot glue to secure the end flaps.

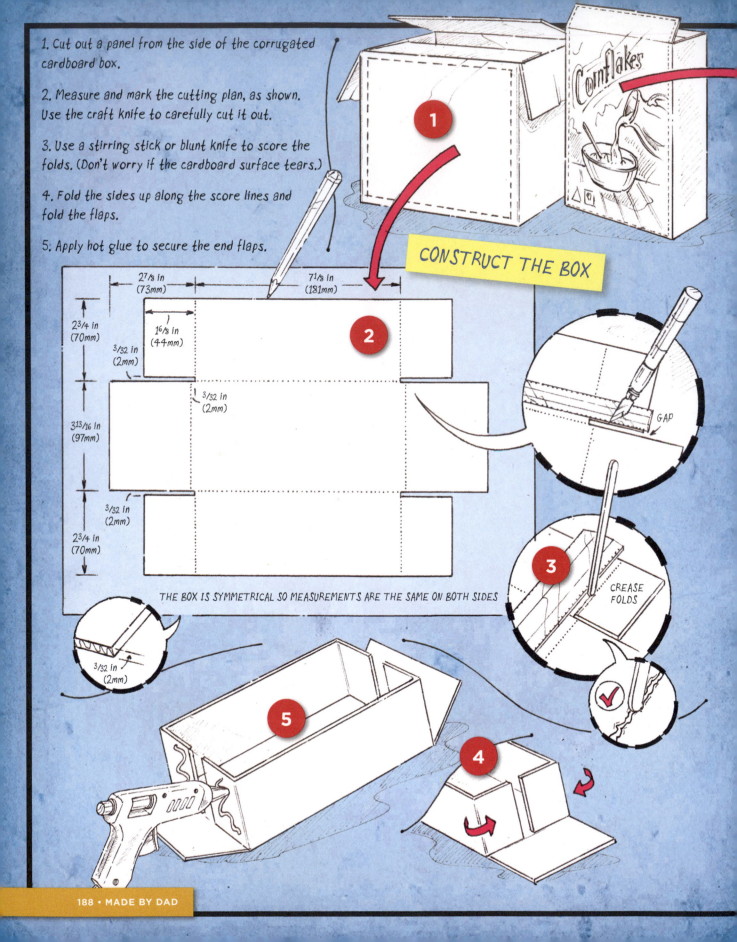

CONSTRUCT THE BOX

2⁷/₈ in (73mm)

7¹/₈ in (181mm)

2³/₄ in (70mm)

1⁶/₈ in (44mm)

³/₃₂ in (2mm)

³/₃₂ in (2mm)

3¹³/₁₆ in (97mm)

³/₃₂ in (2mm)

2³/₄ in (70mm)

THE BOX IS SYMMETRICAL SO MEASUREMENTS ARE THE SAME ON BOTH SIDES

GAP

CREASE FOLDS

³/₃₂ in (2mm)

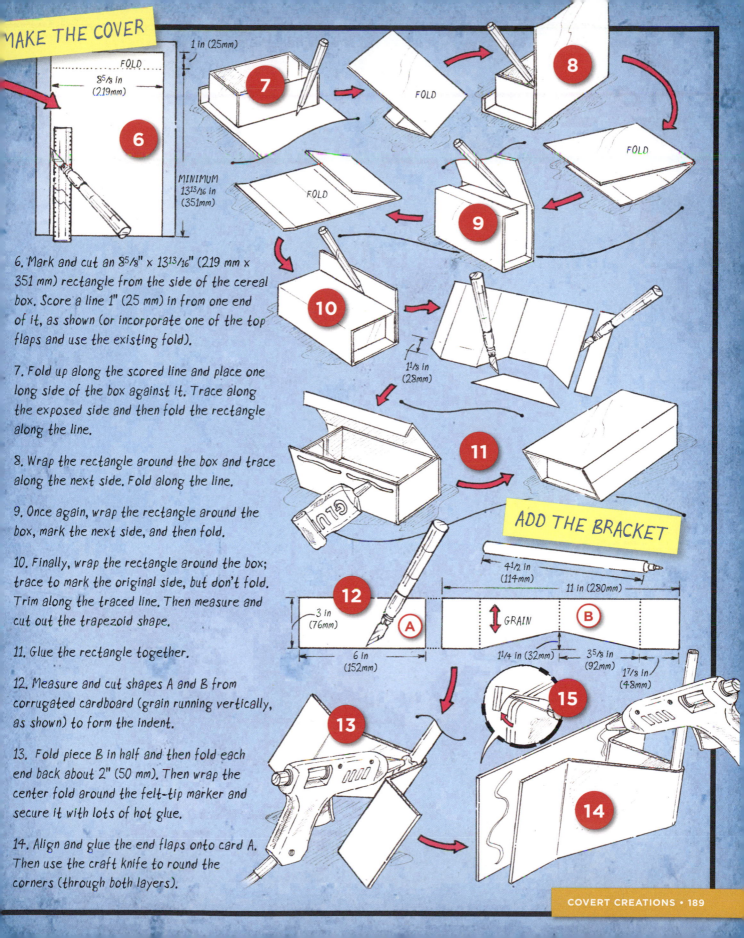

MAKE THE COVER

FOLD

8⅝ in
(219mm)

1 in (25mm)

MINIMUM
13¹³/₁₆ in
(351mm)

FOLD

FOLD

FOLD

1⅛ in
(28mm)

ADD THE BRACKET

4½ in
(114mm)

11 in (280mm)

3 in
(76mm)

A

GRAIN

B

6 in
(152mm)

1¼ in (32mm)

3⅝ in
(92mm)

1⅞ in
(48mm)

6. Mark and cut an 8⅝" x 13¹³/₁₆" (219 mm x 351 mm) rectangle from the side of the cereal box. Score a line 1" (25 mm) in from one end of it, as shown (or incorporate one of the top flaps and use the existing fold).

7. Fold up along the scored line and place one long side of the box against it. Trace along the exposed side and then fold the rectangle along the line.

8. Wrap the rectangle around the box and trace along the next side. Fold along the line.

9. Once again, wrap the rectangle around the box, mark the next side, and then fold.

10. Finally, wrap the rectangle around the box; trace to mark the original side, but don't fold. Trim along the traced line. Then measure and cut out the trapezoid shape.

11. Glue the rectangle together.

12. Measure and cut shapes A and B from corrugated cardboard (grain running vertically, as shown) to form the indent.

13. Fold piece B in half and then fold each end back about 2" (50 mm). Then wrap the center fold around the felt-tip marker and secure it with lots of hot glue.

14. Align and glue the end flaps onto card A. Then use the craft knife to round the corners (through both layers).

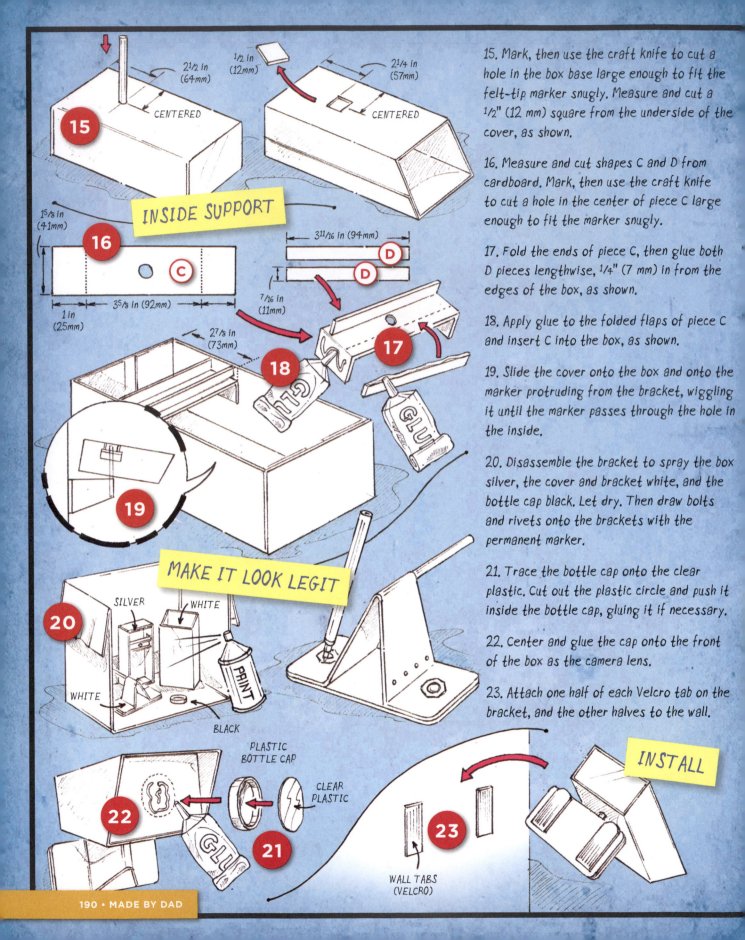

INSIDE SUPPORT

MAKE IT LOOK LEGIT

INSTALL

15. Mark, then use the craft knife to cut a hole in the box base large enough to fit the felt-tip marker snugly. Measure and cut a ½" (12 mm) square from the underside of the cover, as shown.

16. Measure and cut shapes C and D from cardboard. Mark, then use the craft knife to cut a hole in the center of piece C large enough to fit the marker snugly.

17. Fold the ends of piece C, then glue both D pieces lengthwise, ¼" (7 mm) in from the edges of the box, as shown.

18. Apply glue to the folded flaps of piece C and insert C into the box, as shown.

19. Slide the cover onto the box and onto the marker protruding from the bracket, wiggling it until the marker passes through the hole in the inside.

20. Disassemble the bracket to spray the box silver, the cover and bracket white, and the bottle cap black. Let dry. Then draw bolts and rivets onto the brackets with the permanent marker.

21. Trace the bottle cap onto the clear plastic. Cut out the plastic circle and push it inside the bottle cap, gluing it if necessary.

22. Center and glue the cap onto the front of the box as the camera lens.

23. Attach one half of each Velcro tab on the bracket, and the other halves to the wall.

BUNK BED COMMUNICATOR

LEVEL: MEDIUM

WILL YOU STOP SNORING?!

If your children share a bunk bed, they will have endless fun with this bed-to-bed communicator. In fact, even if they are in separate beds, it will still work brilliantly as long as there's space along the wall to run the communicator. (Note: In that event, it may end up looking like the one I've drawn below.)

MATERIALS

- Long cardboard tubes (empty wrapping paper tubes work well)
- Ruler
- Pencil
- Paper
- Craft knife and cutting mat
- Hot glue gun and glue sticks
- White medium-weight cardstock
- Drafting compass
- Poster paint (red and yellow)
- Paintbrush
- Black permanent marker
- Mounting putty or double-sided tape

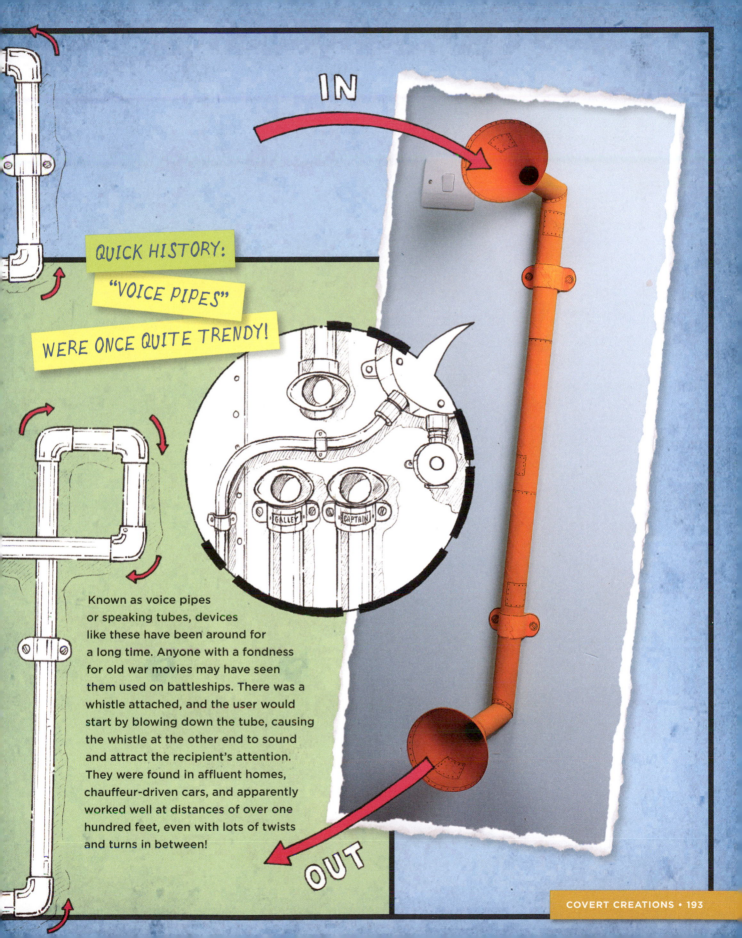

IN

QUICK HISTORY:

"VOICE PIPES"

WERE ONCE QUITE TRENDY!

GALLEY   CAPTAIN

Known as voice pipes or speaking tubes, devices like these have been around for a long time. Anyone with a fondness for old war movies may have seen them used on battleships. There was a whistle attached, and the user would start by blowing down the tube, causing the whistle at the other end to sound and attract the recipient's attention. They were found in affluent homes, chauffeur-driven cars, and apparently worked well at distances of over one hundred feet, even with lots of twists and turns in between!

OUT

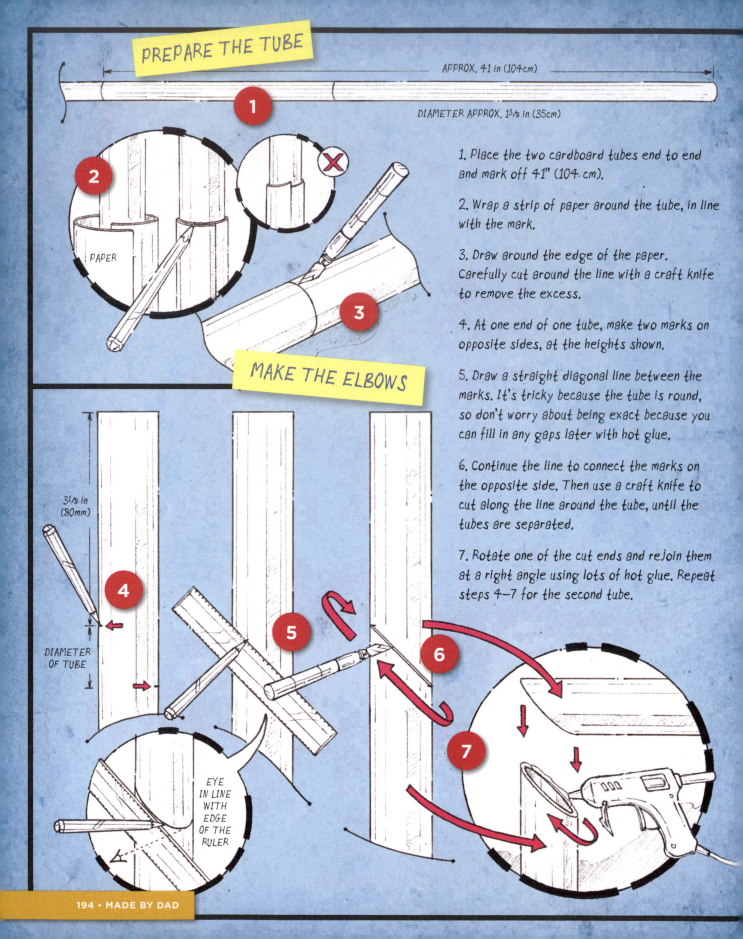

PREPARE THE TUBE

APPROX. 41 in (104cm)

DIAMETER APPROX. 1³⁄₈ in (35cm)

PAPER

MAKE THE ELBOWS

3¹⁄₈ in (80mm)

DIAMETER OF TUBE

EYE IN LINE WITH EDGE OF THE RULER

1. Place the two cardboard tubes end to end and mark off 41" (104 cm).

2. Wrap a strip of paper around the tube, in line with the mark.

3. Draw around the edge of the paper. Carefully cut around the line with a craft knife to remove the excess.

4. At one end of one tube, make two marks on opposite sides, at the heights shown.

5. Draw a straight diagonal line between the marks. It's tricky because the tube is round, so don't worry about being exact because you can fill in any gaps later with hot glue.

6. Continue the line to connect the marks on the opposite side. Then use a craft knife to cut along the line around the tube, until the tubes are separated.

7. Rotate one of the cut ends and rejoin them at a right angle using lots of hot glue. Repeat steps 4–7 for the second tube.

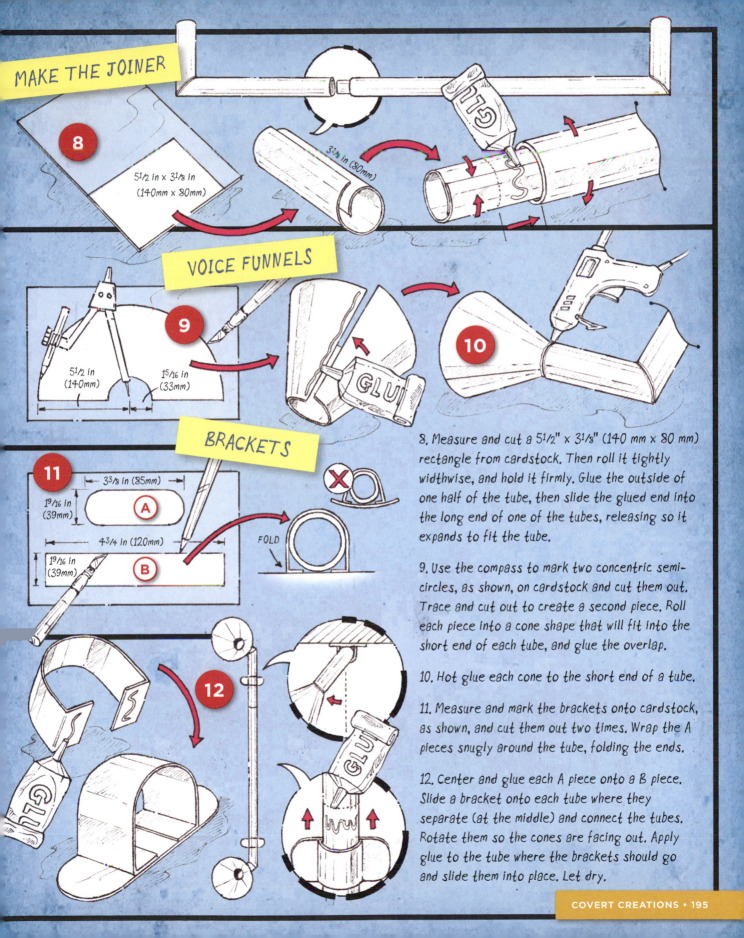

MAKE THE JOINER

8

5½ in x 3⅛ in
(140mm x 80mm)

3⅛ in (80mm)

GLU

VOICE FUNNELS

9

5½ in
(140mm)

1⁵⁄₁₆ in
(33mm)

GLU

10

BRACKETS

11

3³⁄₈ in (85mm)

1⁹⁄₁₆ in
(39mm)

Ⓐ

4³⁄₄ in (120mm)

1⁹⁄₁₆ in
(39mm)

Ⓑ

FOLD

12

GLU

GLU

8. Measure and cut a 5½" x 3⅛" (140 mm x 80 mm) rectangle from cardstock. Then roll it tightly widthwise, and hold it firmly. Glue the outside of one half of the tube, then slide the glued end into the long end of one of the tubes, releasing so it expands to fit the tube.

9. Use the compass to mark two concentric semi-circles, as shown, on cardstock and cut them out. Trace and cut out to create a second piece. Roll each piece into a cone shape that will fit into the short end of each tube, and glue the overlap.

10. Hot glue each cone to the short end of a tube.

11. Measure and mark the brackets onto cardstock, as shown, and cut them out two times. Wrap the A pieces snugly around the tube, folding the ends.

12. Center and glue each A piece onto a B piece. Slide a bracket onto each tube where they separate (at the middle) and connect the tubes. Rotate them so the cones are facing out. Apply glue to the tube where the brackets should go and slide them into place. Let dry.

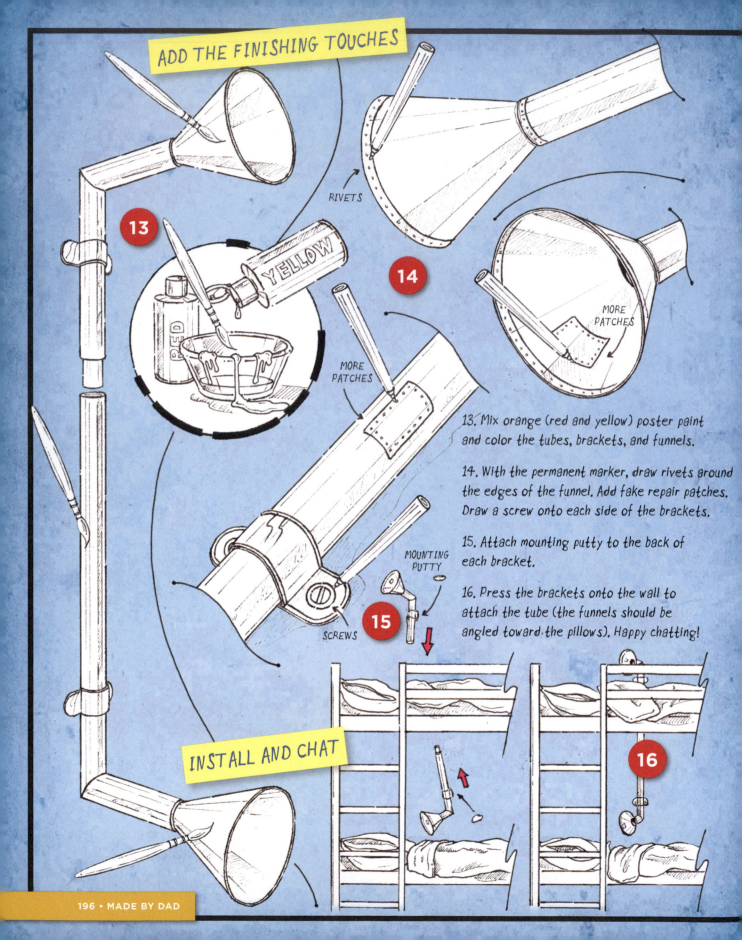

ADD THE FINISHING TOUCHES

13

14

RIVETS

YELLOW

RED

MORE PATCHES

MORE PATCHES

SCREWS

MOUNTING PUTTY

15

13. Mix orange (red and yellow) poster paint and color the tubes, brackets, and funnels.

14. With the permanent marker, draw rivets around the edges of the funnel. Add fake repair patches. Draw a screw onto each side of the brackets.

15. Attach mounting putty to the back of each bracket.

16. Press the brackets onto the wall to attach the tube (the funnels should be angled toward the pillows). Happy chatting!

INSTALL AND CHAT

16

PRICELESS PICTURE SAFE

LEVEL: TRICKY

I DON'T TRUST THAT SMILE....

I've watched so many movies and TV shows with the safe-hidden-behind-the-picture scenario (probably too many *Columbo* episodes) that I've always wanted to make one. Of course, I needed a solution that didn't require knocking a large hole in the wall, so here it is. And the most heavy-duty tool you'll need is a drafting compass.

MATERIALS

- Ruler
- Pencil
- Craft knife and cutting mat
- Small corrugated cardboard box
- Medium-sized corrugated cardboard box
- Paper glue
- Spray paint (silver and brown)
- White medium-weight cardstock
- Drafting compass
- Black permanent marker
- Stirring stick or blunt knife
- Paper
- Felt-tip markers
- Mounting putty
- Access to a photocopier or printer (optional)

I KNEW HE WAS HIDING SOMETHING!

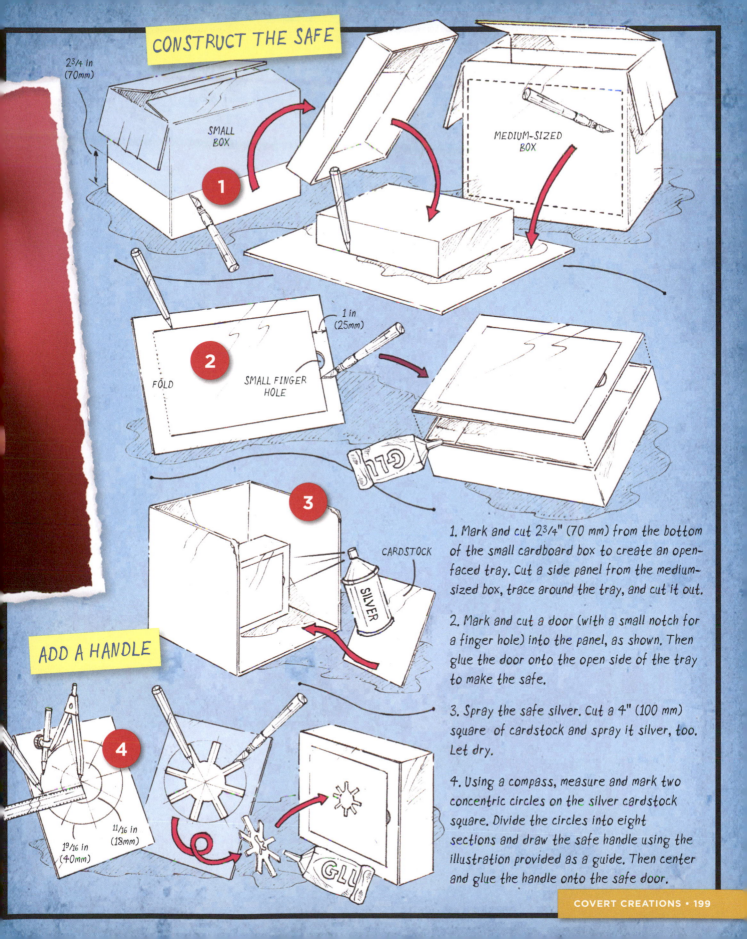

CONSTRUCT THE SAFE

2¾ in
(70mm)

1

SMALL BOX

MEDIUM-SIZED BOX

2

FOLD

SMALL FINGER HOLE

1 in (25mm)

GLU

3

CARDSTOCK

SILVER

ADD A HANDLE

4

1⁹⁄₁₆ in
(40mm)

11⁄16 in
(18mm)

GLU

1. Mark and cut 2¾" (70 mm) from the bottom of the small cardboard box to create an open-faced tray. Cut a side panel from the medium-sized box, trace around the tray, and cut it out.

2. Mark and cut a door (with a small notch for a finger hole) into the panel, as shown. Then glue the door onto the open side of the tray to make the safe.

3. Spray the safe silver. Cut a 4" (100 mm) square of cardstock and spray it silver, too. Let dry.

4. Using a compass, measure and mark two concentric circles on the silver cardstock square. Divide the circles into eight sections and draw the safe handle using the illustration provided as a guide. Then center and glue the handle onto the safe door.

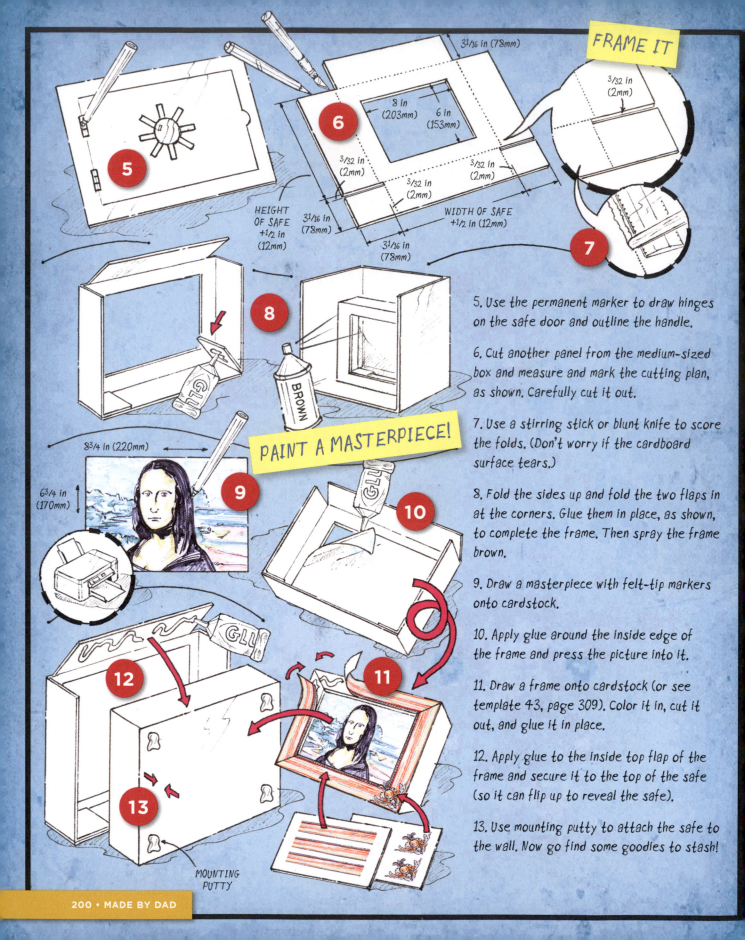

8 in (203mm)

6 in (153mm)

3¹⁄₁₆ in (78mm)

3/32 in (2mm)

3/32 in (2mm)

3/32 in (2mm)

3/32 in (2mm)

3/32 in (2mm)

HEIGHT OF SAFE +¹⁄₂ in (12mm)

3¹⁄₁₆ in (78mm)

3¹⁄₁₆ in (78mm)

WIDTH OF SAFE +¹⁄₂ in (12mm)

BROWN

GLUE

8¾ in (220mm)

6¾ in (170mm)

PAINT A MASTERPIECE!

GLUE

GLUE

MOUNTING PUTTY

5. Use the permanent marker to draw hinges on the safe door and outline the handle.

6. Cut another panel from the medium-sized box and measure and mark the cutting plan, as shown. Carefully cut it out.

7. Use a stirring stick or blunt knife to score the folds. (Don't worry if the cardboard surface tears.)

8. Fold the sides up and fold the two flaps in at the corners. Glue them in place, as shown, to complete the frame. Then spray the frame brown.

9. Draw a masterpiece with felt-tip markers onto cardstock.

10. Apply glue around the inside edge of the frame and press the picture into it.

11. Draw a frame onto cardstock (or see template 43, page 309). Color it in, cut it out, and glue it in place.

12. Apply glue to the inside top flap of the frame and secure it to the top of the safe (so it can flip up to reveal the safe).

13. Use mounting putty to attach the safe to the wall. Now go find some goodies to stash!

ARTY PARTY

CHEEKY FORTUNE-TELLER

LEVEL: EASY

This project is based on the classic paper fortune-teller. But there's one important twist: The fortunes inside aren't written—they're hand-drawn renderings of outrageous scenarios.

MATERIALS
- Printer paper
- Pencil
- Craft knife and cutting mat
- Ruler
- Felt-tip markers
  (in at least four colors)

2. Crease the square across the other diagonal, and unfold. (If you printed the template, place it on the folding surface, drawing-side down. Fold and crease it along both diagonals, and unfold.)

1. Fold up the corner of a sheet of paper to meet the opposite edge, as shown. Trace the edge of the paper with a pencil and unfold the paper. Using the ruler as a straightedge, cut out the square with the craft knife and cutting mat (or see template 44, page 310, and trim the excess paper from the square template).

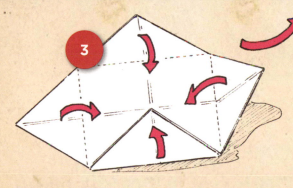

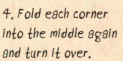

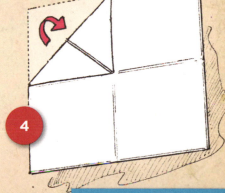

4. Fold each corner into the middle again and turn it over.

3. Fold each corner into the middle to make a smaller square. Turn the square over.

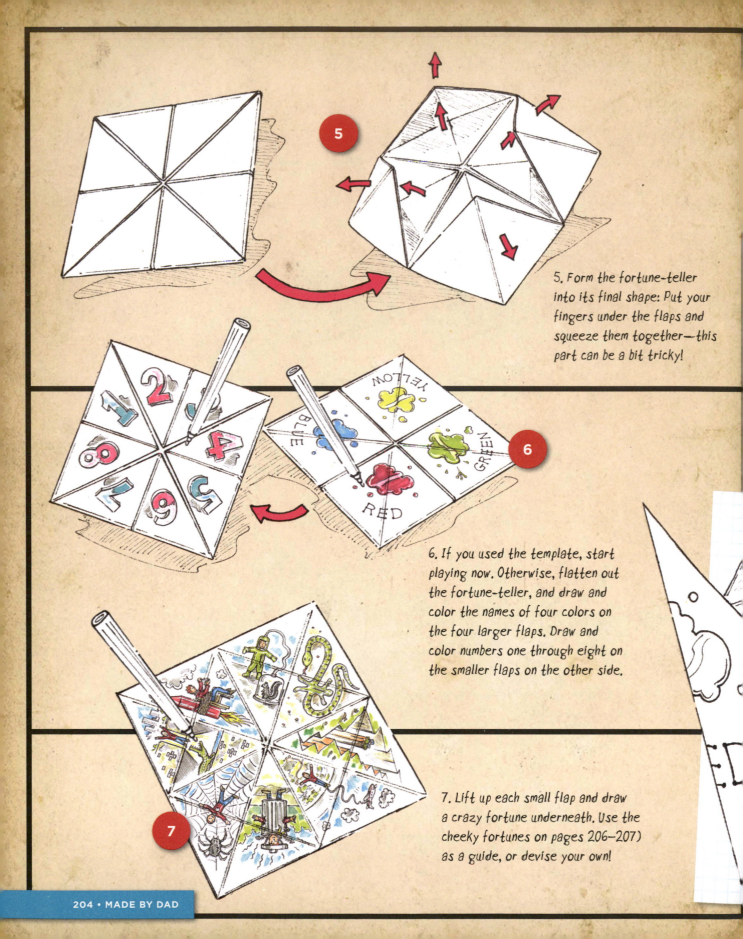

5. Form the fortune-teller into its final shape: Put your fingers under the flaps and squeeze them together—this part can be a bit tricky!

6. If you used the template, start playing now. Otherwise, flatten out the fortune-teller, and draw and color the names of four colors on the four larger flaps. Draw and color numbers one through eight on the smaller flaps on the other side.

7. Lift up each small flap and draw a crazy fortune underneath. Use the cheeky fortunes on pages 206–207) as a guide, or devise your own!

HOW TO PLAY

Find a willing participant and ask him to pick a color. Spell out the color, opening and closing the fortune-teller in alternate directions for each letter. Reveal the numbers inside the fortune-teller to the person. Ask him to pick a number. Lift up the flap under the number to reveal the person's fate.

COLOR-COORDINATE YOUR TREATS!

PRO-DAD TIP: Here's a cool idea. Flip your fortune-teller upside down and turn it into a cool jelly bean storage container. It's perfect for birthday parties!

A GUIDE TO YOUR CHEEKY FORTUNE

1. HIGH CHAIR

Next time you eat breakfast, you'll be sitting in a high chair . . . a very high chair!

2. SKUNK SUIT

Hold your nose! You'll be spending a day in the dreaded skunk suit.

3. SNAKE SNACK

You'll be taking quite a long lunch! A giant anaconda will swallow you alive.

4. CANYON BED

An earthquake will leave you stranded on a precarious pillar of rock for six nights.

5. THE WEB

You'll be stuck on the web for a week, but not the sort of web you're used to!

6. CROC DROP

You better watch your step . . . because soon you'll find yourself in the mouth of a sewer croc!

7. FULL-METAL JACKET

It's a coat of many odors! And it's going to be on your back for two weeks.

8. JUMBO BUNGEE

Your next trip on a plane will result in a harrowing bungee skydive!

LEVEL: MEDIUM

MOUSE-EPHANT

Bigger than an elephant, this mouse is a cat's worst nightmare! Come between him and his favorite food (cheese and grass) and expect to feel the full force of those fearsome tusks!

NAME
MOUSE-EPHANT

SPEED

STRENGTH

SIZE

AGGRESSION

TRI-BITE

This mean-looking snake is not the speediest, but he doesn't have to be— fluffy chicks are his favorite food! You don't think that's very nice? Then make your own mouthy monster . . . one that eats Tri-Bites.

NAME
TRI-BITE

SPEED

STRENGTH

SIZE

AGGRESSION

MATERIALS

- Printer paper
- Ruler
- Pencil
- Scissors
- Felt-tip markers

- Paper glue
- Access to a photocopier or printer (optional)

It's amazing what you can do with a little bit of paper and lots of imagination. These monster mash-ups will keep your kids busy for hours. And they're a double whammy of crafting pleasure: fun to make *and* fun to collect.

SNOTEROUS
Don't stand too close, this mucus-covered blob is more dangerous than you might think. Just one sneeze and that'll be the end of you! He's also rather partial to eyeballs, so don't stare. It's rude . . . and dangerous.

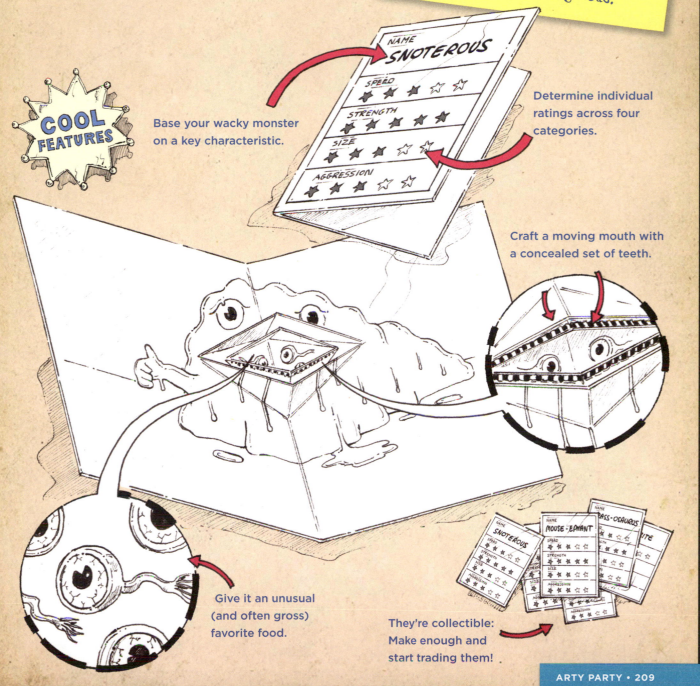

COOL FEATURES

Base your wacky monster on a key characteristic.

Determine individual ratings across four categories.

NAME
SNOTEROUS
SPEED
STRENGTH
SIZE
AGGRESSION

Craft a moving mouth with a concealed set of teeth.

Give it an unusual (and often gross) favorite food.

They're collectible: Make enough and start trading them!

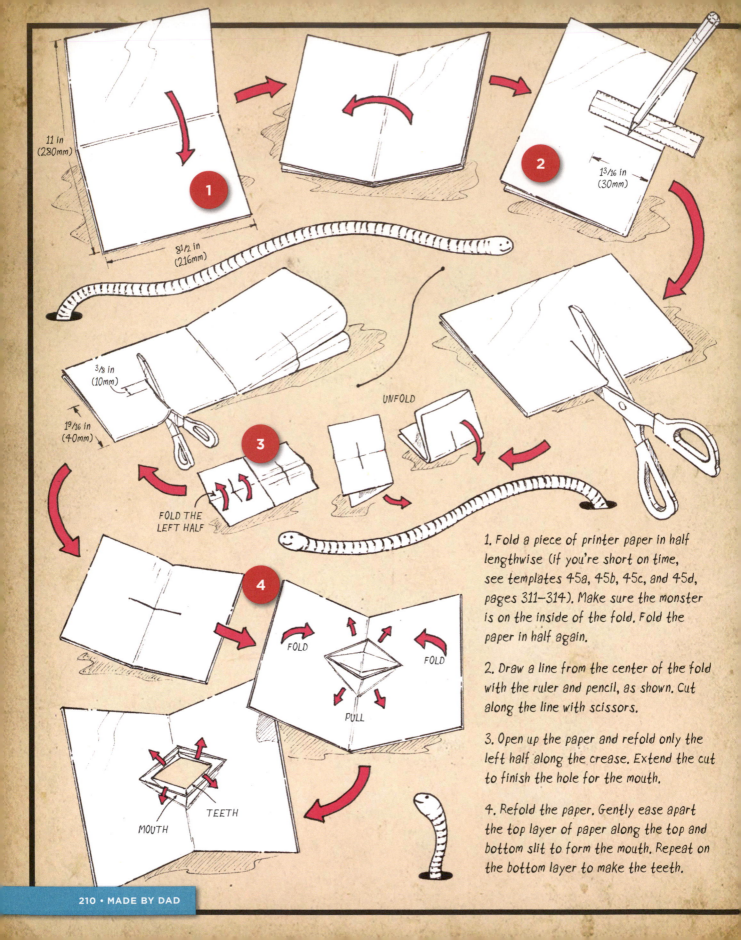

11 in
(280mm)

8½ in
(216mm)

1³/₁₆ in
(30mm)

③/₈ in
(10mm)

1⁹/₁₆ in
(40mm)

UNFOLD

FOLD THE
LEFT HALF

FOLD

FOLD

PULL

TEETH

MOUTH

1. Fold a piece of printer paper in half
lengthwise (if you're short on time,
see templates 45a, 45b, 45c, and 45d,
pages 311–314). Make sure the monster
is on the inside of the fold. Fold the
paper in half again.

2. Draw a line from the center of the fold
with the ruler and pencil, as shown. Cut
along the line with scissors.

3. Open up the paper and refold only the
left half along the crease. Extend the cut
to finish the hole for the mouth.

4. Refold the paper. Gently ease apart
the top layer of paper along the top and
bottom slit to form the mouth. Repeat on
the bottom layer to make the teeth.

GRASS-OSAURUS

He may not be the strongest (Mouse-Ephant would win in an arm wrestle), but this hunk of turf is very grumpy. So approach carefully . . . Although worms are his favorite food, he's been known to scarf up little boys and girls as well!

NAME
GRASS-OSAURUS

SPEED

STRENGTH

SIZE

AGGRESSION

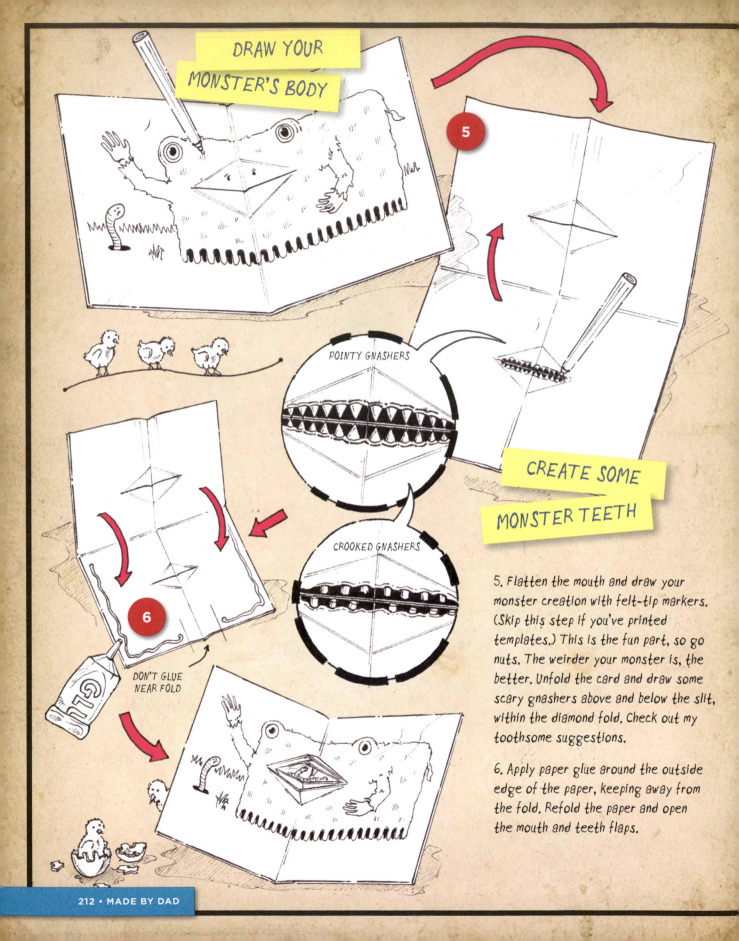

DRAW YOUR MONSTER'S BODY

5

POINTY GNASHERS

CROOKED GNASHERS

6

DON'T GLUE NEAR FOLD

GLU

CREATE SOME MONSTER TEETH

5. Flatten the mouth and draw your monster creation with felt-tip markers. (Skip this step if you've printed templates.) This is the fun part, so go nuts. The weirder your monster is, the better. Unfold the card and draw some scary gnashers above and below the slit, within the diamond fold. Check out my toothsome suggestions.

6. Apply paper glue around the outside edge of the paper, keeping away from the fold. Refold the paper and open the mouth and teeth flaps.

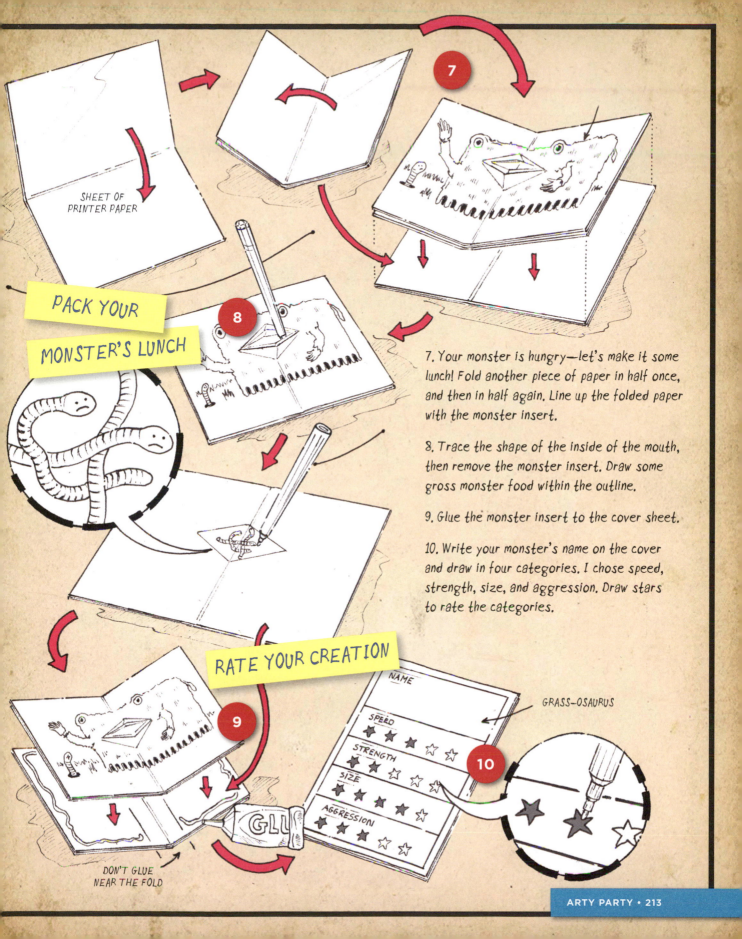

SHEET OF
PRINTER PAPER

7

PACK YOUR

MONSTER'S LUNCH

8

9

7. Your monster is hungry—let's make it some lunch! Fold another piece of paper in half once, and then in half again. Line up the folded paper with the monster insert.

8. Trace the shape of the inside of the mouth, then remove the monster insert. Draw some gross monster food within the outline.

9. Glue the monster insert to the cover sheet.

10. Write your monster's name on the cover and draw in four categories. I chose speed, strength, size, and aggression. Draw stars to rate the categories.

RATE YOUR CREATION

NAME

GRASS-OSAURUS

SPEED

STRENGTH

SIZE

10

AGGRESSION

GLU

DON'T GLUE
NEAR THE FOLD

BEE SWARM CHANDELIER

LEVEL: EASY

The latest must-have decor item: an insect infestation! Originally, I wanted to hang a canopy of flies over my boys' beds, but I thought the pesky nature of the bugs might limit its appeal. So, here's a cute bee version instead. It's a simple technique, though, so feel free to make your own unique swarms.

MATERIALS

- Craft knife and cutting mat
- Medium-sized corrugated cardboard box
- Drafting compass
- Ruler
- Pencil
- Thread
- Hot glue gun and glue sticks
- Velcro wall tabs
- White lightweight cardstock
- Felt-tip markers (black and yellow)
- Scissors
- Access to a photocopier or printer (optional)

1. Use the craft knife to cut out a large panel from the cardboard box.

2. Draw the cutting plan of three concentric circles on the panel with the drafting compass. Cut around the outer circle on the cutting mat.

3. Mark eight evenly spaced lines on each circle, offsetting the marks so that they are not in line. Make a hole at each intersection with the pencil.

CIRCLE RADII
5¹³/16 in (147mm)
4¹⁵/16 in (125mm)
2¹²/16 in (70mm)

60 in (152cm)

4. Cut a length of thread (about 60", 152 cm), push it through one of the holes, and secure with hot glue. Repeat for the remaining fifteen holes.

5. Attach one half of each Velcro tab on the top of the circle, and the other halves to the ceiling. Then press it up to hang.

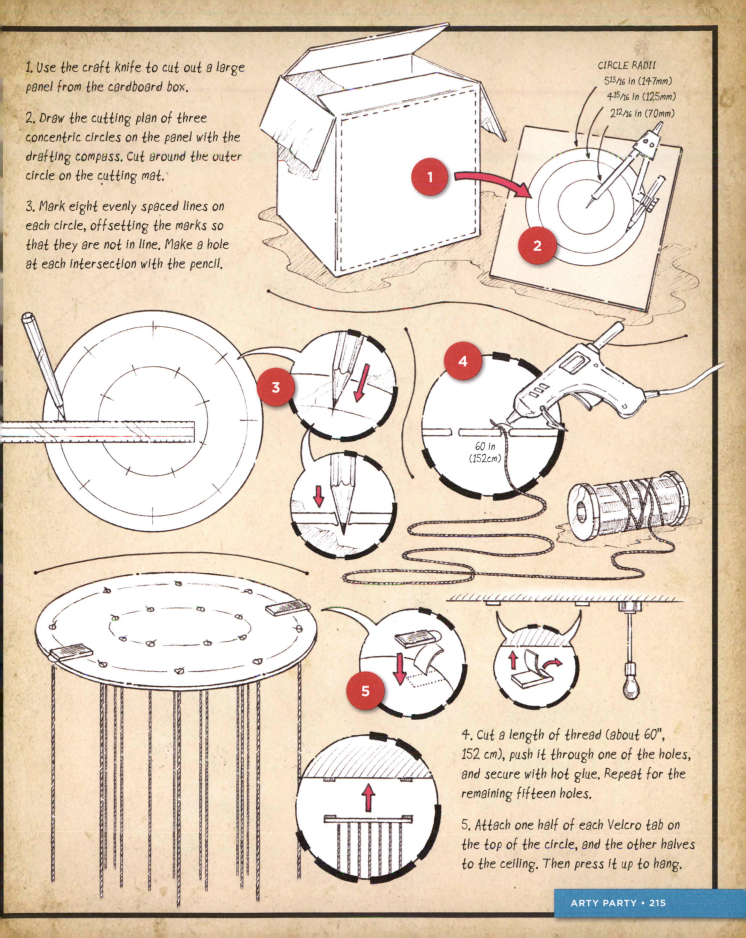

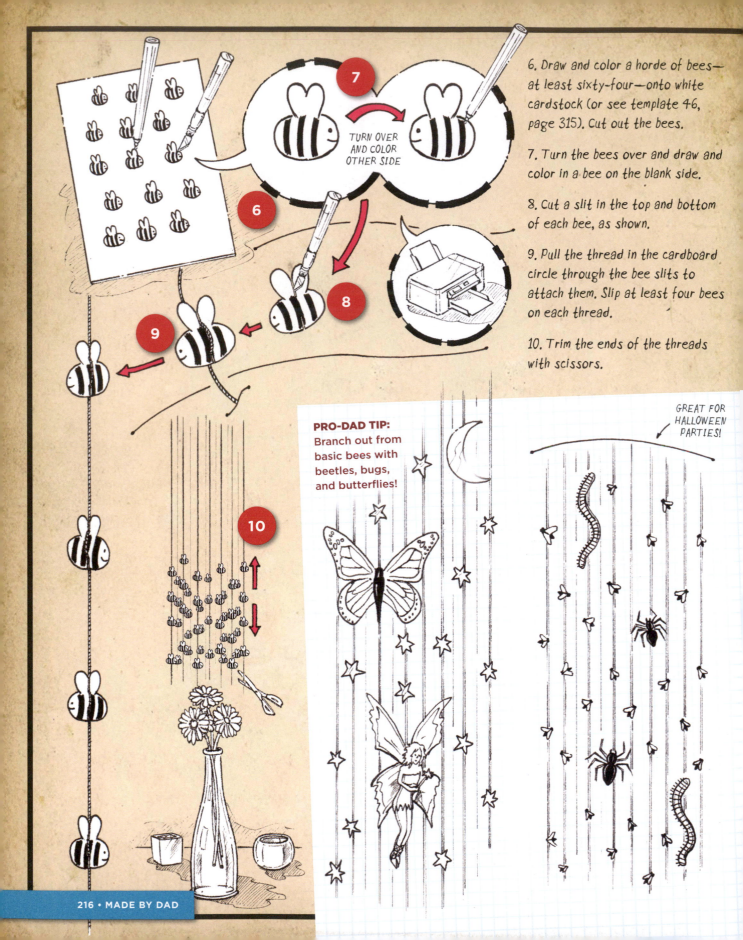

6. Draw and color a horde of bees— at least sixty-four—onto white cardstock (or see template 46, page 315). Cut out the bees.

7. Turn the bees over and draw and color in a bee on the blank side.

8. Cut a slit in the top and bottom of each bee, as shown.

9. Pull the thread in the cardboard circle through the bee slits to attach them. Slip at least four bees on each thread.

10. Trim the ends of the threads with scissors.

TURN OVER AND COLOR OTHER SIDE

PRO-DAD TIP: Branch out from basic bees with beetles, bugs, and butterflies!

GREAT FOR HALLOWEEN PARTIES!

SNEAKY CAKE THIEF

LEVEL: EASY

I think the sneaky thief on pages 173, 187, and 197 has finally given up looking for hidden treasures and turned his attention to something easier: cupcakes! This creeping crook will definitely encourage a smile at mealtimes—especially children's parties. And what's more, it's easy to make!

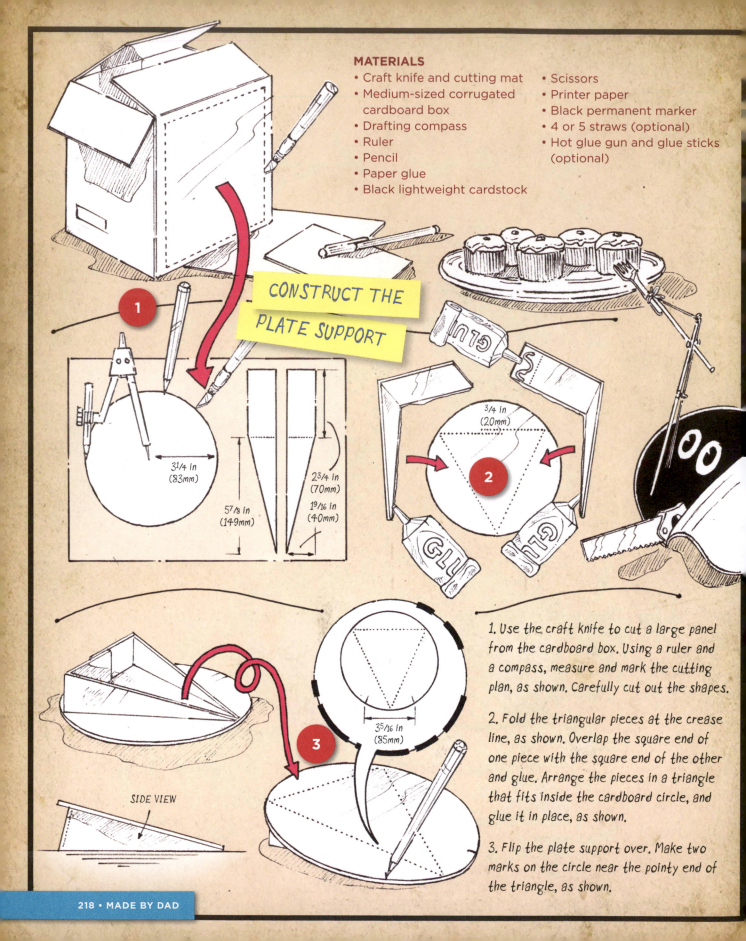

MATERIALS

- Craft knife and cutting mat
- Medium-sized corrugated cardboard box
- Drafting compass
- Ruler
- Pencil
- Paper glue
- Black lightweight cardstock
- Scissors
- Printer paper
- Black permanent marker
- 4 or 5 straws (optional)
- Hot glue gun and glue sticks (optional)

CONSTRUCT THE PLATE SUPPORT

1

3¼ in (83mm)

5⅞ in (149mm)

2¾ in (70mm)

1⁹/₁₆ in (40mm)

2

¾ in (20mm)

3

SIDE VIEW

3⁵/₁₆ in (85mm)

1. Use the craft knife to cut a large panel from the cardboard box. Using a ruler and a compass, measure and mark the cutting plan, as shown. Carefully cut out the shapes.

2. Fold the triangular pieces at the crease line, as shown. Overlap the square end of one piece with the square end of the other and glue. Arrange the pieces in a triangle that fits inside the cardboard circle, and glue it in place, as shown.

3. Flip the plate support over. Make two marks on the circle near the pointy end of the triangle, as shown.

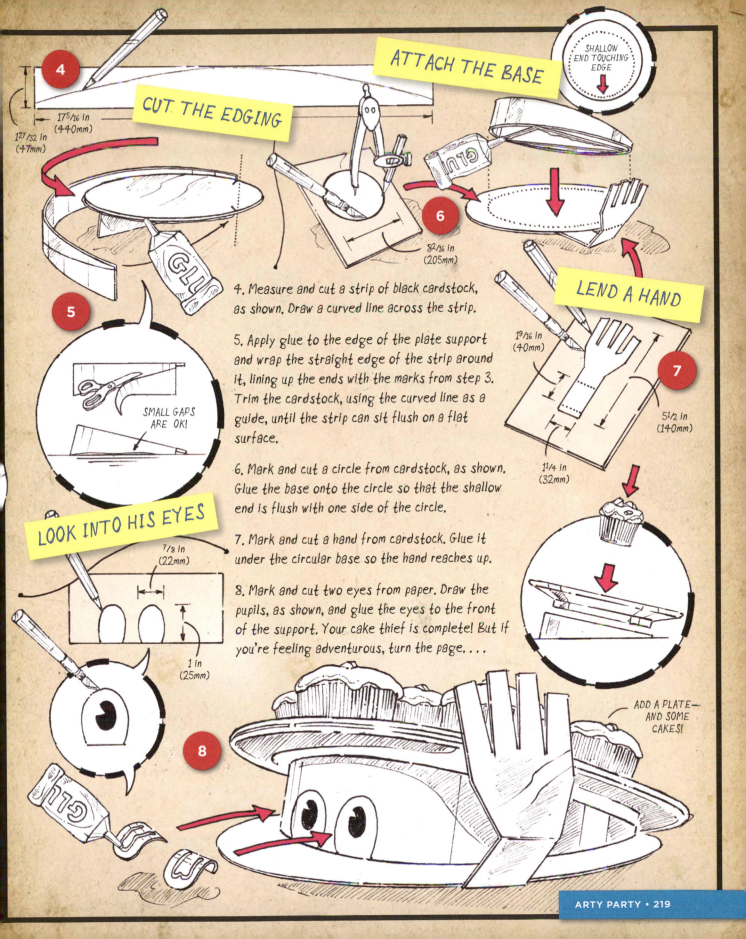

4

17⁵/₁₆ in (440mm)

1²⁷/₃₂ in (47mm)

CUT THE EDGING

ATTACH THE BASE

SHALLOW END TOUCHING EDGE

GLU

6

8²/₁₆ in (205mm)

LEND A HAND

1⁹/₁₆ in (40mm)

7

5¹/₂ in (140mm)

1¹/₄ in (32mm)

5

SMALL GAPS ARE OK!

GLU

LOOK INTO HIS EYES

⁷/₈ in (22mm)

1 in (25mm)

8

GLU

ADD A PLATE— AND SOME CAKES!

4. Measure and cut a strip of black cardstock, as shown. Draw a curved line across the strip.

5. Apply glue to the edge of the plate support and wrap the straight edge of the strip around it, lining up the ends with the marks from step 3. Trim the cardstock, using the curved line as a guide, until the strip can sit flush on a flat surface.

6. Mark and cut a circle from cardstock, as shown. Glue the base onto the circle so that the shallow end is flush with one side of the circle.

7. Mark and cut a hand from cardstock. Glue it under the circular base so the hand reaches up.

8. Mark and cut two eyes from paper. Draw the pupils, as shown, and glue the eyes to the front of the support. Your cake thief is complete! But if you're feeling adventurous, turn the page. . . .

PRO-DAD TIP: Add a long, sneaky straw! Mark and cut a second hand and glue it to the base opposite the first. Then flatten one end of a straw and fold it widthwise to form a point. Push the point into the end of a second straw. Repeat to make a "chain" of straws. Cut a small hole between the cake thief's eyes. Insert one end of the long straw. Then bend the straw into a crazy squiggle, securing each bend with a dollop of hot glue. The final touch: a glass of juice to wash down the cake!

RADIOACTIVE SPORTS DRINKS

LEVEL: EASY

If you think sugar makes your kids hyper, wait until they get their hands on these radioactive water bottles. Your little superheroes will get the ultimate energy boost, courtesy of the placebo effect. Perfect for passing out at parties, or for making a scene during school lunch break or gym class!

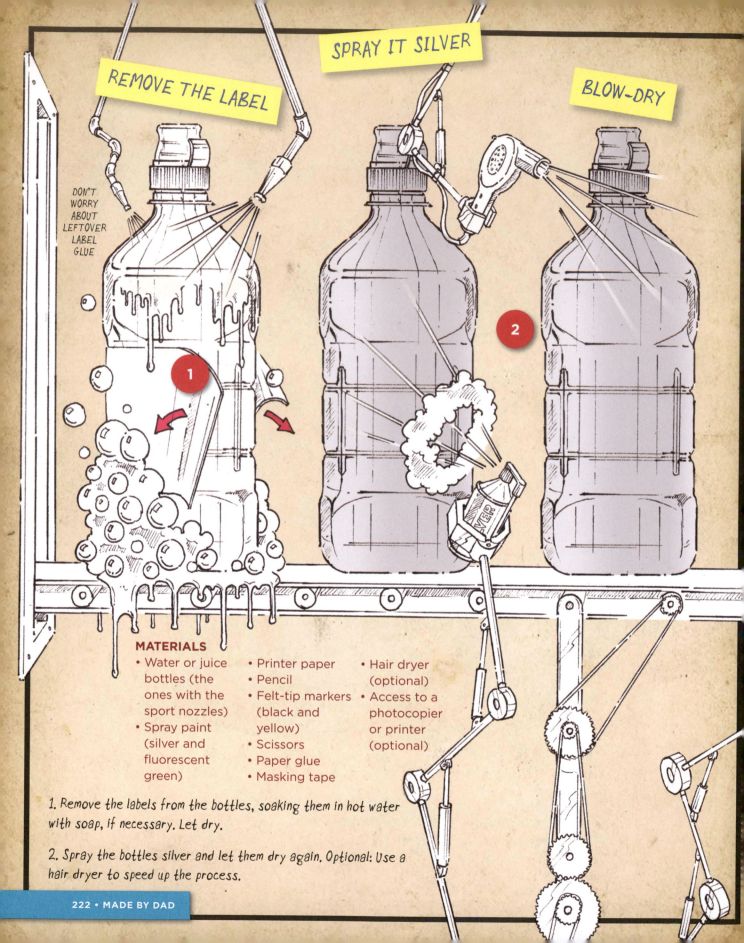

REMOVE THE LABEL

SPRAY IT SILVER

BLOW-DRY

DON'T WORRY ABOUT LEFTOVER LABEL GLUE

MATERIALS

- Water or juice bottles (the ones with the sport nozzles)
- Spray paint (silver and fluorescent green)
- Printer paper
- Pencil
- Felt-tip markers (black and yellow)
- Scissors
- Paper glue
- Masking tape
- Hair dryer (optional)
- Access to a photocopier or printer (optional)

1. Remove the labels from the bottles, soaking them in hot water with soap, if necessary. Let dry.

2. Spray the bottles silver and let them dry again. Optional: Use a hair dryer to speed up the process.

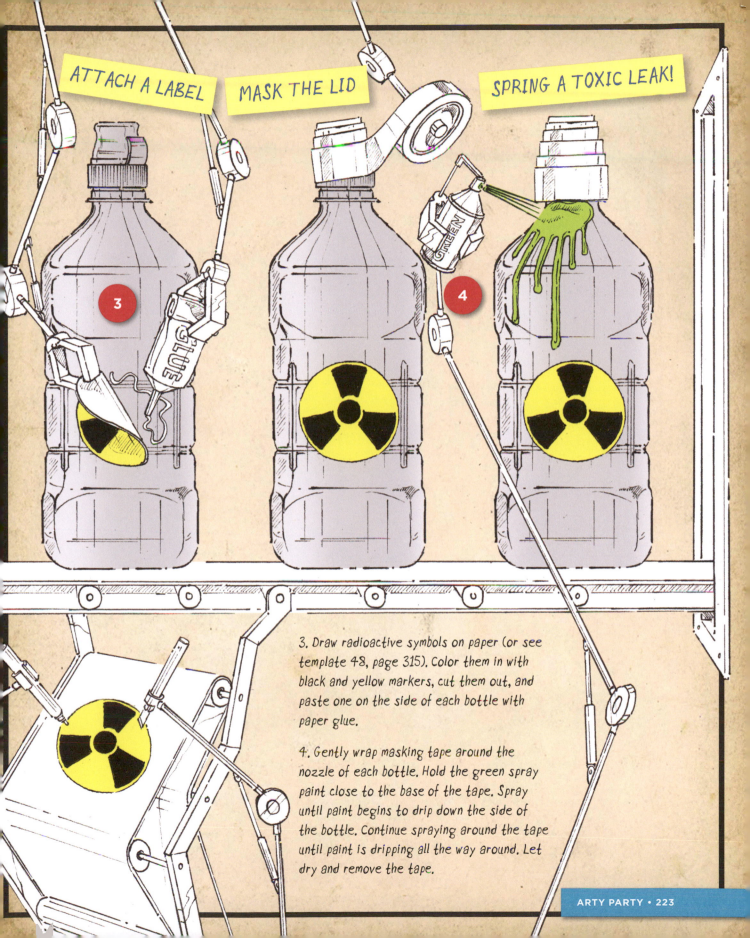

ATTACH A LABEL

MASK THE LID

SPRING A TOXIC LEAK!

3

4

3. Draw radioactive symbols on paper (or see template 48, page 315). Color them in with black and yellow markers, cut them out, and paste one on the side of each bottle with paper glue.

4. Gently wrap masking tape around the nozzle of each bottle. Hold the green spray paint close to the base of the tape. Spray until paint begins to drip down the side of the bottle. Continue spraying around the tape until paint is dripping all the way around. Let dry and remove the tape.

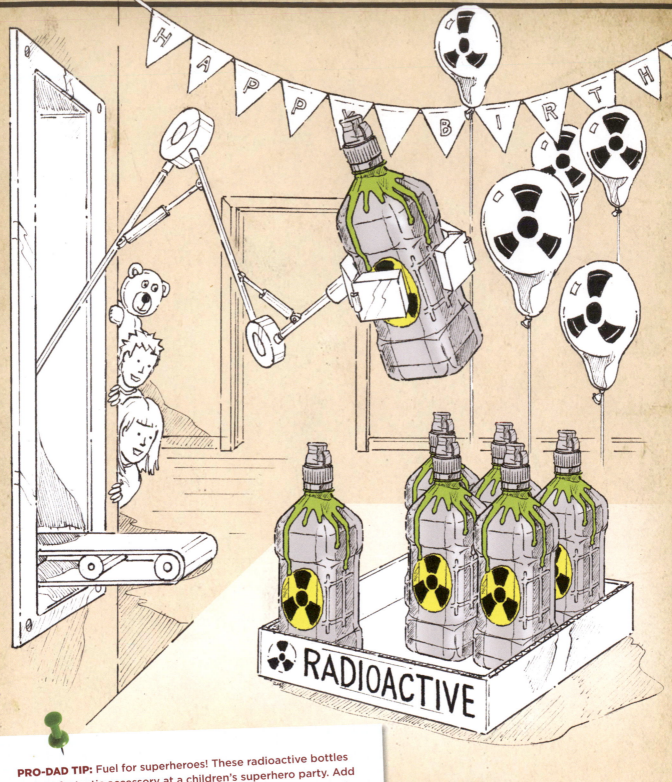

PRO-DAD TIP: Fuel for superheroes! These radioactive bottles make a fantastic accessory at a children's superhero party. Add to the effect by making a tray from a cardboard box to hold the bottles. Label it "RADIOACTIVE" for maximum impact!

SNAKES AND LADDERS

LEVEL: MEDIUM

Snakes and Ladders might be a classic children's game, but the fact that the ladders never *actually* went up and the snakes never *technically* went down always bothered me. Here's my chance to put that right! The good news is that you need look no farther than your food cupboard for the construction equipment. Don't worry about following my design too closely—the beauty of this project is that it can be adapted to include whatever you have in the pantry.

MATERIALS

- Selection of cans and cereal boxes (I used one large cereal box, one small cereal box, four bean tin cans, and one tuna fish tin can.)
- Printer paper
- Scissors
- Paper glue or clear tape
- Black permanent marker
- Felt-tip markers
- White lightweight cardstock
- Access to a photocopier or printer (optional)

1. Cover the cereal boxes and cans with paper. Secure the paper with tape or glue.

2. Arrange the boxes and cans, as shown, on a sheet of paper.

3. Use the black permanent marker to draw the game board and numbers on the paper. (I fit sixty-two.) Start at the bottom and work to the top.

4. Use felt-tip markers to draw four to five snakes and four to five ladders onto white cardstock (or see template 49, page 316). Cut them out and glue them to the game board to create various intersections.

5. Draw and color some fun game pieces on the cardstock and cut them out. Include a foldover tab at the bottom so they can stand up.

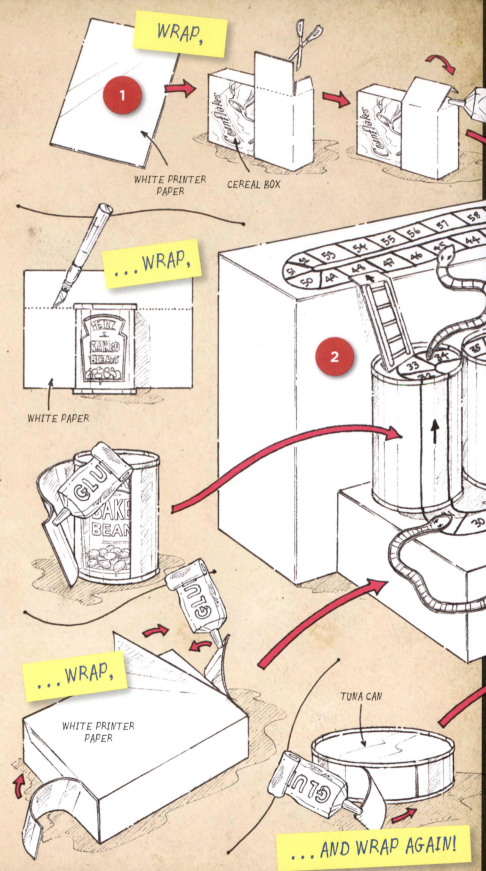

WRAP,

WHITE PRINTER PAPER

CEREAL BOX

... WRAP,

WHITE PAPER

... WRAP,

WHITE PRINTER PAPER

TUNA CAN

... AND WRAP AGAIN!

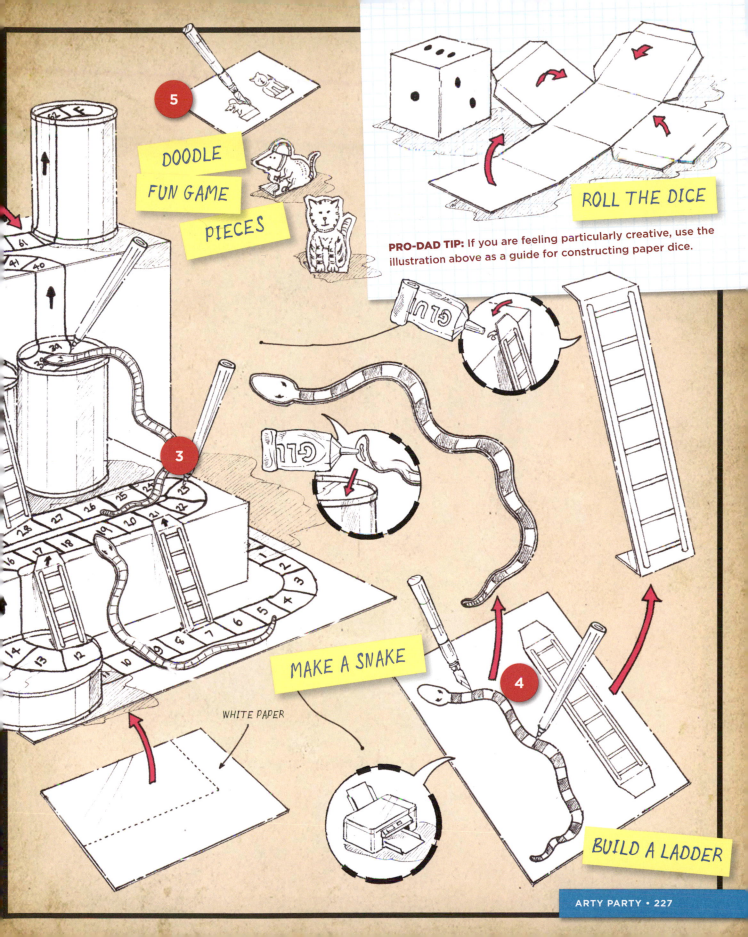

ROLL THE DICE

PRO-DAD TIP: If you are feeling particularly creative, use the illustration above as a guide for constructing paper dice.

DOODLE FUN GAME PIECES

MAKE A SNAKE

WHITE PAPER

BUILD A LADDER

WHACKY GADGET ARMY PAPER TARGETS

LEVEL: EASY

GOOD SHOT!

Tired of dodging high-velocity Nerf gun darts? If so, you'll need to show your kids something that's more fun to shoot at than Mom and Dad (and that's not easy). These whacky targets are no guarantee, but they should buy you at least half an hour!

MATERIALS

- Ruler
- Pencil
- 5 toilet paper tubes
- Printer paper
- Craft knife and cutting mat
- Silver spray paint

- White light- or medium-weight cardstock
- Felt-tip markers
- Scissors
- Paper glue
- Access to a photocopier or printer (optional)

TAKE A STAND

1½/16 in
(50mm)

PAPER STRAIGHT-EDGE

FOLD

1½/16 in
(50mm)

7/8 in
(22mm)

1

2

1. Mark two vertical lines with a ruler and pencil, as shown, on opposite sides of a toilet paper tube. Use the straight edge of a piece of paper to draw a line between the two marks.

2. Cut along the horizontal line with the craft knife. Cut out a small vertical section at the middle of the horizontal line to make two flaps. Fold the flaps in to make a backstop for the targets.

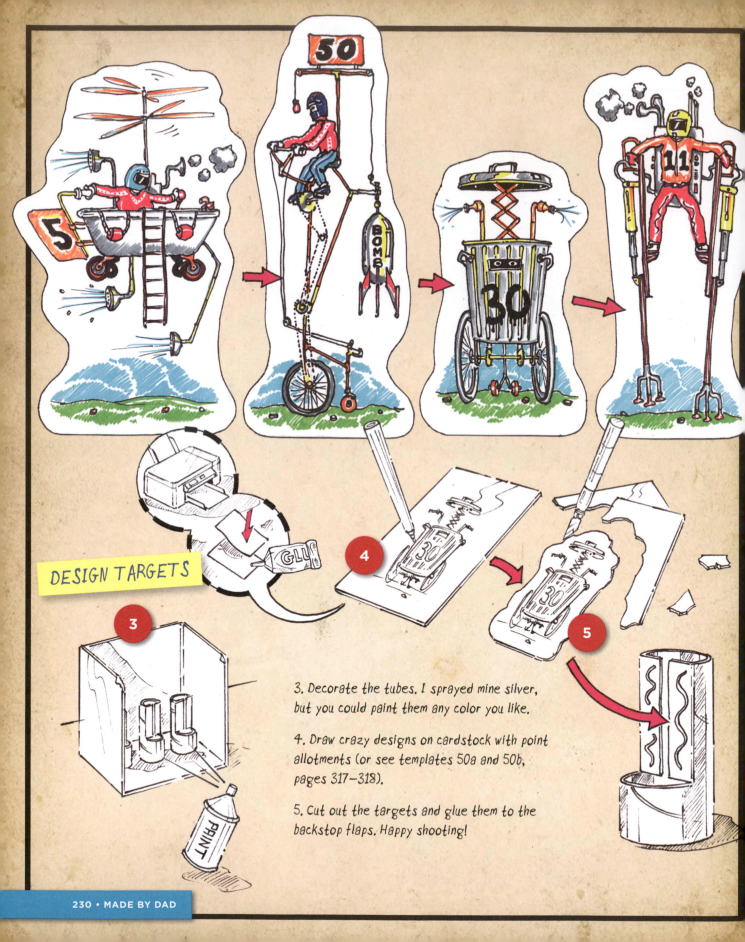

DESIGN TARGETS

3. Decorate the tubes. I sprayed mine silver, but you could paint them any color you like.

4. Draw crazy designs on cardstock with point allotments (or see templates 50a and 50b, pages 317–318).

5. Cut out the targets and glue them to the backstop flaps. Happy shooting!

SABER-TOOTHED SPIDERS

LEVEL: EASY

I f you think fruit flies are a nuisance, you obviously haven't encountered fruit spiders! With razor sharp teeth and lightning reflexes, these guardians of the fruit bowl are guaranteed to scare off the flies . . . *and* Mom!

MATERIALS
- 8 large paper clips (for each spider)
- Hot glue gun and glue sticks
- Black plasticine
- Blunt knife
- Craft knife and cutting mat or scissors
- Ruler
- Printer paper
- Pencil
- Black permanent marker
- Access to a photocopier or printer (optional)

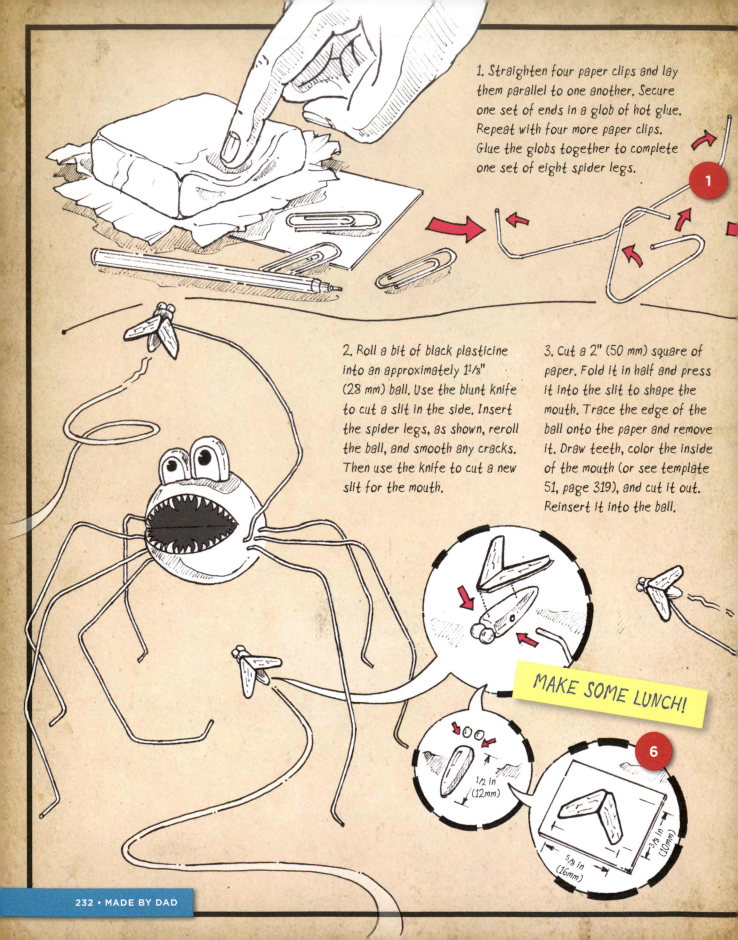

1. Straighten four paper clips and lay them parallel to one another. Secure one set of ends in a glob of hot glue. Repeat with four more paper clips. Glue the globs together to complete one set of eight spider legs.

1

2. Roll a bit of black plasticine into an approximately 1⅛" (28 mm) ball. Use the blunt knife to cut a slit in the side. Insert the spider legs, as shown, reroll the ball, and smooth any cracks. Then use the knife to cut a new slit for the mouth.

3. Cut a 2" (50 mm) square of paper. Fold it in half and press it into the slit to shape the mouth. Trace the edge of the ball onto the paper and remove it. Draw teeth, color the inside of the mouth (or see template 51, page 319), and cut it out. Reinsert it into the ball.

MAKE SOME LUNCH!

½ in (12mm)

6

⅜ in (10mm)

⅝ in (16mm)

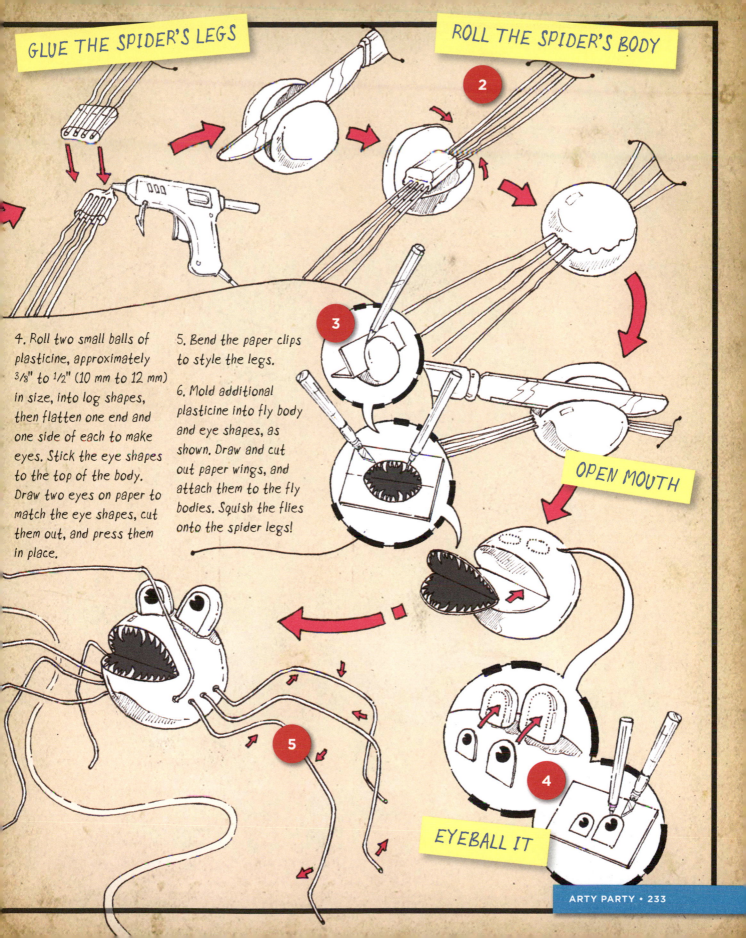

GLUE THE SPIDER'S LEGS

ROLL THE SPIDER'S BODY

2

4. Roll two small balls of plasticine, approximately ³⁄₈" to ¹⁄₂" (10 mm to 12 mm) in size, into log shapes, then flatten one end and one side of each to make eyes. Stick the eye shapes to the top of the body. Draw two eyes on paper to match the eye shapes, cut them out, and press them in place.

5. Bend the paper clips to style the legs.

6. Mold additional plasticine into fly body and eye shapes, as shown. Draw and cut out paper wings, and attach them to the fly bodies. Squish the flies onto the spider legs!

3

OPEN MOUTH

EYEBALL IT

5

4

MODERN FOSSILS

LEVEL: MEDIUM

MATERIALS

- Aluminum foil or several clean, disposable pie pans
- Small object(s) to fossilize
- Plaster of paris
- Mixing bowl and stirring stick
- Poster paint (yellow, red, and blue)
- Paint brush
- Water glass
- PVA glue

A BOBOSAURUS BUILDERCUS!

You don't need to wait hundreds of years in unique environmental conditions to make these fossils. . . . All you need is an everyday object, plaster of paris, water, and about fifteen minutes. Anything with a distinctive shape can easily become a fossil: crushed soda cans, undesirable toys from a fast-food restaurant, toy guns or water pistols past their prime, and rusty tools.

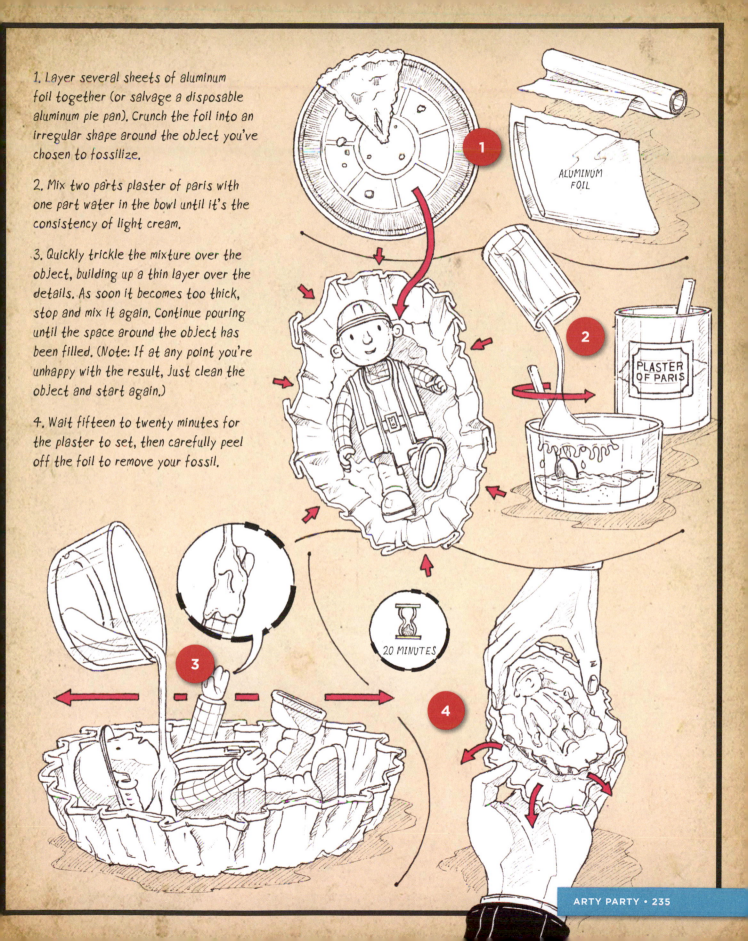

1. Layer several sheets of aluminum foil together (or salvage a disposable aluminum pie pan). Crunch the foil into an irregular shape around the object you've chosen to fossilize.

2. Mix two parts plaster of paris with one part water in the bowl until it's the consistency of light cream.

3. Quickly trickle the mixture over the object, building up a thin layer over the details. As soon it becomes too thick, stop and mix it again. Continue pouring until the space around the object has been filled. (Note: If at any point you're unhappy with the result, just clean the object and start again.)

4. Wait fifteen to twenty minutes for the plaster to set, then carefully peel off the foil to remove your fossil.

ALUMINUM FOIL

PLASTER OF PARIS

20 MINUTES

PRO-DAD TIP: Coat a toy dinosaur to make a more conventional fossil. Then party like it's 1999 B.C.! For a fun party activity, bury some fossils in a backyard sandbox and have the kids dig for them Indiana Jones–style!

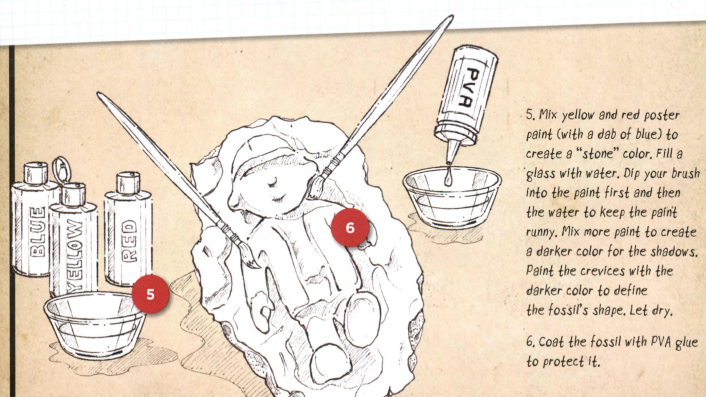

5. Mix yellow and red poster paint (with a dab of blue) to create a "stone" color. Fill a glass with water. Dip your brush into the paint first and then the water to keep the paint runny. Mix more paint to create a darker color for the shadows. Paint the crevices with the darker color to define the fossil's shape. Let dry.

6. Coat the fossil with PVA glue to protect it.

SHARK BITE PAPER PLATE

LEVEL: EASY

MOM, THERE'S A SHARK ON MY SANDWICH!

Next time you make a peanut butter and jelly sandwich, why not serve it up with a little danger? Tell your little ones that if they don't eat their sandwich, Jaws will scarf it up, and you're sure to get back empty plates.

MATERIALS
- Paper plate
- Ruler
- Pencil
- Craft knife and cutting mat
- Black medium-weight cardstock
- Paper glue
- PB&J (or other filling) sandwich
- Table knife
- Access to a photocopier or printer (optional)
- Extra jam (optional)

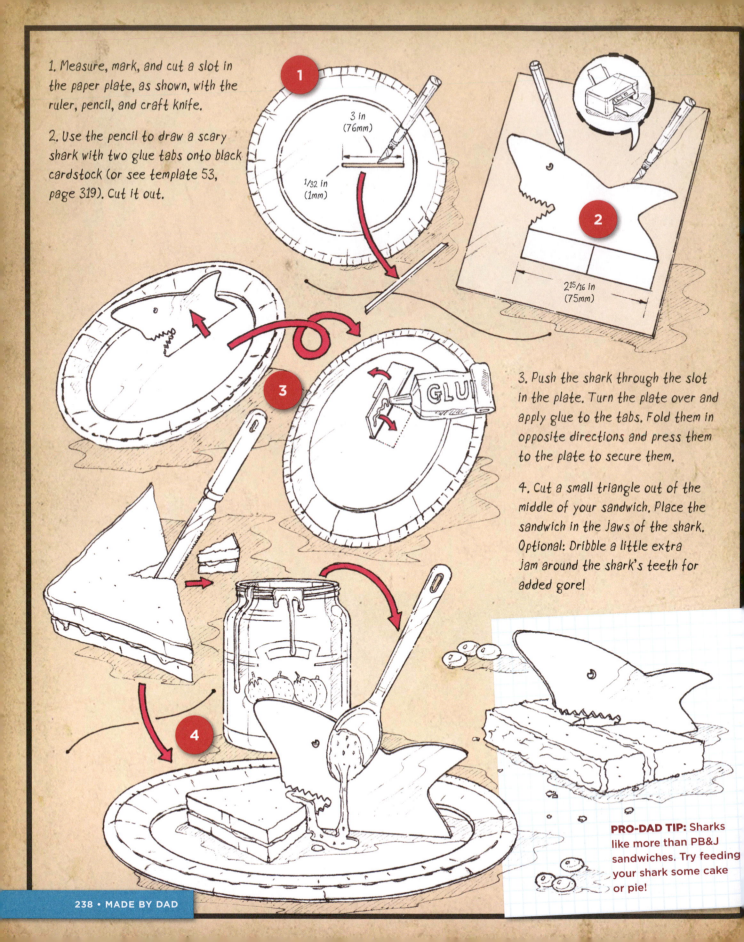

1. Measure, mark, and cut a slot in the paper plate, as shown, with the ruler, pencil, and craft knife.

2. Use the pencil to draw a scary shark with two glue tabs onto black cardstock (or see template 53, page 319). Cut it out.

3 in (76mm)

1/32 in (1mm)

2 15/16 in (75mm)

GLUE

3. Push the shark through the slot in the plate. Turn the plate over and apply glue to the tabs. Fold them in opposite directions and press them to the plate to secure them.

4. Cut a small triangle out of the middle of your sandwich. Place the sandwich in the jaws of the shark. Optional: Dribble a little extra jam around the shark's teeth for added gore!

PRO-DAD TIP: Sharks like more than PB&J sandwiches. Try feeding your shark some cake or pie!

PLAYFUL PARENTING

GIRAFFE GROWTH CHART

LEVEL: EASY

A giraffe knows all about being tall, so he's the perfect character to help chart your child's height. (He's also not bad looking, so you get the benefit of some great wall art that has a practical application.) Next time the grandparents exclaim, "You've grown so much since I last saw you," your child will be able to reply, "Yes, one and three quarter inches to be precise!"

MATERIALS

- Craft knife and cutting mat
- Medium-sized corrugated cardboard box
- Ruler
- Pencil
- White lightweight cardstock (poster size)
- Cardboard tube about 27" (686 mm) long (an empty wrapping paper tube works well)
- Paper glue
- Hot glue gun and glue sticks
- Poster paint (orange, brown, and black)
- Paintbrush
- Black permanent marker
- Velcro tabs
- Access to a photocopier or printer (optional)

1. Use the craft knife to cut off one flap from the cardboard box.

2. Draw a giraffe's head onto the flap, keeping the bottom edge straight (or see template 54, page 320). Cut it out on the cutting mat.

3. Then use the craft knife to cut two sides (they may be joined by a fold, as shown) from the cardboard box.

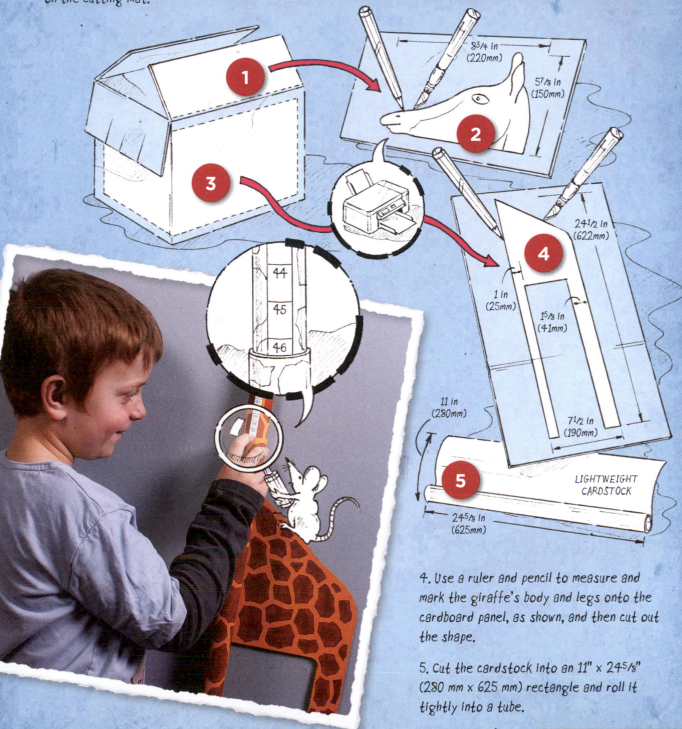

8³/₄ in (220mm)

5⁷/₈ in (150mm)

24¹/₂ in (622mm)

1 in (25mm)

1⁵/₈ in (41mm)

11 in (280mm)

7¹/₂ in (190mm)

24⁵/₈ in (625mm)

LIGHTWEIGHT CARDSTOCK

4. Use a ruler and pencil to measure and mark the giraffe's body and legs onto the cardboard panel, as shown, and then cut out the shape.

5. Cut the cardstock into an 11" x 24⁵/₈" (280 mm x 625 mm) rectangle and roll it tightly into a tube.

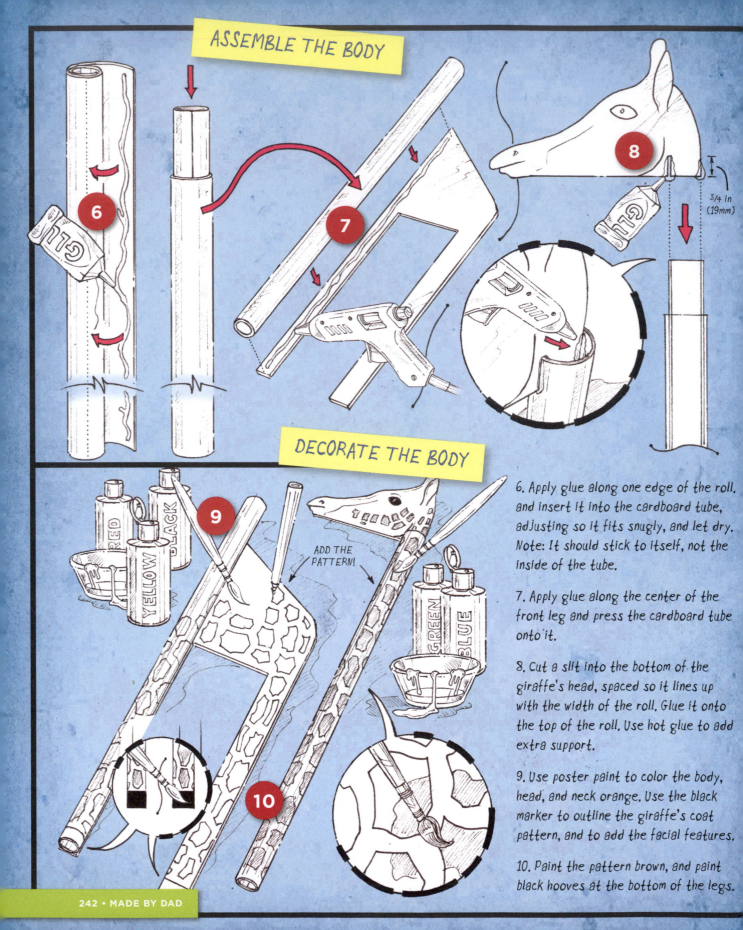

ASSEMBLE THE BODY

6

7

8

3/4 in (19mm)

GLU

DECORATE THE BODY

9

10

RED

YELLOW

BLACK

GREEN

BLUE

ADD THE PATTERN!

6. Apply glue along one edge of the roll. and insert it into the cardboard tube, adjusting so it fits snugly, and let dry. Note: It should stick to itself, not the inside of the tube.

7. Apply glue along the center of the front leg and press the cardboard tube onto it.

8. Cut a slit into the bottom of the giraffe's head, spaced so it lines up with the width of the roll. Glue it onto the top of the roll. Use hot glue to add extra support.

9. Use poster paint to color the body, head, and neck orange. Use the black marker to outline the giraffe's coat pattern, and to add the facial features.

10. Paint the pattern brown, and paint black hooves at the bottom of the legs.

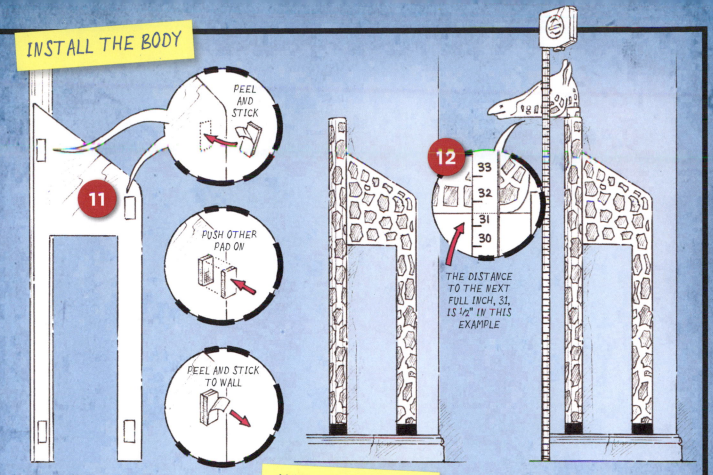

PEEL AND STICK

PUSH OTHER PAD ON

PEEL AND STICK TO WALL

11

12

33
32
31
30

THE DISTANCE TO THE NEXT FULL INCH, 31, IS ½" IN THIS EXAMPLE

MAKE IT MEASURE

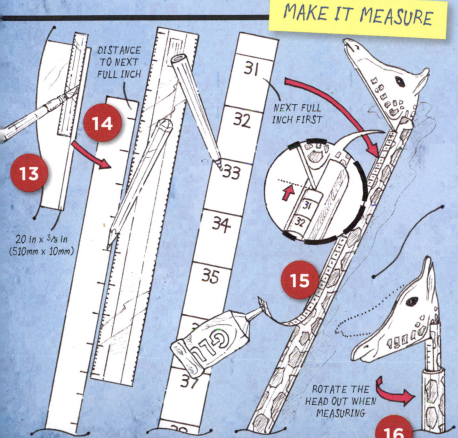

DISTANCE TO NEXT FULL INCH

13

14

20 in x ³⁄₈ in (510mm x 10mm)

31
32
33
34
35
37

NEXT FULL INCH FIRST

31
32

15

16

ROTATE THE HEAD OUT WHEN MEASURING

11. Attach Velcro tabs to the back of the giraffe. Then position the giraffe against the wall and push firmly to secure.

12. With the head at its lowest position, measure the height from the floor to the bottom edge of the head. Note the distance to the next full inch, as shown. Remove the head and neck.

13. Measure and cut a long ³⁄₈" (10 mm)–wide strip of lightweight cardstock.

14. Use a ruler to mark the distance to the next full inch from the top, then mark off full inches for the rest of its length.

15. Add the corresponding numbers, then glue the strip onto the neck, aligning it with the bottom edge of the head.

16. Insert the neck back into the body and you are now ready to start measuring!

MAKE IT ~ FOR ~ MOMMY

·MOMMY·
·REWARDS·

·1 FREE·
**BREAKFAST
IN BED**
SERVED ON RECEIPT
OF THIS CARD

·MOMMY·
·REWARDS·

·1 FREE·
**HOT
BEVERAGE**
SERVED ON RECEIPT
OF THIS CARD

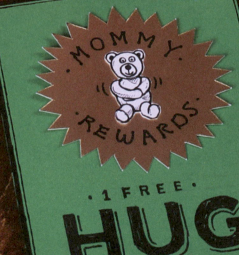

·MOMMY·
·REWARDS·

·1 FREE·
HUG
GIVEN ON RECEIPT
OF THIS CARD

MATERIALS

- Ruler
- Pencil
- Scissors
- Colored lightweight cardstock
  (red, green, yellow, and gold)
- Drafting compass
- Craft knife and cutting mat
- Printer paper
- Paper glue
- Black permanent marker
- Access to a photocopier
  or printer (optional)

Forget perfume, flowers, and chocolates, give Mommy the ultimate present—coupons! Redeemable on the spot (no excuses), these coupons offer Mommy everything from breakfast in bed to a hug, or just a compliment. Note to kids: These work for dads, too (hint, hint).

1. Measure, mark, and cut a 3¹¹⁄₁₆" × 6" (94 mm × 152 mm) rectangle from colored cardstock.

2. Using a compass, draw two concentric circles, as shown, on the back of the gold cardstock. Then draw a zigzag between the two circles and cut along the line to make a medallion.

3. Draw a small picture (or see template 55, page 321), and cut it out. Center and glue it onto the medallion and glue the medallion to the rectangle.

4. Use the marker to write "mommy rewards" on the medallion and the reward on the coupon, as shown.

ZEN NAPKINS

LEVEL: EASY

HEY! THOSE STONES LOOK LIKE MUFFIN CRUMBS!

MATERIALS
• Food crumbs
• Napkins
• Black felt-tip marker

This super simple coffee shop activity will induce a few minutes of Zen-like peace and quiet from the most animated child. My son enjoyed it so much I had to grab a couple of extra napkins for him to use at home, which extended the calm even further!

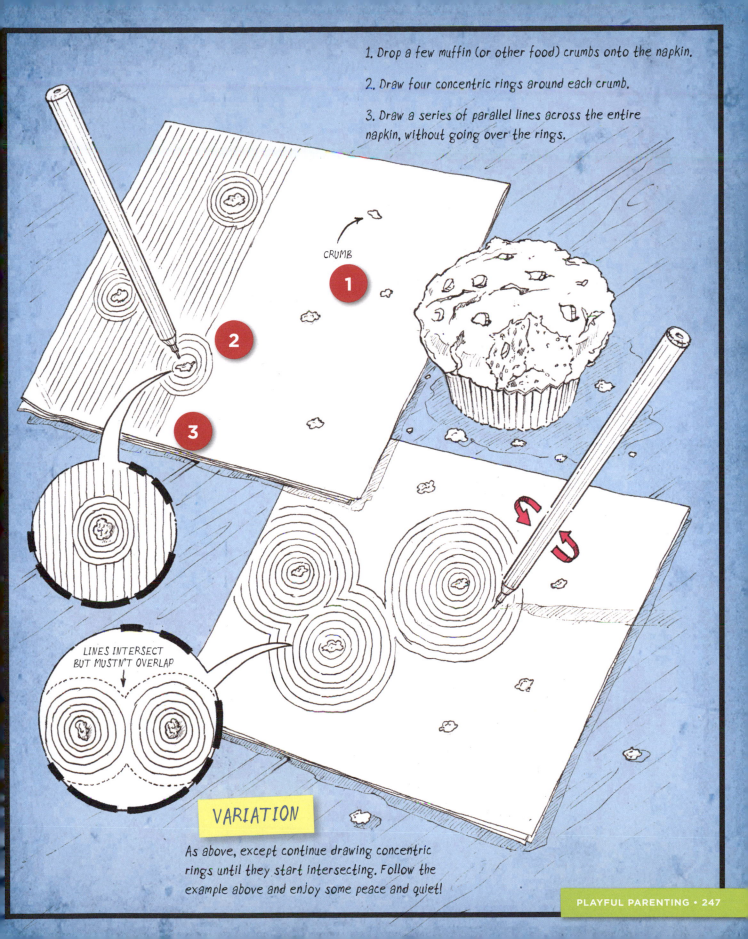

1. Drop a few muffin (or other food) crumbs onto the napkin.

2. Draw four concentric rings around each crumb.

3. Draw a series of parallel lines across the entire napkin, without going over the rings.

CRUMB

1

2

3

LINES INTERSECT BUT MUSTN'T OVERLAP

VARIATION

As above, except continue drawing concentric rings until they start intersecting. Follow the example above and enjoy some peace and quiet!

FRANKENSTEIN FLING

LEVEL: EASY

MATERIALS
- Ruler
- Pencil
- Craft knife and cutting mat
- Paper cup (16 oz, 454 g)
- Stirring stick
- Paper
- Felt-tip markers
- Paper glue
- Penny or other coin(s)
- Scissors (optional)
- Access to a photocopier or printer (optional)

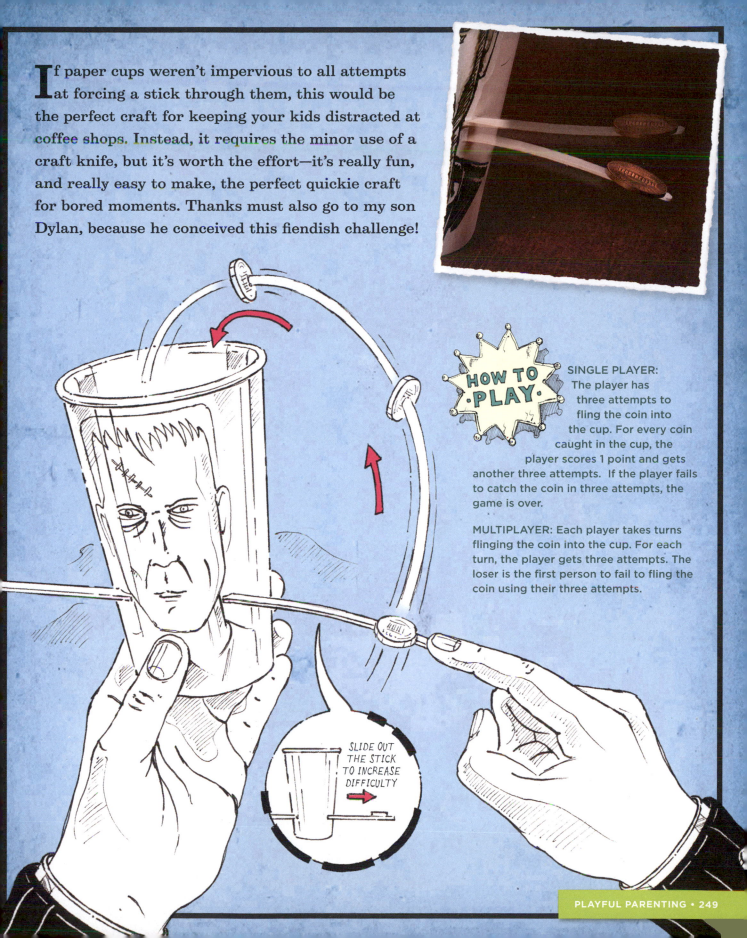

If paper cups weren't impervious to all attempts at forcing a stick through them, this would be the perfect craft for keeping your kids distracted at coffee shops. Instead, it requires the minor use of a craft knife, but it's worth the effort—it's really fun, and really easy to make, the perfect quickie craft for bored moments. Thanks must also go to my son Dylan, because he conceived this fiendish challenge!

HOW TO PLAY

SINGLE PLAYER: The player has three attempts to fling the coin into the cup. For every coin caught in the cup, the player scores 1 point and gets another three attempts. If the player fails to catch the coin in three attempts, the game is over.

MULTIPLAYER: Each player takes turns flinging the coin into the cup. For each turn, the player gets three attempts. The loser is the first person to fail to fling the coin using their three attempts.

SLIDE OUT
THE STICK
TO INCREASE
DIFFICULTY

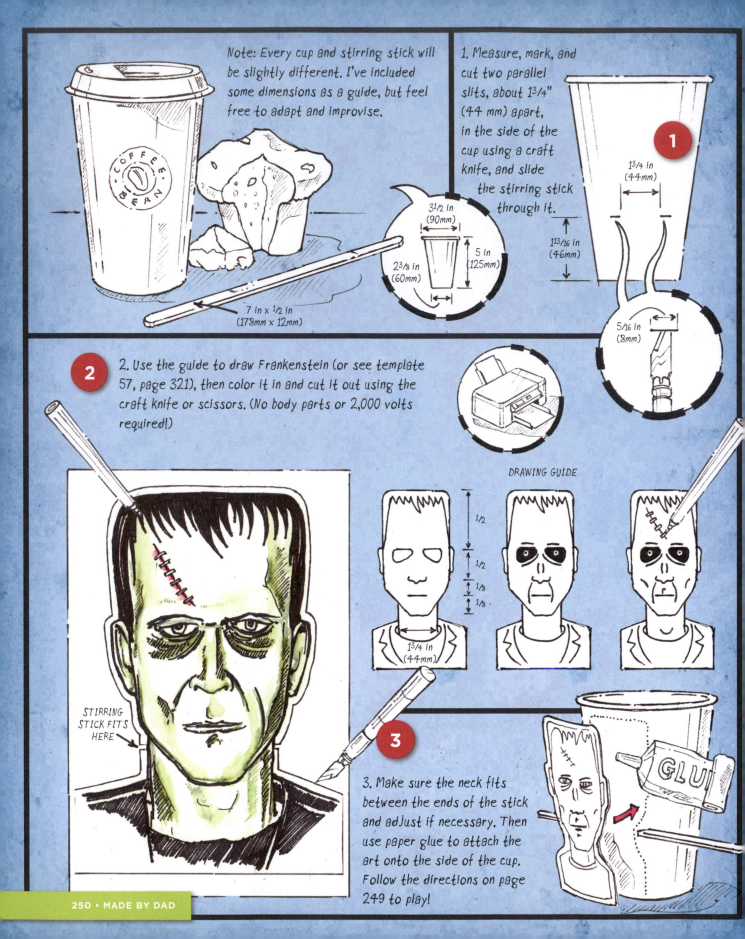

Note: Every cup and stirring stick will be slightly different. I've included some dimensions as a guide, but feel free to adapt and improvise.

1. Measure, mark, and cut two parallel slits, about 1³/₄" (44 mm) apart, in the side of the cup using a craft knife, and slide the stirring stick through it.

1

1³/₄ in (44mm)

1¹³/₁₆ in (46mm)

5/₁₆ in (8mm)

3¹/₂ in (90mm)

2³/₈ in (60mm)

5 in (125mm)

7 in x ¹/₂ in (178mm x 12mm)

2

2. Use the guide to draw Frankenstein (or see template 57, page 321), then color it in and cut it out using the craft knife or scissors. (No body parts or 2,000 volts required!)

DRAWING GUIDE

¹/₂

¹/₂

¹/₈

¹/₈

1³/₄ in (44mm)

STIRRING STICK FITS HERE

3

3. Make sure the neck fits between the ends of the stick and adjust if necessary. Then use paper glue to attach the art onto the side of the cup. Follow the directions on page 249 to play!

GLU

The trouble with giving flowers is that you can't wrap them up so they're never really a surprise. This ingenious little project will change all that: The outside of the box is an empty vase, but open it up and out pops a bunch of beautiful roses! It's fairly simple mechanics, but you'll need to get acquainted with the magical properties of foam core.

POP-UP ROSES

LEVEL: MEDIUM

MAKE IT ~ FOR ~ MOMMY

MATERIALS

- Ruler
- Pencil
- One sheet foam core
- Craft knife and cutting mat
- Paper glue
- Thin rubber band (3″, 76 mm long)
- Printer paper
- Felt-tip markers
- Large empty matchbox (minimum size 4¾″ x 2⅝″ x 1″, 121 mm x 67 mm x 25 mm)
- White lightweight cardstock
- Scissors (optional)
- Access to a photocopier or printer (optional)

OH! HOW SWEET OF YOU!

MESSAGE:

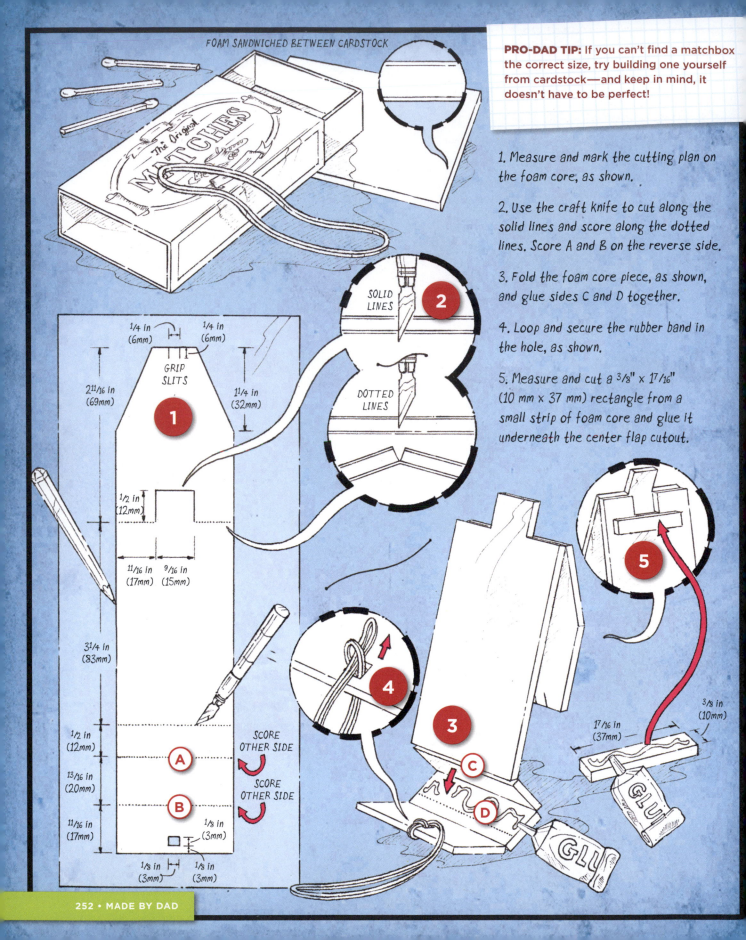

FOAM SANDWICHED BETWEEN CARDSTOCK

PRO-DAD TIP: If you can't find a matchbox the correct size, try building one yourself from cardstock—and keep in mind, it doesn't have to be perfect!

1. Measure and mark the cutting plan on the foam core, as shown.

2. Use the craft knife to cut along the solid lines and score along the dotted lines. Score A and B on the reverse side.

3. Fold the foam core piece, as shown, and glue sides C and D together.

4. Loop and secure the rubber band in the hole, as shown.

5. Measure and cut a 3/8" x 1 7/16" (10 mm x 37 mm) rectangle from a small strip of foam core and glue it underneath the center flap cutout.

The Original MATCHES

SOLID LINES

DOTTED LINES

GRIP SLITS

1/4 in (6mm)   1/4 in (6mm)

2 11/16 in (69mm)

1 1/4 in (32mm)

1/2 in (12mm)

11/16 in (17mm)   9/16 in (15mm)

3 1/4 in (83mm)

1/2 in (12mm)

A

SCORE OTHER SIDE

13/16 in (20mm)

B

SCORE OTHER SIDE

11/16 in (17mm)

1/8 in (3mm)

1/8 in (3mm)   1/8 in (3mm)

1 7/16 in (37mm)

3/8 in (10mm)

GLU

GLU

6¼ in (162mm)

5¼ in (134mm)

6

7

CREASE

CREASE

GLUE

8

KNOT

CENTERED

10

MESSAGE

3⅜ in (85mm)

2⅜ in (60mm)

9

MESSAGE

OPEN

OPEN

GLUE

GLUE

6. Draw roses on the paper (or see template 58, page 322), and color them in. Center and glue them onto the foam core piece, as shown.

7. Fold the foam core at the cutout, creasing the paper (right side in). Glue the bottom two segments of the long piece and insert them, centered, into one end of the matchbox, as shown.

8. Loop the end of the rubber band through the two grip slits (add a knot if the band is too loose).

9. Draw a vase onto cardstock (or see template 58, page 322), color it in, and measure and cut it to fit on the box sleeve.

10. Cut a 3⅜" x 2⅜" (85 mm x 60 mm) rectangle, write a message on it, and place it in the box. Then, with the top flower section folded down, fold the sides in. Fold it into the box, and slide it into the sleeve. Now go find Mom!

TARGET PLACE MAT

LEVEL: EASY

SCORE

1×20

1×15

1×10

3×5

TOTAL 60

Shh . . . don't tell the kids, but they'll do anything if you turn it into a game. But even beyond getting them to eat their veggies, this keeps them from making a mess! Start with 100 points and subtract for each spill (those farthest from the plate cost them more points)—they'll soon start watching how they eat!

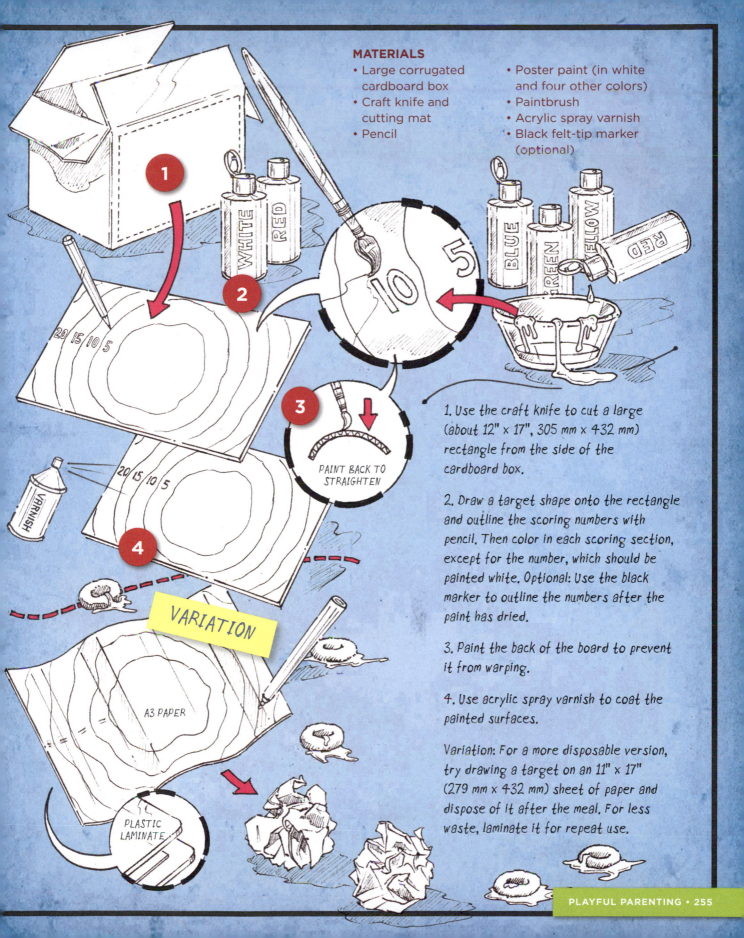

MATERIALS

- Large corrugated cardboard box
- Craft knife and cutting mat
- Pencil
- Poster paint (in white and four other colors)
- Paintbrush
- Acrylic spray varnish
- Black felt-tip marker (optional)

PAINT BACK TO STRAIGHTEN

VARIATION

A3 PAPER

PLASTIC LAMINATE

1. Use the craft knife to cut a large (about 12" x 17", 305 mm x 432 mm) rectangle from the side of the cardboard box.

2. Draw a target shape onto the rectangle and outline the scoring numbers with pencil. Then color in each scoring section, except for the number, which should be painted white. Optional: Use the black marker to outline the numbers after the paint has dried.

3. Paint the back of the board to prevent it from warping.

4. Use acrylic spray varnish to coat the painted surfaces.

Variation: For a more disposable version, try drawing a target on an 11" x 17" (279 mm x 432 mm) sheet of paper and dispose of it after the meal. For less waste, laminate it for repeat use.

MARS POP-UP CARD

LEVEL: EASY

This project was originally conceived as a way of keeping my kids occupied on a trip to a noodle bar. I used the back of a paper place mat for the drawing, and used the tip of a pen to punch around the pictures (MacGyver-style). Here's how to make one with slightly better equipment. Just follow some simple guidelines and add imagination—or green aliens. Or both.

MATERIALS

- White lightweight cardstock or printer paper
- Ruler
- Pencil
- Felt-tip markers
- Paintbrush
- Craft knife and cutting mat
- Access to a photocopier or printer (optional)

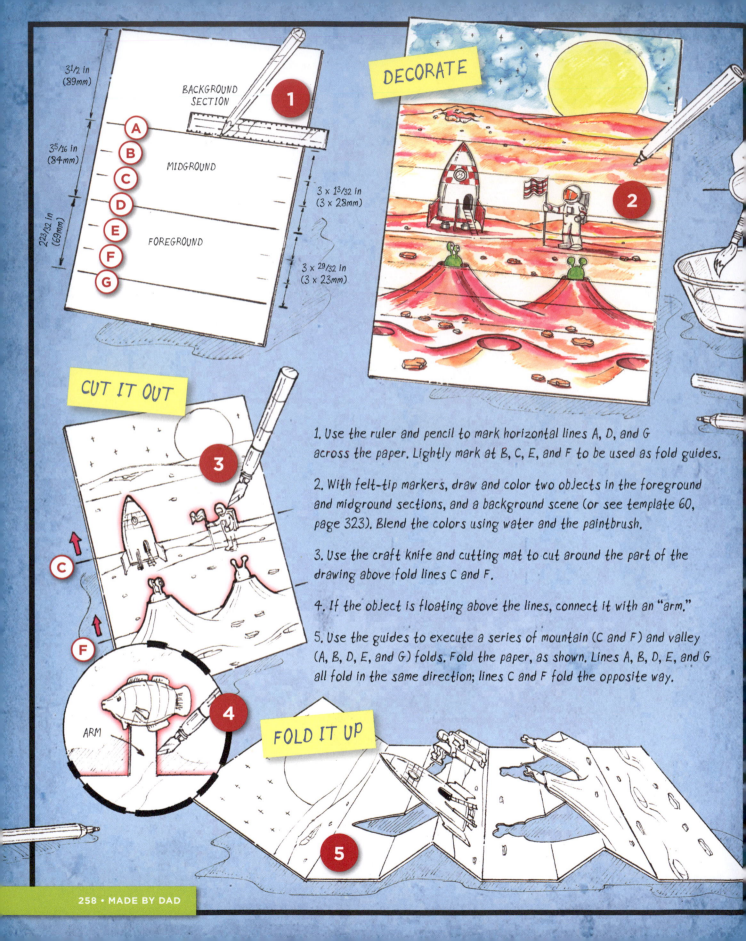

3½ in
(89mm)

3⁵/₁₆ in
(84mm)

2²³/₃₂ in
(69mm)

BACKGROUND SECTION

(A)
(B)
(C)
(D)
(E)
(F)
(G)

MIDGROUND

FOREGROUND

3 x 1³/₃₂ in
(3 x 28mm)

3 x ²⁹/₃₂ in
(3 x 23mm)

1

DECORATE

2

CUT IT OUT

3

(C)

(F)

ARM

4

FOLD IT UP

5

1. Use the ruler and pencil to mark horizontal lines A, D, and G across the paper. Lightly mark at B, C, E, and F to be used as fold guides.

2. With felt-tip markers, draw and color two objects in the foreground and midground sections, and a background scene (or see template 60, page 323). Blend the colors using water and the paintbrush.

3. Use the craft knife and cutting mat to cut around the part of the drawing above fold lines C and F.

4. If the object is floating above the lines, connect it with an "arm."

5. Use the guides to execute a series of mountain (C and F) and valley (A, B, D, E, and G) folds. Fold the paper, as shown. Lines A, B, D, E, and G all fold in the same direction; lines C and F fold the opposite way.

TRY BLENDING THE COLORS WITH A PAINTBRUSH AND WATER

COLLECT THEM ALL!

6. Set up the card for presentation.

7. Get your creative juices flowing and repeat as many times as desired with alternative themes.

TO SEE NEMO GETTING EATEN TURN TO PAGE 147!

LEVEL: EASY

MOUNTING PUTTY

A lmost every parent has the "how many sleeps until . . .?" conversation with their child, particularly as the countdown to a birthday or Christmas approaches. This easy project helps make the counting fun—and the wait less dreary. Simply attach a Z for each day and allow the child to remove one every morning, until the big day arrives.

MATERIALS
- Large corrugated cardboard box
- Craft knife and cutting mat
- Black permanent marker
- Poster paint
- Paintbrush
- Scissors
- Mounting putty

WARNING:

MOUNTING PUTTY

IS KID TREASURE!

The day after attaching the Zs to the wall, I went into the boys' bedroom and noticed they were all missing. After getting on my hands and knees, I discovered they were hidden under the bed, minus the putty—which I later learned had been painstakingly collected by my younger son and rolled into a big ball! (Or maybe he was just trying to rig the system.)

1. Cut one side of the cardboard box to open it up and lay it flat.

2. Use the marker to draw a series of ten to twelve Zs on the cardboard that range in size from about 8" to 1" (203 mm to 25 mm) tall.

3. To add stripes to the Zs, select three poster paint colors. Use the first color to paint two thick vertical stripes, two stripe widths apart (don't worry about painting over the lines).

4. Use the second color to paint two stripes adjacent to the first two, and repeat for the third color. (Note: Small Zs require fewer stripes.)

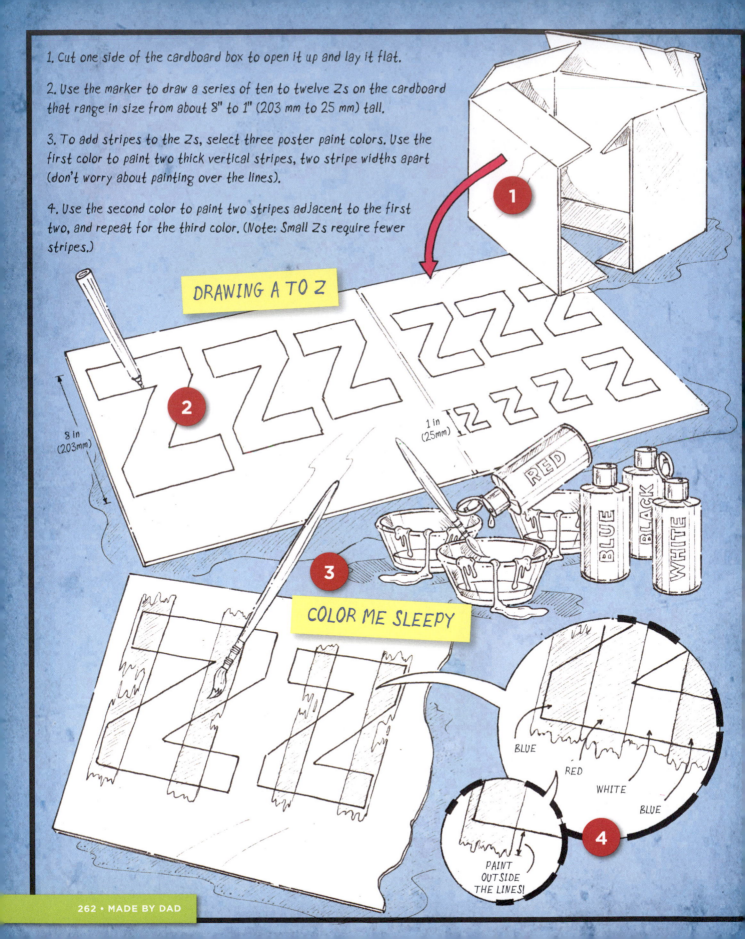

DRAWING A TO Z

1

2

8 in (203mm)

1 in (25mm)

RED

BLUE

BLACK

WHITE

3

COLOR ME SLEEPY

4

BLUE

RED

WHITE

BLUE

PAINT OUTSIDE THE LINES!

MAKE AN OUTLINE

5

NEAT CORNERS

UNTIDY CORNERS

BLACK

CUT IT OUT

MOUNTING PUTTY

6

7

8

STICK 'EM UP!

5. Paint a black outline around each Z. Make sure the two inside corners are painted neatly (all outside corners can be overlapped).

6. Use scissors to cut around the outline of each Z.

7. Press small wads of mounting putty on the back of each Z and arrange them on the wall in descending size order.

8. When it's time to start a countdown, remember to let the kids remove one each morning!

← LARGEST   SMALLEST →

ROCK, PAPER, SCISSORS DICE

LEVEL: EASY

BLUE WINS . . .
. . . SCISSORS CUT PAPER!

RED WINS . . .
. . . ROCK CRUSHES SCISSORS!

1. Measure and mark the cutting plan, on a sheet of red cardstock, as shown.

2. Cut it out using a craft knife, score the fold lines, and then fold it into a cube.

3. Use scissors to cut six 2⅝" (67 mm) squares from the transparency film.

4. Glue them along the inside edges of each cube panel.

Easily settle any family disagreement with these rock, paper, scissors dice. Simply choose your color (blue or red) and then let 'em roll. Remember: Rock beats scissors, scissors beats paper, and paper beats rock. The symbols will dictate the winner and loser.

MATERIALS

- Colored lightweight cardstock (red and blue)
- Ruler
- Pencil
- Craft knife and cutting mat
- Scissors
- Transparency film or any clear plastic
- Paper glue
- Black permanent marker

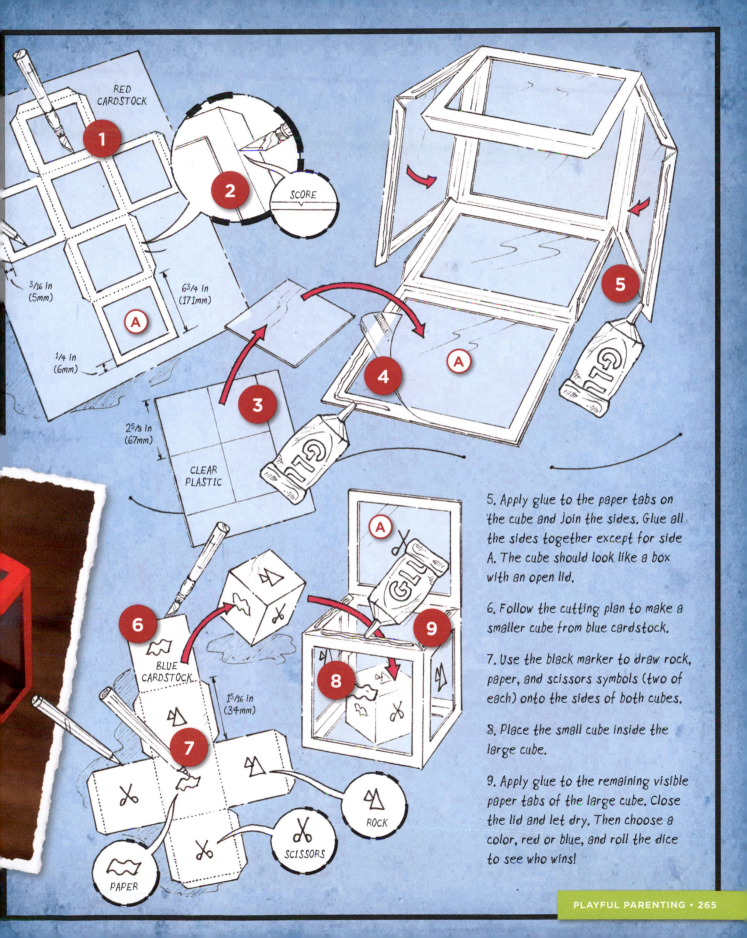

RED CARDSTOCK

1

2

SCORE

3/16 in (5mm)

6 3/4 in (171mm)

A

1/4 in (6mm)

2 5/8 in (67mm)

CLEAR PLASTIC

3

4

A

5

GLUE

A

GLUE

BLUE CARDSTOCK

1 5/16 in (34mm)

6

7

8

9

GLUE

PAPER

SCISSORS

ROCK

5. Apply glue to the paper tabs on the cube and join the sides. Glue all the sides together except for side A. The cube should look like a box with an open lid.

6. Follow the cutting plan to make a smaller cube from blue cardstock.

7. Use the black marker to draw rock, paper, and scissors symbols (two of each) onto the sides of both cubes.

8. Place the small cube inside the large cube.

9. Apply glue to the remaining visible paper tabs of the large cube. Close the lid and let dry. Then choose a color, red or blue, and roll the dice to see who wins!

HUGS AND KISSES CARD

MAKE IT ~FOR~ MOMMY

This might just be the perfect Mother's Day card. But it's also the perfect "any day" card—because any day is the right day to tell Mom how much she is loved! It's easy to make, and you can add as many hugs and kisses as you like.

MATERIALS

- Red lightweight cardstock
- Ruler
- Pencil
- Craft knife and cutting mat
- White lightweight cardstock
- Transparency film or any clear plastic
- Paper glue
- Black felt-tip marker
- Scissors (optional)
- Access to a photocopier or printer (optional)

AND LOTS !

WE LOVE YOU LO

6 in (152mm)

TRIM OFF

RED CARDSTOCK

1. Measure and cut the red cardstock. Draw lines to divide it into five equal sections, then accordion-fold it along the lines.

2. Draw XOXO on the front panel, connecting each letter to the folded edges (or see template 63, page 324). Cut out the letters.

3. Fold the white cardstock in half lengthwise. Then center and trace the folded red XOXO onto the front panel of the white cardstock.

4. Draw XOXO inside the traced line, leaving space between the letters. Cut them out and keep the centers of the Os. Write "We love you lots" on the cardstock, above the cutout.

5. Cut and then glue a 6½" x 2¾" (165 mm x 70 mm) rectangle of plastic onto the inside front cover of the card. Close the card, and glue the centers of the Os into place on top of the plastic.

6. Glue the folded red XOXO inside the card and write "and lots!" above it. Now share the love!

WHITE CARDSTOCK

WE LOVE YOU LOTS

CLEAR PLASTIC (TRANSPARENCY FILM)

GLU

AND LOTS!

"HOW DEEP IS YOUR LOVE?" CARD

LEVEL: EASY

MAKE IT ~ FOR ~ MOMMY

This interactive Valentine's Day card was originally knocked together in fifteen minutes (but don't tell my wife that). It's better than buying a card from a shop, so give it a go, and remember you don't have to wait for Valentine's Day to spread the love.

MATERIALS

- Pencil
- Long cardboard tube (an empty wrapping paper tube works well)
- Colored lightweight cardstock (various hues)
- Craft knife and cutting mat
- Paper glue
- Colored paper (various hues)
- Double-sided tape
- Ruler
- Black felt-tip marker
- Scissors
- Thread
- Hot glue gun and glue sticks
- 3 coins

1. Trace the end of the tube twice onto cardstock. Add a tab to the edge of one of the circles. Then cut them out and glue the tabbed circle to the outside edge of one end of the tube. Glue the tabless circle to the opposite end.

2. Wrap sheets of colored paper around the tube. Secure them with double-sided tape.

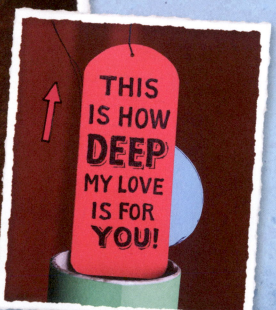

THIS IS HOW **DEEP** MY LOVE IS FOR YOU!

PULL

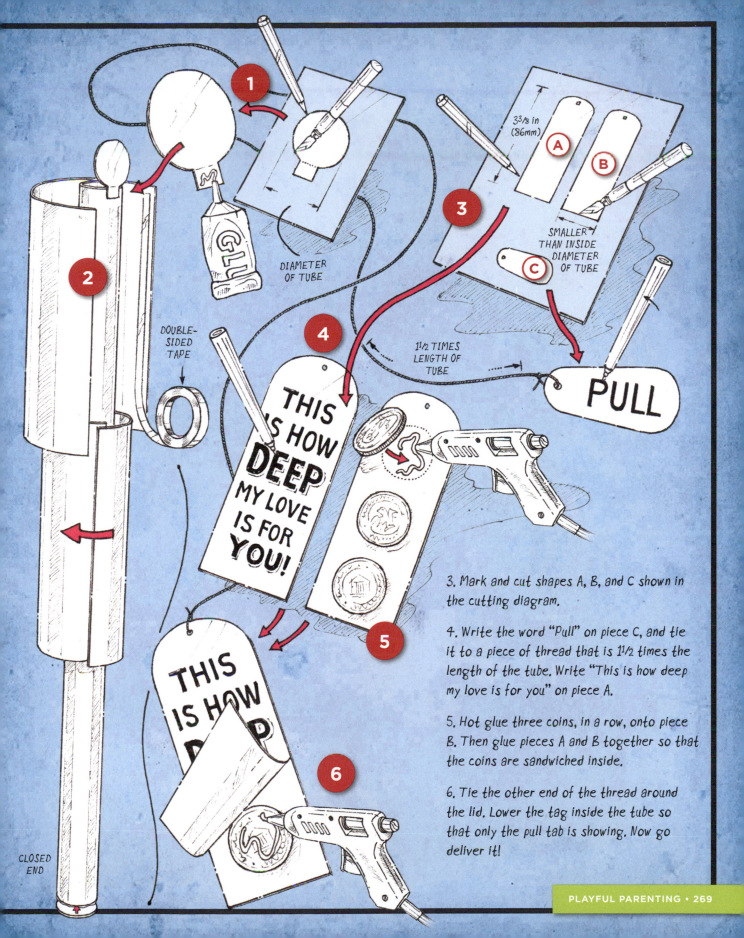

1

DIAMETER OF TUBE

GLUE

2

DOUBLE-SIDED TAPE

CLOSED END

3³⁄₈ in (86mm)

A **B**

3

SMALLER THAN INSIDE DIAMETER OF TUBE

C

4

1½ TIMES LENGTH OF TUBE

PULL

THIS IS HOW **DEEP** MY LOVE IS FOR **YOU!**

5

THIS IS HOW ~~D~~

6

3. Mark and cut shapes A, B, and C shown in the cutting diagram.

4. Write the word "Pull" on piece C, and tie it to a piece of thread that is 1½ times the length of the tube. Write "This is how deep my love is for you" on piece A.

5. Hot glue three coins, in a row, onto piece B. Then glue pieces A and B together so that the coins are sandwiched inside.

6. Tie the other end of the thread around the lid. Lower the tag inside the tube so that only the pull tab is showing. Now go deliver it!

SPIDER SURPRISE CARD

LEVEL: MEDIUM

MAKE IT ~ FOR ~ MOMMY

It's always fun to give Mom a surprise, and I don't mean an "I'll do the laundry for a week" type of surprise—more of a "there's a spider on your head" sort of surprise. Okay, we're not being that cruel, but if you think a spider in a card is a little mean, use it to make scary Halloween party invitations.

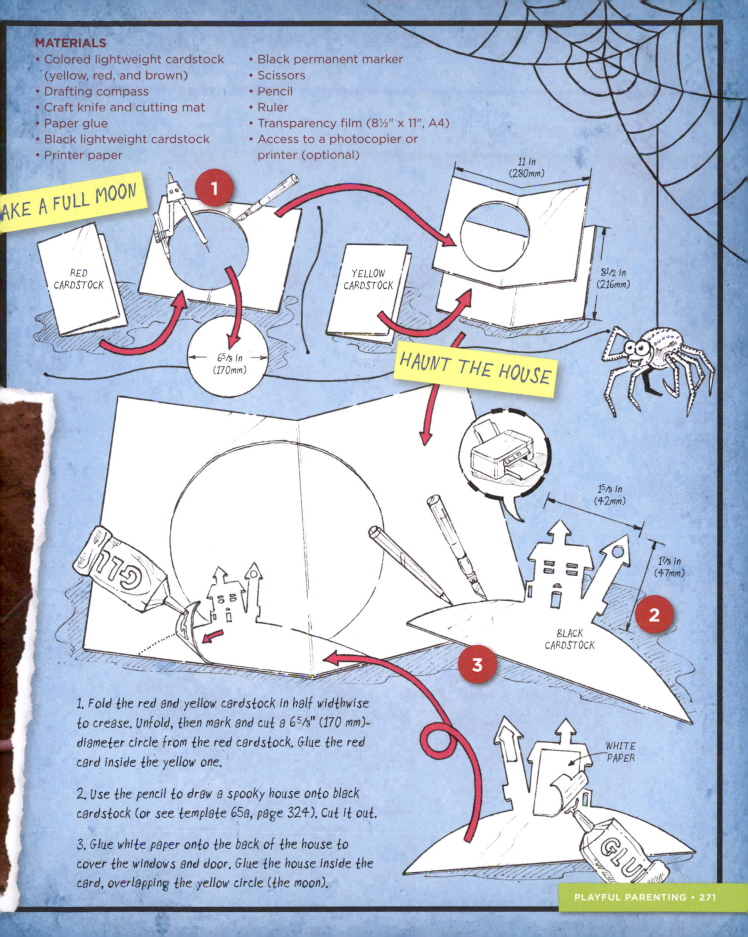

MATERIALS

- Colored lightweight cardstock (yellow, red, and brown)
- Drafting compass
- Craft knife and cutting mat
- Paper glue
- Black lightweight cardstock
- Printer paper
- Black permanent marker
- Scissors
- Pencil
- Ruler
- Transparency film (8½" x 11", A4)
- Access to a photocopier or printer (optional)

MAKE A FULL MOON

RED CARDSTOCK

YELLOW CARDSTOCK

11 in (280mm)

8½ in (216mm)

6⅝ in (170mm)

HAUNT THE HOUSE

1⅝ in (42mm)

1⅞ in (47mm)

BLACK CARDSTOCK

WHITE PAPER

1. Fold the red and yellow cardstock in half widthwise to crease. Unfold, then mark and cut a 6⅝" (170 mm)-diameter circle from the red cardstock. Glue the red card inside the yellow one.

2. Use the pencil to draw a spooky house onto black cardstock (or see template 65a, page 324). Cut it out.

3. Glue white paper onto the back of the house to cover the windows and door. Glue the house inside the card, overlapping the yellow circle (the moon).

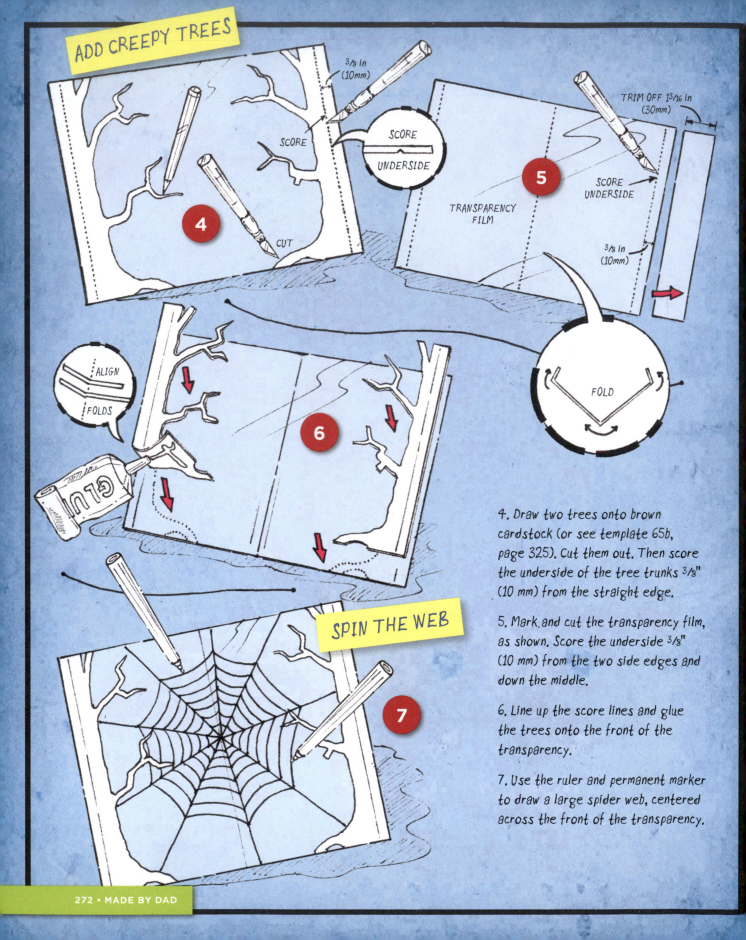

ADD CREEPY TREES

³/₈ in (10mm)

SCORE

SCORE UNDERSIDE

CUT

4

5

TRANSPARENCY FILM

TRIM OFF 1³/₁₆ in (30mm)

SCORE UNDERSIDE

³/₈ in (10mm)

FOLD

ALIGN

FOLDS

GLUE

6

SPIN THE WEB

7

4. Draw two trees onto brown cardstock (or see template 65b, page 325). Cut them out. Then score the underside of the tree trunks ³/₈" (10 mm) from the straight edge.

5. Mark, and cut the transparency film, as shown. Score the underside ³/₈" (10 mm) from the two side edges and down the middle.

6. Line up the score lines and glue the trees onto the front of the transparency.

7. Use the ruler and permanent marker to draw a large spider web, centered across the front of the transparency.

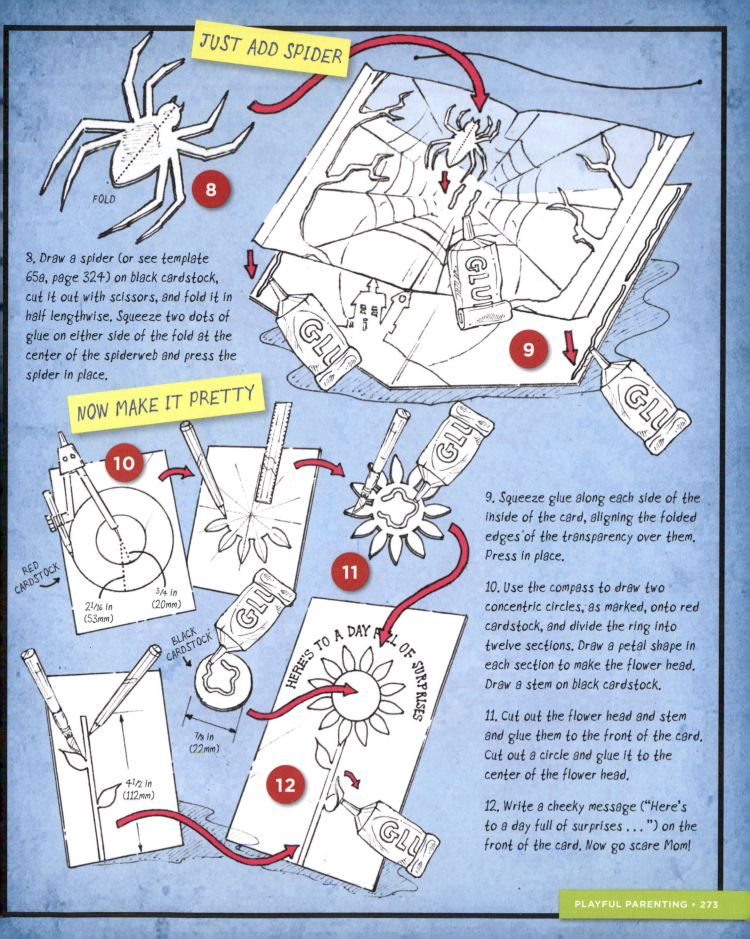

FOLD

8. Draw a spider (or see template 65a, page 324) on black cardstock, cut it out with scissors, and fold it in half lengthwise. Squeeze two dots of glue on either side of the fold at the center of the spiderweb and press the spider in place.

NOW MAKE IT PRETTY

RED CARDSTOCK

2 1/16 in (53mm)

3/4 in (20mm)

BLACK CARDSTOCK

7/8 in (22mm)

4 1/2 in (112mm)

HERE'S TO A DAY FULL OF SURPRISES

9. Squeeze glue along each side of the inside of the card, aligning the folded edges of the transparency over them. Press in place.

10. Use the compass to draw two concentric circles, as marked, onto red cardstock, and divide the ring into twelve sections. Draw a petal shape in each section to make the flower head. Draw a stem on black cardstock.

11. Cut out the flower head and stem and glue them to the front of the card. Cut out a circle and glue it to the center of the flower head.

12. Write a cheeky message ("Here's to a day full of surprises . . . ") on the front of the card. Now go scare Mom!

JELLY BEAN REWARD ROCKET

LEVEL: MEDIUM

Most kids respond very positively to reward charts, so imagine how keen they'll be to impress if you make them a Reward Rocket. From my personal experience, they'll do anything, even clean up their bedroom, just to pull out a stick and get one step closer to a handful of jelly beans!

EVERY STICK THAT IS REMOVED GETS YOU ONE STEP CLOSER . . .

MATERIALS

- Craft knife and cutting mat
- 6 stirring sticks
- Ruler
- Pencil
- 2 cardboard parcel tubes (about 19", 483 mm long; at least 2", 51 mm diameter)
- White lightweight cardstock
- Paper glue
- 6 coins
- Hot glue gun and glue sticks
- Drafting compass
- Small corrugated cardboard box
- Poster paint
- Paintbrush
- Felt-tip markers
- Velcro tabs
- Jelly beans or other small candy

CONSTRUCT THE FUSELAGE

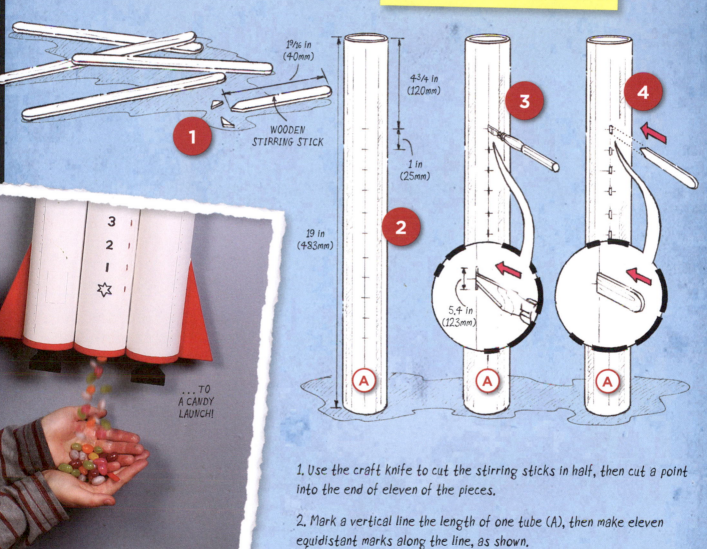

1$^{9/16}$ in (40mm)

WOODEN STIRRING STICK

4$^{3/4}$ in (120mm)

1 in (25mm)

19 in (483mm)

5.4 in (123mm)

...TO A CANDY LAUNCH!

1. Use the craft knife to cut the stirring sticks in half, then cut a point into the end of eleven of the pieces.

2. Mark a vertical line the length of one tube (A), then make eleven equidistant marks along the line, as shown.

3. Make a small vertical slit at the intersection of each mark.

4. Push a sharpened stick into each slit, making sure it fits snugly.

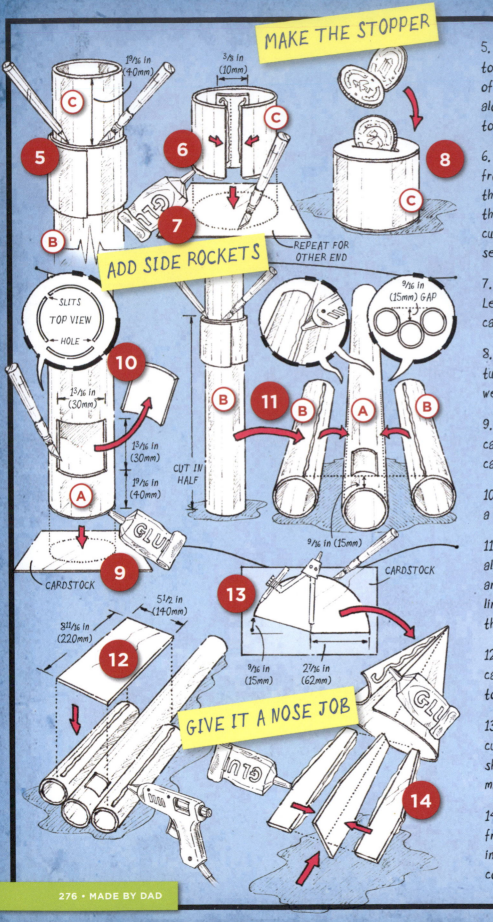

ADD SIDE ROCKETS

GIVE IT A NOSE JOB

5. Make a mark 1⁹/₁₆" (40 mm) from the top of the second tube (B), wrap a strip of cardstock at the mark, and draw along the edge. Then cut along the mark to separate a short piece of tube (C).

6. Mark and cut out a ³/₈" (10 mm) section from the side of tube C. Apply glue to the cutout, press the open edges of the tube back together, and press the cutout onto the inside of the tube to seal the seam.

7. Glue both ends of tube C to cardstock. Let dry, then cut away the excess cardstock around the edges.

8. Cut a slit into the cardstock end of tube C, and insert five or six coins for weight.

9. Glue the bottom end of tube A to cardstock, and cut away the excess cardstock around the edges.

10. Using the visual guide, mark and cut a rectangle near the bottom of tube A.

11. Cut tube B in half. Squeeze hot glue along the side of each half of tube B and press them onto tube A so that they line up with the bottom edge and frame the rectangular cutout.

12. Mark and cut a rectangle from cardstock and glue it over the cutout to connect the B tubes.

13. Using the compass, measure, mark, and cut a near half circle from cardstock, as shown. Curl it into a cone, so its diameter matches the tubes', and glue the overlap.

14. Cut three angled pieces of cardboard from the box, and arrange and glue them into an X, as shown, to insert into the cone and fit into the top of the tubes.

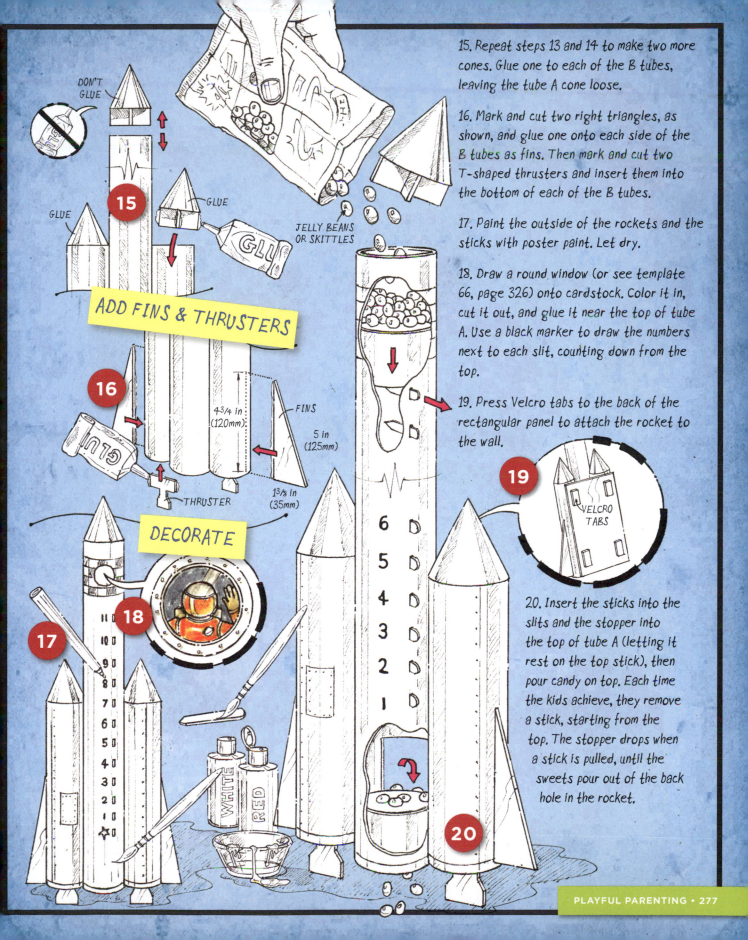

DON'T GLUE

15

GLUE

GLUE

GLU

JELLY BEANS OR SKITTLES

ADD FINS & THRUSTERS

16

GLU

4³/₄ in (120mm)

FINS

5 in (125mm)

THRUSTER

1³/₈ in (35mm)

DECORATE

17

18

WHITE

RED

6
5
4
3
2
1

19

VELCRO TABS

15. Repeat steps 13 and 14 to make two more cones. Glue one to each of the B tubes, leaving the tube A cone loose.

16. Mark and cut two right triangles, as shown, and glue one onto each side of the B tubes as fins. Then mark and cut two T-shaped thrusters and insert them into the bottom of each of the B tubes.

17. Paint the outside of the rockets and the sticks with poster paint. Let dry.

18. Draw a round window (or see template 66, page 326) onto cardstock. Color it in, cut it out, and glue it near the top of tube A. Use a black marker to draw the numbers next to each slit, counting down from the top.

19. Press Velcro tabs to the back of the rectangular panel to attach the rocket to the wall.

20. Insert the sticks into the slits and the stopper into the top of tube A (letting it rest on the top stick), then pour candy on top. Each time the kids achieve, they remove a stick, starting from the top. The stopper drops when a stick is pulled, until the sweets pour out of the back hole in the rocket.

20

"I LOVE YOU THIS MUCH" CARD

Just about every parent has had the "I love you more than . . ." conversation. It normally starts with outstretched arms and escalates to "I love you more than there are stars in the sky." But what if you could stretch your arms farther apart? Well, now you can.

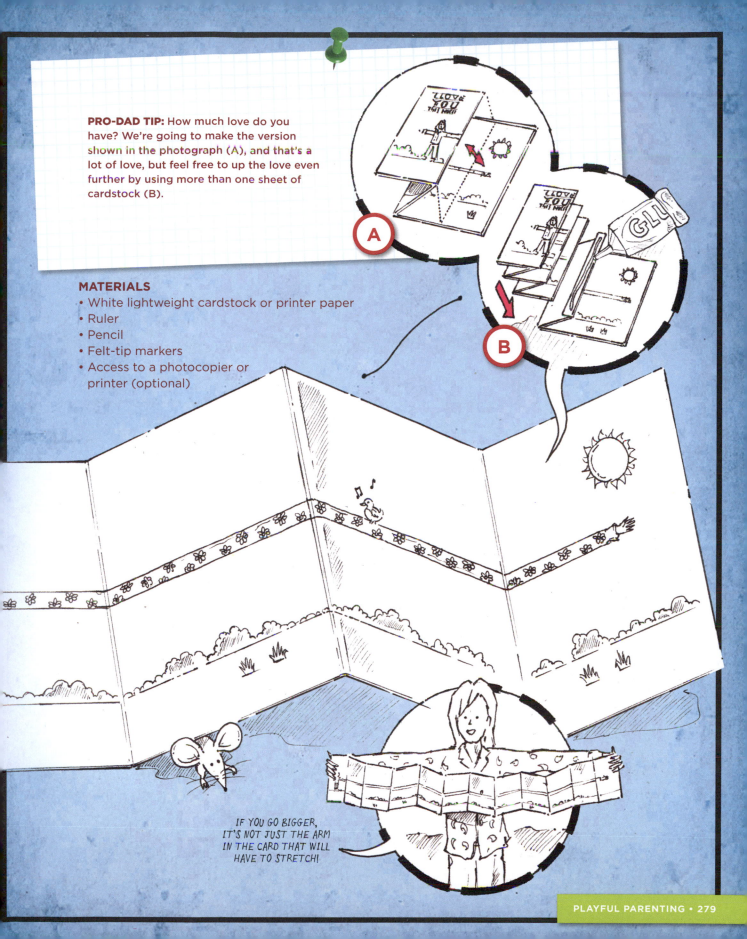

PRO-DAD TIP: How much love do you have? We're going to make the version shown in the photograph (A), and that's a lot of love, but feel free to up the love even further by using more than one sheet of cardstock (B).

MATERIALS
- White lightweight cardstock or printer paper
- Ruler
- Pencil
- Felt-tip markers
- Access to a photocopier or printer (optional)

IF YOU GO BIGGER, IT'S NOT JUST THE ARM IN THE CARD THAT WILL HAVE TO STRETCH!

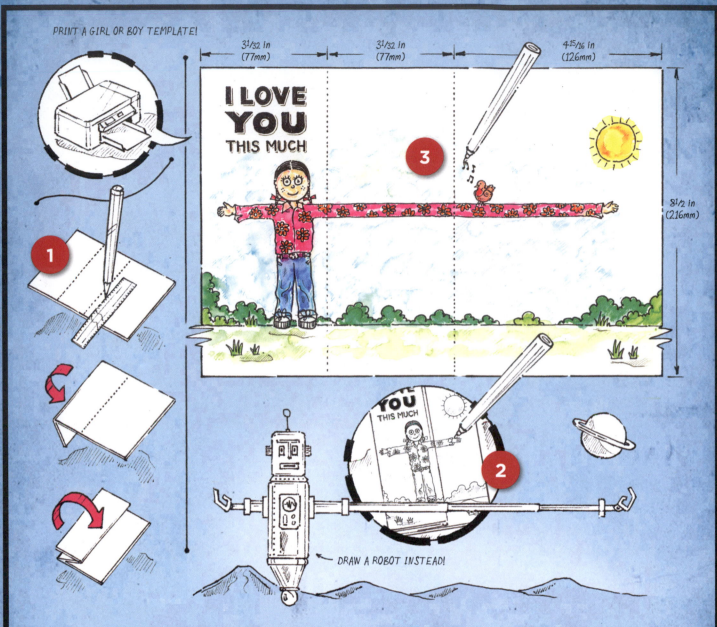

1

2

3

3¹/₃₂ in (77mm)   3¹/₃₂ in (77mm)   4¹⁵/₁₆ in (126mm)

8¹/₂ in (216mm)

I LOVE YOU THIS MUCH

DRAW A ROBOT INSTEAD!

1. Measure and mark two fold lines on the cardstock, as shown in step 3, and accordion fold along the lines (or see templates 67a and 67b, pages 327–328, and skip to step 3).

2. Draw a picture of a person (or a robot, or a friendly monster, or . . .) on the front panel, with one arm extending past the fold to the back panel (or the far right panel, when unfolded). Write the words "I Love You This Much" on the front panel.

3. Unfold the card and join the right arm to the far right extension of the arm through the center panel. Then color in the card, personalize it however you'd like, refold it, and go deliver it!

APPENDIX

PROJECT TEMPLATES

In every project, I wholeheartedly encourage you to draw your own elements (or get the kids to do it!), but for those of you who welcome a shortcut or are shy about drawing, I've included the following pages with templates (think of them as training wheels on a bike—stop using them when you start to feel more confident). As noted throughout, you may photocopy these templates to use with the projects—they're printed on both sides of the page, so you won't be tempted to cut them straight from the book. (Technically, I suppose you *could* cut the pages, but then you'll have only half the templates *and* big holes in your book, so I don't advise it.) For your further convenience, these templates are also available online for downloading and printing at workman.com/madebydad (because unless you're working on these projects at the office or the library, I don't know many folks with an industrial photocopier at home). Photocopy or print all templates at 100% unless indicated otherwise.

LIST OF TEMPLATES

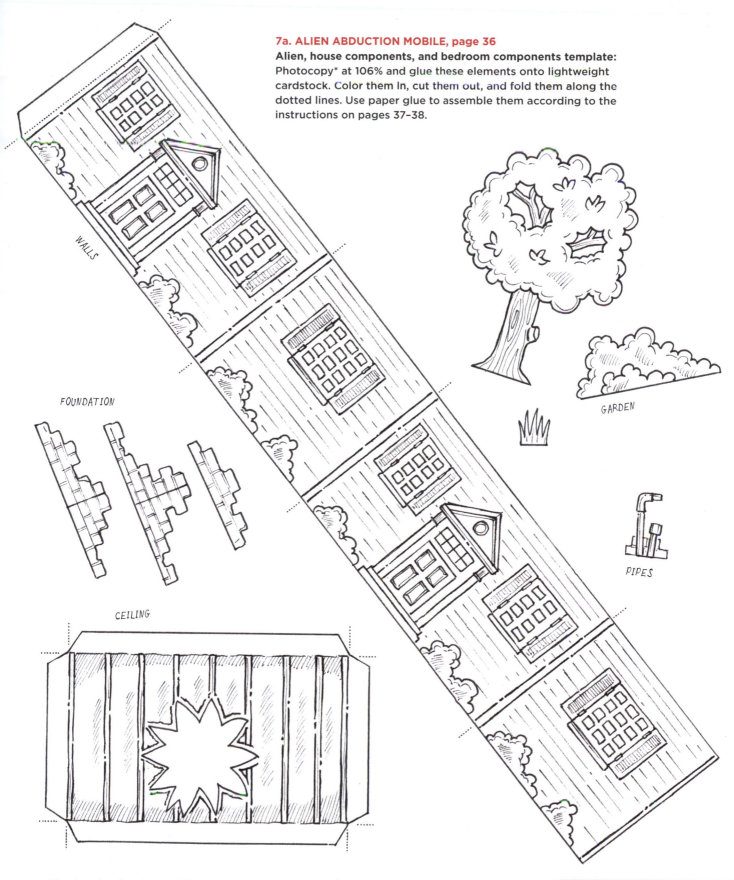

7a. ALIEN ABDUCTION MOBILE, page 36
Alien, house components, and bedroom components template:
Photocopy* at 106% and glue these elements onto lightweight
cardstock. Color them in, cut them out, and fold them along the
dotted lines. Use paper glue to assemble them according to the
instructions on pages 37–38.

WALLS

FOUNDATION

CEILING

GARDEN

PIPES

*Or download and print this template at workman.com/madebydad

7b. ALIEN ABDUCTION MOBILE, page 36

House and garden components template: Photocopy* and glue these elements onto lightweight cardstock. Color them in, cut them out, and fold them along the dotted lines. Use paper glue to assemble them according to the instructions on pages 38–39.
Note: To save time, photocopy or print the template directly onto cardstock.

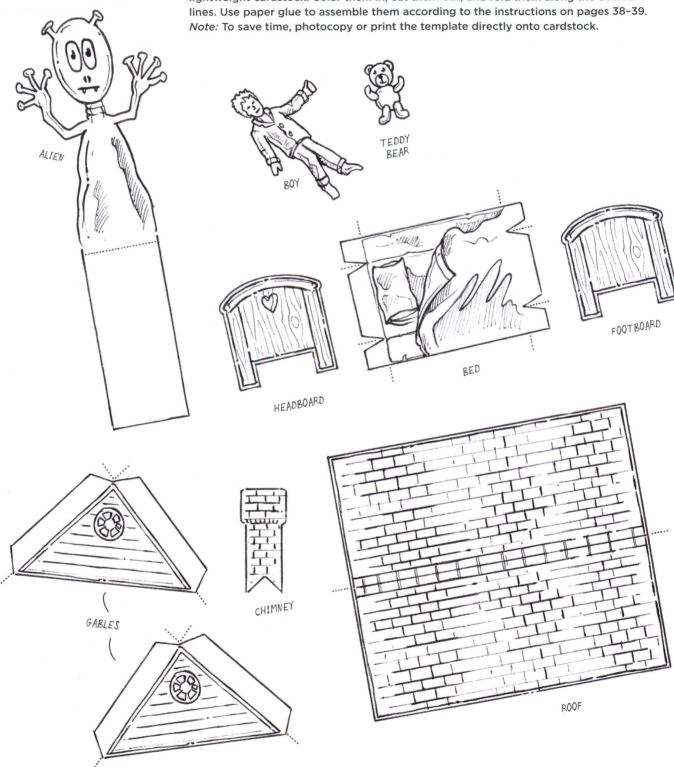

ALIEN

BOY

TEDDY BEAR

HEADBOARD

BED

FOOTBOARD

GABLES

CHIMNEY

ROOF

*Or download and print this template at workman.com/madebydad

11. SNAPPY TOAST RACK, page 50

Crocodile template: Photocopy*, cut out, and trace the pieces for the mouth and splash according to the instructions starting on page 50. Photocopy and glue the eyes and snout onto medium-weight cardstock. Color them in, cut them out, and fold them along the dotted lines. Use paper glue to assemble the pieces according to the instructions starting on page 50. *Note:* To save time, photocopy or print the template directly onto cardstock. You may need to reduce or enlarge the template sizes depending on the size of paper cup used.

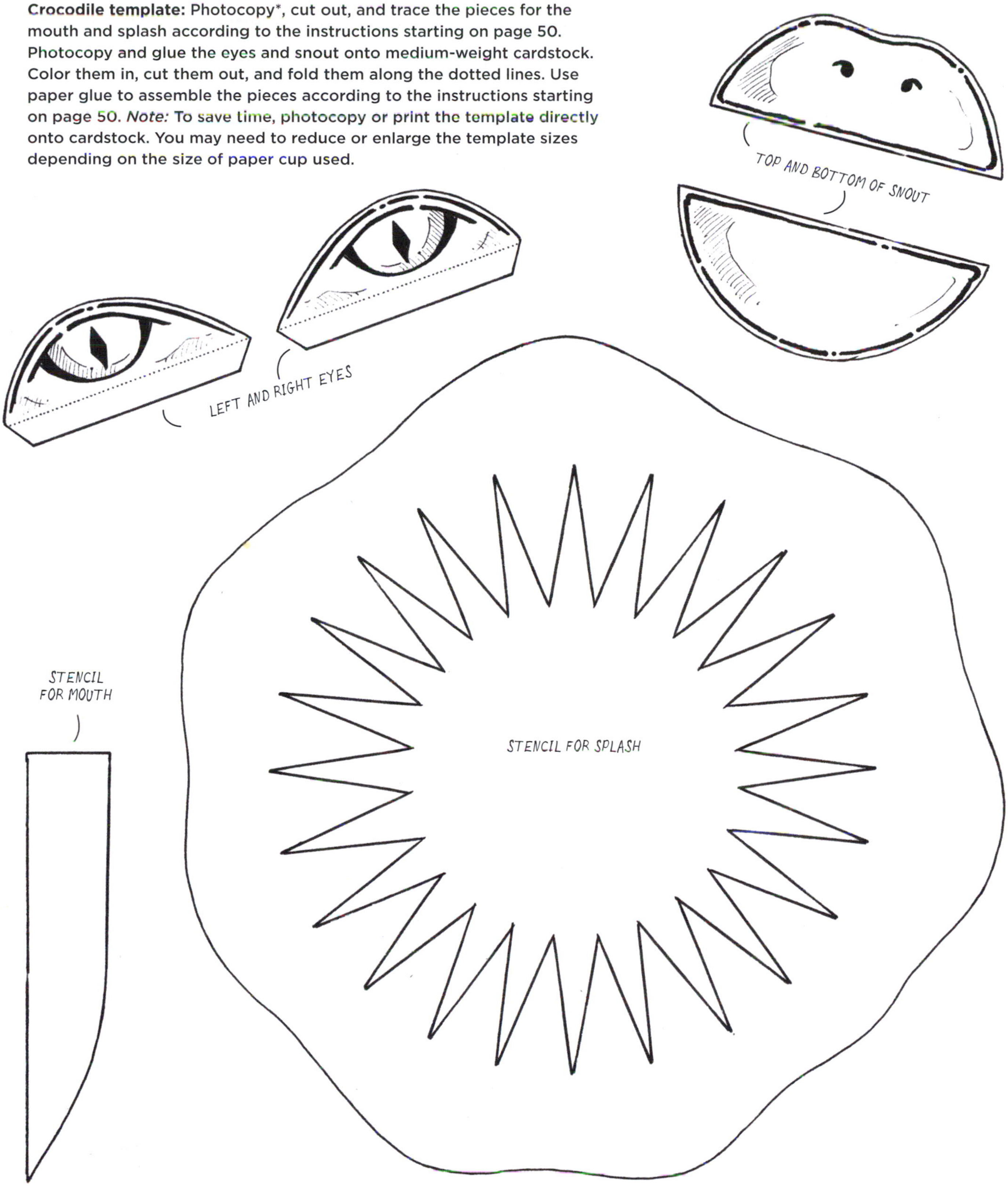

TOP AND BOTTOM OF SNOUT

LEFT AND RIGHT EYES

STENCIL FOR MOUTH

STENCIL FOR SPLASH

*Or download and print this template at workman.com/madebydad

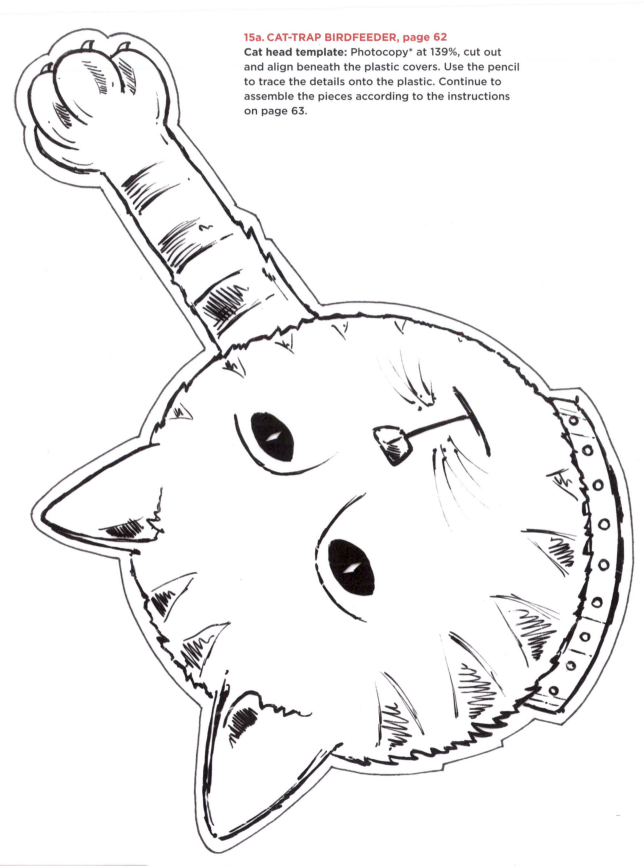

15a. CAT-TRAP BIRDFEEDER, page 62

Cat head template: Photocopy* at 139%, cut out and align beneath the plastic covers. Use the pencil to trace the details onto the plastic. Continue to assemble the pieces according to the instructions on page 63.

Or download and print this template at workman.com/madebydad

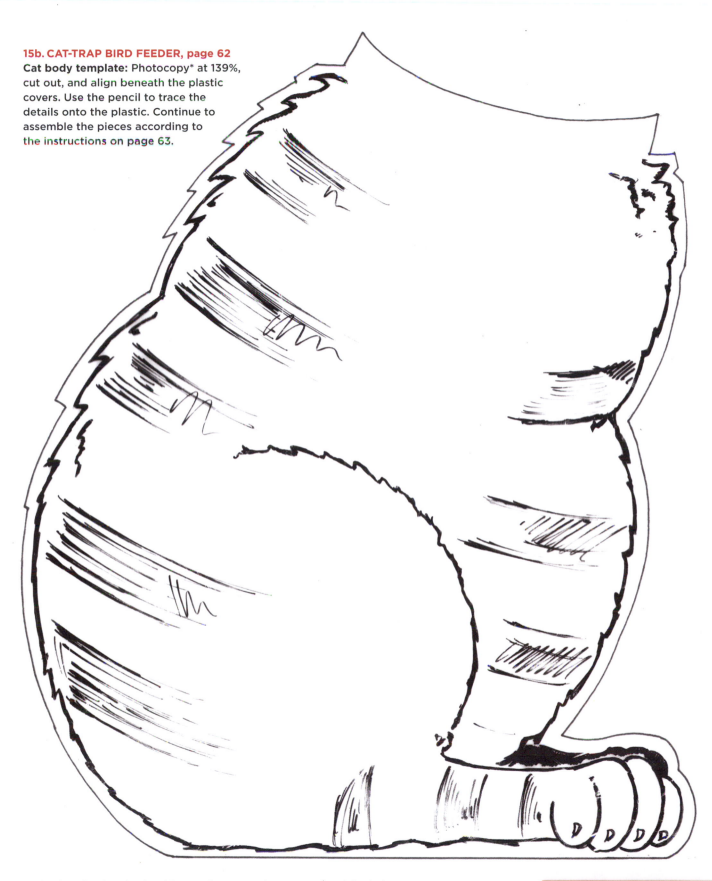

15b. CAT-TRAP BIRD FEEDER, page 62
Cat body template: Photocopy* at 139%, cut out, and align beneath the plastic covers. Use the pencil to trace the details onto the plastic. Continue to assemble the pieces according to the instructions on page 63.

Or download and print this template at workman.com/madebydad

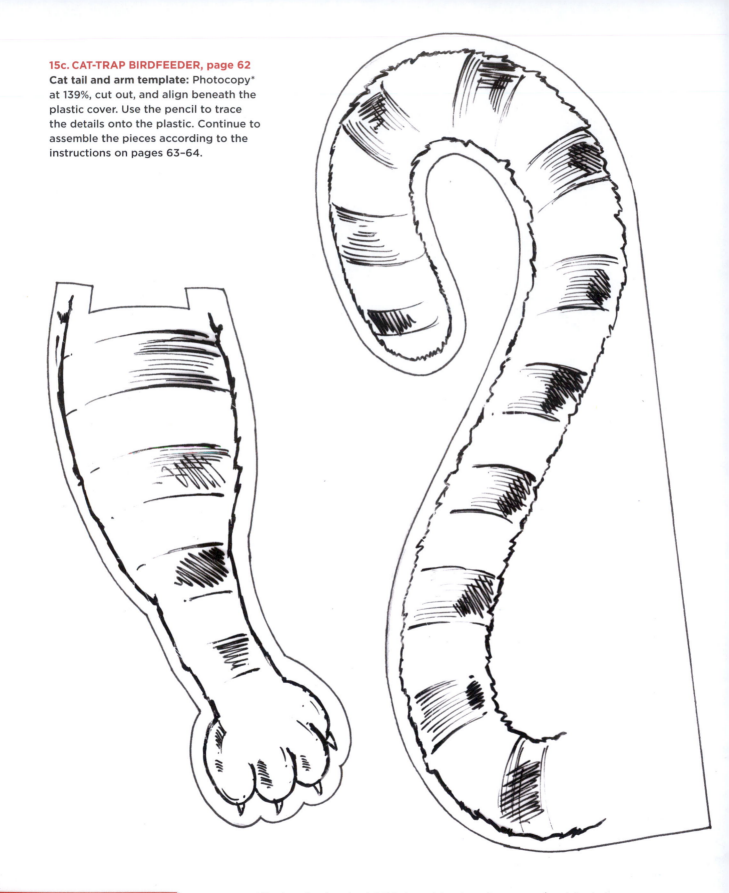

15c. CAT-TRAP BIRDFEEDER, page 62
Cat tail and arm template: Photocopy*
at 139%, cut out, and align beneath the
plastic cover. Use the pencil to trace
the details onto the plastic. Continue to
assemble the pieces according to the
instructions on pages 63–64.

Or download and print this template at workman.com/madebydad

16. "STOP THE PIGEON" WEATHER VANE, page 65

Pilot and pigeon template: Photocopy*, cut out, and align it beneath the plastic cover. Use the marker to trace the characters onto the plastic. Cut them out and assemble them according to the instructions on page 68.

PILOT

PIGEON

18. SLINGSHOT CAR LAUNCHER, page 76

Flames template: Photocopy*, cut out, and trace the flame pieces onto colored cardstock and assemble according to the instructions on page 79. *Note:* To save time, photocopy or print the template directly onto colored cardstock.

RED CARDSTOCK

ORANGE CARDSTOCK

*Or download and print this template at workman.com/madebydad

Wheat fields template: Photocopy*, color in, and cut out the field pieces. Use paper glue to attach them to the base according to the instructions on page 86.

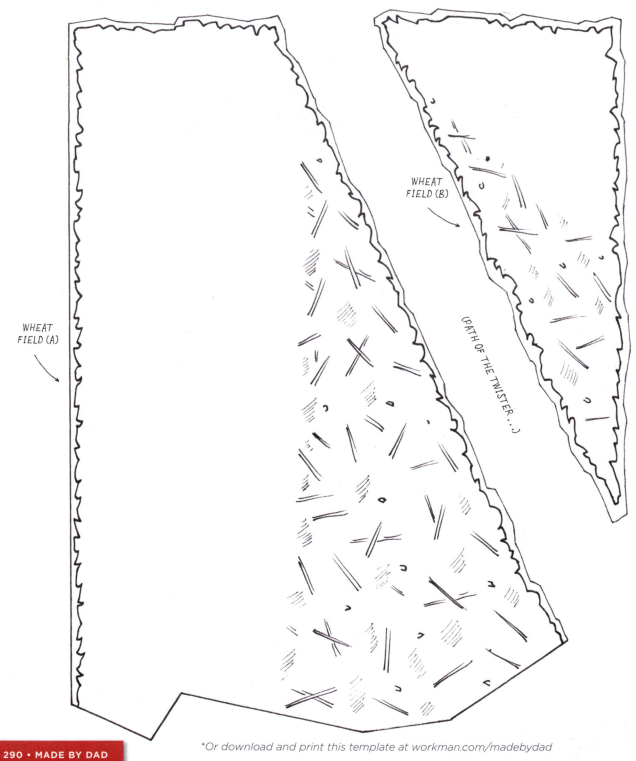

WHEAT FIELD (A)

WHEAT FIELD (B)

(PATH OF THE TWISTER . . .)

*Or download and print this template at workman.com/madebydad

20b. NO PLACE LIKE HOME TWISTER, page 84

Tree, shrub, and animal template: Photocopy* and glue the trees, grass tufts, and animals onto cardstock. Color them in and cut them out. Use paper glue to assemble them according to the instructions on page 86. Photocopy and cut out the grass field piece. Use paper glue to attach it to the base.

BUSH

COWS

FLYING TREE

STANDING TREE

BIRDS

MORE BUSHES!

GRASS TUFTS

GRASS

Or download and print this template at workman.com/madebydad

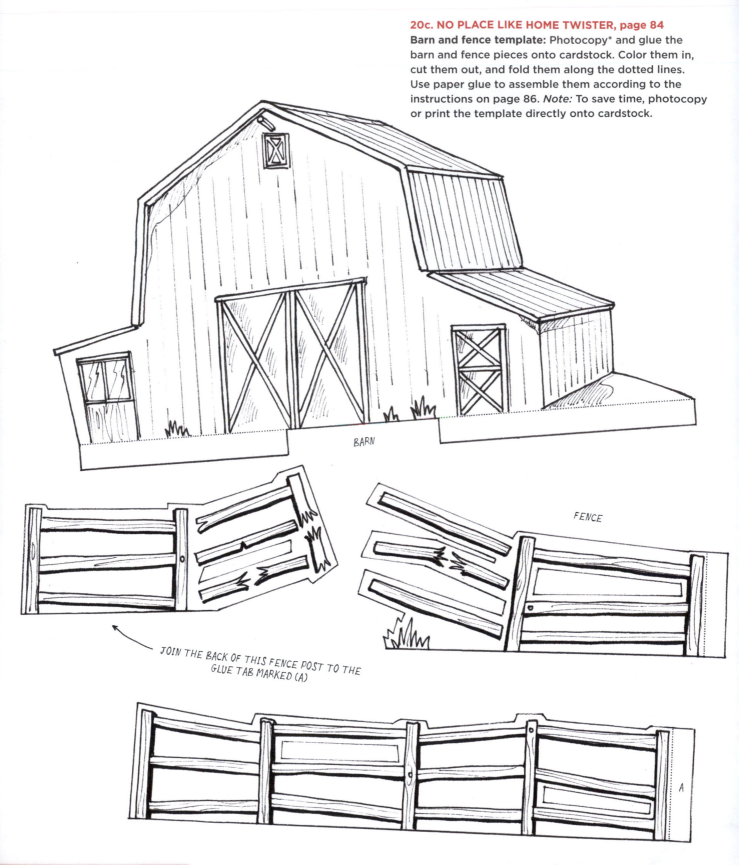

Barn and fence template: Photocopy* and glue the barn and fence pieces onto cardstock. Color them in, cut them out, and fold them along the dotted lines. Use paper glue to assemble them according to the instructions on page 86. *Note:* To save time, photocopy or print the template directly onto cardstock.

BARN

FENCE

JOIN THE BACK OF THIS FENCE POST TO THE GLUE TAB MARKED (A)

A

*Or download and print this template at workman.com/madebydad

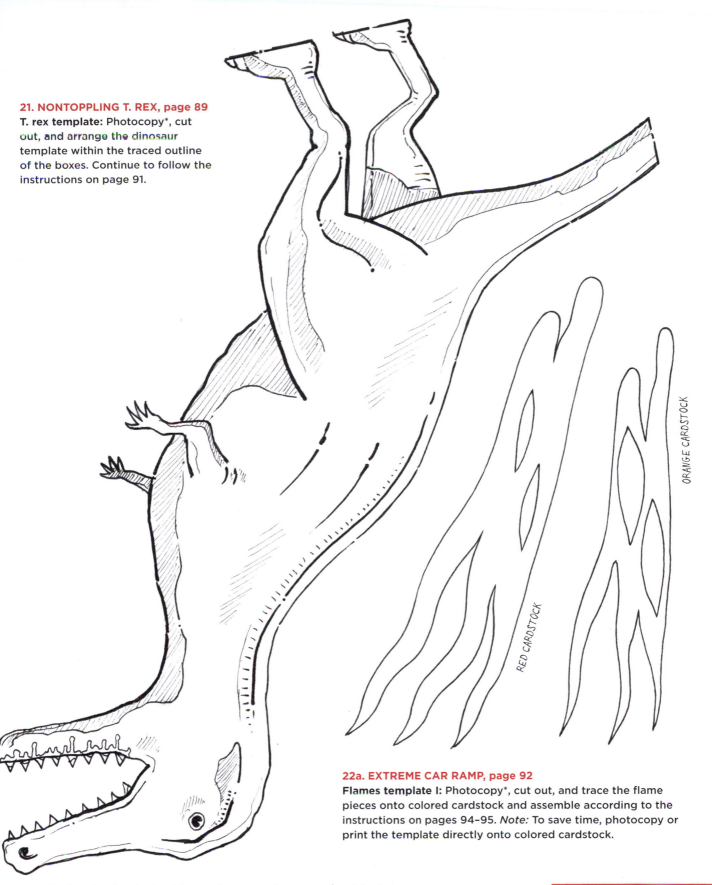

21. NONTOPPLING T. REX, page 89
T. rex template: Photocopy*, cut out, and arrange the dinosaur template within the traced outline of the boxes. Continue to follow the instructions on page 91.

ORANGE CARDSTOCK

RED CARDSTOCK

22a. EXTREME CAR RAMP, page 92
Flames template I: Photocopy*, cut out, and trace the flame pieces onto colored cardstock and assemble according to the instructions on pages 94–95. *Note:* To save time, photocopy or print the template directly onto colored cardstock.

*Or download and print this template at workman.com/madebydad

22b. EXTREME CAR RAMP, page 92

Flames template II: Photocopy*, cut out, and trace the flame pieces onto colored cardstock and assemble according to the instructions starting on page 94. *Note:* To save time, photocopy or print the template directly onto colored cardstock.

ORANGE
CARDSTOCK

RED
CARDSTOCK

Or download and print this template at workman.com/madebydad

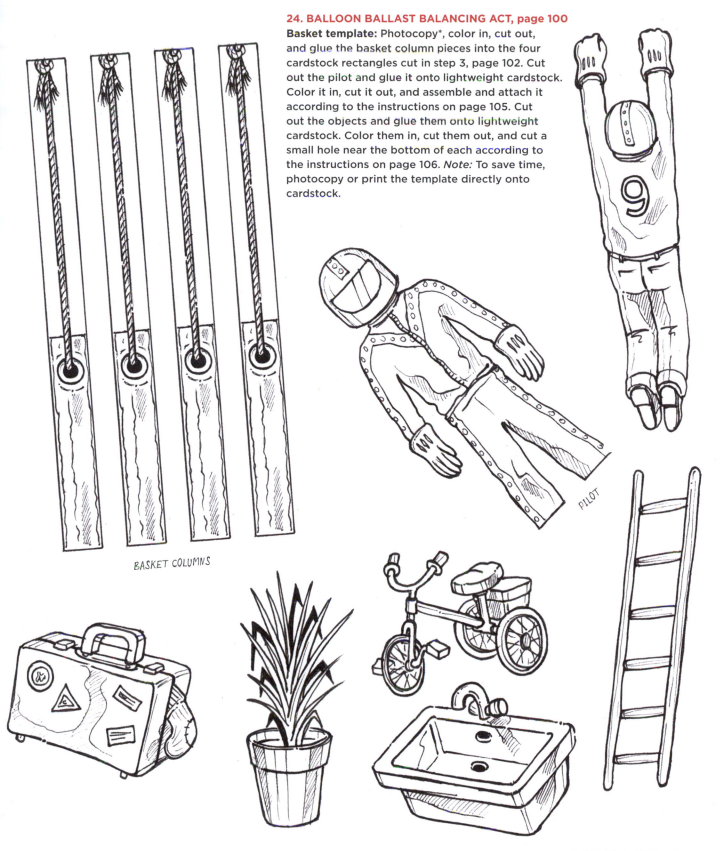

24. BALLOON BALLAST BALANCING ACT, page 100

Basket template: Photocopy*, color in, cut out, and glue the basket column pieces into the four cardstock rectangles cut in step 3, page 102. Cut out the pilot and glue it onto lightweight cardstock. Color it in, cut it out, and assemble and attach it according to the instructions on page 105. Cut out the objects and glue them onto lightweight cardstock. Color them in, cut them out, and cut a small hole near the bottom of each according to the instructions on page 106. *Note:* To save time, photocopy or print the template directly onto cardstock.

BASKET COLUMNS

PILOT

*Or download and print this template at workman.com/madebydad

25. TEDDY THROUGH THE CENTER OF THE EARTH, page 107

Teddy template: Photocopy* and glue the teddy bears and supports onto lightweight cardstock. Color them in, cut them out, and assemble according to the instructions on page 109. *Note:* To save time, photocopy or print the template directly onto cardstock.

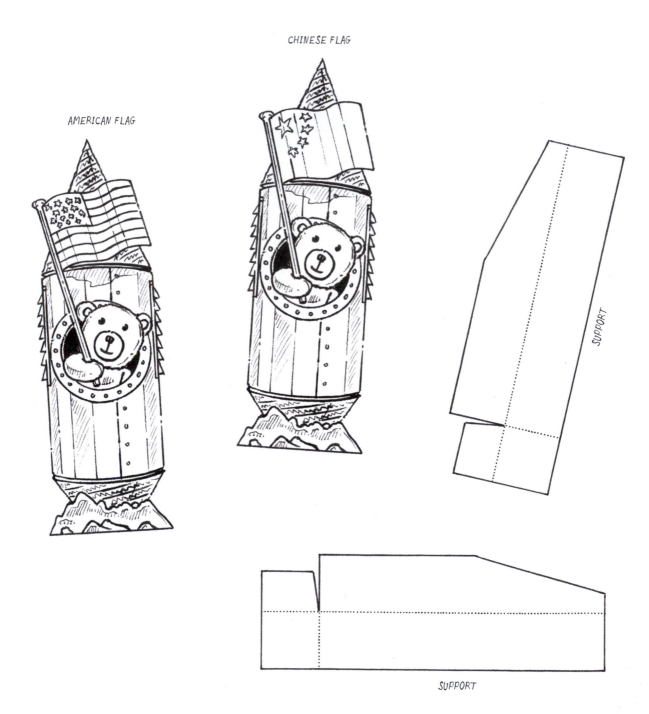

CHINESE FLAG

AMERICAN FLAG

SUPPORT

SUPPORT

*Or download and print this template at workman.com/madebydad

26a. RUBBER BAND ROCKET CAR, page 110
Rocket car template: Photocopy* at 106% and glue the rocket car onto cardstock. Color it in, cut it out, and assemble according to the instructions on pages 115–116. *Note:* To save time, photocopy or print the template directly onto cardstock. If you want to decorate both sides of the car, you'll need to create a mirror copy.

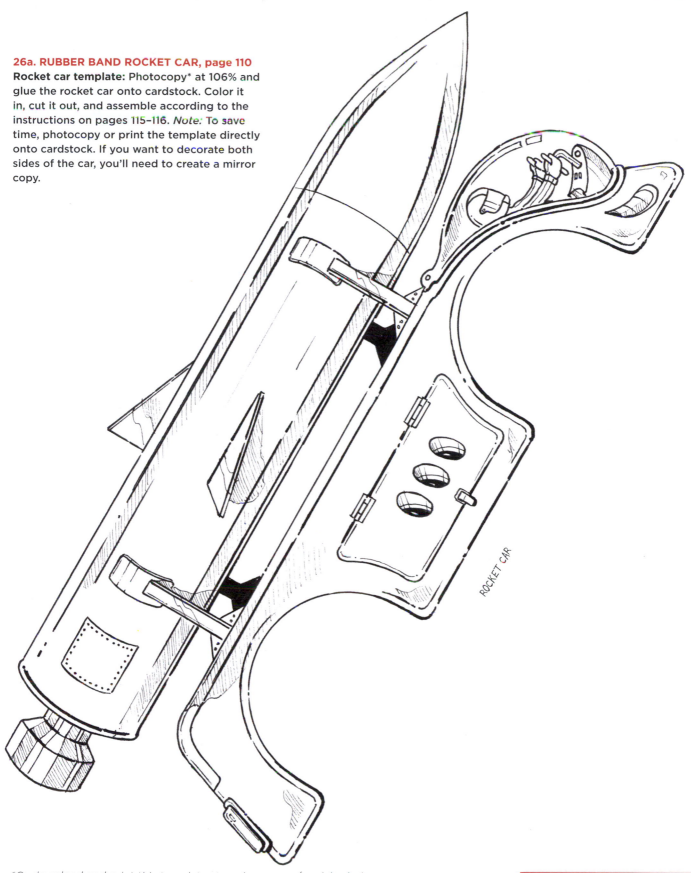

ROCKET CAR

26b. RUBBER BAND ROCKET CAR, page 110

SUV racer template: Photocopy* and glue the racer onto cardstock. Color it in, cut it out, and assemble according to the instructions on page 116. *Note:* To save time, photocopy or print the template directly onto cardstock. If you want to decorate both sides of the racer, you'll need to create a mirror copy.

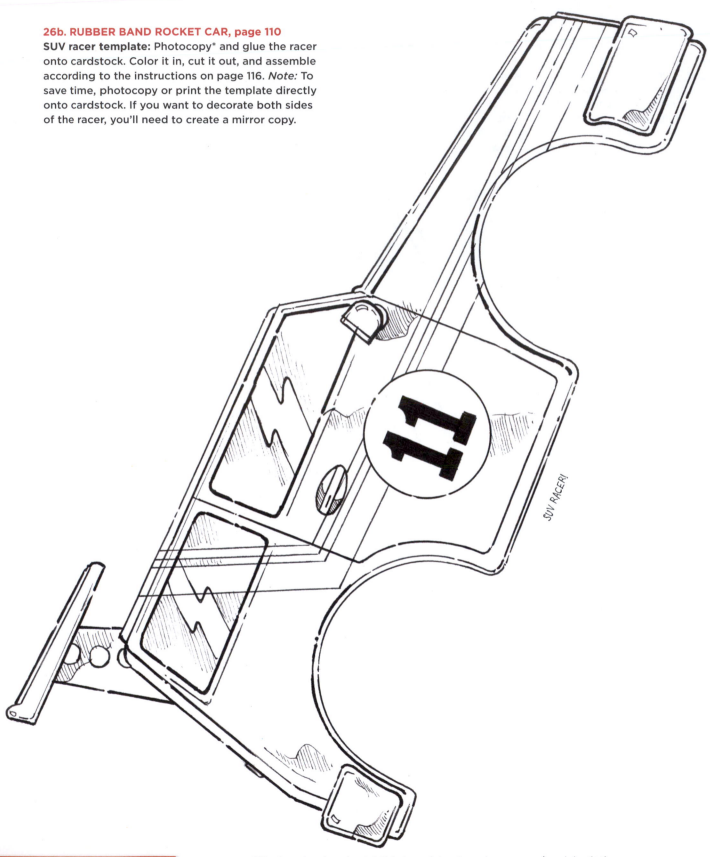

SUV RACER!

Or download and print this template at workman.com/madebydad

Volcano template I: Photocopy*, cut out, and trace the eruption pieces onto lightweight cardstock. Cut them out, fold them along the dotted lines, and assemble them according to the instructions on page 119. *Note:* To save time, photocopy or print the templates directly onto colored cardstock.

RED CARDSTOCK

ERUPTION

YELLOW CARDSTOCK

Or download and print this template at workman.com/madebydad

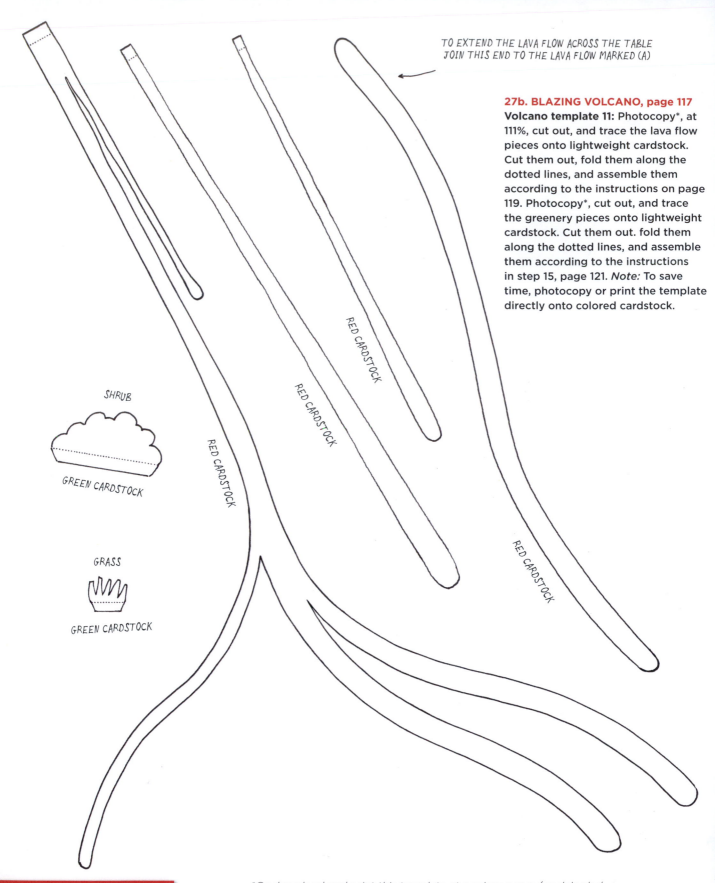

TO EXTEND THE LAVA FLOW ACROSS THE TABLE
JOIN THIS END TO THE LAVA FLOW MARKED (A)

27b. BLAZING VOLCANO, page 117
Volcano template 11: Photocopy*, at 111%, cut out, and trace the lava flow pieces onto lightweight cardstock. Cut them out, fold them along the dotted lines, and assemble them according to the instructions on page 119. Photocopy*, cut out, and trace the greenery pieces onto lightweight cardstock. Cut them out. fold them along the dotted lines, and assemble them according to the instructions in step 15, page 121. *Note:* To save time, photocopy or print the template directly onto colored cardstock.

RED CARDSTOCK

RED CARDSTOCK

RED CARDSTOCK

RED CARDSTOCK

RED CARDSTOCK

SHRUB

GREEN CARDSTOCK

GRASS

GREEN CARDSTOCK

*Or download and print this template at workman.com/madebydad

27c. BLAZING VOLCANO, page 117

Volcano template 111: Photocopy*, cut out, and trace the tree trunk and tree top pieces onto lightweight cardstock. Cut them out, fold them along the dotted lines, and assemble them according to the instructions in step 10, page 121. Photocopy*, cut out, and trace the flame pieces onto lightweight cardstock. Cut them out and assemble them according to the instructions in step 12, page 121. *Note:* To save time, photocopy or print the templates directly onto colored cardstock.

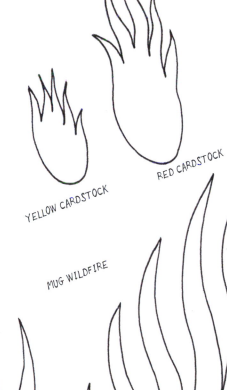

YELLOW CARDSTOCK

RED CARDSTOCK

MUG WILDFIRE

TREE TOP

GREEN CARDSTOCK

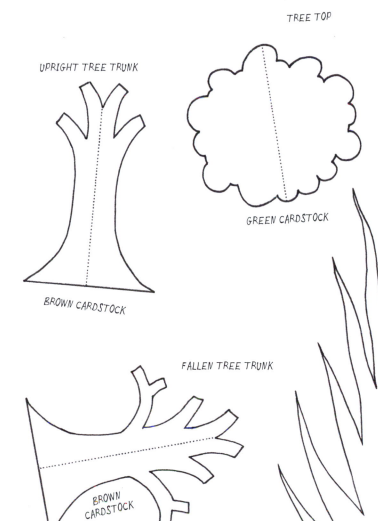

UPRIGHT TREE TRUNK

BROWN CARDSTOCK

FALLEN TREE TRUNK

BROWN CARDSTOCK

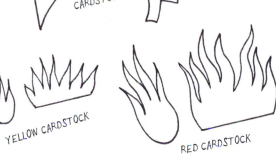

YELLOW CARDSTOCK

RED CARDSTOCK

YELLOW CARDSTOCK

RED CARDSTOCK

*Or download and print this template at workman.com/madebydad

28. GRAVITY-DEFYING BLACK HOLE, page 122

Black hole template: Photocopy*, at 118%, cut out, and trace the black hole piece onto lightweight cardboard according to the instructions on page 123.

PIVOT

*Or download and print this template at workman.com/madebydad

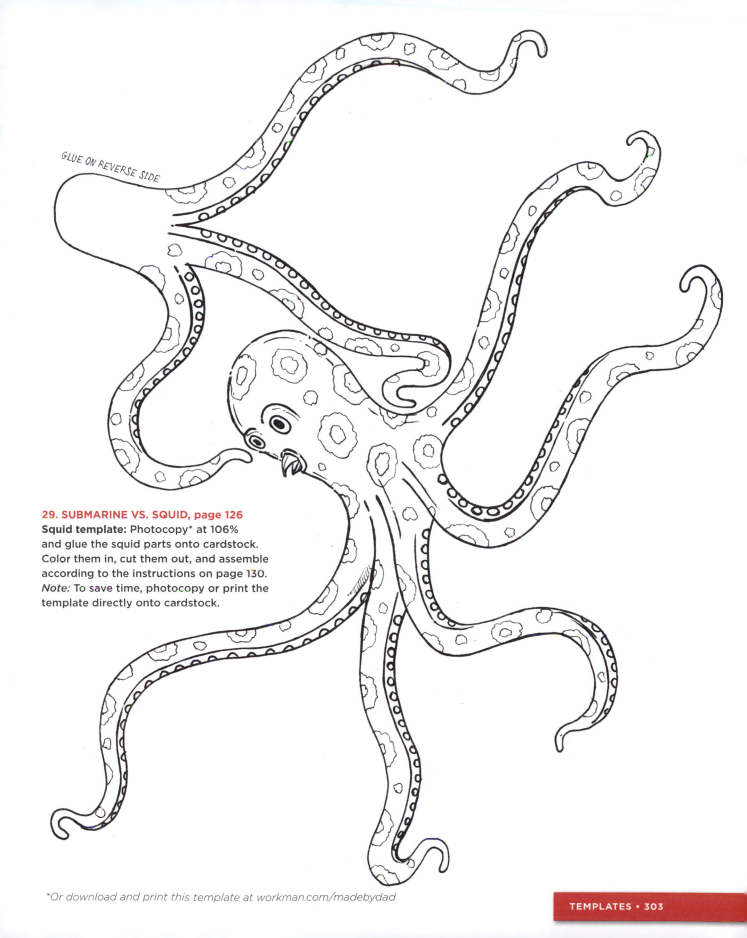

GLUE ON REVERSE SIDE

29. SUBMARINE VS. SQUID, page 126
Squid template: Photocopy* at 106%
and glue the squid parts onto cardstock.
Color them in, cut them out, and assemble
according to the instructions on page 130.
Note: To save time, photocopy or print the
template directly onto cardstock.

Or download and print this template at workman.com/madebydad

30. MILK SHAKE MONSTER, page 131

Milk shake template: Photocopy* and glue the face and drip pieces onto lightweight cardstock. Color them in, cut them out, and assemble according to the instructions on page 134. *Note:* To save time, photocopy or print the template directly onto cardstock.

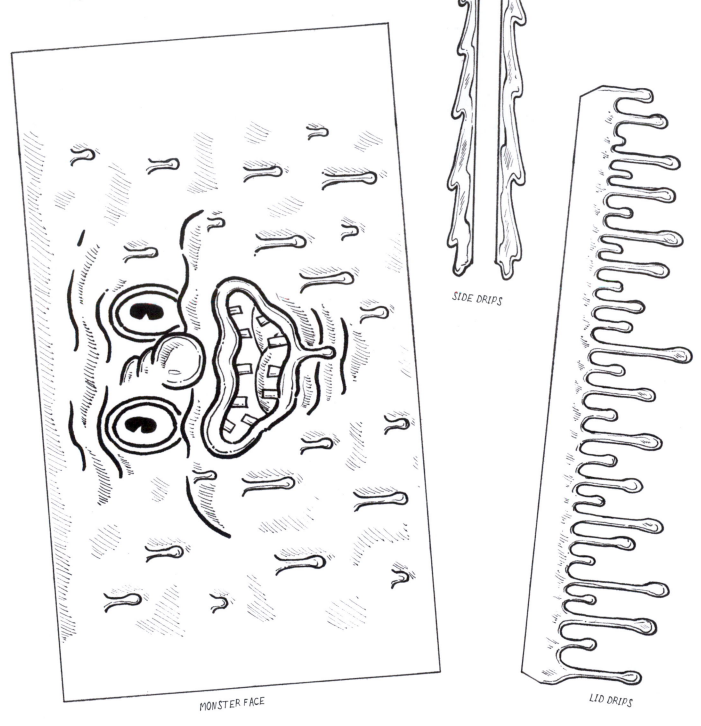

SIDE DRIPS

MONSTER FACE

LID DRIPS

*Or download and print this template at workman.com/madebydad

31. RATAPULT, page 135

Rat template: Photocopy* and glue the rat onto cardstock. Color it in, cut it out, and assemble according to the instructions on page 139. *Note:* To save time, photocopy or print the template directly onto cardstock. If you want to decorate both sides of the rat, you'll need to create a mirror copy.

34. EATING NEMO, page 147

Under the sea template: Photocopy* and glue the two fish and the fish burp onto medium-weight cardstock. Color them in, cut them out, and assemble according to the instructions on page 152. *Note:* To save time, photocopy or print the template directly onto cardstock. Photocopy, color in, and cut out the remaining undersea pieces. Glue them to the project according to the instructions on page 152.

CLOWNFISH

BIG FISH

SPEECH BUBBLE

*Or download and print this template at workman.com/madebydad

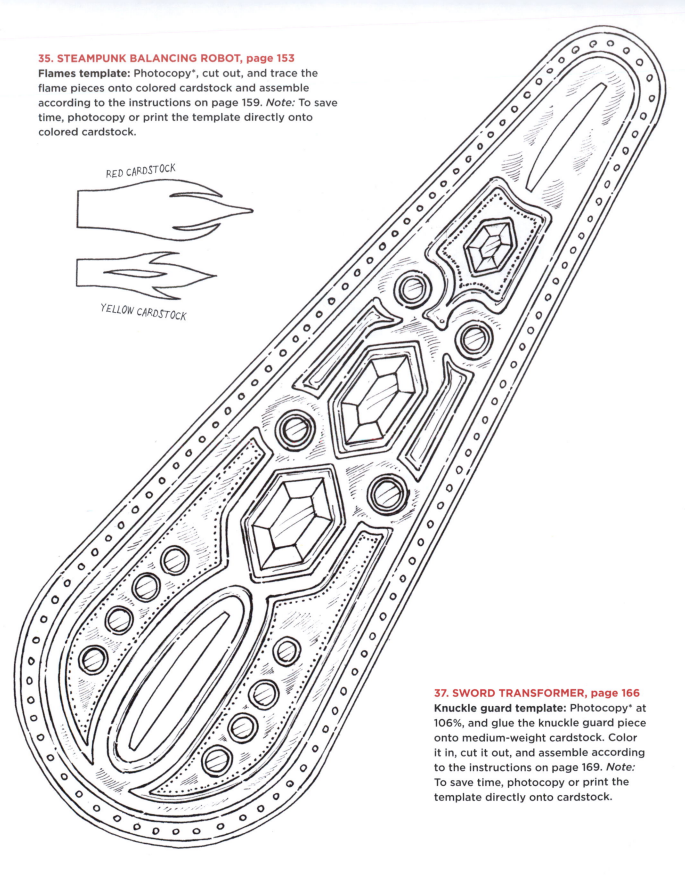

35. STEAMPUNK BALANCING ROBOT, page 153

Flames template: Photocopy*, cut out, and trace the flame pieces onto colored cardstock and assemble according to the instructions on page 159. *Note:* To save time, photocopy or print the template directly onto colored cardstock.

RED CARDSTOCK

YELLOW CARDSTOCK

37. SWORD TRANSFORMER, page 166

Knuckle guard template: Photocopy* at 106%, and glue the knuckle guard piece onto medium-weight cardstock. Color it in, cut it out, and assemble according to the instructions on page 169. *Note:* To save time, photocopy or print the template directly onto cardstock.

*Or download and print this template at workman.com/madebydad

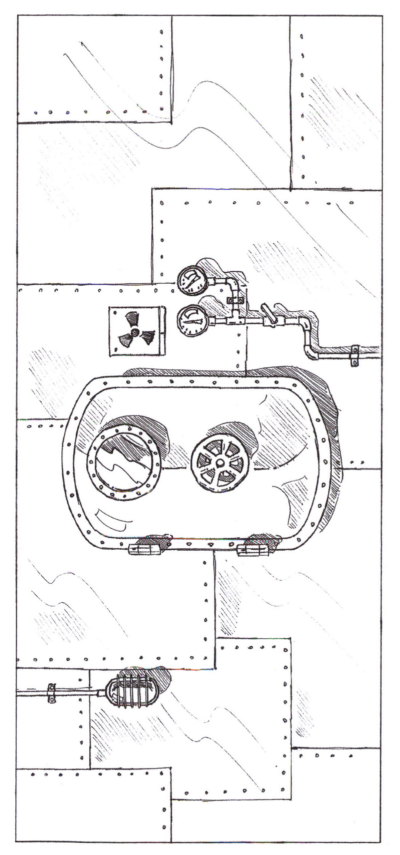

38a. SNAIL SOUP DECOY, page 173
Safe template: Photocopy* at 106%
color in, and cut out the safe decal.
Glue it onto the cylinder, avoiding
positioning the door over the seam,
and continue to assemble according to
the instructions starting on page 178.

SAFE DECAL

Or download and print this template at workman.com/madebydad

38b. SNAIL SOUP DECOY, page 173

Soup can template: Photocopy* at 106%, color in, and cut out the soup label. Glue it onto the outside of the can and continue to assemble according to the instructions on page 179.

SNAIL SOUP LABEL →

Or download and print this template at workman.com/madebydad

43. PRICELESS PICTURE SAFE, page 197

Frame template: Photocopy* at 133% and glue the straight and corner pieces onto medium-weight cardstock. Color them in, cut them out, and assemble the straight and corner pieces (the pieces may be trimmed or extended to fit any size). Glue them in place and continue to assemble according to the instructions on page 200. *Note:* To save time, photocopy or print the template directly onto cardstock.

CORNER PIECES

STRAIGHT PIECES

Fortune-teller template: Photocopy* at 118%, color in, and cut out the fortune-teller. To assemble, fold according to the instructions on pages 203–204.

Or download and print this template at workman.com/madebydad

*Or download and print this template at workman.com/madebydad

Grass-osaurus template: Photocopy* at 133%, color in, and cut
and fold according to the instructions on page 210.

*Or download and print this template at workman.com/madebydad

45c. MOUTHY MONSTER TRADING CARDS, page 208

Mouse-ephant template: Photocopy* at 133%, color in, and cut
and fold according to the instructions on page 210.

Or download and print this template at workman.com/madebydad

45d. MOUTHY MONSTER TRADING CARDS, page 208

Tri-Bite template: Photocopy* at 133%, color in, and cut and
fold according to the instructions on page 210.

*Or download and print this template at workman.com/madebydad

46. BEE SWARM CHANDELIER, page 214

Bees template: Photocopy*, color in, and cut out the bees. Assemble according to the instructions on page 216. *Note:* Every other row includes mirror images; glue the bees back to back so each bee is illustrated on both sides.

48. RADIOACTIVE SPORTS DRINKS, page 221

Label template: Photocopy*, color in, and cut out the radioactive labels. Glue one to the side of each bottle and continue to assemble according to the instructions on page 223.

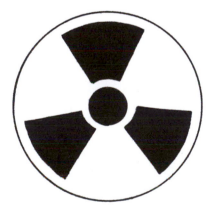

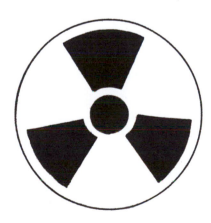

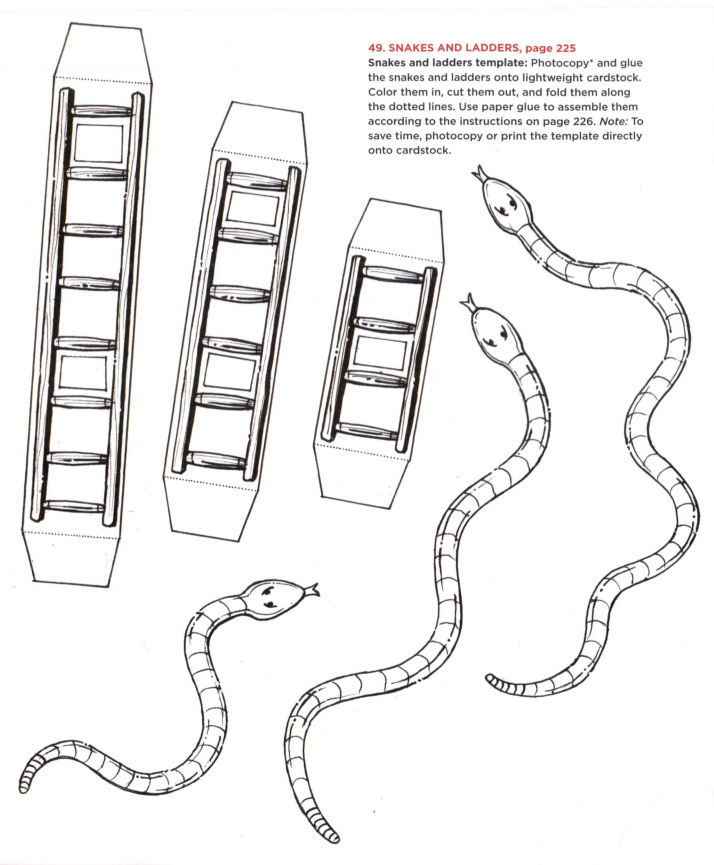

49. SNAKES AND LADDERS, page 225
Snakes and ladders template: Photocopy* and glue
the snakes and ladders onto lightweight cardstock.
Color them in, cut them out, and fold them along
the dotted lines. Use paper glue to assemble them
according to the instructions on page 226. *Note:* To
save time, photocopy or print the template directly
onto cardstock.

Or download and print this template at workman.com/madebydad

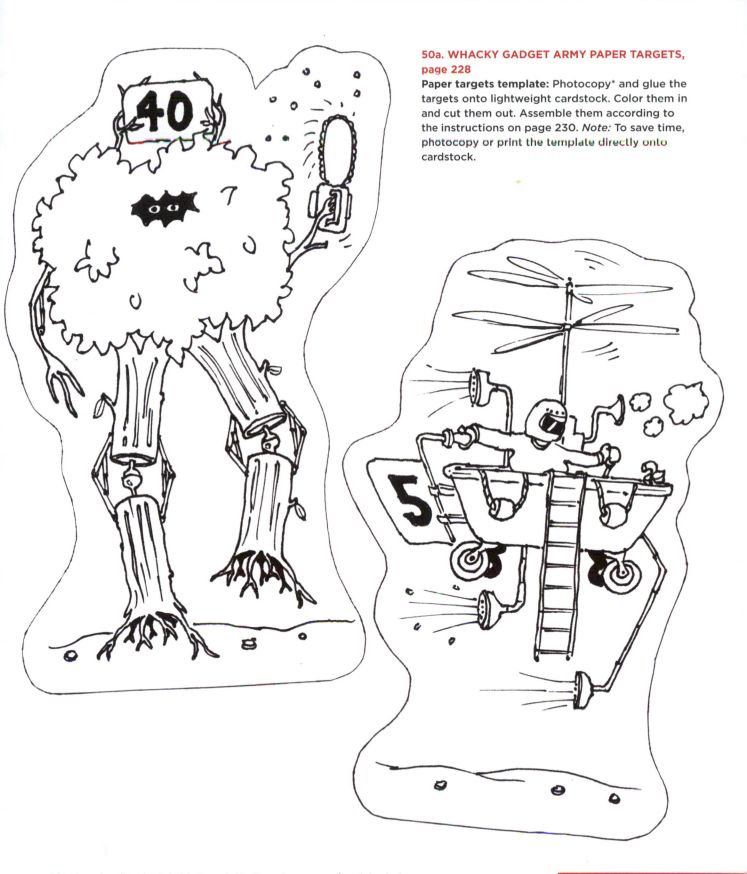

50a. WHACKY GADGET ARMY PAPER TARGETS, page 228

Paper targets template: Photocopy* and glue the targets onto lightweight cardstock. Color them in and cut them out. Assemble them according to the instructions on page 230. *Note:* To save time, photocopy or print the template directly onto cardstock.

Or download and print this template at workman.com/madebydad

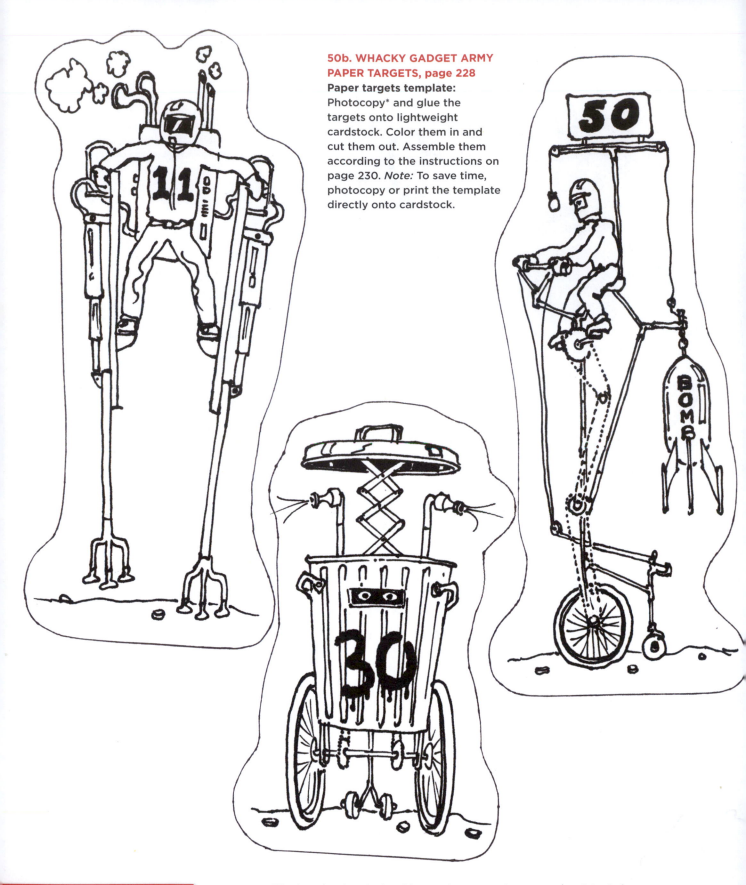

Paper targets template:
Photocopy* and glue the
targets onto lightweight
cardstock. Color them in and
cut them out. Assemble them
according to the instructions on
page 230. *Note:* To save time,
photocopy or print the template
directly onto cardstock.

*Or download and print this template at workman.com/madebydad

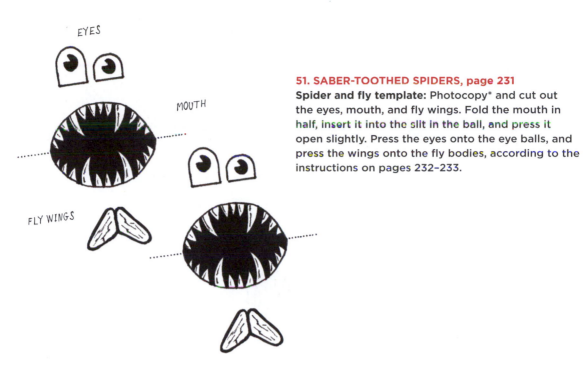

EYES

MOUTH

FLY WINGS

51. SABER-TOOTHED SPIDERS, page 231

Spider and fly template: Photocopy* and cut out the eyes, mouth, and fly wings. Fold the mouth in half, insert it into the slit in the ball, and press it open slightly. Press the eyes onto the eye balls, and press the wings onto the fly bodies, according to the instructions on pages 232–233.

53. SHARK BITE PAPER PLATE, page 237

Shark template: Photocopy*, cut out, and trace the shark piece onto black cardstock. Cut it out, fold along the dotted lines, and assemble according to the instructions on page 238.

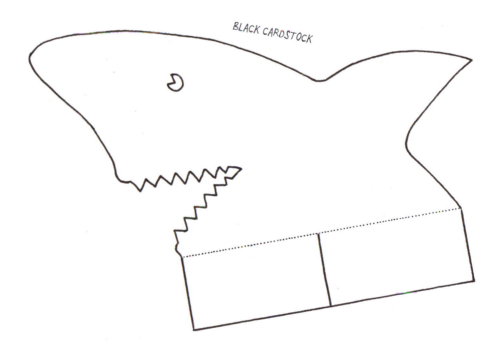

BLACK CARDSTOCK

Or download and print this template at workman.com/madebydad

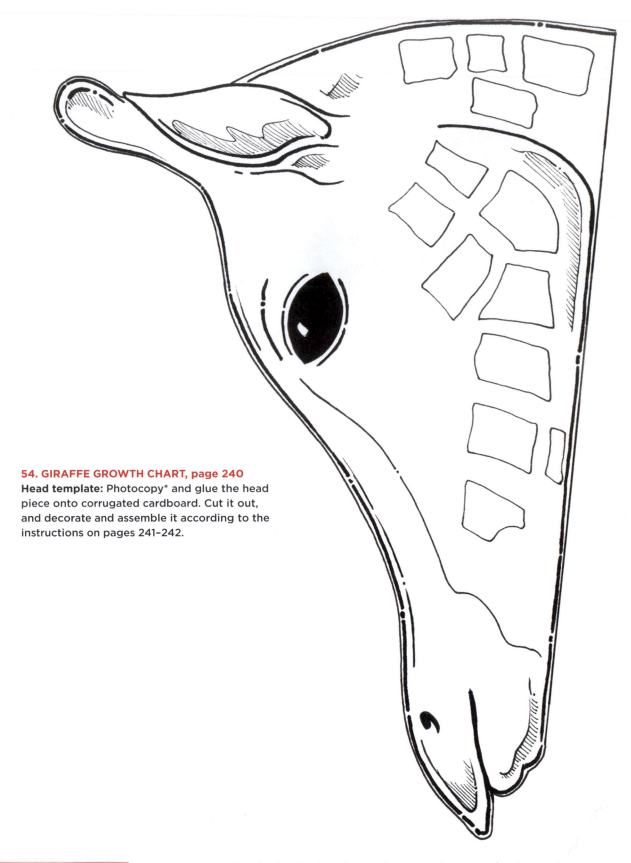

54. GIRAFFE GROWTH CHART, page 240
Head template: Photocopy* and glue the head piece onto corrugated cardboard. Cut it out, and decorate and assemble it according to the instructions on pages 241–242.

Or download and print this template at workman.com/madebydad

BREAKFAST IN BED

HOT COFFEE OR TEA

55. MOMMY REWARDS, page 244
Small picture template: Photocopy*
and cut out the pieces. Glue them,
centered, onto the coupon medallions,
and continue to assemble according
to the instructions on page 245.

HUGS!

DO THE IRONING

DO THE SHOPPING

10 MINUTES OF SILENCE!

PUT AWAY TOYS

57. FRANKENSTEIN FLING, page 248
Frankenstein template: Photocopy*, color in,
and cut out the head piece. Glue the head
onto the side of the cup according to the
instructions on page 250.

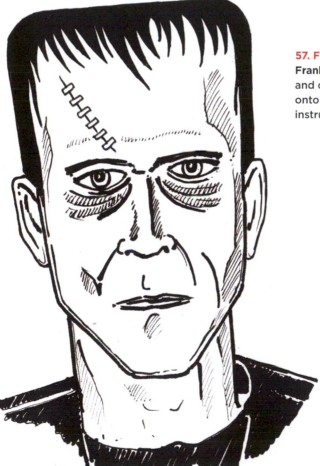

*Or download and print this template at workman.com/madebydad

58. POP-UP ROSES, page 251

Roses and vase template: Photocopy*, color in, and cut out the roses and vase pieces. Glue the roses, centered, onto the foam core piece and glue the vase onto the box sleeve according to the instructions on page 253.

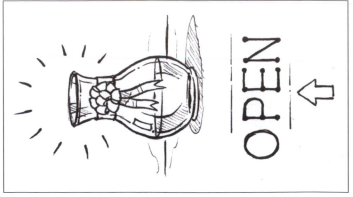

Or download and print this template at workman.com/madebydad

Mars template: Photocopy* at 133% and color in the card. Fold according to the instructions on page 258.

Or download and print this template at workman.com/madebydad

63. HUGS AND KISSES CARD, page 266

XOXO template: Photocopy*, cut out, and trace the XOXO piece onto the front panel of the folded red cardstock. Cut it out and continue to assemble according to the instructions starting on page 267.

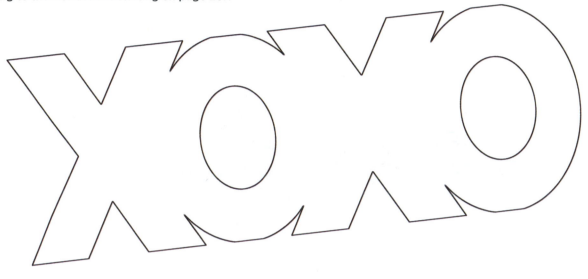

65a. SPIDER SURPRISE CARD, page 270

Surprise template I: Photocopy*, cut out, and trace the house and spider pieces onto black cardstock. Cut them out and assemble according to the instructions starting on page 271.

HOUSE

BLACK CARDSTOCK

SPIDER

Or download and print this template at workman.com/madebydad

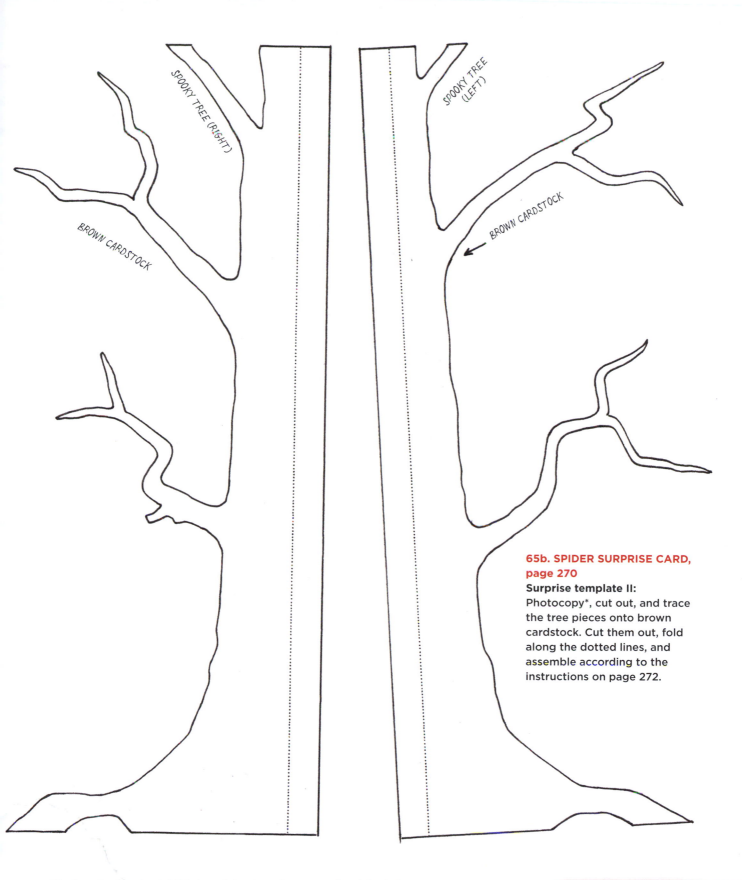

SPOOKY TREE (RIGHT)

SPOOKY TREE (LEFT)

BROWN CARDSTOCK

BROWN CARDSTOCK

BROWN CARDSTOCK

65b. SPIDER SURPRISE CARD, page 270

Surprise template II:
Photocopy*, cut out, and trace the tree pieces onto brown cardstock. Cut them out, fold along the dotted lines, and assemble according to the instructions on page 272.

*Or download and print this template at workman.com/madebydad

65c. SPIDER SURPRISE CARD, page 270

Surprise template III: Photocopy*, cut out, and trace the flower petals, flower head, and stem pieces onto red and black cardstock, as noted. Cut them out and assemble according to the instructions on page 273.

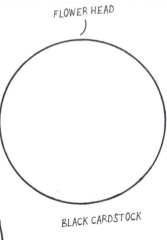

FLOWER HEAD

BLACK CARDSTOCK

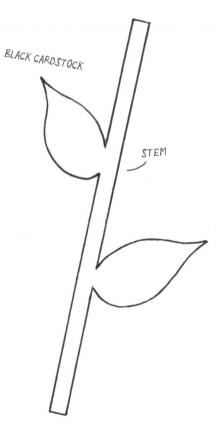

BLACK CARDSTOCK

STEM

FLOWER PETALS

RED CARDSTOCK

66. JELLY BEAN REWARD ROCKET, page 274

Window template: Photocopy*, color in, cut out, and glue the window piece to the top of tube A according to the instructions on page 277.

*Or download and print this template at workman.com/madebydad

Girl template: Photocopy* at 133%, color in, and cut out the card. Fold at the dotted lines, according to the instructions on page 280.

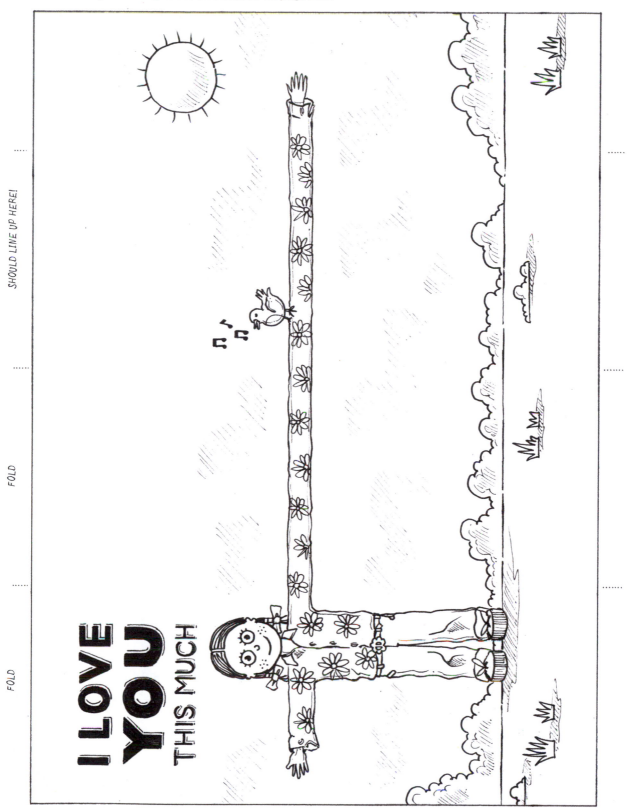

SHOULD LINE UP HERE!

FOLD

FOLD

I LOVE YOU THIS MUCH

Or download and print this template at workman.com/madebydad

Boy template: Photocopy* at 133%, color in, and cut out the card. Fold at the dotted lines according to the instructions on page 280.

Or download and print this template at workman.com/madebydad

ACKNOWLEDGMENTS

I was fortunate enough to have a mother who encouraged my creative endeavors from when I was very young, even when it meant falling victim to my trip-wire alarms on a fairly regular basis. So I'd like to formally apologize and say thank you at the same time. I also had a father who graciously allowed me to take over his workshop, and never asked why the shed roof suddenly sprouted a huge weathervane. (It's just as well he never found the rat trap!)

A big thanks must go to my wife Sharon, who kept things going as the house slowly disappeared under a pile of paper, cardboard, and glue during the time it took me to create all of the projects for this book. And, of course, my two boys, Dylan and Joshua, who rekindled my love for making things—I hope they never lose their joy for creativity.

Lastly, I'd like to thank my agent, Adam Schear, and the whole team at Workman—especially my editor, Megan Nicolay and designer Becky Terhune, along with the rest of the team (Liz Davis, Ian Gross, Kate Karol, Barbara Peragine, Jarrod Dyer, Julie Primavera, Jessica Weiner, Molly Kay Frandson, and Maggie Gleason) who worked very hard to bring "my world" to life in book form.

ABOUT THE AUTHOR

Scott Bedford has loved making things ever since he won a national drawing competition at age 7 for his quirky interpretation of a Kraft Cheese Factory. Today he is creative director at a London-based mobile and digital marketing agency that caters to some of the world's most well-known brands. By nights and weekends, his talents are reserved exclusively for his most discerning A-list clients: his kids. They are the inspiration for his illustrated blog, which has garnered two Webby Awards and a devoted following since its founding in 2010. For more projects beyond the pages of this book, visit Scott at whatimade.com.